Microcomputers as Decision Aids in Law Practice

MICROCOMPUTERS AS DECISION AIDS IN LAW PRACTICE

Stuart S. Nagel

Q

Quorum Books

NEW YORK • WESTPORT, CONNECTICUT • LONDON

Library of Congress Cataloging-in-Publication Data

Nagel, Stuart S., 1934-
Microcomputers as decision aids in law practice.

Bibliography: p.
Includes index.
1. Information storage and retrieval systems—Law—United States. 2. Practice of law—United States. 3. Microcomputers—United States. I. Title.
KF242.A1N24 1987 347.73'504'02855369 86-16873
347.30750402855369
ISBN 0-89930-197-5 (lib. bdg. : alk. paper)

Library of Congress Catalog Card Number: 86-16873
ISBN:0-89930-197-5

First published in 1987 by Quorum Books

Greenwood Press, Inc.
88 Post Road West, Westport, Connecticut 06881

Printed in the United States of America

The paper used in this book complies with the Permanent Paper Standard issued by the National Information Standards Organization (Z39.48-1984).

10 9 8 7 6 5 4 3 2 1

To more systematic decision-making in law practice
With the aid of microcomputers
For the benefit of clients, lawyers, and the general public

Contents

III. JUDICIAL PREDICTION

IV. LITIGATION CHOICES

Figures

Tables

Preface

The purpose of this book is to describe four important uses of microcomputers as decision-making aids in law practice. The book was originally developed as a set of materials for distribution to the participants in the invitational conference "Using Personal Computers for Decision-Making in Law Practice" sponsored by the Committee on Professional Education of the American Law Institute and the American Bar Association in Chicago on May 10–11, 1985.

In developing the conference, it was decided that the emphasis should be on litigation strategy and judicial prediction. The conference should minimize the discussion of microcomputer uses such as word processing, file management, information retrieval, accounting, and other office-practice or law-library uses in contrast to the processing of information to aid in predicting or making decisions. Materials on legal-policy evaluation should also be largely excluded since they are directed more toward legal policy-makers than practicing lawyers. In light of those criteria, a four-part division was adopted consisting of these sections:

1. General microcomputer materials, including a summary of the main decision-aiding software, a detailed analysis of that software, and comparisons with other relevant software.

2. Judicial prediction, including case prediction by way of an approach that emphasizes working with a set of (a) criteria for predicting case outcomes, (b) previous relevant cases, and (c) relations between the criteria and the cases in order to choose a predictive decision-rule for predicting all prior cases accurately.
3. Litigation choices, including general decision science ideas, making choices with multiple unknowns, the microcomputer application, and the alternative decision-tree approach. The choice system involves working with a set of (a) goals to be achieved, (b) alternatives for achieving them, and (c) relations between the goals and the alternatives in order to choose an alternative that maximizes benefits minus costs.
4. The allocation of scarce resources, especially time per individual case, time across cases, money to places and activities, and people to tasks. The allocation system involves working with a set of (a) criteria for evaluating alternative allocations; (b) budget categories, places, activities, people, or other objects to which the scarce resources are being allocated; and (c) relations between the categories and the criteria in order to choose an allocation that provides the most benefits for the resources being allocated.
5. Negotiation and mediation. The software facilitates dispute resolution by quickly clarifying for the disputants the effects of proposed changes in (a) the goals each side is seeking to achieve, (b) the alternatives each side is proposing, and (c) the relations between the alternatives and the goals in order to arrive at a new alternative that will enable both sides to feel they are coming out ahead.

That is the way this book is organized with a summarizing section in the beginning.

This organization differs substantially from that of the earlier American Law Institute-American Bar Association (ALI-ABA) professional development course given on April 30, 1984, in Washington, D.C., and the corresponding book *Applying Decision Science to Law Practice*. That earlier course was more abstract, and the materials were organized mainly in terms of forms of optimizing analysis, including:

1. Optimum-choice analysis or basic benefit-cost analysis, which involves lump-sum alternatives that do not allow for adopting a fraction of an alternative or more than one of the same alternative
2. Optimum-risk analysis or decision theory, which also involves lump-sum alternatives, but the extent to which they produce benefits or costs is contingent on the occurrence of one or more probabilistic or risky events
3. Optimum-level analysis, which involves a policy that can take many positions along a continuum but in which doing too much or too little is considered undesirable
4. Optimum-mix analysis or allocation theory, which involves multiple policies, places, activities, persons, or other entities to which a budget, time, or other scarce resources are to be allocated
5. Optimum-time analysis, which mainly involves applying choice, risk, level, and mix analysis to minimizing time consumption

The new organization in this book emphasizes subject matters rather than decision-making forms. The forms are interspersed within the subject matters. Between the 1984 course and the 1985 conference, a third way of organizing the material was experimented with. It involves emphasizing the kinds of methodological problems and decision-making principles that lawyers and others are most likely to encounter when trying to apply systematic decision-making. Those problems are:

1. Multiple dimensions for measuring goals, such as dollars, years in jail, 0–10 scales, and other measures
2. Multiple missing information, such as the probability of victory, the damages if the plaintiff wins, and the litigation costs
3. Multiple alternatives to choose among, which include thousands of alternatives as in the ways of allocating $10,000 to three activities
4. Multiple constraints, including minimums and maximums on the goals, the alternatives, and the other decision-making inputs
5. Simple presentation when multiple ideas are present

Those problems are also interspersed within the lawyer subject matters. That interspersing is especially clarified in the first part, which summarizes the use of microcomputers as decision aids in law practice.

Five of the six parts in this book contain an introduction to the chapters that are included within the particular part. Those chapters generally include some discussions of quantitative methods that do not explicitly mention microcomputers but could easily be converted to microcomputer applications. The chapters also include explicit microcomputer material. Another way of classifying items is in terms of describing the microcomputer applications available now, in contrast to those that are still in the process of being developed. The future, however, is rapidly becoming the present in this growing field of microcomputers as decision-making aids in law practice.

I gratefully acknowledge the helpfulness and inspiration of Mark Mendenhall and Paul Wolkin of the ALI-ABA Committee on Continuing Professional Education. Paul Wolkin published my first relevant article in *The Practical Lawyer* in 1961 under the title "Using Simple Calculations to Predict Judicial Decisions." We patiently waited almost 25 years for the development and widespread adoption of microcomputers among law firms to make feasible the implementation of those ideas. Thanks are also due Betsy Turner, the chair of the ABA Computer Division. She provided me with the first opportunity to present my ideas before an ABA convention, even though it meant a last-minute change in the program. A special acknowledgment should be given to the discussion leaders for the ALI-ABA conference "Using Personal Computers for Decision-Making in Law Practice," consisting of Paul Bernstein from Paul Bernstein and Associates of Chicago; John Cooley, an arbitrator and mediator from Evanston, Illinois; John Finan, professor of law at the University of Akron; Fremont Magee of Piper and Marbury in Baltimore; and Michael White, professor of public administration at the University of Southern California. Thanks are also due to Ronald Staudt, James Sprowl, and Bernard Farber of the Chicago-Kent-IIT Law School for the use of the facilities of the Center on Law and Computers.

Other people who were important in developing these materials include John Long and Philip Goldberg of the University of Illinois who worked with me in developing the relevant software. Owen Hall of the Management Science Program at Pepperdine University was helpful in developing Chapter 14, ''Using Management Science to Assign Judges or Lawyers to Types of Cases.'' Credit is also due to Miriam ''Cassie'' Mills for her work as a research associate, especially in developing Chapter 14 and Chapter 15, ''Microcomputers, P/G%, and Dispute Resolution.'' Benjamin Radcliff has been an excellent research and teaching assistant. Thanks are also owed to the University Research Board of the University of Illinois for making R&D funds available for this and related projects. I am especially grateful to Joyce Nagel for many hours of hard work assembling, coordinating, and otherwise arranging for these materials to come into existence. The reader should note that some of the chapters in this book also appear in S. Nagel, *Causation, Prediction, and Legal Analysis* (1986) and *Law, Policy, and Optimizing Analysis* (1986).

I

Introduction

1

A Prehistory of Microcomputers as Decision Aids in Law Practice

The purpose of this material is to describe some basic concepts concerning the use of personal computers for decision-making in law practice. Those basic concepts are divided into three groups: (1) law-practice applications, (2) methodological problems, and (3) optimizing forms.

The law-practice applications include general, litigation strategy; negotiation/mediation; judicial prediction; attorney-resource allocation; and legal-policy evaluation. The methodological problems include dealing with multiple goals measured on multiple dimensions, multiple missing information, multiple alternatives that are too many to determine the effects of all of them, multiple and possibly conflicting constraints, and the need for simplicity in spite of all that multiplicity. The optimizing forms include decision-making, which involves finding an optimum choice among lump-sum alternatives, an optimum risk when probabilities are involved, an optimum level when doing too much or too little is undesirable, an optimum risk in allocating scarce resources, and optimum timing or sequencing of events.

In terms of the development of personal computers for decision-making in law practice, the most recent developments relate to the law-practice applications.

They require knowledge of legal substance and some awareness of principles of decision-making. Before those applications could be developed, it was necessary to deal with the methodological problems involved in systematic decision-making. That is where decision analysis or decision science comes in, especially with a concern for the psychology of human thinking. Before those decision-analysis developments, there were foundation developments in operations research and management science concerning how an all-knowing being would do optimum decision-making.

Using personal computers for decision-making in law practice is thus a product of psychological decision analysis, which in turn is a product of management science/operations research. One might also say that the field is partially a product of the development of computer science and office-management applications. The law applications like litigation strategy, however, have relatively little in common with word processing or file management but a lot in common with decision-making under conditions of risk. Likewise, judicial prediction is more closely related to statistical prediction, although substantially different. Attorney-resource-allocation problems are a direct descendant of the allocation problems associated with benefit-cost analysis, linear programming, and econometrics, even though lawyer-users do not have to know anything about those techniques to make use of their personal-computer versions.

The description of the applications, the principles for dealing with the problems, and the optimizing forms will become clearer when presented later in further detail with concrete examples. This introduction is a prehistory in that it attempts to describe the most relevant concepts before those of the present. It is not a prehistory in the sense of events preceding record keeping or in that nothing has happened until now. Lawyers and other humans have been making decisions ever since they came into existence, which was probably about the same time if law is defined broadly enough. What is revolutionary about the present time is that methods, software, and hardware are now being developed that enable lawyers and other people who are not such great decision-makers to emulate the processes that good decision-makers implicitly use and thereby become more effective and efficient in their own decision-making.

APPLICATIONS OF MICROCOMPUTERS TO DECISION-MAKING IN LAW PRACTICE

General

The main general application of microcomputers to decision-making in law practice consists of processing a set of (1) goals or criteria to be achieved, (2) alternatives or policies for achieving them, and (3) relations between goals and alternatives in order to choose the best alternative or combination in light of the goals, alternatives, and relations.

To facilitate that kind of decision-making, a program has been developed for use on personal computers called Policy/Goal Percentaging (P/G%). It is called that because it relates policies or decisions to goals or criteria and because it uses a form of percentaging to handle the problem of goals being measured on different dimensions.

Litigation Strategy

The software facilitates litigation strategy by working with a set of (1) benefits to be achieved and costs to be avoided, (2) alternative courses of action such as going to trial or accepting a settlement, and (3) relations between the payoffs and the alternatives in order to choose an alternative that maximizes benefits minus costs. The software is especially useful in indicating what it would take to bring a second-place alternative up to first place.

Negotiation/Mediation

The software facilitates dispute resolution by quickly clarifying for the disputants the effects of proposed changes on (1) the goals each side is seeking to achieve, (2) the alternatives each side is proposing, and (3) the relations between the alternatives and the goals in order to arrive at a new alternative that will enable both sides to feel they are coming out ahead.

Judicial Prediction

The software deals with judicial prediction through an approach that emphasizes working with a set of (1) criteria for predicting case outcomes, (2) previous relevant cases, and (3) relations between the criteria and the cases in order to choose a predictive decision-rule for predicting all of the prior cases accurately.

Attorney-Resource Allocation

Attorney-resource allocation issues include allocating (1) time for individual cases, (2) time across cases, (3) money to places and activities, and (4) people to tasks. The software system involves working with a set of (1) criteria for evaluating alternative allocations; (2) budget categories, places, activities, people, or other objects to which the scarce resources are being allocated; and (3) relations between the categories and the criteria in order to choose an allocation that provides the most benefits for the resources being allocated.

Legal-Policy Evaluation

In legal-policy evaluation, one is trying to decide the judicial decision that ought to be adopted in light of the goals and the factual circumstances, in contrast to predicting the decision that will be adopted in light of the prior precedents.

Legal-policy evaluation can also involve trying to decide which one among the alternative proposed statutes, regulations, or budgets is best in light of the goals, alternatives available, and relations.

METHODOLOGICAL PROBLEMS ENCOUNTERED IN SYSTEMATIC DECISION-MAKING

Multiple Goals Measured on Multiple Dimensions

To facilitate dealing with the problem of multiple goals, determine their relative importance by noting which goal is the least important and then note how many more times as important each other goal is compared to the base goal. Those relative weights can then be used to multiply the raw scores of each policy on each goal. A more comfortable alternative might involve first converting the raw scores into part/whole percentages. Do this by dividing each raw score by the sum of the raw scores on each goal. That creates a set of dimensionless numbers for dealing better with the problem of adding apples and oranges.

Multiple Missing Information

To facilitate dealing with the problem of multiple missing information, arrange for software that can do "what-if" analysis. Goals and alternatives can then be changed so that one can quickly see the effects of the changes on the bottom line of each potential alternative. If the weight of a goal or the score of a policy/goal relation is unknown, arrange for software that can do threshold analysis, whereby the threshold value of the weight of each goal or relation score is determined. The bottom-line conclusion concerning which alternative to adopt depends on whether one is above or below the threshold value on a weight or relation. It is easier to determine whether one is above or below a threshold value than it is to determine the exact value of a weight or relation. If multiple weights or relations are unknown, arrange for software that can do an indifference-curve analysis. The computer screen then shows a curve or set of curves above which one alternative is better and below which another alternative is better. It is easier to determine whether a combination of unknowns is above or below such a curve than it is to determine the exact values of the weights and relations.

Multiple Alternatives That Are too Many to Determine the Effects of All of Them

One may need to deal with the problem of deciding among an infinite number of alternatives on a continuum that goes from zero to 100 or 1 to infinity or on another continuum. To do this, divide the continuum into intervals or categories, with the end intervals being under and over a certain number if necessary. One may need to deal with the problem of deciding among an infinite number of alternative ways of allocating scarce resources to various objects. To do this, give relative scores to the allocation objects and then use those relative scores as allocation percentages.

Multiple and Conflicting Constraints

To facilitate dealing with minimum or maximum constraints on the alternatives or goals, follow the above principles for optimizing without considering the constraints. Then observe whether any of the constraints are unsatisfied and make adjustments to satisfy them. If some of the constraints are conflicting, prioritize them so as to satisfy the more important ones fully or partially.

The Need for Simplicity in Spite of All That Multiplicity

To facilitate simplicity in drawing and presenting conclusions, use a policies/goals table. The policy alternatives are shown on the rows, and the goals/criteria are shown on the columns. Go down one goal-column at a time to relate each of the policies to each goal. Use words or symbols rather than numbers if necessary to express the relation. Then later convert the words or symbols into numbers. After recording each relation, go across each policy row to make an overall statement about each policy. Conclude by noting which policy or combination of policies is best in light of the goals and relations. This kind of PG analysis can be aided by a microcomputer whereby the TV screen provides prompting and shows how the results change as a result of changing the goals, their weights, the policies, their constraints, the relations, and their measurement.

FORMS OF OPTIMUM DECISION-MAKING

Optimum Choice among Lump-Sum or Discrete Alternatives

The simplest kind of decision-making involves a set of discrete alternatives with no inherent order. This occurs when choosing among alternative legislative-redistricting patterns, when choosing among alternative ways of providing legal counsel to the poor, and in deciding whether or not to adopt a policy of excluding illegally seized evidence from criminal proceedings. The general rule is to pick the alternative that maximizes benefits minus costs, taking into consideration multi-dimensionality, missing information, multiple constraints, and other methodological problems.

Optimum Risk with Contingent Probabilities

Contingent probabilities in this context means probabilities that events will occur and will influence the benefits or the costs that alternative projects or decisions produce. Thus if a project produces $10 in benefits, but only if something happens that has a 0.60 probability of occurring, that project has expected benefits of only $6, which equals the $10 discounted by the 0.60 probability that the contingent event will occur. The general rule is to pick the alternative that maximizes expected or discounted benefits minus expected or discounted costs.

Optimum Level When Doing too Much or too Little Is Undesirable

Optimum-level situations involve policies that produce increasing benefits or net benefits at first, but the benefits reach a peak and start to go down. The object in such situations is to find the point on a policy continuum at which the benefits are maximized. That can be done by graphing and eyeballing the hill-shaped curve or by more complicated methods that involve calculus and algebra. Optimum-level situations may also involve policies that reduce costs at first, but past a certain point the costs reach their lowest level and start to rise. The objective then becomes finding the point on a policy continuum at which the costs are minimized.

Optimum Mix in Allocating Scarce Resources

Optimum-mix situations involve allocating money, time, people, or other scarce resources across activities, places, people, or other allocation objects. The ideal mix under such circumstances is to give to each object an amount that will satisfy a set of simultaneous equations in which one equation involves having the sum of the amounts add to the total amount available. The other equation involves equalizing the marginal rates of return of each object, taking into consideration the principle of diminishing returns. Nothing can then be gained by shifting resources from one object to another under the ideal mix.

Optimum Timing

Time-optimization models are decision-making systems designed to minimize time consumption. Such models often involve variations on optimum choice, risk, level, or mix but applied to situations in which the goal is to minimize time. Some time-optimization models are peculiar to a temporal subject matter such as (1) queuing theory for predicting and reducing waiting time and backlogs using information on arrival and service rates, (2) optimum sequencing for determining the order in which matters should be processed so as to minimize the average waiting time, and (3) critical-path analysis for determining which paths from start to finish are especially worth attention with regard to delay-reduction efforts.

EXAMPLES

One of the main purposes of this book and the ALI-ABA conference on which it is based is to summarize and stimulate new examples of these ideas concerning (1) forms of optimum decision-making, (2) principles for dealing with problems encountered in systematic decision-making, and (3) law-practice applications. The datafiles appendix to this book provides almost 100 examples. They are classified in terms of the applications, problems, and forms that they illustrate. I hope that the participants in the conference and the readers of this book will add to those examples by sending documentation to me at 361 Lincoln Hall, University of Illinois, Urbana, Illinois 61801. The new examples can then be mentioned with appropriate credits in future editions of the datafiles appendix and the interpretive materials. Through that kind of building, we should be able to develop an even more meaningful structure with regard to using personal computers for decision-making in law practice.

Readers who would like to see how a story ends before reading the contents can turn to the epilogue in this book, although it is really a commencement rather than an ending. The epilogue deals with principles that cut across the law applications such as:

1. The importance of sensitivity analysis for determining the effects of input changes on decisions
2. The importance of traditional lawyer knowledge in using personal computers as decision aids
3. The value of computer software for dealing with goals that are measured on multiple dimensions
4. The value of computer software for converting complicated problems into relatively simple ones but not simplistic ones that leave out the important considerations
5. The need for being more sensitive to ethical and related problems when doing an explicit decision analysis

The epilogue also deals with the problems of getting personal computers adopted as supplements for decision-making in law practice. Doing this involves overcoming a number of objections by emphasizing that:

1. Personal computers are not necessary to lawyer decision-making, but they can be helpful such that the benefits of using them generally outweigh the costs.
2. Personal computers cannot replace lawyers. They can only supplement them to add to their effectiveness and efficiency.
3. Decision-aiding software can allow for working with qualitative and verbal, as well as quantitative, considerations and both non-monetary and monetary considerations.
4. The relevant software is in a state of flux in being constantly improved, but it is already usable.

Table 1–1

Examples That Illustrate Optimizing Problems and Legal Applications

PROBLEMS OR PRINCIPLES / SUBJECTS	General P/G% Analyses	Predicting Court Cases	Litigation Choices	Allocation, Especially Time
Multiple Dimensions on Multiple Goals	1 (1-2) Speed versus Respect in Resolving Cases	6 (5-7,5-9) Housing Discrimination Cases	11 (1-4) Prosecuting a Criminal Case	16 (1-7) Shortest Cases First vs. First-Come, First-Served
Multiple Missing Information	2 (1-2) Threshold and Convergence Analysis	7 (5-3,5-10) Redistricting Cases	12 (1-5) Suing in a Civil Case	17 (1-3) Money to Activities
Multiple Alternatives	3 (1-2) Allocating Cases to Trials and Pleas	8 (5-4,5-5) International Law Cases	13 (7-3) Prosecutor's Concern for Bail Level	18 (7-15) Allocating Time to Multiple Projects
Multiple Constraints	4 (1-2) Minimum % of Trials and Maximum % of Pleas	9 (5-2) Cases on Religion in Public Schools	14 (7-4,7-5) Settling a Flat Fee or Hourly Rate Case	19 (7-14) Time Allocating for a Flat Fee or Hourly Rate Case
Simple Presenting. A P/G% Table Created From:	5 (1-2) Primary Results	10 (7-13) A Scattergram	15 (7-2) A Decision Tree	20 (7-19) A Flowchart

NOTE: The numbers in parentheses at the top of each cell are numbers from the Appendix at the back of the book.

Table 1–2

Examples That Illustrate Optimizing Forms and Legal Applications

DECISION MAKERS / FORMS	Choice	Risk	Level	Mix
Police and Crime Reduction	1 (7-1) Excluding Illegally Obtained Evidence	2 (6-1) Decreasing Illegal Behavior	3 Optimum Crime Level	4 (1-3) Allocating Anti-crime Dollars
Courts and Pretrial Release	5 (7-7) Notification Methods	6 (7-10) Releasing vs. Holding Prior to Trial	7 (7-3) Percent to Hold or Bond the Set	8 (7-7) Methods to Encourage Appearance
Courts and Delay	9 (1-7) Optimum Sequencing	10 Incentives for Time-saving Decisions	11 (7-20) Optimum Delay Level	12 Court Personnel
Corrections and Sentencing	13 Reducing Judicial Disparities	14 (7-10) Releasing on Probation	15 Optimum Sentencing Level	16 Prison Space Allocation Jail vs. Parole
Practicing Lawyers	17 (1-7) Order of Cases	18 (1-5) Settlement vs. Trial	19 (7-13) Time per Case	20 (7-15) Allocation Across Cases
Criminal Justice in General	21 (7-1) Excluding Illegally Obtained Evidence	22 (6-1) Decreasing Illegal Behavior	23 Optimum Sentencing Level	24 (6-9) Anti-crime Allocation to Places

NOTES:
The purpose of this matrix is to show the variety of examples from the legal process to which the concepts of optimum choice, risk, level, and mix can apply.

5. To appreciate the value of personal computers for decision-making in law practice, it is helpful to try out the relevant software. A key purpose of this book and the conference on which it is based is to facilitate that experience.

Table 1–1 summarizes parts II–V of this book in the form of a set of five visual aids for each. These four parts relate to the subject matters of (1) general microcomputer materials (P/G% analysis), (2) judicial prediction, (3) litigation choices, and allocating scarce resources, especially time. The five visual aids relate to the methodological problems of (1) multiple dimensions on the goals to be achieved, (2) multiple missing information, (3) multiple alternatives, (4) multiple constraints, and (5) simple presentation of multiple ideas. That four-by-five analysis lends itself well to a matrix in which each cell refers to an illustrative example. The matrix shows the datafiles where further details can be found for each example and for the related principles.

Table 1–2 organizes the datafiles in a different way. In that table the emphasis is on forms of decision analysis such as optimum choice, risk, level, and mix. This is in contrast to the emphasis on problems in Table 1–1 such as multiple dimensions, missing information, multiple alternatives, multiple constraints, and simplicity. Table 1–2 divides the substance in terms of the decision-makers, such as police, courts, corrections, and lawyers. This is in contrast to law-practice activities such as predicting cases, deciding whether to settle or go to trial, and allocating resources.

II

General Microcomputer Materials

The following materials describe a general microcomputer program that is capable of processing a set of (1) goals to be achieved, (2) alternatives for achieving the goals, and (3) relations between goals and alternatives in order to choose the best alternative or combination for maximizing benefits minus costs. The alternatives can be litigation choices, alternative ways of allocating time, or other decision-making alternatives. The goals can be benefits (which are effects to be increased) or costs (which are effects to be decreased). The goals can also be monetary or non-monetary. The relations can be positive or negative, high or low, measured in categories like red, green, and purple or in numbers on a 0–100 scale. The same general microcomputer program can also be used to process a set of (1) prior cases, (2) predictive criteria for distinguishing among the cases, and (3) the relations between each prior case and each criterion in order to arrive at an accurate predictive decision-rule.

Chapter 2 is a short summary of the microcomputer program describing its basic components and its applications. Chapter 3 provides a more detailed description including the input variables of alternatives, goals, and relations and the variations on the basic analysis. These variations include being able to deal with (1) one or two versus many alternatives and goals; (2) mutually exclusive choices or combinations or allocating along a continuum of possibilities; (3) raw-score aggregating or part/whole percentaging to deal with multi-dimensional goals; (4) threshold and convergence analysis to deal with missing information; (5) constraint analysis to deal with minimums and maximums; and (6) residual analysis to deal with discrepancies between what should be and what is. Chapter 4 refers to other microcomputer programs and related methods that have also been mentioned in the literature as possibly being capable of dealing with multiple-criteria decision-making.

2

A Summary of the Main Decision-Aiding Software

THE PROGRAM IN GENERAL

This chapter briefly describes a new microcomputer program called Policy/Goal Percentaging Analysis (P/G%). The program is designed to process a set of (1) goals to be achieved, (2) alternatives for achieving the goals, and (3) relations between goals and alternatives in order to choose the best alternative or combination for maximizing benefits minus costs. It is called ''Policy/Goal Percentaging Analysis'' because it relates alternative policies to goals, and it makes use of part/whole percentages to handle the problem of goals being measured on different dimensions. The measurement units are converted into a system of percentages showing relative achievement of each policy on each goal, rather than a system of inches, dollars, apples, days, or other measurement scores.

To facilitate applications of part/whole percentaging, an appropriate microcomputer program has been developed. It can be applied to any problem involving one or more policies and one or more goals. The program is especially useful when one is working with many policies, many goals, various measurement units, and other constraints and conditions. The program can run on an IBM PC

Figure 2–1
An Abbreviated Version of the Main Menu of the P/G% Program

```
CHOOSE AN OPTION:

1. Enter total budget
   Currently set at $   947.00
2. Review Alternatives

3. Review Criteria

4. Enter Alternative scores
        for each Criteria

5. Perform primary analysis

6. Threshold analysis

7. Save present model
```

or an IBM-compatible microcomputer. Figure 2–1 shows the main menu of the microcomputer program.[1]

COMPONENTS OF THE PROGRAM

The program can perform a variety of useful decision-making analyses such as (1) choosing, ranking, or allocating to alternative categories; (2) working with goals that have a common measurement unit or that are multi-dimensional; (3) doing what-if variations on the goals, alternatives, and relations; (4) doing a threshold or convergence analysis to indicate the scores on the goals, alternatives, or relations that will make a difference in the winning alternative or how resources are allocated; (5) adjusting results for minimums, maximums, and other constraints; and (6) comparing optimum choices with actual choices to reduce the gap between the actual and the optimum.

The decision-aiding system involves basically the following steps:

1. Listing the alternatives from which a choice needs to be made or to which an allocation needs to be made
2. Listing the criteria or goals that one wants to achieve and their relative importance
3. Scoring each alternative on each criterion with as precise or as rough a relation-score as is available
4. Converting the scores into part/whole percentages or other scores that can show the relative relations of the alternatives on each criterion
5. Aggregating the relative scores for each alternative across the criteria to arrive at an overall score or allocation coefficient for each alternative
6. Drawing a conclusion about which alternative or combination is best or how much of a budget or a set of scarce resources should be allocated to each alternative

7. Changing the alternatives, criteria, relations, and other inputs to see how such changes affect the conclusion

The computer program is divided into five parts or options covering the following:

1. The accessment, creation, or deletion of a datafile of information relevant to resolving a decision problem
2. The insertion or change of the inputs regarding the alternatives, goals, relations, or amount of scarce resources to be allocated
3. The initial results based on the alternatives, goals, and relations
4. The post facto analyses, which include threshold analysis and convergence analysis
5. The provision for saving and storing datafiles that one might want to refer to in the future

The post facto analyses are especially useful to aid in resolving disputes about what the weights or relation-scores should be. *Threshold analysis* is one option, whereby the computer shows what it would take in changing the goals-weights or the relation-scores to bring the second-place alternative up to first place or any alternative up to any other alternative. For example, if there is a dispute about whether a relation-score is a 2 or an 8, and the threshold value is a 10, there should be no need to dispute the matter further since neither a 2 nor an 8 will make any difference in terms of the second-place alternative moving to first place. *Convergence analysis* is another option, whereby the computer shows at what level the weight for a goal becomes high enough to produce results that are close to the results that would occur if that goal were the only goal. For example, if there is a dispute about whether a goal weight is a 5 or a 10 and the convergence value is a 3, there should be no need to dispute that matter further.

APPLICATIONS AND LIMITATIONS

The P/G% approach differs from other decision-aiding approaches by virtue of being able to deal meaningfully with all of the following decision-making situations: (1) setting multi-dimensional goals; (2) choosing the one best alternative; (3) choosing the best combination of alternatives; (4) making choices where risks and probabilities are involved; (5) making choices where doing too much or too little is undesirable; (6) allocating scarce resources, even when there are millions of alternative ways of allocating a given budget to a set of budget categories; (7) handling situations with multiple missing information; (8) handling situations involving public policy, law, business, medicine, or personal decision-making; (9) handling situations in which all of the goals are measured on the same dimension; (10) handling situations involving prediction as well as prescription;

and (11) determining minimums or maximums on the alternatives, goals, or other constraints.

The approach also differs from other approaches by virtue of having the following characteristics:

1. P/G% can easily go from alternatives, goals, and relations to drawing a conclusion.
2. It has been translated into a highly user-friendly microcomputer program.
3. It is based on mathematical justifications that relate to classical calculus optimization, especially if one views the part/whole percentages as proxies for non-linear regression coefficients.
4. It comes with lots of illustrative applications and years of relevant experience.
5. It is analogous to mathematical programming procedures such as linear, non-linear, integer, goal, and multi-objective programming but without the complexity and unrealistic assumptions.
6. The program can systematically compare optimum choices or allocations with actual choices or allocations in order to bring the optimum closer to the actual and vice versa.

Along with the program, there are a variety of demonstration datafiles. They include applications from the fields of law, public policy, health care, and personal decision-making. They also include applications that involve predicting decisions as well as prescribing decisions. One can easily create new applications by inserting a set of tentative alternatives, goals, and relations for various problems.

The program can be applied to law-practice problems such as deciding (1) whether to go to trial or settle out of court in civil or criminal cases, (2) how to allocate time or other resources across a set of cases, (3) which of various laws should be adopted for achieving a set of goals, (4) what decision should be reached in resolving a legal dispute, (5) what level of activity should be engaged in for a given matter where doing too much or little may be undesirable, and (6) how to handle other decision problems that involve goals, alternatives, and relations between goals and alternatives.

A limitation that the program currently has is the requirement that one have access to an IBM-compatible microcomputer with 192K of memory and a graphics adapter. The program is, however, being developed for running on other microcomputers. A body of experience is also being developed that will be incorporated into a book consisting mainly of various applications, entitled *Public Policy Controversies: Relating Options to Goals*. Those applications are also leading to further improvements in the versatility of the program. The program is mainly limited by the fact that the real world involves multi-dimensional goals, missing information, complex constraints, and other problems, but the program seeks to handle those problems as well as possible.[2]

NOTES

1. This program is related to the field of multi-criteria decision-making. That field includes literature such as Ward Edwards and Robert Newman, *Multi-Attribute Evaluation* (Beverly Hills, Calif.: Sage, 1982); Thomas Saaty, *The Analytic Hierarchy Process: Planning, Priority Setting, and Resource Allocation* (New York: McGraw-Hill, 1980); and Milan Zeleny, *Multiple Criteria Decision Making* (New York: McGraw-Hill, 1982). In comparison to those methods, the P/G% program is both simpler to use and more realistic in its procedures. The program is also related to spreadsheet analysis, but it is more focused on evaluating alternatives and informing the user about what changes will make a difference as well as what difference they will make. See T. Henderson et al., *Spreadsheet Software: From VisiCalc to 1–2–3* (Indianapolis: Que Corp., 1983).

2. For further information concerning this multi-criteria decision-aiding tool, you may write to me at 361 Lincoln Hall, University of Illinois, Urbana, Illinois 61801. The microcomputer program is based on S. Nagel, "Multiple Goals and Multiple Policies," in S. Nagel, *Public Policy: Goals, Means, and Methods* (New York: St. Martin's, 1984). A copy of the P/G% program, the present instruction manual, and periodic updates can be obtained from me for experimental purposes for a moderate fee to cover the cost of a floppy disk and photocopying. Further details are provided in S. Nagel, *Microcomputers, Evaluation Problems, and Policy Analysis* (Beverly Hills, Calif.: Sage, forthcoming).

3

A Detailed Analysis of the Main Decision-Aiding Software

THE BASIC ANALYSIS

The Program in General

The purpose of this chapter is to analyze a floppy-disk program that can process a set of goals or criteria, alternative legal policies or decisions for achieving the goals, and the relations between the goals and legal-policy alternatives in order to arrive at the alternative or combination of alternatives that is best for maximizing benefits minus costs. All of those concepts are explained in this chapter in light of the microcomputer program. To illustrate the use of the program, this chapter uses as an example the evaluation of alternative ways of disposing of criminal cases by trials, plea bargains, and diversion out of the judicial system. The key goals are delay reduction, respect for the law, and expense reduction.

The program is called Policy/Goal Percentaging Analysis (P/G%) because it makes use of part/whole percentages to handle the problem of goals being measured on different dimensions. The measurement units are converted into a system of percentages showing achievement on each goal, rather than a system of inches,

Figure 3–1
The Title Page of the Program

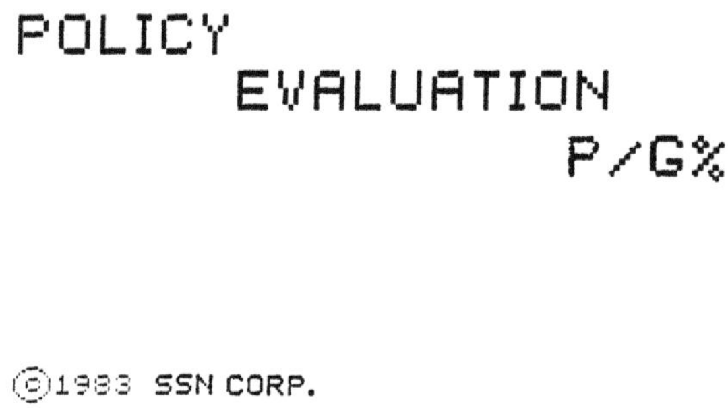

dollars, apples, days, or other measurement scores. This program was written by John Long of Champaign, Illinois, based on a decision-making methodology that I developed at the University of Illinois. The programming benefited from a program previously written on the basis of my methodology by David Garson of North Carolina State University.

To use the program, one needs the following equipment:

1. A copy of the floppy disk available from me especially for experimenting and demonstrating.
2. An IBM personal computer or an IBM-compatible computer that has at least 192K of memory and is equipped with a color graphics adapter and a color or non-color monitor that works with the adapter. A version of the P/G% program written by David Garson is also available for use on an Apple lle or ll+ microcomputer.
3. A copy of this chapter, possibly supplemented by some of the references given in the bibliography.
4. Optional items, including a dot-matrix graphics printer if one wants a printout rather than just a screen display.

To start the program, use the following procedures:

1. Insert the floppy disk into disk drive A.
2. Press Control-Alternate-Delete to boot up the program onto the screen. A notice will appear indicating that the program is written in the ENCORE language, which is part of the PLATO system for interactive learning.
3. Press Carriage Return, which is also referred to as "Enter" or "Next" in this program and this chapter.
4. On the screen will appear Figure 3–1 showing the title page of the program.
5. Press Carriage Return, and the first menu will appear.

Figure 3–2
Menu 1 for Determining a File

```
Current data file =

Available files:
ASPA        diversn




Enter name of data file desired and
press NEXT to select,
shift-NEXT to create,
shift-HELP to delete.
NEXT alone for ASPA
    ▶
```

The Initial Menus

Figure 3–2 shows Menu 1 for determining a file. That menu requires the user to type either the name of an existing file or create a new file. When this computer run was being made, there were two existing files named "ASPA" and "diversn." As many as eight letters can be used to name a file. After typing the name of a file, one has four choices:

1. Press Next or Return. This shows that the user has selected one of the existing files.
2. Press the Shift key and Return. This shows that the user wants to create a new file.
3. Press the Shift key and F8 on the left of the keyboard. This shows that the user wants to delete the existing file named. Key F8 is also the "help" key for this program. When it is pressed without the Shift key, the main menu usually appears as is shown in Figure 3–3. To create a new file, one may have to delete an old file since the present program allows for only three files in storage at one time.
4. Press Return without naming a file. This shows that the user wants to work with the ASPA file.

Exercising choices 1, 2, or 4 on Menu 1 will bring the user to Menu 2, which is shown in Figure 3–4. It is used for indicating what is to be done with the file. There are three choices:

1. Press Return. This shows that the user wants an analysis of the existing file whose name was typed in response to Menu 1. The example shows that "diversn" was selected.
2. Press Shift and Return. This shows that the user wants to edit either the existing

Figure 3–3
Menu 3 for Inserting, Changing, Processing, or Saving Data

```
Current data file =diversn

Available files:
ASPA          diversn



Selected/Added file = diversn
NEXT alone to analyze
SHIFT-NEXT to edit
DATA to reselect
```

Figure 3–4
Menu 2 for Indicating What Is to Be Done with the File

```
CHOOSE AN OPTION:

1. Enter total budget
   Currently set at $      0.00
2. Review Alternatives

3. Review Criteria

4. Enter Alternative scores
         for each Criteria

5. Perform the analysis

6. Present results

7. Save present model
```

file or a new file. Edit means either inserting new data or changing old data as to the alternatives, criteria, or relations.

3. Press F7 to go back to Menu 1. This shows that the user wants to select a different existing file or create a different new file. F7 is also called the "data button."

Exercising option 1 on Menu 2 will display Menu 3, which is shown in Figure 3–3. Menu 3 is useful for inserting, changing, processing, or saving data. It is the main menu in the program and provides the following seven options:

1. Press 1. The user can then enter or change a total budget to be allocated. That is only applicable to optimum-mix problems in which scarce resources are being divided among alternatives, in contrast to an optimum-choice problem in which one wants to know the alternative that is best or the rank order of the alternatives.

Figure 3–5
Two Alternatives

	Budgets	
Alternative	Minimum	Actual
1trials	0.00	0.00
2pleas	0.00	0.00

Select a number to modify- ▶

2. Press 2. The user can then enter or change the criteria, as is explained by Figure 3–5.
3. Press 3. The user can then enter or change the criteria, as is explained by Figure 3–6.
4. Press 4. The user can then enter or change the scores of each alternative on each criteria, as is explained by Figures 3–7 and 3–8.
5. Press 5. The computer will then (1) calculate weighted part/whole percentages for each alternative on each criterion, (2) sum the percentages across each alternative, (3) convert the sums into a 100 percent scale, and (4) apply the percentages to whatever the total budget is, as is explained by Figure 3–9.
6. Press 6. The computer will display the results of the analysis performed when option 5 is chosen. In a future version of the program, options 5 and 6 may be combined since one would not want to perform the analysis without presenting the results or present the non-results without performing the analysis.
7. Press 7. This shows that the user wants to save the alternatives, the criteria, the relation-scores, and the budget from whatever problem or file has been selected for editing or analysis.

The Input Variables

Describing the Alternatives. Exercising option 2 in Menu 3 or pressing Shift and Return in Menu 2 will generate a display like that in Figure 3–5. That display is in effect prompting the user to do the following:

1. Press 1 and Return or Enter. This mainly tells the computer that the user wants to give a label or a name to the first alternative. After pressing Enter, the cursor-arrow will move from the bottom of the display to the left of the first row to show the user where the typing will be displayed. In the present program, the cursor-arrow sometimes covers the first letter or number of the typing but moves to the right when Next is pressed.
2. Type the name of the first alternative and press Enter. For example, type "trials" in choosing between trials and plea bargains as a means of resolving criminal cases.

Figure 3–6
Two Criteria

Criterion	Meas.Unit	Weight
1DELAY	DAYS	-1.00
2RESPECT	0-10 SCALE	1.00
3EXPENSE	DOLLARS	-1.00

Select a number to modify- ▶

3. Type the minimum allocation to the first alternative when there is a minimum allocation. If there is no minimum allocation, just press Enter.
4. Type the previous or actual allocation. It will be subsequently compared with the optimum allocation. If there is no previous allocation or if this is not an allocation problem, just press Enter.

After entering that information for the first alternative, type 2 and press Enter. This informs the computer that the user wants to enter analogous information for the second alternative, which in this example is "pleas." The user could then go on to 3 or more alternatives up to 15, but for the sake of simplicity, we will start with 2 alternatives. Therefore, when the display asks you to select another number to modify, just press Return. At that point, the display will state, "Toggle an alternative—on/off." *Toggle,* as a verb, means to turn something on when it is off and to turn something off when it is on. An alternative is stopped (or off) if its label appears red (or is relatively dark). An alternative is go (or on) if its label appears in blue (or is relatively bright). When creating a new datafile, the alternatives are off until the user indicates which ones should be turned on for comparison purposes. To turn an alternative on, simply give its number in response to the toggle prompt and press Enter. If one wants to turn all of the alternatives on, press Next and no number in response to the toggle prompt.

Describing the Goals. If in response to the toggle prompt on the alternatives one presses Next without giving another number, Menu 3 returns. At that point it would be appropriate to choose option 3 to insert or change data concerning the criteria. Doing so will cause a display like that in Figure 3–6 to appear on the screen. That display in effect prompts the user to do the following:

1. Press 1 and Enter. This mainly tells the computer that the user wants to give a label or a name to the first criterion or goal.
2. Type the name of the first criterion and press Enter. For example, type "Delay" when the goals are delay reduction and respect for the law.
3. Type the measurement unit. This is useful for understanding the scoring of the relations that appear in Figures 3–7 and 3–8.

Figure 3–7
Relations for the First Alternative on the Two Criteria

```
        ALTERNATIVE / CRITERIA SCORING

          Enter a score for each criterion
             on the alternative presented.
trials
   delay                                120.00
   respect                                6.00



Press: DATA to redo - BACK when done
```

4. Type the relative weight of the first goal relative to the other goals. The easiest way to do this is to give no weight to the goals until they are all listed. Then give a weight of 1 to the least important goal. Then give a weight to each other goal in terms of how many more times it is important than the least important goal is. A weight of 3 means that an improvement of 10 percentage points on the goal to which it pertains is worth roughly as much as an improvement of 30 percentage points on the least important goal. Along with the relative weight of the goal, type a minus sign for each goal that is like golf, in which a high score is bad, and a plus sign or no sign for a goal that is like bowling, in which a high score is good.

After entering that information for the first criterion, type 2 and press Enter to inform the computer that the user wants to enter analogous information for the second criterion. The user can then go on to other criteria up to five criteria. After the criteria have been exhausted by pressing Next without giving a criterion number, respond to the toggle prompts to turn on or activate certain goals selectively or to turn on all of them.

Describing the Relations between the Alternatives and the Goals. If in response to the toggle prompt on the criteria one presses Next without giving another number, Menu 3 returns. It would then be appropriate to choose option 4 to insert or change data concerning the relations. Doing this will generate a display like that in Figure 3–7. It in effect prompts the user to do the following:

1. Give a score to the first alternative on the first goal in light of the measurement units previously mentioned.
2. Give a score to the first alternative on the second goal.
3. Give a score to the first alternative on the next goal and so on. If a score involves more than three digits, stars will appear on the display because the display is now

Figure 3–8
Relations for the Second Alternative on the Two Criteria

```
     ALTERNATIVE / CRITERIA SCORING

        Enter a score for each criterion
           on the alternative presented.
pleas
   delay                              30.00
   respect                             2.00




Press: DATA to redo - BACK when done
```

only wide enough to hold three numbers to the left of a two-place decimal point, although larger numbers can be entered but not displayed.

After scoring the first alternative on the last goal, press Next, and a display like that in Figure 3–8 will appear. It states that the computer wants the following information:

1. A score on the second alternative on the first goal
2. A score on the second alternative on the second goal
3. A score on the second alternative on the next goal and so on

After inserting the scores for one alternative on all of the goals, one can make corrections by pressing F7 (the data key) to redo any or all of the scores. When the rescoring is complete, press F6 (the back key) to go to Menu 3. The F6 key is useful for going back to Menu 1 on other occasions.

The Primary Results

After scoring the last alternative on the last goal, press Next and Menu 3 will reappear. At this point you could go back and review the alternatives, the criteria, and the relation-scores to make sure everything is right. If you are satisfied that the data has been properly entered or changed, exercise option 5 to perform the analysis. The display will then indicate that the computer is complying by stating, "Analyzing the data." Then press 6 and Next to request that the computer present the results. A display like that in Figure 3–9 will appear. It shows that trials is the better way of resolving cases in light of the goals, the alternatives,

Figure 3–9
Results of Relating Two Alternatives to Two Criteria

```
        Total Resources =        0.00
Alternative                   Alloc.   %Budget
 trials                         0.00    72.50
 pleas                          0.00    27.50
```

and the relations. To be more exact, if we were allocating 100 points between trials and pleas, trials would receive 72.50, and pleas would receive 27.50, as is shown in Figure 3–9. There are zeros in the allocation column since no budget is being allocated in this problem.

To provide a better understanding of what happens between the data on alternatives, goals, and relations and the results, the program will be modified to show intermediate values. Those intermediate values can be seen in Table 3–1. The table shows that trials receives a part/whole percentage of −80 percent on delay and +75 percent on respect. If the +75 percent is tripled to show a weight of 3 for respect, the sum of the weighted part/whole percentages for trials is 225 percent minus 80 percent, which equals 145 percent. Table 3–1 also shows that pleas receives a part/whole percentage of −20 percent on delay and +25 percent on respect. Tripling the 25 percent means adding +75 percent to −20 percent to give a sum of the weighted part/whole percentages equal to 55 percent for pleas. The sum of the weights of −1 and +3 is 2. Dividing 145 percent by 2 gives the bottom-line adjusted percentage of 72 to trials (rounding to the nearest even number) and 28 to pleas.

Adding More Alternatives and More Goals

We could easily show additional displays with additional alternatives and goals. That, however, would be redundant for methodological purposes although maybe of interest for substantive purposes or to test one's understanding of the basic analysis. If we start with two alternatives and two goals, a logical extension would be to three alternatives and two goals. A third alternative might be to divert cases out of the judicial system. Assume that diversion on the average takes 20 days and that it receives a respect score of 4 on a 0–10 scale. Then the adjusted percentages for the three alternatives would be 40, 16, and 44, respectively. Notice that diversion becomes the winner because it does so well on delay and is middling on respect.

We could also have two alternatives and three goals (Table 3–2). A third goal might be expense with a weight of −1 like delay. Suppose that trials on the average cost $3,000 and pleas cost $600. Then the adjusted percentages for the two alternatives would be 62 and 38, respectively. Notice that trials comes down because it does not do so well on the negative goal of expense.

We could also have three alternatives and two goals (Table 3–3) or three alternatives and three goals (Table 3–4). The latter option requires just adding

Table 3–1
Data Illustrating Percentaging Analysis

CRITERIA / ALTERNATIVES	Time Consumption (Weight = 1)		Respect for Law (Weight = 3)		Choosing Score		Allocating Score
	Raw Score (Days)	Part/Whole Percent	Raw Score (1-10)	Part/Whole Percent	Unweighted Sum	Weighted Sum	Part/Whole Percent
Trials	120	-80%	6	75%	- 5%	+145%	+ 72%
Pleas	30	-20%	2	25%	+ 5%	+ 55%	+ 28%
Totals	150	100%	8	100%	0%	200%	100%

Note: The above percentaging analysis can be applied to any number of goals and alternatives. It can be used to choose:

1. The one best alternative where the alternatives are mutually exclusive. It is the one which has the highest weighted percentage.

2. The best combination of alternatives. Determine the sum of the weighted percentages for each possible or feasible combination. Pick the combination that has the highest weighted sum of percentages. Sometimes it might be meaningful to rank order the alternatives in terms of their weighted percentages and then pick the better ones until the budget runs out.

3. The best alternative where doing too much or too little is undesirable. The alternatives are arranged on a continuum from doing a little to doing a lot. The one best alternative is the one where the weighted percentages reach a peak if the goals are positively stated, or reach a bottom if the goals are all negatively stated.

4. The best mix across alternatives. Multiply the weighted percentages in the last column by the total available budget after allocating minimums to each alternative.

Table 3–2
Handling Two Policies and Three Goals

GOALS / POLICIES	Delay (W = -1)		Respect (W = 3)		Sum of Weighted P/W %'s	Adjusted Sum	Allocation
	Raw Score (Days)	Part/Whole Percent	Raw Score (0-10)	Part/Whole Percent			
Trials	120	- 70%	6	50%	79%	40%	$ 80
Pleas	30	- 18	2	17	33	16	32
Diversion	20	- 12	4	33	88	44	88
Total	170	100%	12	100%	200%	100%	$200 (Total Budget)

Table 3–3
Handling Three Policies and Two Goals

GOALS / POLICIES	Delay (W = -1)		Respect (W = 3)		Expense (W = -1)		Sum of Weighted P/W %'s	Adjusted Sum	Allocation
	Raw Score (Days)	Part/Whole Percent	Raw Score (0-10)	Part/Whole Percent	Raw Score (Dollars)	Part/Whole Percent			
Trials	120	-80%	6	75%	3,000	-83%	62%	62%	$123
Pleas	30	-20	2	25	600	-17	38	38	77
Total	150	100%	8	100%	$3,600	100%	100%	100%	$200 (Total Budget)

Table 3–4
Handling Three Policies and Three Goals

GOALS / POLICIES	Delay (W = -1)		Respect (W = 3)		Expense (W = -1)		Sum of Weighted P/W %'s	Adjusted Sum	Allocation
	Raw Score (Days)	Part/Whole Percent	Raw Score (0-10)	Part/Whole Percent	Raw Score (Dollars)	Part/Whole Percent			
Trials	120	- 71%	6	50%	$3,000	- 77%	2%	2%	$ 5
Pleas	30	- 18	2	17	600	- 15	17	17	34
Diversion	20	- 12	4	33	300	- 8	81	81	161
Total	170	100%	12	100%	$3,900	100%	100%	100%	$200 (Total Budget)

the additional piece of information as to the average expense incurred in using diversion to resolve cases. Suppose that the answer is $300. The adjusted percentages for the three alternatives in light of the three goals then become 2, 17, and 80. Notice that diversion moves substantially up and trials moves down when expense to the judicial system is considered. One could interpret those results as meaning that for certain types of cases like public drunkenness or juvenile matters, about 80 percent of the cases should be diverted, 17 percent should be resolved through out-of-court settlements, and 2 percent should go to full trials.

VARIATIONS ON THE BASIC ANALYSIS

Allocation Analysis

We could easily show additional displays that involve allocating scarce resources across budget categories. That, however, would also be redundant. The main differences from what we have shown are:

1. In describing the alternatives, minimum allocations and past allocations are usually given. Each alternative gets its minimum as the first step in the allocation process. The sum of the minimums is then subtracted from the total budget and the residue is allocated in proportion to the weighted part/whole percentages for each alternative.
2. When one comes to Menu 3, press 1 to enter a total budget to be allocated. Doing this states that one is to spend that figure rather than more or less. The program could be changed to allow for budget allocating that would spend as little as possible while achieving a minimum satisfaction level on one or more goals. To change the budget requires having at least some alternatives and criteria turned on. The budget cannot be set for an amount less than 1. Nor can any alternative or criterion be numbered less than 1.
3. The results provide allocation amounts or recommended appropriations as well as adjusted percentages. The display shows the allocations in a column before the column showing the percentages, implying that the percentages are derived from the allocations. In reality, the percentages determine the allocations by multiplying the total budget (minus the sum of the minimums) by the percentages, which have been adjusted to a 100 percent scale.

As a brief example of how the program handles an allocation problem, Figure 3–10 shows how the program allocated the $947,000 available in 1983 for allocating to 15 activities of the American Society for Public Administration (ASPA). Table 3–5 shows the membership attitude scores that each activity received on a scale of +2, +1, 0, −1, and −2. The *Public Administration Times* (P.A. Times), for example, received an average score of 1.40, which translates into a part/whole percentage of 14.8 percent when 1.40 is divided by 9.43, which is the sum of the 13 positive attitude scores. If one multiplies 0.148 by $947,000, one gets $140,156, or 140 monetary units with each monetary

Figure 3–10
Multiple Alternatives with Budget Allocations

Total Resources =	947.00	
Alternative	Alloc.	%Budget
Study tours	0.10	0.01
Insurance programs	0.10	0.01
awards program	3.01	0.32
Affirmative action	33.13	3.50
Section activities	42.17	4.45
Training programs	44.18	4.66
Regional conferences	57.23	6.04
Position taking	60.24	6.36
Prof. standards	72.29	7.63
National Confs.	81.33	8.59
Special Publications	83.33	8.80
Job listings	100.40	10.60
Chapter activities	111.45	11.77
PAR	117.47	12.40
P.A. times	140.56	14.84

unit worth $1,000. One could go up the list on Figure 3–10 to see that the part/whole percentages under "Budget" match column 2 in Table 3–5 and to see that the dollar amounts under "Alloc." match column 3 in Table 3–5. The one small discrepancy is that the program (as currently written) gives a minimum allocation percentage of 1/100 of 1 percent, as was done with study tours and insurance programs.

A future version of the P/G% program will provide a column comparing each actual or past budget allocation with the optimum or proposed allocation, as Table 3–5 does. That comparison is helpful here in analyzing why some budget activities receive more or less than one would expect in light of their popularity among the ASPA membership. It is helpful in general to question why the actual allocations of each alternative differ from the optimum scores. The answers may help the actual decision-makers revise their decisions. The answers can also help the program users revise the goals, alternatives, and relations to make the optimums more realistic or empirically valid.

Raw-Score Analysis

Figure 3–11 provides a raw-score analysis of the data shown in Figures 3–7 and 3–8. The −102 for the trials alternative was arrived at by subtracting 3 times 6 for the respect benefits (measured on a 0–10 scale) from the −1 times 120 for the delay costs (measured in days). The −24 for pleas was arrived at by subtracting 3 times 2 from the −1 times 30. The +3 is the weight of respect, and the −1 is the weight of delay. Those two weights mean that respect as a dimensionless criterion is three times as important as delay. They also mean that being high on respect is plus, or desired, and that being high on delay is negative, or undesired.

Table 3–5

Allocating the 1983 ASPA Budget in Proportion to the Attitude Scores

Rank	Current Activity	Attitude Score (Parts) 1	Part/ Whole % 2	% Times Budget ("Optimum") 3	Actual Budget Allocation 4	Budget Page 5	Actual Minus Optimum 6	
1	P.A. Times	1.40	14.8	$140	$123	p. 21	$-17(8)	1
2	Public Admin. Review	1.17	12.4	117	208	19	91(2)*	2
3	Chapter activities	1.11	11.8	112	152	11, 13, 31	40(3)*	3
4	Job listings	1.00	10.6	100	60	26	-40(3)	4
5	Informal networking	--	--	--	--	--	--	5
6	Special publications	.83	8.8	83	46	23	-37(4)	6
7	National conferences	.81	8.6	81	198	15	117(1)*	7
8	Professional standards	.72	7.6	72	35	16	-37(5)	8
9	Position taking	.60	6.4	61	35	16	-26(7)	9
10	Regional conferences	.57	6.0	57	~0	none	-57(1)	10
11	Training programs	.44	4.7	45	35	16	-10(9)	11
12	Section activities	.42	4.5	43	~0	13	-43(2)	12
13	Affirmative action	.33	3.5	33	~0	none	-33(6)	13
14	Awards program	.03	.32	3	35	16	32(4)*	14
15	Study tours	neg.	0	0	~0	none	0	15
16	Insurance programs	neg.	0	0	20	30	20(5)*	16
Totals		9.43 =whole	100%	$947 =budget	$947 =budget		$0	

Notes:

1. The attitude scores are translated into numbers as follows: ++ = +2, + = +1, 0 = 0, - = -1, and -- = -2.
2. All columns with dollars have been rounded to the nearest $1,000.
3. Informal networking is not given a separate allocation since it is part of chapter/section activities, national/regional conferences, and PA Times/other publications.
4. The $974,000 to be allocated comes from the $1,441,000 proposed total budget minus $494,000 in anticipated ASPA expenses that are not allocated to the 16 activities.
5. The allocation for program development has been divided equally between the six activities of policy issues, training, professional standards, awards, promoting public administration, and promoting ASPA.
6. The budget allocations come from the fiscal year 1983 proposed budget.
7. The numbers to the right of column 6 show the rank order for the underfunded and the overfunded items. Asterisks appear next to the overfunded items.

Figure 3–11
Results of a Raw-Score Analysis

Alternative	Combined Rawscores	%
1trials	-102.00	-80.95
2pleas	-24.00	-19.05

Figure 3–11 is mainly meaningful when all of the criteria under consideration are measured in the same measurement units such as days, 0–10 scales, dollars, or some other common unit. To generate Figure 3–11, one must change Figure 3–6 or the criteria display so that the measurement unit of respect is changed to "days" or so that the measurement unit of delay is changed to "0–10 scale" with the same capitalization, spacing, and punctuation. An alternative approach is to blank out the measurement units for each alternative that is involved in the raw-score analysis. One could also obtain the equivalent of a raw-score analysis by weighting the raw scores by their column totals, which has the effect of defeating the part/whole percentaging.

Figure 3–11 could also be meaningful if one could state that RW days of delay (e.g., 25 days) is worth one unit of respect on a 0–10 scale. If one can make such a statement, RW (e.g., 25) should be substituted for the %W of 3 in the criteria display. *RW* stands for the raw weight, showing the relative importance of goals when working with raw scores, and *%W* stands for the percentage weight, showing the relevant importance of goals when working with part/whole percentages.

When goals have a common unit, it is more meaningful to work with raw scores than part/whole percentages. When goals do not have a common unit, it is generally easier to work with percentages, although one can still work with raw scores. In either way of working with multi-dimensional criteria, one needs to use raw-score weights or percentage weights to show the relative importance of the criteria.

Threshold Analysis

To aid in arriving at raw-score weights, percentage weights, or raw scores, it is often useful to know the threshold value of such inputs. The *threshold value* is the numerical value of an input item that causes the sum of the weighted P/W%'s of the second-place alternative to become tied with the first-place alternative or that causes any alternative to become tied with any other specified alternative. Knowing the threshold value of a weight or other input enables one to simplify a difficult question about the correct weight of a goal or a relation-score. Such a question can be converted into a threshold question, whereby one asks whether the actual value of a weight is more or less than the threshold value. Such a question enables one to avoid arguing over whether the weight is 5 or 10 if both values are higher than the threshold value or if both values are lower than the threshold value.

Figure 3–12
Results of a Threshold Analysis

THRESHOLD ANALYSIS

	delay	respect
trial	-150.00	3.00
pleas	-24.00	4.00
Weight	-2.50	1.20

Figure 3–12 shows a threshold analysis of the problem of trials versus pleas as a means of resolving criminal cases. The most important numbers are −2.50 for the weight of delay and 1.20 for the weight of respect. If the −2.50 is substituted for the −1.00 in Figure 3–6, and all of the other numbers are held constant, the allocation percentages in Figure 3–9 will be tied at 50 percent each for trials and pleas. A weight of −1.00 to delay results in trials winning 72 to 28 percent. Giving a greater weight to delay (on which trials does not do as well as pleas) causes the allocation percentage of trials to go down and the allocation percentage of pleas to go up. The same effect can be achieved by lowering the weight of respect from 3.00 in Figure 3–6 to its threshold value of 1.20.

Likewise, decreasing the respect score of trials from a 6.00 (as shown in Figure 3–7) to a 3.00 (as shown in the threshold analysis) will generate a tie, and so will increasing the respect score of pleas from a 2.00 (as shown in Figure 3–8) to a 4.00 (as shown in Figure 3–12). The negative threshold values for trials and pleas on delay tell us that there is no actual value that either trials or pleas could have on delay that would cause a tie. On the basis of respect alone, trials begins with a part/whole percentage of 225 (i.e., 75 percent multiplied by 3), and pleas begins with a P/W% of 75 (i.e., 25 percent multiplied by 3). Thus even if trials were to be 100 percent responsible for delay, trials would still have an overall P/W% of 125 (i.e., 225 percent − 100 percent), and pleas would still have an overall P/W% of 75 (i.e., 75 percent − 0 percent). Thus there is no positive number of days of delay to which trials could increase or to which pleas could decrease in order to generate an overall tie in the worth of those two alternatives.

Figure 3–12 shows a threshold analysis in which each input item is allowed to vary while the other input items are held constant in order to determine the threshold value of each input item. One might, however, ask what it would take to bring the second-place alternative to a tie with the first-place alternative if two, three, or more input items could vary simultaneously. To determine that, one should experiment with changing the goal weights in Figure 3–6 and the relation-scores in Figures 3–7 and 3–8. To bring pleas up to a tie with trials, one would logically (1) increase the weight of delay, (2) decrease the weight of respect, (3) increase the delay of trials, (4) decrease the respect of trials, (5) decrease the delay of pleas, (6) increase the respect of pleas. The threshold analysis of Figure 3–12 is useful even when more than one input is allowed to vary because it shows how much variation can be allowed before overcompensation occurs. Thus if the respect of trials is lowered from 6.00 to below 3.00, pleas will become the clear winner rather than just tie with trials.

The program is also capable of doing a threshold analysis with the raw scores. For example, Figures 3–7 and 3–8 show the raw score of trials on delay and respect to be 120 and 6 and the raw scores of pleas to be 30 and 2. The net or aggregated raw scores are thus −102 for trials and −24 for pleas, as is shown in Figure 3–11 when delay has a weight of −1 and pleas has a weight of +3. One can show that the threshold values for the raw data of Figures 3–7 and 8 are 42 (down from 120) and 32 (up from 6) to improve trials to −24. The threshold values for pleas are 108 (up from 30) and −24 (down from 2) to worsen pleas to −102. That is useful threshold information when the goals are measured in the same units.

The raw threshold weight of respect is 22.5. That means if 22.5 days of delay are worth equally as much as one unit of respect, trials and pleas have equal worth. If 22.5 days is more desired than one unit of respect, pleas is the better alternative because it gives more days saved. If one unit of respect is more desired than 22.5 days saved, trials is the better alternative because it generates more respect. That is useful threshold information even when the goals are not measured in the same units. The threshold weight of delay is −0.13 meaning that at the tied threshold, about a tenth of a unit of respect is worth a day on delay. It is, however, easier to grasp a tradeoff of one unit of respect on a 0–10 scale for 22.5 delay days saved.

Convergence Analysis

Threshold analysis is a highly useful tool for determining the changes in the raw scores or weights that can make a difference as to who is in first place when choosing the best alternative. Threshold analysis is, however, not so useful when the P/G% program is being used for allocation purposes. In an allocation, the bottom line does not involve determining which alternative is best. Instead, it involves determining how much of something to allocate to each alternative. Thus when there are two alternatives, the second-place alternative may receive as much as 49 percent of the scarce resources and therefore not be an all-or-nothing loser like the second-place alternative in an optimum-choice situation. Under those allocation circumstances, the kind of sensitivity analysis that is analogous to threshold analysis is called "convergence analysis."

Convergence analysis involves determining the point at which each weight causes the allocation percentages to be almost the same as they would be if

Figure 3–13
Results of a Convergence Analysis

```
                    CONVERGENCE ANALYSIS


        Enter a delta for incrementing the weights.
              (default = 1.00)
             1.00

        Enter a stopping difference.
            (default = 5 percentage points)
          Stopping difference set at   5.0 percentage points.



                   delay       respect
Weight - -          -2.00        2.00
```

infinity were assigned to the weight. For example, Figure 3–13 shows that if the weight of respect were infinity rather than a 3, the allocation percentages between trials and pleas would be 75 and 25 percent. This means that the allocation percentages on the far right would be the same as the part/whole percentages for the goal of respect because that goal would totally dominate all of the other goals. One, however, does not have to raise the weight of respect all the way to infinity to come close to the 75 versus 25 percent allocation. One can define ''coming close'' as being within 5 percentage points, or 0.05 expressed as a decimal. The 0.05 level has considerable respectability in statistical analysis as the cutoff between a small difference that is not worth being concerned about and a big difference.

What then is the convergence value of the weight of respect that is capable of producing allocation percentages that are within 5 percentage points of the limits of 75 and 25 percent? The answer is that a weight as low as 2 will do it. A weight of 2 means that the P/W% of 75 is doubled to 150, and the P/W% of 25 is doubled to 50. If one then adds the weighted P/W% of 150 for trials on respect to the −80 percent for trials on delay, one obtains an allocation percentage of 70. Likewise, if one adds the weighted P/W% of 50 for pleas on respect to the −20 percent for pleas on delay, one obtains a complementary allocation percentage of 30. Those two allocation percentages of 70 and 30 are both within 5 percentage points of the limits of 75 and 25 percent. There is thus no need to argue over whether a weight of respect relative to delay should be 2, 3, 4, 6, 10, or higher since any weight of 2 or above will yield allocation percentages within the convergence range of 70 to 80 percent on trials and within 20 to 30 percent on pleas.

Knowing that the convergence value of the weight of respect is 2 (given the

−1 weight of delay and given the four relation-scores) enables us to resolve the problem (of the percentage of cases to allocate to trials and pleas) much easier than if we had to argue over a variety of alternative weights for respect. All we have to decide is that respect is at least twice as important as delay and the allocation problem is resolved, given the way the problem is structured here. We might not, however, like the structure, because it does not consider the relative expense of trials and pleas. If an expense goal were considered, we would allocate a much smaller percentage of cases to trials than pleas, but the goals to include is a separable problem for the weights to assign the goals that are included.

Display 13 shows the results of a convergence analysis applied to the input data of the problem of trials versus pleas. The display is divided into five parts. The first part asks the user by how large an amount each of the weights should be changed or incremented. The default is to increment the weights by one whole number at a time. If one suspects that the existing weight is already above the convergence value (as a weight of 3 for respect would be), one should reset the original weight at 1. The second part of the display asks the user how much of a percentage-point difference will be considered a small or convergent difference. The default is 5 percentage points (as was used in Display 13) or 5.01 to get the computer to stop when the difference is exactly 5.00 percentage points. The program also gives the user the option of defining "coming close" as being within 95 or 105 percent of the limits, which is different from being 5 percentage points below or above the limits. That alternative way of defining "coming close" is the third part of the convergence analysis, although not shown in Figure 3–13.

The fourth part is also not shown on this figure. It involves the computer showing the percentage-points difference for each increment until the stopping difference has been reached or until the user stops the incrementing by hitting Carriage Return. The fifth part consists of the bottom-line results. They show that the convergence value for the weight of respect is 2.00, as explained above. They also show that the convergence value for the weight of delay is −2.00. This means that if respect has a weight of 1 and given the relation-scores, the weight of delay only has to go as high as a −2.00 to generate allocation percentages within 5 points of 80 and 20 percent. Those two percentages are the limits that would be reached if the weight of delay were negative infinity.

As a practical matter, most people are likely to agree that respect for law is more important than delay. They are, therefore, likely to be willing to set the weight of delay at 1 or −1 if one considers the direction as well as the magnitude. They would then ask how much more important is the weight of respect. Twice as important? Three times as important? Or higher? Thus the normative subjectivity is not likely to be expressed in terms of the weight of delay relative to respect but rather the weight of respect relative to delay when delay is anchored at a value of 1. The above analysis tells us that the key value judgment reduces to whether respect is equal to delay or is more important than delay, where

Figure 3–14
Results of a Constraint Analysis

```
        Total Resources =    100.00
   Alternative               Allbo.      P/W %
 1trials                      39.00      72.50
 2pleas                       61.00      27.50



      Press: SHIFT-NEXT for P/W's
```

"more" means at least twice as much if we express weights in whole numbers. That is the basic issue if one is trying to decide which is the better alternative or what percentage of the cases should be allocated to each alternative in light of the goals, alternatives, and relations.

Constraint Analysis

Two additional variations on the policy/goal percentaging analysis that have recently been developed include constraint and residual analysis. They have in common that they both involve information inserted into the alternatives-input, which is shown in Figure 3–5. Constraint analysis involves inserting minimums or maximums for each alternative. Residual analysis involves inserting previous actual allocations for each alternative. The insertions can be percentages, dollars, or other units as long as one is consistent.

For example, suppose that we indicate on Figure 3–5 that there should be a minimum of 10 percent for trials as a matter of basic fairness and a minimum of 50 percent for pleas in view of the need to avoid the expense of trials. Working with minimums normally means giving equity allocations, as contrasted to efficiency allocations, although minimums may sometimes be justified for reasons other than equity or fairness reasons. Figure 3–14 shows how inserting those minimums affects the results. The column on the far right shows the allocation percentages if the minimums are ignored. Those percentages are 72 and 28 rounded to the nearest even whole number. The percentages taking the minimums into consideration are 39 and 61. Those two percentages come from summing the two minimums of 10 and 50 percent and thereby arriving at 60 percent in minimum allocations. That leaves 40 percent available to be allocated on the basis of the goals and relations, meaning on the basis of efficiency in achieving those goals. The 39 percent comes from giving trials a minimum of 10 percent and then giving trials 0.725 of the 40 percent, which is an additional 29 percent for a total of 39 percent. The 61 percent comes from giving pleas a minimum of 50 percent and then giving pleas 0.275 of the 40 percent, which is an additional 11 percent for a total of 61 percent. One should also note that the total resources to be allocated in Figure 3–14 are 100 percent or the sum of 39 and 61 percent.

The total resources and the allocations are generally expressed in dollars, but they could be hours, people, or percentage points as here. This kind of constraint analysis can be called "preoptimizing constraint analysis" because the constraints are satisfied before the optimizing is done.

An alternative way of dealing with minimums, maximums, or other constraints on the allocations or choices is to ignore those constraints until after the allocations or choices have been made solely on efficiency. Thus one would allocate 72 percent of the cases to trial and 28 percent to pleas. The 72 percent satisfies the constraint of requiring a minimum of 10 percent. The 28 percent, however, does not satisfy the constraint requiring a minimum of 50 percent. We therefore take 22 percent from trials and give it to pleas. The result is 50 percent for trials and 50 percent for pleas, which satisfies both of the constraints and comes closer to the optimum of 72 and 28 percent than 39 and 61 percent did. That kind of constraint analysis can be called "postoptimizing constraint analysis" because the constraints are satisfied after the optimizing is done.

Another way of handling constraints within the P/G% program is a combination of preoptimizing and postoptimizing. Suppose, for example, that there are three alternatives of trials, pleas, and diversion with minimums of 10, 50, and zero percent. Suppose further that the unconstrained allocations are 40, 16, and 44 percent as previously mentioned in discussing multiple alternatives. Pleas needs to be brought up by 34 percent from 16 to 50 percent. That can be handled by allocating 50 percent to pleas and whatever other minimums need to be covered that are not covered by the initial optimizing. The residue is then optimally allocated to the other alternatives in accordance with their allocation percentages. In other words, we part/whole percent the 40 and 44 percent, which add to a whole of 84 percent. Thus trials would get $^{0.40}/_{.84}$ or 0.48 of the remaining 50 percent, which is 24 percent. Diversion would get $^{0.44}/_{.84}$ or 0.52 of the 50 percent, which is 26 percent. The most efficient allocations that satisfy the constraints are thus 24, 50, and 26 percent. This is a combination approach to satisfying the constraints since it involves optimizing, constraint satisfying, and then reoptimizing the residue. The best method depends on the nature of the facts, including the constraints, the alternatives, the criteria, and the relations.

Residual Analysis

To illustrate residual analysis, suppose that we insert on Figure 3–5 that 20 percent of all cases actually go to trial and 80 percent are actually settled by plea bargains. That is roughly the distribution in most jurisdictions when dealing with felony and misdemeanor cases. Figure 3–15 shows how inserting those actual allocations affects the results. The first numerical column repeats the actuals as being 20.0 and 80.0 percent. The second column shows that the optimum percentages in light of the goals, alternatives, and relations is 72.5 and 27.5 percent. The third column shows the residuals. That column indicates trials are being

Figure 3–15
Results of a Residual Analysis

Total Resources = 0.00

Alternative	Actual	Alloc.	Resid
1trials	20.00	72.50	-52.50
2pleas	80.00	27.50	52.50

Press: SHIFT-NEXT for P/W's

underallocated by 52.5 percentage points, and pleas are being overallocated by 52.5.

The residual analysis here is expressed in percentage points. In other problems, it might be expressed in terms of dollars or other resources being allocated. One could also do a residual analysis with an optimum-choice problem in which the object is to choose the one best alternative. The actual score of the previous best alternative would be a one, and the other alternatives would have actual scores of zero. The new best alternative would receive a one in the allocations, and the other alternatives would receive zeros. One could likewise express the actuals and the optimums as rank orders. The residuals would then be the differences between the actual and the optimum rank orders of the alternatives.

Residual analysis raises the logical questions of why the residuals are as low as they are and why they are as high as they are. They are relatively low since they could have been −100 and +100 percent if the actuals had been zero and 100 percent and if the optimum allocation percentages had been 100 and zero percent. The reason that the residuals are not bigger or worse is because the goals and relations do partially capture the values and perceptions of the decision-makers who determine the actual percentages. The reason that the residuals are not smaller or better is because the goals and relations do not sufficiently capture the goals and perceptions of the decision-makers. In particular, no goal was included in this two-by-two analysis for the relative expense of trials versus pleas. If that goal would have been included, the percentage allocation to trials would drop and the percentage allocation to pleas would rise, thereby decreasing the residuals.

There are basically two kinds of reasons why the actual percentages or allocations differ from the optimums. One is that the optimums are not adequately capturing the goals and perceived relations of the decision-makers. The other reason may be that the decision-makers are not accurately perceiving the relations between the alternatives and the goals or between the intermediate goals and the higher goals. Thus residual analysis has both theoretical value for explaining variations and practical value for aiding in improving decision-making. Indeed, the whole policy/goal percentaging analysis is designed primarily to aid in improving or explaining decision-making.

Additional Improvements

Since the July 1984 drafting of the original chapter, the following additional improvements have been made:

1. Instead of Figures 3–7 and 3–8 to show the relations between the alternatives and the criteria, the program now provides a data matrix with alternatives on the rows and criteria on the columns. One can change any of the cells by using the cursor-arrows at the right of the IBM PC.
2. In addition to showing the sum of the weighted part/whole percentages and the adjusted allocation percentages for each alternative, the program can now also show for each goal the part/whole percentages, the weighted part/whole percentages, and the weighted raw scores.
3. A variation on Policy/Goal Percentaging Analysis written in the BASIC language (rather than the ENCORE/PLATO language) provides for multiplying as well as adding in order to aggregate some goals. This is useful when one is calculating expected values with probabilities or discounting raw scores for the passage of time before those raw scores can be received. This variation program was written by Philip Goldberg of the University of Illinois.
4. If the sum of the weighted P/W%'s is negative, the alternative is now allocated nothing or its minimum, and the other alternatives share the total resources in proportion to their sums of weighted P/W%'s after allocating the minimums.
5. If one or more inputs are expressed as ranges, do the analysis twice. For the first time, work with the extreme points that favor the first alternative. For the second time, work with the extreme points that favor the second alternative. Observing the two analyses can facilitate compromises.
6. The program does not automatically show the results of working with the 1, 2, or N policies and 1, 2, or N goals. That would result in an overload of information. It is better for the users to pick out those policies and those goals that they want to have especially considered.

CONCLUSIONS

One might ask how the microcomputer program adds to the basic methodology combined with a hand calculator. The microcomputer program has the following advantages, which the above description helps to clarify:

1. The micro can make the calculations quickly and accurately better than one could do by hand or with a hand calculator.
2. The micro can handle many goals, alternatives, and relations simultaneously.
3. The micro can prompt the user into thinking out more clearly as to what are the alternatives, goals, relations, weights, and minimums.
4. The micro facilitates the adding or deleting of alternatives and goals and the changing of relations, weights, minimums, and budgets.

5. The micro can show various kinds of threshold analysis as to what each input value has to be changed to in order to make a second-place alternative into a tie with the first-place alternative.
6. The micro can show the bottom-line adjusted percentages as a range if each weight and relation is entered as a range with a minimum and a maximum.
7. The interactive nature of microcomputer programs can accelerate learning and retention greater than trying to learn through lectures, reading, or discussion.
8. By eliminating the drudgery of calculations and record keeping, the micro frees and stimulates the user to do more creative and experimental thinking about policy problems and decision-making.

To add to the list of improvements, the authors of this program welcome hearing from users concerning suggestions for making the program even more useful. The authors are also interested in learning about new applications to add to the bibliography of examples. Through that kind of use and feedback, the program should become even more capable of developing and processing sets of goals, alternatives, and relations in order to arrive at the alternative or combination that is best in light of those goals, alternatives, and relations. Doing this can be beneficial to better decision-making in government, business, and law; to better personal decision-making; and to other uses.

APPENDIX A: POINTERS FOR THE SMOOTH WORKING OF THE P/G% PROGRAM

1. In dealing with file creation, access, or deletion, be sure to give a file name before you indicate what is to be done with the file.

2. If an instruction states to hit Shift-Next, it means hit both keys simultaneously, not sequentially.

3. If the program gets stuck and does not seem to want to move, (1) hit Next (also known as the "Carriage Return" or "Enter" key), (2) hit Back (also known as the "F9" key), (3) hit Control-Alternate-Delete simultaneously or as a last resort, or (4) turn the computer off and then back on again.

4. Before entering the name of an alternative, be sure to give it a number and hit Enter. Doing this moves the cursor up to the correct row number for entering the alternative. The same thing must be done for each criterion.

5. After listing your alternatives, indicate that you have no more alternatives by hitting Next. Doing this will bring forth the second alternative display. That display should show asterisks next to each alternative that you want actively considered. If you want to deactivate an alternative, type its number and hit carriage return. Do the same thing after listing your criteria.

6. To enter your data in the data matrix, use the cursor-arrows at the right of the keyboard to move the cursor to the left, right, up, or down. If you have more than five criteria, move the right arrow to the right after the fifth criterion, and the screen will display the sixth through the tenth criterion.

7. When you are listing each alternative, hit Next twice to bypass the minimum and previous budget allocations if you are not doing a budgeting problem.

8. Avoid hitting Next more times than you want. Otherwise, you will be propelled further into the program than you want to be.

9. The above pointers and others can be learned by reading the manual, reading the screen, or through practice, but they are put here to save time and frustration.

10. Access an existing file by selecting a master file and then selecting a datafile. Hit Carriage Return between each selection. Create a master file or a specific datafile by typing the new name and then hitting Shift-Next.

11. Give the budget $0 if you are not allocating a budget on the data management menu.

12. Choose raw-score analysis by hitting option 5 on the data-management menu. Do this when all of your criteria are measured in the same units or if you can indicate how much more one unit or one criterion is worth compared to one unit on a second criterion. Choose percentaging analysis for dealing with multidimensionality when your criteria are not measured in the same units.

13. When you want to see the A prompt, hit F1 or Shift-F1. When the A prompt appears, type "POLICY" if you are at a terminal that has a graphics adapter. Type "TPOLICY" (for "text policy") if you are at a terminal that lacks a graphics adapter.

APPENDIX B: RECENT ADDED FEATURES TO THE P/G% PROGRAM

1. There is now a new datafiles-management system that allows for a separate datafiles disk. It can hold as many as 320 datafiles with 20 datafiles per master file and 16 master files. See the appendix at the end of this book for details.

2. A raw-score analysis can now be done by exercising option 5 on the data-management menu instead of showing that the measurement units for all of the criteria are the same.

3. Indicate for each datafile whether it is being established for prescriptive or predictive purposes. If prescription is chosen, the alternatives display asks for minimums for a constraint analysis and actuals for a residual analysis. If prediction is chosen, the alternatives display asks for the outcomes of the previous cases for use in developing a predictive decision-rule.

4. After getting the primary results, one can press Shift-Next to see the part/whole percentages for each alternative on each criterion. By pressing Shift-Next again, one can see the weighted part/whole percentages for each alternative on each criterion. That information explains how the summation scores were derived for each alternative.

5. The initial "help" statements show how each function key can be used. The most important function key is F9, which will always take one back to the main menu.

6. The program now assumes that any alternative or criterion that is inputted

is meant to be activated unless the alternative or criterion is toggled off by entering the number of the alternative or criterion in response to the question about toggling on or off the alternatives or the criteria for sensitivity analysis. One still needs to enter the set of alternatives and the set of criteria to have them activated, but that can be done collectively by pressing Next or Enter in response to the toggling request without having to enter each alternative and criterion separately.

7. So that no input data will be lost as a result of prematurely exiting from the program, call the main menu by pressing F9 after inputting the alternatives, the goals, the relations, and other input data. When the main menu appears, exercise option 5 to save what has been inputted before that point.

8. To run the main P/G% program requires an IBM-compatible microcomputer with 192K memory and a graphics adapter. We do have an alternative program available on request that can run with 128K memory and no graphics adapter. Many of its characteristics, however, are not covered by the P/G% manual, which may make it more difficult to use.

9. To facilitate working with the P/G% program, the book-length manual *Microcomputers, Evaluation Problems, and Policy Analysis* has been published by Sage Publications. It is organized in terms of the methodological problems of how to deal with (1) multiple dimensions on multiple goals, (2) multiple missing information, (3) multiple alternatives that are too many to determine the effects of each one, (4) multiple and possibly conflicting constraints, and (5) the needs for simplicity in spite of all that multiplicity.

10. To print any display, one needs to (1) attach a graphics printer with a male plug to a printer board at the back of the computer which has a female outlet, (2) plug the printer into the wall and turn it on, (3) arrange for the desired display to appear on the TV monitor, and (4) press Shift-Printscreen.

APPENDIX C: NEW P/G% SCREEN DISPLAYS

Figure 3–16
The New Main Menu

```
        POLICY EVALUATION  P/G%
        *** Choose an option ***
          1. File management
              Master file = demo1
              Data file = diversn

          2. Data management

          3. Primary analysis

          4. Threshold / Convergence
                    analyses

          5. Save present data

    Press: BACK for Title page
           INDEX to return to this menu
```

Figure 3–17
The New File-Management Menu

```
                 FILE MANAGEMENT

          *** Choose an option ***

            1. Master file selection
               Current file = demo1

            2. Data file selection
               Current file = diversn

            3. Disk drive - - B


      Press: BACK, NEXT, or INDEX
             to return to MAIN menu
```

Figure 3–18
The New Data-Management or Input Menu

REVIEW / MODIFY

1. Total Budget
   Currently set at $ 0.00

2. Alternatives

3. Criteria

4. Alternatives / Criteria
   scores

5. Method = Percentaging

Figure 3–19
The New Relations or Raw-Data Matrix

ALTERNATIVE / CRITERIA SCORING

	delay	respect	expense
trials	120.00	6.00	3000.00
pleas	30.00	2.00	600.00
diversion	20.00	4.00	300.00

Figure 3–20
The New Part/Whole Percentages Matrix

PART / WHOLE %

	delay	respect	expense
trials	70.59	50.00	76.92
pleas	17.65	16.67	15.38
diversion	11.76	33.33	7.69

Figure 3–21
The New Weighted Part/Whole Percentages Matrix

WEIGHTED PART / WHOLE %

	delay	respect	expense
trials	-70.59	150.00	-76.92
pleas	-17.65	50.00	-15.38
diversion	-11.76	100.00	-7.69

RELEVANT BIBLIOGRAPHY

For further details concerning the methodology behind the Policy/Goal Percentaging Analysis Program, see S. Nagel, *Public Policy: Goals, Means, and Methods,* (New York: St. Martin's, 1984), pp. 343–354; idem, "Part/Whole Percentaging as a Form of Multiple-Criteria Decision-Making," *Evaluation and Program Planning* 8 (1985): 107–120; and S. Nagel and B. Malis, "Using Percentaging Analysis to Aid in Allocating a Budget," *Public Productivity Review* (forthcoming).

For further examples that use the Policy/Goal Percentaging Analysis Program, see S. Nagel, *Microcomputers, Evaluation Problems, and Policy Analysis,* (Beverly Hills, Calif.: Sage, forthcoming); idem, ed., *Equity as a Policy Goal* (Bowling Green, Ohio: Bowling Green State University, 1983), pp. 1–6; idem, ed., *Policy Evaluation: Making Optimum Decisions* (New York: Praeger, 1982), pp. 225–229; and idem, "Maximizing Social Impact in Allocating Across Cities," in Peter Hom and Rodger Griffeth, eds., *American Institute for Decision Sciences: Proceedings,* (Akron, Ohio, 1984), pp. 165–67.

For background material on other approaches to multiple-criteria decision-making, see A. Easton, *Complex Managerial Decisions Involving Multiple Objectives* (New York: Wiley, 1973); Ward Edwards and Robert Newman, *Multi-Attribute Evaluation* (Beverly Hills, Calif.: Sage, 1982); Ralph Keeney and H. Raiffa, *Decisions with Multiple Objectives: Preferences and Value Tradeoffs* (New York: Wiley, 1976); Thomas Saaty, *The Analytic Hierarchy Process: Planning, Priority Setting, and Resource Allocation* (New York: McGraw-Hill, 1980), and Milan Zeleny, *Multiple Criteria Decision Making* (New York: McGraw-Hill, 1982).

For materials specifically relevant to legal-policy evaluation and microcomputers, see H. Bohigian, *The Foundations and Mathematical Models of Operations Research with Extensions to the Criminal Justice System* (Yonkers, N.Y.: Gazette, 1971); W. Hirsch, *Law and Economics: An Introductory Analysis* (New York: Academic Press, 1979); S. Nagel and M. Neef, *Decision Theory and the Legal Process* (Lexington, Mass.: Lexington-Heath, 1979); idem, *Legal Policy Analysis: Finding an Optimum Level or Mix* (Lexington, Mass.: Lexington-Heath, 1977); S. Nagel, ed., *Policy Evaluation: Making Optimum Decisions* (New York: Praeger 1982); Richard Posner, *Economic Analysis of Law* (Boston: Little, Brown, 1977); Daniel Remer, *Computer Power for Your Law Office* (Berkeley, Calif.: Sybex, 1983); C. Tapper, *Computers and the Law,* (New York: Longman, 1973); Gordon Tullock, *The Logic of the Law* (New York: Basic Books, 1971); G. Becker and William Landes, eds., *Essays in the Economics of Crime and Punishment* (New York: Columbia University Press, 1974); and Ronald Roesch and R. Corrado, eds., *Evaluation and Criminal Justice Policy* (New York: Russell Sage, 1981).

III

Judicial Prediction

The following material describes various judicial-prediction methods applicable to predicting court-case outcomes by practicing lawyers in light of their knowledgeable insights, the data generally available, and their quantitative abilities. Chapter 4 is entitled "Case Prediction by Staircase Tables and Percentaging." That methodology involves first showing one predictive criterion along the horizontal axis of a two-dimensional matrix. Its categories are shown as columns in ascending order toward winning. A second predictive criteria is shown along the vertical axis. Its categories are shown as rows also in ascending order toward winning. The actual or presumed outcomes are then shown in the cells for each combination of categories. One can express the outcomes in words, symbols, or numbers. As one moves from the southwest corner of the matrix toward the northeast the probability of losing changes to a probability of winning. One can section off the losing cells from the winning cells with a thick, kinked line that looks like a staircase.

Chapter 5 builds on the basic ideas of staircase prediction in order to develop a microcomputer variation. That variation is easier to use in view of the aid that microcomputers can give in terms of doing arithmetic quickly and accurately. Microcomputers also have the ability to facilitate trying out different inputs to resolve inconsistencies and develop more powerful predictive decision-rules. The methodology can work well with only a few cases, with a variety of predictive criteria, with different weights for the variables, and with predicting either winning/losing or a variable that has degrees like damages, sentences, or probabilities. A variety of concrete examples are given from fields such as welfare, civil rights, housing, international law, criminal law, schools, and legislative redistricting.

Chapter 6 is more concerned with predicting trial-court decisions than appellate-court decisions, although the same methods to some extent apply in both contexts. Trial-court prediction emphasizes probabilities of plaintiffs or prosecutors winning under varying circumstances. It also emphasizes average damages or average sentences under varying circumstances. Appellate-court prediction emphasizes whether or not something will be found to be in conformity with federal or state constitutions, statutes, or common-law principles. Both kinds of predictions rely on previous judicial behavior, generally at the appellate-court level since appellate-court behavior is more easily determined.

4

Case Prediction by Staircase Tables and Percentaging

The purpose of this chapter is to discuss two new methods for predicting systematically the outcome of court cases. These methods are simple and easy to use. They also have the advantage over more traditional prediction methods of providing causal insights into why the cases are decided the way they are. These prediction methods could be used to predict outcomes in situations that do not necessarily involve predicting how court cases are decided, but this chapter uses court cases for illustrative purposes.[1]

The chapter is organized in terms of (1) staircase prediction, which applies when two key predictive variables are used; and (2) percentaging, which especially applies when there are more than two key predictive variables. The examples mainly relate to due process, equal protection, and the First Amendment.

CASE PREDICTION BY STAIRCASE TABLES

Eight Basic Steps

There are eight steps involved in staircase prediction.

1. Have one or more key *cases* from the field of law in which one is interested.
2. Decide what *variables* or case characteristics tend to be associated with winning or losing in those cases. *Winning* in this context can mean deciding in favor of the liberal position, and *losing* can mean deciding in favor of the conservative position. Winning and losing, however, can be defined in any manner as long as one is consistent across the cases from the field of law in which one is interested.
3. Decide what *categories* or subdivisions are on each variable.
4. Decide the *order* of the categories from the category that least favors to the one that most favors the liberal side. *Liberal* refers to siding with the interests associated with unions, poor people, minorities, consumers, environmentalists, tenants, personal injury plaintiffs, criminal defendants, and so on. *Conservative* refers to siding with the interests associated with management, well-to-do people, dominant ethnic groups, sellers, developers, landlords, personal injury defendants, prosecutors, and so on.
5. Prepare a two-dimensional *matrix* showing one variable along the top and a second variable along the side. Each column corresponds to a different category on the first variable, and each row corresponds to a different category on the second variable.
6. Insert into each of the *cells* the predicted outcome for that combination of categories.
7. Draw a *staircase* blocking off the cells showing in what situations the liberal side is likely to win above the staircase and lose below the staircase. There may also be some cells that are questionable as to which way those situations or combinations of categories would be likely to go. The staircase is a distinctive aspect of this kind of table. One can define a *staircase prediction table* as being a two-dimensional matrix in which there is a predictive variable on each dimension and in which the categories on each variable are arranged so that by moving from the southwest to the northeast, one moves toward situations in which a given position is more likely to prevail, especially above a straight, curved, or jagged line.
8. *Revise* the staircase table in light of new cases as they are decided.

Table 4–1 provides a good illustration of these eight steps in the context of welfare cases. A key case dealing with welfare procedures is *Goldberg v. Kelly*. It held that individual welfare recipients could not have their welfare payments terminated if they were denied a confrontation hearing with notice of wrongdoing, opportunity to present witnesses, opportunity to cross-examine opposition witnesses, and a reasonably neutral judge before the termination occurs.

One variable in this analysis is substance severity and the other is procedural severity. The first variable refers to what is being taken away from the welfare recipient, and the second variable refers to how it is being taken away. The categories on substance severity are eligibility denial, benefits reduction, welfare termination, and criminal prosecution in that order of increasing severity. The categories on procedural severity are being denied an appointed attorney, a confrontation hearing, or even reasons in that order of increasing severity.

As the substance severity increases, the welfare recipients are more likely to

Table 4–1
Welfare Cases

V₁. SUBSTANCE SEVERITY

V_2. PROCEDURAL SEVERITY	C_1. Eligibility Denial	C_2. Benefits Reduction	C_3. Welfare Termination	C_4. Criminal Prosecution
C_3. Denied Reasons	1 W	2 W	(3) W	(4) W
C_2. Denied Confrontation Hearing	5 L	6 ?	(7) W *Goldberg*	(8) W
C_1. Denied Appointed Attorney	9 L	10 L	11 L	12 W *Argersinger*

Favors W (→ across columns; ↑ up rows)

V = Variable.
C = Category.

W = Welfare recipient wins.
L = Welfare recipient loses.

win because they are *entitled* to more rights. As the procedural severity increases, the welfare recipients are also more likely to win because they have been *denied* more rights. One can see from the two-dimensional table that as one goes from southwest to northeast, a welfare recipient's chances of winning are increased because one is then going up on both variables. If welfare recipients are considered winners by being denied a hearing in a termination case (Cell 7), surely the recipients would be even more likely to win in Cell 8, where they have been denied a hearing in a criminal prosecution. Likewise the recipients should be more likely to win if, in addition to being denied a hearing (Cell 7), they are denied reasons for the welfare termination (Cell 3). On the basis of the *Goldberg* case, one can thus fill in cells 7, 3, 4, and 8. Cell 12 does not follow from the *Goldberg* case, but from other Supreme Court cases like the *Argersinger* case, which provides right to counsel in misdemeanor cases. The staircase shows that cells 1, 2, 3, 4, 7, 8, and 12 are likely to be situations in which the welfare recipient wins. Cells 5, 9, 10, and 11 are situations in which the recipient is likely to lose. Cell 6 is questionable, given the cases on which this table is based. Also, the table can be easily revised as new cases are decided.[2]

A closely related set of cases are the public-housing procedure cases. The staircase matrix is similar but with the following differences: The columns might be labeled eligibility denial, rent increase, non-renewal of lease, eviction during the lease, and criminal prosecution. The rows are the same. A key case is *Thorpe v. Durham Housing Authority,* which held that reasons must be given for the non-renewal of a lease. Also relevant is *Holmes v. New York City Housing Authority,* which held that reasons must be given for eligibility denials. Those two cases tell us that reasons must be given in all five substance severity categories. We know from forcible entry and detainer statutes that there is a right to a court hearing in an eviction proceeding. We also know that right to counsel and a court hearing are required in either a public-housing or a public-aid prosecution. We thus have the same set of win cells, lose cells, and question-mark cells as in Table 4–1, except for Cell 7, since neither of these two cases clearly states that there is a right to a hearing when a public-housing lease is not renewed.[3]

Another related set of cases are those dealing with right to court-appointed counsel. The staircase matrix there involves the following differences from Table 4–1: The columns can deal with substance severity. The categories (in order of increasing severity) would be civil proceeding, juvenile proceeding, misdemeanor, felony, and capital punishment. The rows can deal with procedural severity. The categories (in increasing severity) would be availability of counsel in prison, on appeal, at pretrial, and at trial. The key cases include, in chronological order, *Powell v. Alabama* (capital-punishment trial), *Gideon v. Wainwright* (felony trial), *Douglas v. California* (felony appeal), *Miranda v. Arizona* (felony pretrial), *Argersinger v. Hamlin* (misdemeanor trial), *In re Gault* (juvenile trial), and *Johnson v. Avery* (felony prison). Since there are four procedural categories and five substantive categories, we have a four-by-five matrix. All of the northeast cells provide for court-appointed counsel, especially the trial row and the felony and capital columns. Most of the southwest cells do not provide for court-appointed counsel, especially the civil column and the prison row. The cells in the middle are less clear, especially the pretrial and appeal rows and the juvenile and misdemeanor columns.[4]

The eight general steps can be broadened to include a great variety of cases or non-case prediction situations. The examples used in this chapter emphasize constitutional law cases because they are among the most widely known court cases. One can, however, apply the same kind of analysis to common law cases in fields such as contracts, property, torts, and family law. This chapter sometimes uses the term *plaintiff* instead of *liberal side*. Doing this recognizes that civil court cases tend to involve personal injury matters in which the plaintiff is usually the liberal side. This, however, is not always true. For example, in merchant-consumer cases, the plaintiff is sometimes the consumer seeking repairs or a refund but sometimes the merchant seeking payment. In merchant-consumer cases, one could also have a merchant that is a small business and a consumer that is a big business, although if the principle in the case favors big consumers, it is likely to favor consumers in general in future cases. The term *plaintiff* has a different meaning in criminal cases (where it is synonomous with the *prosecutor*) than it has in civil cases (where it tends to refer to an injured party suing an insurance company). The term *plaintiff* is often used in this chapter because it is a less emotional term than *liberal position*. The reason for using terms like *liberal* and *conservative position* is that those terms are often meaningful in predicting case outcomes.

Staircase prediction is already familiar to most lawyers, law students, and pre-law students, although they may not realize it. The staircase matrix idea is the main format in which predictions of law school admissions have been made for about the past 15 years. In each edition of *The Pre-Law Handbook*, there is generally one such two-dimensional matrix for each law school. Along the top is the variable of Law School Admission Test (LSAT) score, which formerly could range from 200 to 800. That variable can be divided into seven columns with each column covering a 100–unit interval of test scores. Along the side is the variable of grade-point average, which can range from 1.00 to 4.00. That variable can also be divided into seven rows with each row covering a .50 interval of grade-point averages (GPA). Each cell shows the probability of being admitted to law school under consideration with the LSAT score of the column and the GPA of the row. With that cell information, one can draw a staircase above which one has more than a 50/50 probability of being accepted and below which one has less than a 50/50 probability. One could draw two sets of staircases. The upper staircase could indicate situations in which one has better than a .75, or P, probability of being admitted and the lower staircase, less than a .25, or $1 - P$, probability. As one moves from the southwest to the northeast, one's probability of being admitted increases regardless of which law school one is analyzing. That is the equivalent of predicting that one will be a likely winner with combinations of the categories that are in the upper right hand corner and a likely loser with combinations in the lower left hand corner.

Four Basic Principles

In addition to the eight basic steps for developing a staircase prediction table, there are four basic principles for interpreting one:

1. If the foundation or binding case is decided *in favor of the plaintiff,* the plaintiff should *win* in all cases to the direct north, northeast, or direct east of the cell in which the case is located. All of the other cells or situations are ambiguous unless there is more than one case in the data base. This principle and the others assume that the staircase prediction table has been developed in accordance with the previously described steps. The phrase "should win" in this context does not mean the outcome is good. It means the outcome should happen or is predicted to happen to preserve consistency with the nature of the staircase table.
2. If the case is decided *in favor of the defendant,* the defendant should *win* in all cases to the direct west, southwest, or direct south of that cell. All other cells are ambiguous or questionable. This principle follows logically from the first principle in that two negatives make a positive. Converting "plaintiff wins" to "defendant wins" is one negative. Converting cells to the north, northeast, and east into cells to the south, southwest, and west is the second negative.
3. If the case is decided *in favor of the plaintiff,* the defendant should *lose* in all cases to the direct north, northeast, and direct east of that cell. This principle logically follows from the first principle. Converting "plaintiff should win" to "defendant should lose" is the equivalent of a double negative.
4. If the case is decided *in favor of the defendant,* the plaintiff should *lose* in all cases to the direct west, southwest, or direct south of that cell. This principle logically follows from the second principle. Converting "defendant should win" to "plaintiff should lose" is a double negative.

Applying those four principles to the welfare cases in Table 4–1, we first note that the *Goldberg* case was decided in favor of the plaintiff or the liberal side, which means it is covered by the first and third principles. The first principle in effect states that in light of the *Goldberg* decision, the plaintiff should also win in the situations to the direct north (Cell 3), the northwest (Cell 4), and the direct west (Cell 8). The cell numbers are circled in those three cells as well as the *Goldberg* cell to show that those predictions stem directly from the result in the *Goldberg* case. W's and L's are inserted in other cells either because the *Goldberg* case mentions those other situations as an aside or *obiter dictum* or because we are aware that other cases have so held. The only other landmark case that is included here is the *Argersinger* case, which held that it is unconstitutional to convict an indigent defendant in a criminal prosecution without a court-appointed attorney, even if only a welfare misdemeanor is involved.

Comparison with Social Science and Legal Prediction

One interesting aspect of staircase prediction is that it enables one to make predictions on the basis of a single case. This can be contrasted with traditional social science, which usually requires large roughly random samples of cases to make predictions. If one is interested in predicting welfare cases, one is likely to be more successful by just knowing *Goldberg v. Kelly* than by having data on a random sample of welfare cases from the past 20 years. That is especially true if many of the cases precede *Goldberg v. Kelly*. The *Goldberg* case has the characteristic of being a *foundation case*. That means it is a landmark precedent that is binding on all future cases regardless of prior cases. Foundation cases (1) are decided by high level appellate courts like the U.S. Supreme Court (or one's own state supreme court where a common law matter is involved), (2) are explicit in replacing prior cases or in indicating that they are breaking new ground, and (3) are commented on extensively in the law review and treatise literature.

Along related lines, staircase prediction differs from traditional social science prediction in emphasizing deductive rather than inductive analysis. The basic deductive principle behind staircase analysis is the principle of "a fortiori." That principle states that if one knows that (1) when *X* fact is present that *Y* decision will be reached, one also will know that (2) when *X* and *Z* are present that *Y* decision is even more likely to be reached, assuming that both *X* and *Z* aid in justifying *Y*. An alternative formulation is to state that if one knows that (1) when *X* fact is absent that $-Y$ decision is reached, one also will know that (2) when *X* and *Z* are both absent that a $-Y$ decision is even more likely to be reached, assuming the absence of both *X* and *Z* detracts from justifying *Y*. In terms of simple arithmetic logic, if $X = Y$, then $X + 1$ is greater than *Y*. Likewise, if $-X = -Y$, then $-X - 1$ is less than $-Y$.

The inductive logic of *traditional social science* involves generalizing from many cases by observing patterns such as (1) in ten cases *X* was present and *Y* was present; (2) in five cases *X* was present and *Y* was absent, (3) in two cases *X* was absent and *Y* was present, and (4) in eight cases *X* was absent and *Y* was absent. From that pattern, one can conclude that 67 percent of the time when *X* is present, there is a *Y* victory; whereas in only 20 percent of the time when *X* is absent is there a *Y* victory. One can further conclude that as *X* goes from absent to present, the probability of victory moves up 47 percentage points from a base of .20 to .67.

There are several advantages of the staircase deduction over traditional social science prediction. The staircase deduction avoids (1) the problems of finding a truly random sample from which to generalize; (2) having to compile and process data on so many cases; (3) the fact that the empirical-inductive relation between *X* and *Y* may be confounded by the presence of other variables, which can be isolated deductively; and the fact that previous decisions (*Y*) may greatly influence the subsequent facts (*X*) that are presented to the courts, as well as having the facts influence the decisions. Deductive analysis can also isolate that kind of reciprocal causation. The staircase deduction also stimulates more careful thinking about what the relevant variables are than does a statistical analysis, which tends to include many irrelevant variables. It stimulates more careful thinking about the relevant categories on the variables and their order in influencing a favorable decision. Statistical regression analysis, on the other hand, cannot even deal with categories that do not have inherent order and preferably interval measurement, rather than rank-order measurement.

Staircase prediction should also be compared with *traditional legal prediction*. That kind of prediction comes closer to staircase prediction than statistical analysis does. Legal prediction, however, tends to emphasize predicting to a specific case under consideration. Staircase prediction is concerned with being able to predict to all cases in the field in terms of all possible combinations of key facts. Legal prediction also tends to be highly verbal, whereas staircase prediction is at least graphic and is capable of being easily quantified, as will be demonstrated when we discuss the percentaging variation on basic staircase prediction.

Those differences lead to several advantages of staircase prediction over traditional legal prediction. Staircase prediction has the capability of being able to predict to a greater variety of case types, although some types will be ambiguous as in Table 4–1. It has the capability of dealing with variables that are entitled to different weights, as will be shown shortly. It has the capability of being able to handle more than two important variables simultaneously, as will also be shown shortly. It forces one to think more clearly about the relevant variables and the categories on the variables. It is capable of being communicated in an objective manner, whereas traditional legal prediction tends to be more subjective, personalized, and based on non-explicit hunches. It stimulates more causal thinking about why cases are decided the way they are, as contrasted to merely predicting an undecided case or future cases.

One might note that certain aspects of legal research are just as applicable to staircase as to traditional legal prediction. One aspect is the finding of relevant cases. One uses the same legal research tools for either approach, although the staircase approach tends to emphasize finding foundation, or landmark, cases, rather than lots of cases. Likewise, one uses basically the same methods for briefing or determining the details of the cases, although the staircase approach tends to emphasize determining what each case indicates about related situations even if those statements are not part of the holding. The two approaches differ regarding what one does with the cases. The traditional legal approach predicts by reasoning from analogy, whereby one reasons that if the previous case said fact *X* leads to decision *Y* and the present case has facts like *X*, one predicts *Y*. The staircase approach puts the previous case through the eight basic steps to develop a predictive framework like Table 4–1 into which the case to be predicted is placed.

One might also note that staircase prediction and traditional legal prediction are both concerned with clarifying legal rules through a process that partially involves inducing or generalizing from specific cases. This kind of prediction can be contrasted with predicting the facts that courts will find present under various circumstances, such as who arrived at the intersection first, where the defendant was on the night of the crime, or what the parties probably interpreted the contract to mean. Most legal disputes are over facts rather than rules. Thus most legal disputes involve the form (1) if facts F are present, rule R prevails and (2) are facts F present? The issue of which rule prevails when a given set of facts are present is, however, probably more important qualitatively (if not quantitatively) because resolving those issues influences so many future cases. Thus one can state that both rule issues and fact issues are important without having to choose which type of issues are more important.

Expanding to More Categories and Cases

To clarify further what is involved in staircase prediction, Table 4–2 applies the same general ideas to the field of equal protection rather than welfare cases. This table is slightly more complex because it contains 6 × 4 cells rather than 3 × 4 cells. It also involves more cases on which the cells are based. The foundation case involves a Supreme Court decision for the conservative side, unlike the *Goldberg* case, which involved a Supreme Court decision for the liberal side. The foundation case here is *San Antonio v. Rodriguez*. The essence of the holding is that the equal protection clause of the Constitution is not violated if a state does not subsidize low-funded schools, even if the lack of subsidies means big differences in the quality of the schools across different geographic regions and economic classes. Table 4–2 provides a staircase analysis of that case and how it relates to the equal protection field. The variable along the top refers to the group that is allegedly being given unequal treatment, with the main groups relating to region, economic class, sex, and race in that order toward favoring the plaintiff, the liberal side, or the finding of unconstitutionality. The variable along the side refers to the rights that are allegedly being denied with the main rights relating to consumers, employment, housing, schools, criminal justice, and voting in that order toward favoring the plaintiff.

Since the *Rodriguez* case was decided in favor of the defendant, the second and fourth rather than the first and third principles apply to interpreting Table 4–2. The second principle states in effect that in light of the *Rodriguez* decision the defendant should also win in situations to the direct south, which includes cells 9, 10, 13, 14, 17, 18, 21, and 22. Those cell numbers are circled. The principle would also include any cells to the direct west or southwest, but there are no such cells since the *Rodriguez* case is in the southwest corner of the two-dimensional matrix. P's and D's are inserted in other cells either because the *Rodriguez* case mentions those other situations as an aside or because other landmark cases have so held. There are landmark cases for every rights category in the race column and for every group category in the voting row. The situation is more ambiguous when we get below the voting row or to the left of the race column, at least with regard to constitutional rights as contrasted to statutory

Table 4–2
Equal Protection Cases

V_1. THE GROUP THAT IS ALLEGEDLY BEING GIVEN UNEQUAL TREATMENT

V_2. THE RIGHTS THAT ARE ALLEGEDLY BEING DENIED	C_1. Region	C_2. Economic Class	C_3. Sex	C_4. Race
C_6. Voting	1 P *Reynolds v. Sims*	2 P *Harper v. Virginia*	3 P *Nineteenth Amendment*	4 P *Gomillion v. Lightfoot*
C_5. Criminal Justice	5 ?	6 P *Gideon v. Wainwright*	7 P *Taylor v. Louisiana*	8 P *Powell v. Alabama*
C_4. Schools	(9) D *Rodriguez*	(10) D *Rodriguez*	11 ?	12 P *Brown v. Board of Ed.*
C_3. Housing	(13) D	(14) D	15 D	16 P *Shelley v. Kramer*
C_2. Employment	(17) D	(18) D	19 D	20 P *Jones v. Mayer*
C_1. Consumers	(21) D	(22) D	23 D	24 P *Jones v. Mayer*

Favors P (→ right; ↑ up)

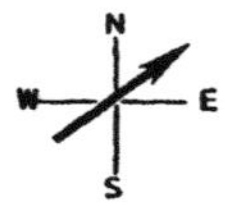

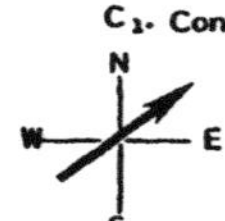

V = Variable.
C = Category.

P = Plaintiff.
D = Defendant.

rights such as those of the 1964 Civil Rights Act. For example, is it unconstitutional for one part of the state of Illinois to provide better right to counsel through a salaried public defender system than another part of the state provides through a volunteer legal aid system? The *Rodriguez* case states that the state has no obligation to legalize schools across regions, but criminal justice may be more important than education. Likewise, the Supreme Court has held that the state has an obligation to equalize between poor and rich defendants with regard to having access to an attorney. What about poor and rich regions? Cell 11 is another questionable cell regarding the rights of males and females to attend the same educational institutions and receive equal treatment regarding school activities such as interscholastic athletic teams. A stepwise prediction table is a bit like the Mendeleyev table of chemical elements. They both can aid in determining what elements are missing that need discovering or clarifying.

Table 4–2 could be expanded to include even more categories and cases or to rephrase the categories. For example, instead of focusing on region, economic class, sex, and race, one might more meaningfully focus on the side of those dimensions that is most likely to allege unequal treatment, namely, poor regions, poor people, women, and blacks. There are also more groups than just region, economic class, sex, and race, such as those that relate to age, disability, sexual preference, legitimacy, national citizenship, and state citizenship, but those groups are less frequently before the courts. There are also more constitutional rights, such as those that relate to health, welfare, family rights, and entrepreneurial rights, but they are also less frequent. Both the additional groups and the additional rights could be included, but doing that would make Table 4–2 more complicated than necessary to illustrate working with many categories. There are also additional landmark cases in the equal protection field, although some deal with the constitutionality of congressional legislation rather than the constitutionality of discriminatory activities. Some of the groups and rights can be subdivided. Race, for example, could be referred to as ethnic group and subdivided into race, religion, and ancestral nationality. Likewise, schools could be subdivided into discriminatory admissions versus equalization of funding, with discriminatory admissions being higher on the rights scale.[5]

CASE PREDICTION BY PERCENTAGING AND FURTHER LOGIC

Case prediction by percentaging is based on the same general principles as case prediction by staircase tables. Both approaches involve the same initial four steps of (1) finding one or more key cases, (2) deciding the variables or case characteristics that tend to be associated with winning or losing in those cases, (3) deciding the categories or subdivisions on each variable, and (4) deciding the order of the categories from the category that least favors the liberal or related side to the category that most favors the liberal or related side. The approaches differ because at that point the percentaging approach assigns percentages to the categories such as zero and 100 percent when there are two categories; zero, 50, and 100 percent when there are three categories; and zero, 33, 67, and 100 percent when there are four categories.

Dealing with a Third Variable

One might ask, why bother to assign percentages to the categories if we can predict so meaningfully with tables 4–1 and 4–2, which have no percentages or numbers assigned to the categories? One answer is that a staircase table is confined to predicting from two variables. Adding a third variable would require drawing a three-dimensional table and staircase. That is difficult to do and impossible when predicting from four variables. By doing simple percentaging, one can accommodate any number of additional variables.

A good example is shown in Table 4–3, which analyzes cases dealing with religion in the public schools. There are three variables shown. They are whether the religious teaching is (1) for indoctrination (i.e., instilling or strengthening religious beliefs) or education, as in a course on comparative literature or cultural geography; (2) during regular school hours; and (3) within the school building. Each variable has two categories. The category that is more associated with a declaration of unconstitutionality is given a score of 100 percent, and the other category on each variable, zero percent. With three variables each having two categories, there are eight possible factual situations, as indicated by the eight cells in Table 4–3. Each cell shows how many points the factual situation receives by adding the percentage scores of the three categories associated with each cell.

From a legal perspective, the most important aspect of Table 4–3 is showing for each cell whether that situation was held constitutional or unconstitutional. There are two foundation cases. One is *McCollum v. Board of Education* in which the Supreme Court held that it was unconstitutional to have religious indoctrination on school time in school buildings, even if the indoctrination was truly voluntary. The second foundation case is *Zorach v. Clausen* in which the Court held that it was constitutional to release school children who requested a release during school time to go elsewhere for religious indoctrination. Those two cases together indicate where the line can be drawn in the point system between constitutionality and unconstitutionality. In terms of the percentaging analysis, the *McCollum* case indicates that any situation that can generate 300 percentage points or more will be declared unconstitutional. The *Zorach* case comes close to stating that any situation that generates only 200 percentage points or less will be held constitutional. That, however, assumes that 200 points obtained by being out of the school building on school time is equal to 200 points obtained by being in the school building after school time, which may not be true. In other words, by applying the a fortiori test, cells 1, 5, and 7 would surely be constitutional, since *Zorach* was held constitutional and those cells have even stronger facts in the direction of constitutionality plus what *Zorach* had. Cells 2, 6, and 8 cannot be deduced from Zorach unless we know

Table 4–3
Cases Dealing with Religion in the Public Schools

TIME AND PLACE

V_1. SCHOOL TIME	C_1. Off (0%)	C_1. Off (0%)	C_2. On (100%)	C_2. On (100%)
V_2. SCHOOL BUILDING	C_1. Out (0%)	C_2. In (100%)	C_1. Out (0%)	C_2. In (100%)
V_3. PURPOSE: C_2. Indoctrination (100%)	(1) 100% C	2 200% C	3 200% C *Zorach v. Clausen*	4 300% U *McCollum*
V_3. PURPOSE: C_1. Educational (0%)	(5) 0% C	6 100% C	(7) 100% C	8 200% C

Favors U (→ across columns; ↑ up rows)

V_i = Variable #.
C_i = Category #.

C = Constitutional.
U = Unconstitutional.

something about the relative importance of the three variables, which will be discussed in talking about unequal variables.[6]

One might note that in the equal protection cases, there is sometimes a third variable, namely, whether the alleged discriminator was a governmental or private entity. Bringing in that third variable, however, does not generate a need for a three-dimensional table or for percentaging analysis. One can simply state on the basis of the landmark case of *Jones v. Mayer* that the only situation in which private discrimination violates the Constitution is in racial cases. In all other cases, private discrimination is constitutionally irrelevant, although it may violate a statute like the 1964 or 1968 Civil Rights Acts.

Dealing with Only One Variable

In discussing percentaging to deal with three variables, as contrasted to staircase prediction for dealing with two variables, one might note case prediction from only one variable. Prediction from a variable is not involved where the one variable is virtually synonomous or tautologous to the outcome being predicted. For example, one could predict well the outcome of personal injury cases if one knew whether or not the defendant was negligent, but that is almost the same as what we are trying to predict, namely, whether the court will find that the defendant was negligent. It is not prediction from a variable simply to classify cases or types of cases as being constitutional, questionable, or unconstitutional without indicating what characteristic or characteristics are useful in predicting the finding of constitutionality.

Table 4–4 shows two examples of a one-dimensional version of staircase/percentaging prediction. The first example deals with aid to parochial schools. The cases or types of cases are first arranged in the three outcome categories of constitutional, questionable, and unconstitutional. Those three outcome categories correspond to the question, "Is the aid for secular matters?" The answer is yes for fire and police protection for parochial schools, but it is no for salaries and building funds. Cases in the middle (in which the Supreme Court has been divided) include bus reimbursement, secular textbooks, and tuition tax deductions, although they have all been decided in favor of constitutionality. Future parochial cases can be predicted by positioning them as being in categories 1, 2, or 3 but leaning toward 1 or 3.[7]

The second example deals with racial hiring and admissions. There are six types of cases covering:

1. Separatism, whereby blacks or other minority groups voluntarily choose to live separately or go to separate schools
2. Affirmative action, whereby recruiters: (a) Advertise in periodicals read by minorities, (b) Mention equal opportunity in recruiting, (c) Locate their physical plants close to minority neighborhoods, (d) Provide training programs to upgrade the

Table 4–4
One-Variable Predictions in Church–State Cases and Racial Discrimination Cases

SUBJECT AND VARIABLE	CATEGORIES ON THE VARIABLE: CONSTITUTIONAL	PREVIOUSLY OR PRESENTLY QUESTIONABLE	UNCONSTITUTIONAL
Aid to Parochial Schools:	C_1. Yes (0%)	C_2. Maybe (20%-30%)	C_3. No (100%)
V_1. Is the aid for secular matters?	Fire protection	Bus reimbursement	Salaries
	Police protection	Secular textbooks	Building funds
		Tuition tax deduction	
Racial Hiring & Admissions:	C_1. Yes (0%)	C_2. Maybe (50%-60%)	C_3. No (100%)
V_1. Is the treatment consistent with allocation by merit?	Separatism	Preferential Hiring	Segregation
	Affirmative action		Discrimination
			Reverse racism or quotas

Cells show cases or types of cases. See text for definition of terms.

qualifications of minorities and others, or (e) Remove job or admission requirements that correlate highly with race but poorly with job or school success

3. Preferential hiring, whereby a qualified minority member is hired or admitted ahead of a more qualified member of the majority, although both are qualified
4. Reverse racism, or quotas, whereby minorities are preferred over members of the majority although the minority members may be substantially less qualified or even unqualified
5. Discrimination, whereby less qualified members of the majority are preferred over substantially more qualified minorities even where members of the majority may be unqualified
6. Segregation, whereby minorities are forced to live, work, or attend schools apart from members of the majority

The three categories for the racial example are yes, questionable, and no on the one variable of "Is the treatment consistent with allocation by merit?" "Consistent" here means the same as "not inconsistent," rather than "positively promoting." The answer to the question is yes to cases 1 and 2 but no to cases 4, 5, and 6. Case 3, which covers preferential hiring, is questionable, with the answer depending on whether the preferential hiring involves (1) private or governmental preferences, (2) past or no past discrimination, (3) a temporary or permanent arrangement, (4) an isolated case or a regular pattern, (5) having or not having a minimum qualification level, (6) allowing a small or large gap between minority and majority hires or admittees, and (7) subjective or objective test scores. The first of each of those two subcategories leans more toward constitutionality and the second toward unconstitutionality of the preferential hiring or admissions.[8]

The kind of one-variable prediction that we are doing might be called "trichotomy prediction." It involves three outcome categories. The middle outcome is always something like questionable, maybe, or uncertain. The other two categories could be something like constitutional/unconstitutional, plaintiff/defendant, or conservative/liberal. One might note that the concepts of conservative/liberal are not equal to constitutional/unconstitutional in the racial example, since anti-black segregation and pro-black reverse racism are both unconstitutional.

Trichotomy prediction is the simplest form of what might be called "ordered-category prediction." That phrase covers trichotomy prediction with one variable, staircase prediction with two variables, and percentaging prediction with three or more variables. They all have in common that they work with ordered categories on one or more variables. All three forms of prediction also have in common that they stimulate the user into thinking more clearly about how to develop a logical system for predicting the outcomes of court cases.

Even with one-variable prediction, percentaging can be helpful. This is true because percentaging can enable us to position the categories better. For example, the first row of Table 4–4 involves working with three categories for predicting constitutionality in parochial aid cases. The second row also involves working with three categories for predicting constitutionality but in racial hiring/admissions cases. The implication (without some form of at least rough percentaging) is that the middle category is equally distant from yes and no on both rows. That, however, is not likely to be true. The middle category on the parochial aid row is close to yes or constitutionality. The middle category on the racial row is more unclear and could go either way depending on the subcategory elements mentioned above. Those differences between the two rows could be partially clarified by assigning 100 percent to "no" and zero percent to "yes" on both rows. Since "no" sounds like a zero percent category, one can substitute "*victory* for the side attacking the practice" for "no" and substitute "*defeat* for the side attacking the practice" for "yes." The middle category on the parochial aid row would score about 20 to 30 percent, meaning closer to constitutional. The middle category on the racial row, however, would score about 50 to 60 percent on a scale, allowing for nine notches between zero and 100 percent, meaning closer to constitutional. The important point is not the exact percentages but rather that using a percentaging continuum aids in predicting more so than thinking in terms of three discrete, equidistant categories.

Dealing with Unequal Variables

A third justification for assigning percentage scores to the categories is to facilitate working with predictive variables that have unequal importance. In Table 4–3, for example, if the variable of indoctrination/education were considered twice as important as the variables of time and place, we should be able to multiply the indoctrination/education scores by 2 to show their importance. We could not do that if there were no numbers assigned to those categories that could be multiplied by 2. If we multiply the percentage scores of indoctrination/education by 2, all four numbers in the top row get 100 percentage points added to them, so they become 200 percent, 300 percent, 300 percent, and 400 percent, respectively. That now tells us that if Cell 3 were held to be constitutional, as it was, the odds have increased that Cell 8 will also be held constitutional since it is now a substantially milder offense of the Constitution in view of the increased importance of indoctrination/education in determining constitutionality.

Looking back at the equal protection analysis of Table 4–2, there is nothing to indicate that the group variables should be given more or less weight than the rights variable. There is one group category, namely, race, and one rights category, namely, voting rights, that the Court favors highly. Likewise, one out of the four group categories is not so favored, namely, region; and two out of the six rights categories are not so favored, namely, employment and consumers. Schools and housing are capable of arousing the Court's concern if the issue is having a right to a public education or having a right to live anywhere in a city. They are, however, not so capable of arousing the Court's concern if the issue is unequal funding across schools or the alleged unconstitutionality of having an election referendum to disallow public housing in a community. When one variable is not clearly favored over another variable, they should be considered as having equal weight.

On the matter of unequal variables, there are some variables that are considered so important by the Supreme Court that being in a certain position on those variables automatically determines the outcome of the case, regardless of how the case is positioned on the other variables. Such a variable might be called a "constraint," where the presence of a category means that a serious enough violation has occurred to make the violator a loser. A good example is from the field of religion in the public schools. A fourth variable that could be added to Table 4–3 is the variable of whether the program is required or voluntary. If the program is required and it involves indoctrination, the program is unconstitutional regardless of whether the program is on or off school time or whether the program is in or out of the school building. This example involves a declaration of unconstitutionality for violating the constraint or prohibition against requiring religious indoctrination.

The opposite kind of variable is one that might be called an "exemption," where the presence of a category is enough to make an alleged wrongdoer into a winner. If, for example, the religious program is truly educational, it can be required on school time and in the school building without violating the Constitution. The fact that the program is required might raise some suspicion that it is an indoctrination rather than educational program. The important point, though, is that if it is truly educational, the program is in effect exempt from being struck down on the grounds that it is compulsory, on school time, and in the school building.

DEALING WITH MULTIPLE VARIABLES AND INTERACTIONS

Table 4–5 carries the analysis a step further by working with a set of cases in which four variables seem important for making predictions. The subject matter is *restrictive racial covenants:* provisions in deeds that require the owner of the property to refrain from renting or selling to blacks, Jews, or other minorities. The key case in the field is *Shelley v. Kraemer*. That case held that if a white neighbor sues a black buyer to enjoin the sale, the courts should refuse to issue the injunction. Issuing it would make the courts a party to the restrictive racial covenant and thus violate the equal protection clause regarding governmental participation in housing discrimination.

Variables, Categories, and Situations

Shelley v. Kraemer involved three variables that relate to the nature of the parties: (1) Is the seller willing to sell? Yes or no. (2) Is an interfering neighbor involved? Yes or no. (3) Is the buyer being overly aggressive or abusive? Yes or no. The above answers or categories to each of those three issues are arranged in the

Table 4–5
Variables and Categories in Racial Covenant Cases

VARIABLE AND CATEGORIES	RANK ORDER	INTERPOLATION PERCENT	PART/WHOLE PERCENT
V_1. Is the seller willing to sell?			
C_2. Yes	2	100%	67%
C_1. No	1	0%	33%
	3	100%	100%
V_2. Is an interfering neighbor involved?			
C_2. Yes	2	100%	67%
C_1. No	1	0%	33%
	3	100%	100%
V_3. Is the buyer being overly aggressive?			
C_2. No	2	100%	67%
C_1. Yes	1	0%	33%
	3	100%	100%
V_4. What is the alleged violation?			
C_4. Constitutional	4	100%	40%
C_3. Breach of contract	3	67%	30%
C_2. Personal injury	2	33%	20%
C_1. Property rights	1	0%	10%
	10	200%	100%

order favoring a victory for the black buyer. Thus the black buyer is favored in terms of winning a lawsuit over the restrictive racial covenant if (1) the seller is willing, (2) there is an interfering neighbor, and (3) the buyer is not abusive. *Shelley* and related cases also involve a fourth issue that relates to the nature of the violation or cause of action that the plaintiff is alleging. The category that most favors the black buyer is a constitutional violation. The other categories can be combined into a category of non-constitutional violations. Table 4–5, however, divides the non-constitutional violations into breach of contract, personal injury, and property rights because doing so enables us (1) to show how to handle a combination of dichotomous and nondichotomous variables, (2) to show that the general methodology is applicable to common law concepts, and (3) because those categories are relevant to explaining some of the variation in the case outcomes.

Shelley v. Kraemer also involved other variables, but they are not so meaningful in explaining variation across the racial covenant cases in terms of whether the pro-integration side wins or loses. For example, in these cases no distinction is made about whether the plaintiff is seeking damages or an injunction directed toward specific behavior, although that distinction might be relevant in another set of cases. The nature of the plaintiff and the defendant is also generally irrelevant. Thus one expects and receives the same result regardless of whether the plaintiff is a neighbor seeking to stop the seller from selling or is the seller seeking to stop the neighbor from interfering with the sale. Along related lines, it is more meaningful to predict whether the pro- or anti-integration side will win, rather than whether the plaintiff or defendant will win. The terms *plaintiff* and *defendant* have no substantive image in this context unlike a typical personal injury case or a criminal case. Likewise, no variable is included to distinguish between a federal and a state lawsuit or between a government and a private seller, since those distinctions are also irrelevant.

With 2, 2, 2, and 4 categories, there are 32 situations that could occur. The 32 situations are shown in Table 4–6. None of those situations is impossible as would be the case if one variable related to whether the plaintiff was the buyer, seller, or neighbor and another variable related to whether the defendant was the buyer, seller, or neighbor. It would be logically inconsistent to have a combination where the buyer is suing the buyer and likewise with the seller or the neighbor. Some of the 32 situations were dealt with in subsequent cases. *Barrows v. Jackson*, for example, held that it made no difference whether the neighbor was suing the seller for damages for breach of contract among the neighbors or suing to enjoin the buyer from moving in as in *Shelley*. Some of the 32 situations are purely hypothetical, such as an abusive buyer inflicting a personal injury on the seller or the neighbor. Under those circumstances, the black buyer is not likely to be given any special consideration for his pro-integration motives.

Table 4–6 could be simplified by eliminating columns that set up case situations or combinations that seem unlikely although not impossible. For example, columns 5 and 7 could be eliminated on the grounds that the buyer is unlikely to be abusive if the seller is willing to sell. Even so, the unlikely hypothetical cases can be left in the table for the insights they might generate. No harm is done even if they are mispredicted since they are not likely to occur. Rows 1, 2, and 3 could be collapsed into one row called "non-constitutional violations," but then we would be losing the benefits previously mentioned, including relevant distinctions.

Percentaging

Percentaging prediction is useful in making a large number of situations like this more manageable for prediction purposes. It does so by assigning each category a percentage score so that the categories on different variables can be added

Table 4–6
Types of Cases Involving Racial Covenants

PARTIES / VIOLATION	V_1. Unwilling Seller (C_1)				Willing Seller (C_2)			
	V_2. No Interfering Neighbor (C_1)		Interfering Neighbor (C_2)		No Interfering Neighbor (C_1)		Interfering Neighbor (C_2)	
	V_3. Abusive Buyer (C_1)	No Abusive Buyer (C_2)	Abusive Buyer (C_1)	No Abusive Buyer (C_2)	Abusive Buyer (C_1)	No Abusive Buyer (C_2)	Abusive Buyer (C_1)	No Abusive Buyer (C_2)
C_4 Constitution Violation	140	173 *Jones*	173	207	173	207	207	240 *Sullivan*
C_3 Breach of Contract	130	163 *Rice*	163	197	163	197	197	230 *Barrows*
C_2 Personal Injury	120	153	153	187	153	187	187	220
C_1 Property Violation	110 *Adderly*	143 *Thornhill*	143	177	143	177	177	*Buchanan* 210 *Shelley*
Column Numbers	(1)	(2)	(3)	(4)	(5)	(6)	(7)	(8)

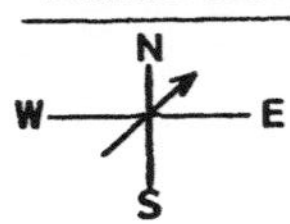

→ Favors Pro-Integration

together. One important issue is how the percentages should be assigned. There are basically two methods that can be used. One is the interpolation method, and the other is the part/whole percentaging method. The interpolation method assigns zero and 100 percent to the categories when there are *two* categories, as with the first three variables; zero, 50, and 100 percent when there are *three* categories; and zero, 33, 67, and 100 percent with *four* categories, as with the alleged violation. The general formula for using the interpolation method for assigning percentages is: Percentage $= -[1/(N-1)] + [1/(N-1)]$ Rank. The N indicates the number of categories on the variable. If there are 2 or N categories, the category that favors victory for the pro-integration side is given a rank of 2 or N and the other category is given a rank of 1 or $N-1$, so the higher category gets more points. The formula can translate the ranks into interpolated percentages no matter how many categories or ranks there are. The formula can also work with ranks or raw scores that start with numbers less than one and end with numbers greater than N. The main alternative percentaging approach involves summing the ranks and then dividing each rank by the sum in its column in order to obtain a part/whole percentage. Each rank is a part, and the sum is the whole. The part/whole percentaging formula is thus: Percentage = Rank/Sum. Both formulas can be checked against the data in Table 4–5.

The part/whole percentaging method has a number of advantages over the interpolation method. It is simpler to apply and explain. The percentages always sum to 100 percent, which is a form of norming that makes the variables more comparable even though they are measured on different dimensions or have different numbers of categories. Weighting the variables becomes easier because the weights only need to consider the predictive importance of the variables. They do not need to consider differences in measurement or the number of categories. Under the interpolation method, a variable that has four categories in effect receives more weight than a variable that has two categories because the four-variable category will add more points to the total points of a case than the two-variable category will. The part/whole percentaging method does not make the unrealistic assumption that categories are equally distant apart. The part/whole percentaging method makes intuitive sense by stating that each variable is like a pie or a whole of predictive power, with pie slices to be allocated to each category depending on its contribution to the whole. The part/whole method can also work with any scores for the categories, not just ranks from 1 to N. The part/whole percentaging method has a supportive literature in the methodology of multi-criteria decision-making.[9]

We can easily apply the part/whole percentages of Table 4–5 to the 32 case situations of Table 4–6. For example, suppose we apply column 3 of Table 4–5 to the foundation case of *Shelley v. Kraemer*. Doing this means adding 67 percent for having a willing seller, 67 percent for an interfering neighbor, 67 percent for not having an abusive buyer, and 10 percent for having an alleged property rights violation. The total number of percentage points is 210, which places the *Shelley* case well into the area of Table 4–6 where the pro-integration side is likely to win.

Moving Across, Up, and Diagonally

As one moves from the west to the east in Table 4–6, the probability of a pro-integration victory generally increases. The progression, however, backtracks at column 5, which involves an abusive buyer when there is no interfering neighbor and a willing seller. There was no backtracking when one moved from west to east in Tables 4–1 and 4–2 because each of those tables involved only one variable on the horizontal axis, whereas Table 4–6 involves three variables. As one moves from south to north, the numbers do continuously move upward since there is only one variable on the vertical axis. One would, however, not always expect a breach-of-contract argument to be more likely to result in a pro-integration victory than a property-violation argument. As was mentioned before, the ordering of the categories on the fourth variable is less justifiable substantively than the ordering of the categories on variables 1, 2, or 3.

As one moves from the southwest to the northeast the probability of a pro-integration decision generally increases. The case with the most points is *Sullivan v. Little Hunting Park*. That case involved both a willing landlord and a non-abusive renter suing an interfering neighbor for damages and an injunction to allow the renter to have access to the recreational facilities associated with the housing project. The co-plaintiffs based their case on a constitutional violation of the Thirteenth Amendment. The case with the least points in the southwest corner involves an unwilling seller, no interfering neighbors, and an abusive buyer who is trespassing in order to force the seller to act favorably toward him. There has been no such actual Supreme Court case, but the case of *Adderly v. Florida* comes close in affirming the conviction of demonstrators who trespass in an area that is considered non-public property.

Between *Sullivan* in the northeast and *Adderly* in the southwest, there are a number of cases in Table 4–6 that are relevant to restrictive racial covenants and to the broader issue of how the courts are likely to decide housing discrimination cases in the absence of fair housing or open occupancy statutes. The *Barrows* case was already mentioned, in which the Supreme Court may have been even more reluctant to interfere with the seller's right to sell than it was with the buyer's right to buy. The Court, however, may have been more favorably disposed toward integration in the *Barrows* case, not because of the factual or legal differences but because the Court had the *Shelley* case to rely upon as a precedent. The time period is not shown as a variable in Tables 4–4 or 4–6, although it is often relevant to explaining variation among past cases. The period is not relevant to predicting future cases, so long as all of the precedent cases in the data base are still current. The *Buchanan* case, like the *Shelley* case, involved a neighbor seeking to enjoin the buyer for violating the plaintiff's property rights. In the

Buchanan case, however, the rights stemmed from an anti-integration zoning ordinance rather than an anti-integration covenant in the deed. The zoning ordinancy represented an even greater unconstitutional government involvement than judicial enforcement of a deed.

At the other side of the table is the landmark case of *Jones v. Mayer*. It involved a buyer seeking to force a sale from an unwilling seller on the successful grounds that refusing to sell to a black buyer for racial reasons is a violation of the Thirteenth Amendment. It was not so strong a case as *Sullivan,* in which the seller and the buyer joined against the interfering neighbor. *Sullivan* (like *Barrows*) also had the benefit of coming later. The *Rice* case involved the purchase of a cemetery plot by a black buyer from a seller who had been willing to sell before he became aware that the buyer was black. This case thus involved the enforcement of a contract consistent with public policy, as contrasted to *Barrows,* which involved the non-enforcement of a contract that was contrary to public policy. The *Thornhill* case is the classic case allowing for peaceful picketing that does not involve personal injuries or trespass, as contrasted to *Adderly,* which did involve trespass.

Drawing the Line

A logical question that Table 4–6 raises is, where does one draw the lines showing the situations that are likely and those that are not likely to be decided in a pro-integration direction? The line seems to be between columns 1 and 2, especially if columns 7 and 5 are eliminated as being unlikely situations. Column 3 is not so unlikely since the buyer could conceivably be abusive when faced with both an unwilling seller and interfering neighbors. The pro-integration side, however, may still be likely to win because the concept of interfering neighbor in this context implies that the neighbor is seeking court action to block the possible sale of the property to a black buyer in alleged violation of (1) the contract between the neighbor and the seller, (2) the possible personal injury abuse by the buyer, and/or (3) the possible property rights violation of the buyer. The contract and property rights are not likely to be recognized, and the personal injury matter is likely to be recommended for separate action. The neighbor's freedom of association is not likely to be recognized ahead of the buyer's right to non-discrimination. The buyer, however, is likely to be a loser in the last column if the buyer seeks to force a sale from the seller whom he has abused or if the seller is only suing for personal injury damages or to enjoin an illegal trespass.[10]

CONCLUSIONS

The outcomes of these hypothetical cases could be predicted better if more facts were available than just knowing whether the seller is willing, whether the neighbor is interfering, whether the buyer is abusive, and what violation is being alleged by the plaintiff. On the other hand, by trying to find underlying variables and ordered categories, one obtains insights into reasons why the past cases were decided as they were and how related future cases might be decided. These six tables provide generalizations that are subject to being revised in light of new decisions in the data base and new factual situations to be predicted. *New* in this context could mean a case that fits into one of the 32 situations or the other combination sets that has not previously had a case. It could also mean a case that shares a cell with a previous case but that brings in a new variable, a new category, or a new variation on an old category. The important point is that through staircase prediction and percentaging, one can obtain insights for supplementing traditional legal and social science analysis. Such insights can be helpful in improving our ability to explain and predict case outcomes in the legal and political process.

One might note that staircase prediction and percentaging do require more thinking than mechanical statistical analysis and more thinking than being concerned with predicting just one undecided case. Encouraging more organized thinking, however, is an advantage rather than a disadvantage over the alternative approaches. The idea of aggregating ordered categories on predictive variables is the essence of trichotomy prediction for one variable, staircase prediction for two variables, and percentaging for three or more variables. That basic idea tends to bring order out of what otherwise would be a mass of disordered cases. The orderliness represents a kind of synthesis between the overemphasis on unique characteristics that is associated with legal analysis and the ignoring of unique characteristics that is associated with statistical analysis. It is hoped that this chapter has brought some order to the idea of ordered-category prediction, which good analytic thinkers may often do intuitively. Perhaps there will be more explicit and beneficial use in the future of methodologies such as staircase prediction and percentaging.

APPENDIX: USING MICROCOMPUTER PROGRAMMING TO AID IN STAIRCASE PREDICTION

To facilitate prediction analysis by staircase tables and percentaging, a microcomputer program has been developed.

The Input

Figure 4–1 shows the 12 types of welfare cases that are shown in the 12 cells of Table 4–1. There are 12 types of cases since there are three procedural categories and four substantive categories into which the cases can be classified. The first half of column 1 shows the three procedural categories in order of increasing severity. They are (1) no attorney (symbolized A), (2) no hearing (H), and (3) no reasons (R) from the bottom up. The second half of column 1 shows the four substantive categories in order of increasing severity. They are

Figure 4–1
The 12 Types of Welfare Cases Scored on Three Procedural and Four Substantive Categories

ALTERNATIVE / CRITERIA SCORING

	SUBSTANC	PROCEDUR
RE	1.00	3.01
RB	2.00	3.01
RT	3.00	3.01
RC	4.00	3.01
HE	1.00	2.00
HB	2.00	2.00
HT	3.00	2.00
HC	4.00	2.00
AE	1.00	0.99
AB	2.00	0.99
AT	3.00	0.99
AC	4.00	0.99

Press: SHIFT-NEXT when finished

(1) eligibility denial (E), (2) benefits reduction (B), (3) termination (T), and (4) criminal prosecution (C).

The second column shows how each case-type is scored on the substance variable on a scale from 1 to 4. The third column shows how each case-type is scored on the procedural variable on a scale from .99 to 3.01 from the bottom up. The scale goes slightly below 1 and slightly above 3 in order to recognize that the RE case is a winner for the welfare recipient and the AT case is a loser. That distinction would be lost if the RE case received 1 + 3 points, rather than 1 + 3.01, and the AT case received 3 + 1 points, rather than 3 + .99. Figure 4–1 is in effect a computer version of briefing the 12 cases or indicating how each case is positioned on relevant predictive characteristics.

The Initial Output

Figure 4–2 shows the primary or initial output from the computer program. That output consists of summing the scores in Figure 4–1 for each case. Figure 4–2 might be improved if the cases were rearranged in rank order and if a third

Figure 4–2
The Primary Output Showing the Overall Scores for 12 Types of Cases

Alternative	Combined Rawscores
1RE	4.01
2RB	5.01
3RT	6.01
4RC	7.01
5HE	3.00
6HB	4.00
7HT	5.00
8HC	6.00
9AE	1.99
10AB	2.99
11AT	3.99
12AC	4.99

Press: SHIFT-NEXT

column were added showing for each case-type whether the welfare recipient is a winner, a loser, or in between. One could then readily see that all of the case-types scoring less than 4.00 are losers; all scoring more than 4.00 are winners; and all scoring exactly 4.00 are questionable as to how they are likely to be resolved. That is the predictive decision-rule that the data in Figures 4–1 and 4–2 logically generate.

This decision-rule can also be expressed as an equation of the form $Y = X_1 + X_2$, where Y is the overall score of a case, X_1 is the score on substance, X_2 is the score on procedure, and 4.00 is the cutoff on Y between winning and losing. That same equation could be generated by inserting the data from Figures 4–1 and 4–2 into a statistical regression analysis program. The program would indicate that for an equation of the form $Y = a + b_1(X_1) + b_2(X_2)$, the value of a would be 0; b_1 would be 1; and b_2 would also be 1. The equation would generate a perfectly fitting correlation coefficient of 1.00. The regression approach, however, is needlessly complicated and not as relevant to deductive legal analysis. The regression approach in this context merely tends to put into equation form the decision rule that has been arrived at deductively rather than to be useful in arriving at the decision-rule.

One could also use the microcomputer program to analyze a set of cases in which one is trying to predict the amount of damages, the length of sentence, or another type of judgment, rather than just winning or losing. The main difference is that one notes the sentences on damages that correspond to each case to the right of the last column in Figure 4–2. One can then see the scores that correspond to various damages or sentences in order to develop a meaningful decision-rule. The microcomputer program can also show the differences between the predicted outcomes and the actual outcomes to aid in reducing those differences by changing the variables or the scoring on them.

Suppose an attorney is representing a welfare recipient in an appellate court in an AE case where there is an eligibility denial and an appointed attorney was refused at the administrative level. How might the computer analysis be used to aid in developing a litigation strategy? Figure 4–2 could inform the attorney that he should probably advise his or her client, employer, or partner that the case is likely to be lost. Figure 4–2 is in effect a computer version of synthesizing the 12 cases to derive and apply a general decision-rule.

Threshold Analysis

Figure 4–3 helps inform the attorney what it would take to turn the AE case into a winner. That display shows the threshold values that would bring an AE case up to the minimum winning level, which is the 4.01 level of the RE case. Figure 4–3 states that the AE case at bar will win if it can move on the substance variable up from a score of 1.00 to a score of 3.02, which is slightly above welfare termination in severity. Figure 4–3 also states that the AE case at bar will win if it can move on the procedural variable up from 1.00 to 3.01, which is slightly above reasons denied. The first row of the threshold analysis also states that the AE case will be at the minimum level with any combination of substantive and procedural improvement that removes the 2.02 gap between the 1.99 score of the AE case and the 4.01 score of the RE case.

The second row of the threshold analysis states that if the RE case were to worsen from 1.00 to −1.02 on substance, there would then be a tie between the two cases. That, however, is impossible since the lowest score on the substance scale is +1.00. There would also be a tie if the RE case were to drop from 3.01 on procedure to .99. Any change in the RE case, however, may be unreasonable since it is an established precedent.

The zeros in the bottom row state that if the procedural variable had no weight, there would be a tie because both the AE case and the RE case received the same score on the substance variable. The question marks in the bottom row state that there is no weight that could be given to the substance variable that would help the AE case to come up to the RE case since they both received the same score on the substance variable.

Figure 4–3
The Threshold Analysis Showing the Input Values That Would Bring the AE Case Up to the RE Case

THRESHOLD ANALYSIS

	SUBSTANC	PROCEDUR
AE	3.02	3.01
RE	-1.02	.99
Weight	??	.00

The Program in General

One can readily see that the analysis shown in Figures 4–1, 4–2, and 4–3 could be extended to Tables 4–1 through 4–6. The microcomputer analysis is helpful when there are many categories on each variable (Table 4–2) or when there are more than two variables (Tables 4–5 and 4–6). The number of case-types is equal to the number of categories on the first variable multiplied by the number of categories on the second variable and so on through the last variable. The number of case-types may be more than the microcomputer program currently allows for alternative cases, but that number is being increased. The microcomputer analysis is especially helpful when there is more than one measurement scale. An example is a 1–2 scale on one variable and a 1–4 scale on another variable (Tables 4–5 and 4–6). Another example is a 1–2 scale on one variable and dollars, years, or some other measurement unit on another variable. Under those circumstances, the program converts the relation scores into part/whole percentages that can then be meaningfully added or subtracted when the original measurement units cannot be.

In addition to having broad applicability, the microcomputer analysis can be particularly helpful for indicating what needs to be done to convert a potential loser into a winner or a potential winner into a loser by changing the scores that relate the cases to the variables or by changing the weights of the variables. The computer program can also help in determining what the variables and categories should be by allowing the user to experiment with different variables and different categorizing or measuring systems to see how well one can separate the winners from the losers.

The program will be further improved by adding the following features: (1) Provision should be made for allowing more cases or case-types. As of now, the program only allows for 15 alternatives. That should be substantially raised. (2) The program should ask the user how each of the previous cases or case-types in the data set have been decided. The cases can be coded 2 for winning and 1 for losing. They can also be coded in terms of the amount of damages awarded, the years of sentencing received, or in terms of other outcome variables. (3) To facilitate arriving at a decision-rule, the output display can show the cases in the order of their summation scores, which can either be combined raw scores or the sum of the weighted part/whole percentages. Next to those summation scores can be shown the outcome scores for the cases. The program should also be capable of doing a bivariate regression analysis with the outcome scores (Y) as the dependent variable to be predicted and the summation scores (X) as the independent variable from which predicting is done. The resulting equation of the form $Y = a + bX$ should be helpful in developing an accurate decision-rule. (4) To facilitate changing the inputs to improve the accuracy of the decision-rule, the summation scores should also be shown to the right of the data matrix that lists the cases on the rows and the predictive criteria on the columns. The accuracy of the decision-rule can often be improved by changing the weights of the criteria, adding criteria, changing the measurement systems on the criteria, deleting incorrectly included cases, deleting incorrectly included criteria, re-scoring some of the cases on some of the criteria, and adding cases.

If the variables and categories have been carefully chosen, there should be a perfect separation of the past winners from losers. In statistical terms, this means that the method is capable of generating a predictive system or decision-rule in which there are no discrepancies between predicted outcomes and actual outcomes at least with the cases that have already been decided. No other predictive system is that accurate. This kind of predictive system, however, does require more careful thinking about variables, categories, and scores than other more mechanical quantitative methods.[11]

NOTES

1. On traditional legal prediction, see Harry Jones et al., *Legal Method* (Mineola, N.Y.: Foundation Press, 1980); K. Llewelleyn, *The Common Law Tradition: Deciding Appeals* (Boston: Little, Brown, 1960); W. Statsky and J. Wernet, *Case Analysis and Funddamentals of Legal Writing* (St. Paul: West, 1977); and W. Thode et al., *Introduction to the Study of Law* (Mineola, N.Y.: Foundation Press, 1970). On behavioral statistical prediction as applied to court cases, see Joel Grossman and Joseph Tanenhaus, *Frontiers of Judicial Research* (New York: Wiley, 1969); Glendon Schubert, ed., *Judicial Behavior: A Reader in Theory and Research* (Chicago: Rand McNally, 1964); Harold Spaeth, *Supreme Court Policy Making: Explanation and Prediction* (San Francisco: Freeman, 1979); and S. Ulmer, *Courts, Law, and Judicial Process* (New York: Free Press, 1981).

2. The cases referred to in Table 4–1 are *Argersinger v. Hamlin*, 407 U.S. 25 (1972); and *Goldberg v. Kelly*, 397 U.S. 254 (1970). The cases dealing with welfare procedures are discussed in A. Berney et al., *Legal Problems of the Poor* (Boston: Little, Brown, 1975), pp. 849–869; G. Cooper et al., *Law and Poverty* (St. Paul: West, 1973), pp. 296–351; and A. LaFrance et al., *Law of the Poor* (St. Paul: West, 1975), pp. 368–376.

3. The cases dealing with public housing procedure are *Thorpe v. Durham Housing Authority*, 386 U.S. 670 (1967); and *Holmes v. New York City Housing Authority*, 398 F.2d 262 (1968). Those cases and related cases are discussed in Cooper et al., *Law and Poverty*, pp. 772–787; Eli Jarmel, *Problems in the Legal Representation of the Poor* (New York: Matthew Bender, 1972), pp. 13–1 to 13–47; and LaFrance et al., *Law of the Poor*, pp. 212–230.

4. The cases dealing with right to court-appointed counsel are *Powell v. Alabama*, 287 U.S. 45 (1932); *Gideon v. Wainwright*, 372 U.S. 335 (1963); *Douglas v. California*, 372 U.S. 353 (1963); *Miranda v. Arizona*, 384 U.S. 436 (1966); *Argersinger v. Hamlin; in re Gault*, 387 U.S. 1 (1967); and *Johnson v. Avery*, 393 U.S. 483 (1969). The right to counsel cases are discussed in P. Lewis and K. Peoples, *The Supreme Court and the Criminal Process* (Philadelphia: Saunders, 1978), pp. 549–593; Herman Pritchett, *Constitutional Civil Liberties* (Englewood Cliffs, N.J.: Prentice-Hall, 1984), pp. 206–216, 232–233, 235–237 (hereinafter cited as Pritchett); and C. Whitebread, *Criminal Procedure: An Analysis of Constitutional Cases and Concepts* (Mineola, N.Y.: Foundation Press, 1980), pp. 514–563.

5. The cases referred to in Table 4–2 are *Taylor v. Louisiana*, 419 U.S. 522 (1975); *San Antonio Independent School District v. Rodriguez*, 411 U.S. 1 (1973); *Jones v. Alfred H. Mayer Co.*, 392 U.S. 409 (1968); *Harper v. Virginia State Board of Elections*, 383 U.S. 663 (1966); *Reynolds v. Sims*, 377 U.S. 533 (1964); *Gideon v. Wainwright; Gomillion v. Lightfoot*, 364 U.S. 339 (1960); *Brown v. Board of Education*, 347 U.S. 483 (1954); *Shelley v. Kraemer*, 334 U.S. 1 (1948); and *Powell v. Alabama*. The equal protection cases are discussed in N. Dorsen et al., *Political and Civil Rights in the United States*, vols. 1 and 2 (Boston: Little, Brown, 1979) pp. 1–1278 (hereinafter cited as Dorsen); J. Nowak et al., *Constitutional Law* (St. Paul: West, 1983), pp. 585–831 (hereinafter cited as Nowak); and Pritchett, pp. 249–283.

6. The cases referred to in Table 4–3 are *Zorach v. Clausen*, 343 U.S. 306 (1952); and *McCollum v. Board of Education*, 333 U.S. 203 (1948). The cases dealing with religion in the public schools are discussed in Dorsen, vol. 1, pp. 953–975; Nowak, pp. 1049–1052; and Pritchett, pp. 150–154.

7. For a discussion of the cases dealing with aid to parochial schools, see Dorsen, vol. 1, pp. 947–952, 976–1006; Nowak, pp. 1030–1048; and Pritchett, pp. 145–160.

8. For a discussion of the cases dealing with racial hiring and admissions, see Dorsen, vol. 2, pp. 1611–1939; Nowak, pp. 631–681; Pritchett, pp. 258–273; and A. Sindler, *Bakke, Defunis, and Minority Admissions: The Quest for Equal Opportunity* (New York: Longman, 1978).

9. On the use of percentaging in multi-criteria decision-making, see W. Edwards and R. Newman, *Multi-Attribute Evaluation* (Beverly Hills, Calif.: Sage Publications, 1982); S. Nagel, *Public Policy: Goals, Means, and Methods* (New York: St. Martin's, 1984), pp. 343–354; and Thomas Saaty, *The Analytic Hierarchy Process: Planning, Priority Setting, Resource Allocation* (New York: McGraw-Hill, 1980).

10. The cases referred to in Table 4–6 are *Sullivan v. Little Hunting Park*, 396 U.S. 229 (1969); *Jones v. Alfred H. Mayer Co.; Alderly v. Florida*, 385 U.S. 39 (1967); *Rice*

v. Sioux City Memorial Park Cemetery, 349 U.S. 70 (1955); *Barrows v. Jackson,* 346 U.S. 24 (1948); *Shelley v. Kraemer; Thornhill v. Alabama,* 310 U.S. 88 (1940); and *Buchanan v. Warley,* 245 U.S. 60 (1917). Those cases and related cases are discussed in Dorsen, vol. 2, pp. 940–946; J. Greenberg, *Race Relations and American Law* (New York: Columbia University Press, 1959), pp. 275–312. D. King and C. Quick, *Legal Aspects of the Civil Rights Movement* (Detroit: Wayne State University Press, 1965), pp. 129–148; and Pritchett, pp. 256–258.

11. For further details concerning the microcomputer program that generated the three displays, see S. Nagel, *Microcomputers as Decision-Making Aids in Law Practice* (Philadelphia: ALI-ABA, 1985), pp. 47–49 or Chapters 2 and 3 of this book. For more traditional computerized prediction that relies on multivariate regression analysis, see S. Nagel, *The Legal Process from a Behavioral Perspective* (Homewood, Ill.: Dorsey, 1969), pp. 125–172.

5

Using Microcomputers and P/G% to Predict Court Cases

The purpose of this chapter is to analyze a microcomputer program that can process a set of (1) prior cases, (2) predictive criteria for distinguishing among the cases, and (3) the relations between each prior case and each criterion in order to arrive at an accurate decision-rule. Such a rule will enable all prior cases to be predicted without inconsistencies and thereby maximize the likelihood of predicting future cases accurately. To illustrate the program, five substantive fields are used, including the predicting of cases dealing with religion in the public schools, legislative redistricting, housing discrimination, international law, and criminal law.[1]

THE GENERAL METHODOLOGY

The predictive methodology on which the computer program is based involves six key elements:

1. Listing the cases or case-types that are to be analyzed.
2. Listing the tentative criteria to aid in explaining why some cases were decided one

way and others differently. That listing might also involve indicating the relative importance of each criterion.

3. Listing how each case scores on each of those predictive criteria. That listing can use whatever measurement units seem comfortable, such as a yes-no dichotomy, a 1–5 scale, years, or dollars.
4. Summing the scores for each case across the criteria to give each case an overall score. Doing this might involve transforming the raw scores into dimensionless part/whole percentages.
5. Relating the set of summation scores for the cases to the actual or presumed outcomes of those past cases or case-types. One can thereby develop a decision-rule indicating the summation scores that are associated with certain kinds of outcomes.
6. Doing a sensitivity analysis, whereby one determines how the decision-rule, the presence of inconsistencies, or a litigation strategy might be affected by changes in the cases, criteria, weights, relations, measurement units, or other inputs.

The program is called Policy/Goal Percentaging Analysis, or P/G%, because it was originally designed to relate alternative legal policies to goals to be achieved. The program can be easily extended to relating prior cases to predictive criteria. The word *percentaging* is used in the title of the program because the program uses part/whole percentages to handle the problem of goals or predictive criteria being measured on different dimensions. The measurement units are converted into a system of percentages showing the relative position of each case on each criterion, rather than working with a system of dollars, apples, years, miles, or other measurement scores.

Each set of substantive cases is designed to illustrate a different variation on the six key elements. The cases dealing with religion in the public schools involve case-types rather than actual cases. They also involve only one way of measuring the predictive criteria, namely, a simple yes-no dichotomy. The legislative redistricting cases involve specific cases rather than case-types. They especially illustrate resolving inconsistencies in how the cases were decided. The housing discrimination cases illustrate how the program deals with multiple ways of measuring the predictive criteria. The international law cases involve a continuum outcome like damages, sentences, or probabilities, rather than just winning or losing. The criminal cases deal with multiple weights for the predictive criteria.

This chapter is designed to discuss a methodology that is helpful in arriving at accurate predictions of court cases. Making accurate predictions, however, depends on a number of factors in addition to having a good predictive methodology. Those factors include a knowledge of the subject matter; previous prediction experiences; the stimulus of having a lot at stake, depending on the accuracy of the predictions; requiring written analysis justifying one's predictions; clarity about what one is predicting; being a positive thinker with regard to one's ability to predict; being explicit about one's predictive criteria; having a relevant set of cases on which to base one's predictions; being accurate in how the cases are positioned on each of the predictive criteria; being capable of seeing relations and reasoning by analogy; and having a knowledge of predictive methodologies, such as P/G%, multiple regression, and staircase prediction, which are compared in this chapter.[2]

CASE-TYPES, UNI-DIMENSIONALITY, AND RELIGION IN THE PUBLIC SCHOOLS

Table 5–1 contains data for predicting cases dealing with religion in the public schools. This simple example can serve well to illustrate the six key elements. They are referred to as "elements," rather than steps, because they are developed in a cyclical rather than a sequential way. This means that subsequent elements tend to lead to revising the previous elements in a series of repeated cycles. The process continues until one is satisfied that the elements make sense in light of the user's purposes and the overall criterion of 100 percent accuracy in predicting or postdicting the cases on which the decision-rule is based.

The cases listed on the rows of Table 5–1 are not specific cases, except for Case 7, which is *Zorach v. Clauson,* 343 U.S. 306 (1952), and Case 8, which is *McCollum v. Board of Education,* 444 U.S. 203 (1948). Instead, the "cases" are case-types formed by combining the categories on the three predictive criteria. The first predictive criterion is whether the religious activity was on school time. A yes scores 2 and a no scores 1. The second predictive criterion is whether the religious activity was within the school building, with a yes scoring 2 and a no scoring 1. The third criterion is whether the purpose of the religious activity is for indoctrination, that is, instilling or strengthening religious beliefs (scored 2), or for education, as in a course on comparative literature or cultural geography (scored 1). A high score or a 2 on each predictive criterion indicates a score in the direction of unconstitutionality for these cases. Thus with three predictive criteria, each of which is a yes-no dichotomy, there can be eight case-types or possible combinations of the categories. Those case-types are listed in the first column in the order of the summation scores for each case-type. When two case-types have the same summation scores, they are listed alphabetically.

After clarifying the cases or case-types and the predictive criteria, the third element involves showing the relations between each case/case-type and each predictive criterion. That is easy here since the definition of each case-type shows how it is positioned on each criterion. The fourth element involves summing the relation scores to obtain an overall score for each case. That is also easy here since the raw scores can be summed, because all of the predictive criteria are measured on the same 1–2 scale. We therefore do not have a problem of multi-dimensionality, which is present when we try to add apples to oranges, years to dollars, or a 1–2 scale to a 1–5 scale.

The fifth element involves relating the summation scores to the outcomes in the form of a decision-rule. Predictive decision-rules in this context have the form, "If a case has a summation score of ____ or more, predict a decision of ____ ; if a case has a summation score of ____ or less, predict an opposite

Table 5–1
Data for Predicting Cases Dealing with Religion in the Public Schools

CASETYPES / CRITERIA	School Time	School Building	Purpose	SUM	OUTCOME
1. Educational Purpose Off School Time Out of School Building	1	1	1	3	C
2. Educational Purpose Off School Time In School Building	1	2	1	4	C
3. Educational Purpose On School Time Out of School Building	2	1	1	4	C
4. Religious Indoctrination Off School Time Out of the School Building	1	1	2	4	C
5. Educational Purpose On School Time In School Building	2	2	1	5	C
6. Religious Indoctrination Off School Time In the School Building	1	2	2	5	C
7. Religious Indoctrination On School Time Out of the School Building	2	1	2	5	C
8. Religious Indoctrination On School Time In the School Building	2	2	2	6	U

NOTES:

1. A "U" in the outcome column means the arrangement is found unconstitutional. A "C" means the arrangement is found constitutional. The Zorach case is Casetype 7, and the McCullom is Casetype 8.
2. The decision rule which the above data generates is:
   (1) If a case dealing with religion in the public schools has a summation score of 5 or less, the arrangements will be found constitutional.
   (2) With a summation score of 6 or more, the arrangements will be found unconstitutional.
3. The leading case is Zorach v. Clauson. It involved a summation score of 5, and the arrangement was found constitutional. Therefore, one would expect constitutionality to be found even more with scores lower than 5.
4. The outcome of Case 4 is known from the case of McCullom v. Champaign, although the outcome could have been known from things said in Zorach.

decision. To aid in developing decision-rules, the computer program arranges the case-types in the order of their summation scores with ties broken alphabetically. Before the computer calculates the summation scores, it asks the user for (1) the labels for the case-types, or the names for the specific cases; (2) the labels for the predictive criteria; (3) an indication whether the criteria are all measured the same way or differently; and (4) the relative importance or weights of the criteria. Here the criteria are weighted equally, meaning that they each receive a weight of 1. When differential weights are involved, those weights are used to multiply the relation scores in order to work with weighted relation scores and thus weighted summation scores.

A sixth and especially important piece of information is the outcome for each case or case-type. That is usually easy information to provide when specific cases are involved. When case-types are involved as here, deductive reasoning may be needed to indicate the outcomes for those case-types that do not correspond to specific cases. For example, in *Zorach,* the Supreme Court upheld religious indoctrination on school time although not in the school building. The Court would then surely uphold religious indoctrination not on school time and not in the school building, which is Case-type 4. In other words, if a case wins with an unfavorable score on Criterion A and a favorable score on Criterion B, it is even more likely to win with a favorable score on Criterion A if all other variables are held constant. This is known as "a fortiori reasoning." One can similarly deduce Case-type 1 when all three variables are favorable and Case-type 3 when two variables, rather than just one, are favorable and the one unfavorable variable has not changed. Another form of a fortiori reasoning, which is not present here, is to state that if a case loses with a favorable score on Criterion A, it will lose even more with an unfavorable score on Criterion A if everything else is held constant.

Likewise, if the Court explicitly states or implies that being on or off school time and in or out of the school building are of approximately equal importance, one can deduce Case-type 2 and Case-type 6 since they interchange the scores on those two variables as compared to the *Zorach* Case-type 7. Also if the Court explicitly states or implies than an educational purpose provides an exemption from unconstitutionality, we can deduce that Case-type 5, as well as case-types 1, 2, and 3, will be found constitutional. Case-type 8 does not have to be deduced since it corresponds to the specific case of *McCullom v. Board of Education.* If that case had not been decided, one could predict unconstitutionality from language that implies that being in an unfavorable position on all three variables crosses the threshold of unconstitutionality. When the outcome column has been completed, one should have no trouble seeing that the data generate a decision-rule stating that if a case has a summation score of 6 or more, predict a decision of unconstitutionality; if a case has a summation score of 5 or less, predict a decision of constitutionality.

As an example of sensitivity analysis in this substantive context, one could add a fourth variable such as whether or not the program is voluntary. We would then have 16 case-types since we would have four dichotomous variables that lend themselves to 2 × 2 × 2 × 2 or 16 case-types. The relations would still be determined by the definitions of the case-types. Adding that fourth variable brings in the concept of violating a constitutional constraint in that all eight case-types in which the program is not voluntary would be unconstitutional. In other words, having a compulsory religious program is enough to generate an unconstitutionality decision, regardless of how the case-type is scored on the other three variables, even if the program is educational rather than doctrinal. A sensitivity analysis, however, is subject to change when the new inputs actually occur in a future case. Those new cases can then become part of the data set that is used to develop and revise the decision-rules.[3]

SPECIFIC CASES, RESOLVING INCONSISTENCIES, AND LEGISLATIVE REDISTRICTING

Analyzing the Specific Cases

Table 5–2 contains data for predicting legislative redistricting cases. The cases listed on the rows are all specific cases rather than case-types. They are the most important legislative redistricting cases decided in the United States by various courts from *Colegrove v. Green,* 328 U.S. 549 (1946), through *Baker v. Carr,* 369 U.S. 186 (1962). The cases are arranged in the order of their summation scores. That happens to be roughly the same as the chronological order of the cases, which shows that the cases became more favorable toward ordering redistricting as one moved from *Colegrove* to *Baker*.

There are four predictive criteria. As with the cases dealing with religion in the public schools, all four criteria here are measured using a yes-no dichotomy. The first variable asks whether the relevant constitution expressly requires districts of equal population per representative. The *Colegrove* case, for example, involved congressional redistricting. The federal Constitution does not expressly require equality. On the contrary, it expressly requires that each state have at least one representative, no matter how small the state might be. Equality for congressional districting has been read into the federal Constitution by way of finding it implicit in the due process clause of the Fifth Amendment and the equal protection clause of the Fourteenth Amendment. The *Baker* case, on the other hand, involved Tennessee State legislative redistricting. The Tennessee Constitution does explicitly require equality, which had been ignored for years by the refusal of the state legislature to redistrict.

The second variable asks whether a state or federal legislature is involved. A state legislature is scored 2, and the federal legislature is scored 1. State legislatures are more likely to be ordered to redistrict because the courts (at least in those early years) seemed to show more respect for not upsetting Congress. Oliver Wendell Holmes had said that the federal system could survive if Congress violated the Constitution but not if the states did so. The third variable refers to

Table 5–2
Data for Predicting Redistricting Cases

CRITERIA / CASES	Equality Requirement	State Legislature	Equality Violation	Federal Court	SUM	OUTCOME
1. Colegrove	1	1	1	2	5	D
2. Grills	2	2	1	1	6	A
3. Maryland	1	2	2	1	6	D
4. Scholle	1	2	2	1	6	D
5. WMCA	1	2	1	2	6	D
6. Asbury	2	2	2	1	7	A
7. Dyer	2	1	2	2	7	A
8. Baker	2	2	2	2	8	A
9. Magraw	2	2	2	2	8	A

NOTES:

1. A 1 in column 1-4 means No. A 2 means Yes. An "A" in the outcome column means the attacker wins. A "D" means the defender wins.

2. The decision rule which the above data generates is:
   (1) If a redistricting case during the time period covered has a summation score of 7 or above, the attacker wins.
   (2) With a summation score of 6 or below, the defender wins.

3. That decision rule generates one inconsistent case. The inconsistency can be eliminated by:
   (1) Changing the decision rule to say a summation score of 6 leads to an unclear outcome.
   (2) Giving the first variable a weight of 2, which would be consistent with the importance of requiring equality.
   (3) Adding a fifth variable called "Decided After the Maryland Case."
   (4) Eliminating the Grills case, but that does not seem justifiable.
   (5) Changing the measurement on the first variable from no-yes to a 1-3 scale and giving Grills a score of 3.
   (6) Finding that Grills really deserves a 2 on the third or fourth variables.

4. When working with cases, rather than case-types, inconsistencies are likely to occur that need resolving.

the degree of equality violation. If less than 35 percent of the state's population can choose more than 50 percent of the state legislature, the equality violation is high (scored 2). If more than 35 percent of the state's population is required to choose more than 50 percent of the state legislature, the equality violation is relatively low (scored 1). The fourth variable asks whether a federal or state court is deciding the case. One would expect a federal court to be more likely to decide in favor of redistricting in view of the lifetime appointment of federal judges, which makes them less susceptible to pressure from the dominant political party.

With nine cases and four predictive criteria, there are 36 relations. They are shown in the cells of Table 5–2. Those relation scores can be objectively determined, as are the relation scores in most court-case prediction. The fourth key element in the predictive analysis involves summing the relation scores for each case and arranging the cases in the order of their summation scores. The minimum summation score is 4 for a case that scores 1 on all four variables. There was no such case, which is a further indication that we are dealing with actual cases rather than case-types. The *Colegrove* case comes closest with a score of 5. The maximum score possible is 8 for a case that scores 2 on all four variables. *Baker* is an example of that case-type.

With actual specific cases, the prior outcomes are generally easy to determine. Of these nine cases, five were decided in favor of the party attacking the existing apportionment and four in favor of the party defending it. The decision-rule that the data generates is that if a redistricting case during the period covered has a summation score of 7 or above, the attacker wins. With a summation score of 6 or below, the defender wins. That decision-rule, however, results in at least one inconsistency. This is true because four cases received scores of 6 apiece, and one of the four resulted in a victory for the attacker when the other three were won by the defender of the existing redistricting.

Resolving the Inconsistencies

The P/G% system provides methods whereby the system can guarantee 100 percent accuracy in predicting the past cases on which the decision-rule is based. This is the equivalent in statistical regression analysis of guaranteeing that there will be no residuals or differences between predicted and actual scores when one is predicting winning or losing. It is possible that there are some real inconsistencies across cases, judges, places, or periods. The philosophy of the P/G% approach, however, assumes that the inconsistencies are only on the surface and that if one does a better analysis of the cases, criteria, relations, weights, measures, and other input, the inconsistencies will disappear. The P/G% approach facilitates such an analysis by enabling the user easily to determine the effects of changes in those inputs and by allowing for variables that refer to when, where, and by whom the cases were decided.

There are at least six ways of resolving what otherwise would be inconsistencies or residuals. Taking them in random order as applied to Table 5–2, one can change the decision-rule to state that a summation score of 7 or above leads to the attacker winning, of 5 or below to the defender winning, and of 6 to an unclear result. There would then be no inconsistencies since a summation score of 6 could then accommodate both an A and a D for its outcome. That approach, is, however, undesirable, because it may declare too many cases to be unpredictable. In this example, an undesirable four out of the nine cases would become unpredictable.

A more meaningful approach is to give the first criterion a weight of 2. That would have the effect of doubling all of the numbers in that column before the summing is done. Doing that would mean the new summation scores would be 6, 8, 7, 7, 7, 9, 9, 10, and 10, respectively. The new decision-rule would then be that a summation score of 8 or above leads to a redistricting order, and a summation of score of 7 or below leads to such an order being denied. In other words, each case that had scored 1 on the equality requirement would move up one extra point on the summation score, and each case that had scored 2 on the equality requirement would move up two extra points on the summation score. This means that the *Grills* case would move up from a 6 to an 8, and the other three cases that started at 6 would move up to a 7, because only *Grills* of the four cases received a 2 on the equality requirement. Giving the requirement of equality a weight of 2 when the other criteria receive a weight of 1 is substantively reasonable, since the question of whether equality is required should be especially fundamental in determining whether a redistricting is ordered for lack of equality. The other criteria are less fundamental in that sense.

Instead of or in addition to changing the weights of the criteria, one could add an additional criterion. For example, the inconsistency would be resolved if we added a time variable that asks whether the case was decided after the *Maryland* case. There were only two cases decided after the *Maryland* case, namely, *Grills* and *Baker*. Thus they would be the only cases receiving a 2 on this new variable. All of the others would receive a 1. This would mean that the new set of nine summation scores would be 6, 8, 7, 7, 7, 8, 8, 9, and 8. Unlike the differential weighting, however, adding that variable is not so substantively reasonable. That time-point was not a watershed in any sense but rather just an arbitrary way of separating *Grills* from the other three cases. That time variable would have been more meaningful if there had been years rather than months separating the *Maryland* case from the *Grills* case or if the *Maryland* case had established an important new precedent favoring redistricting that was applicable to *Grills*.

Another alternative might be to eliminate the *Grills* case. That would eliminate the inconsistency and would be justifiable if the *Grills* case really did not belong by virtue of its being a foreign redistricting case, a redistricting of fire stations rather than legislative districts, or some other substantively meaningful reason.

There is no such reason here. Any approach to eliminating inconsistencies must also be substantively meaningful. Approaches that do not work with Table 5–2 might, however, work with other sets of cases.

Another approach is to change the measurement on one or more predictive criteria. For example, perhaps the requirement of equality could be measured in three categories rather than just yes-no. The three categories might be strongly yes, mildly yes, and no. If the constitution in the *Grills* case strongly requires equality, that case would receive a 3 on the first variable, and the other three cases would remain at 1. The new summation scores would then be 7, 6, 6, and 6 for those four cases, which would separate *Grills* from the other three cases without creating any new inconsistencies. Another example might involve noting that the equality violation is crudely measured with a yes-no dichotomy. A more sophisticated measurement might ask what the minimum percentage of the population is that is needed to elect 51 percent of the legislature. The answer could range from a low of about 10 percent to a high of 51 percent. The *Grills* case, however, would not receive a substantially higher score on the degree of equality violation than those other three cases, since it received a no on the yes-no dichotomy when two of the other three received a yes.

Another alternative relates to finding an error in how the cases have been scored on each criterion. If, for example, *Grills* really deserves a 2 on the third or fourth variables, the inconsistency will be resolved. That approach is more likely when there is more subjectivity in scoring the relations. An error could also occur in calculating the summation scores if they were calculated by hand or with a calculator. The microcomputer, however, is not likely to err in summing the relation scores even if they are multi-dimensional and weighted. The program also shows intermediate values between the raw scores and the summation scores to enable the user to check that the summation was done properly. The intermediate scores show the corresponding part/whole percentages for each raw score to consider multi-dimensionality (which will be discussed shortly) and weighted raw scores or weighted part/whole percentage scores to consider differential weighting.

Sensitivity/Threshold Analysis

The computer program aids the user in determining which alternative is best for eliminating inconsistencies. The program does so in various ways. One way is to inform the user what it would take to move the *Grills* case up to a tie with the lowest scoring case in which the attacker won. That kind of threshold analysis shows how each of the four relation scores or their weights would have to change. Another way is to inform the user what it would take to move the other three cases down to a tie with the highest scoring case beneath them in which the defender won. Probably the best way in which the sensitivity aspects of the program are helpful here is by enabling one to experiment quickly and accurately with different weights, variables, sets of cases, measurement units, and relation scores to see what their effects are in terms of new summation scores and the elimination of previous inconsistencies without introducing new ones.

A special form of sensitivity or threshold analysis in this substantive context could involve asking what would have enabled *Colegrove* to be decided in favor of the attacker the way *Baker* was. The answer is that it would have taken a combination of changes great enough to make up the 3–point gap between the score of 5, which *Colegrove* received, and the score of 8 for *Baker*. The gap could be made up if *Colegrove* could receive a score of 4 on the equality requirement or Baker a score of −1. Neither change, however, is possible since that criterion only provides for scores of 1 and 2. The same thing is true of all other criteria in that no change on any of them is possible that will make up the 3–point gap. The threshold analysis also informs us that the gap could be made up if any one of the first three criterion were to be given a negative weight of −2. Then *Colegrove* would receive weighted relation scores of −2 +1 +1 +2, which sum to +2, and *Baker* would receive scores of −4 +2 +2 +2, adding to +2 just like *Colegrove*. A −2 weight, however, makes no substantive sense for any of the first three variables. No weight will help *Colegrove* for the fourth variable. Both *Colegrove* and *Baker* receive the same raw score on that variable, since they were both decided in federal courts.

The threshold analysis is summarized in Table 5–3. The first row indicates the threshold values for the *Colegrove* case on each of the four variables. The second row indicates the threshold values for the *Baker* case. The third row indicates the threshold weights for each of the four predictive criteria. This analysis informs us that it would have been virtually impossible for *Colegrove* to have been decided any other way in view of the validity and meaning of these predictive variables as well as other variables that also disfavored *Colegrove*.

To apply the decision-rule of Table 5–2 one needs a new case that is not included in the data set from which the decision-rule was generated. If the next case after *Baker* involves no equality requirement, a state legislature, a severe equality violation, and a federal court, the case will have 7 unweighted points. We will then predict victory for the attacker, since 6.5 is the cutoff summation score. If we weight the equality requirement by 2, the new case will have a weighted summation score of 8. We will still predict victory, since the cutoff score with the weights is 7.5. We could test the predictive power of the methodology by predicting Case 3 from the first two, Case 4 from the first three, and so on. If we do that, we will predict accurately each time, provided that we use the weighting system whereby scores on the equality requirement are doubled while the other scores remain unchanged.[4]

MULTI-DIMENSIONALITY AND HOUSING DISCRIMINATION CASES

Table 5–4 contains data for predicting housing discrimination cases in light of *Shelley v. Kraemer*, 334 U.S. 1 (1948). That case held that covenants in deeds

Table 5–3
An Example of the Computer Display: Threshold Analysis

THRESHOLD ANALYSIS

COLEGROVE
VS
BAKER

	EQ. REQU	LEGIS. S	EQ. VIOL	COURT FE
COLEG	4.00	4.00	4.00	5.00
BAKER	-1.00	-1.00	-1.00	-1.00
Weight	-2.000	-2.000	-2.000	????

NOTES:

1. The object here is to determine what it would take to bring Colegrove up to the same summation score as Baker, or to bring Baker down to the same summation score as Colegrove.
2. Each cell shows the threshold value of a relation or a weight. If an actual cell value in Table 1 were to change to its above threshold value, then there would be a tie between Colegrove and Baker, assuming all the other inputs are held constant.
3. No one threshold value can equalize Colegrove and Baker given the four criteria. All the threshold values are above or below the measurement range of 1-2. There is also no substantive sense for the weights of any of those predictive variables to be negative rather than positive.

are unenforceable when they prohibit the owner from selling to a black buyer, at least when a neighbor is seeking an injunction against a willing seller as a matter of the neighbors' property rights. To predict related housing discrimination cases, it is useful to know how each case is positioned on the four predictive criteria of (1) whether the seller is willing to sell, (2) whether there is an interfering neighbor seeking to enjoin the sale, (3) whether the buyer is abusive in some way so that the seller would be legally right in not selling regardless of the racial matter, and (4) whether the claim of the plaintiff is based on a constitutional violation, breach of contract, personal injury, or property violation. The sale is more likely to be upheld if the seller is willing, the plaintiff is an interfering neighbor, and the buyer is not abusive. The sale is also more likely to be upheld if the claim is based on a violation of constitutional law, contract law, tort law, or property law in that order.

To illustrate the problem of multi-dimensionality in predictive criteria, Table 5–4 uses only criteria 1 and 4, which relate to the willingness of the seller and the nature of the claim. The multi-dimensionality problem involves the fact that the willingness of the seller is measured in terms of a yes-no dichotomy, whereas

Table 5–4
Data for Predicting Housing Discrimination Cases

CRITERIA / CASETYPES	(1) Is Seller Willing	(2) Part/Whole % (Weight = 2)	(3) Claim	(4) Part/Whole % (Weight = 1)	(5) Unweighted Sum	(6) Outcome	(7) Sum of Unweighted Part/Whole %'s (2)+(4)	(8) Sum of Weighted Part/Whole %'s 2(2)+1(4)
1. Unwilling Seller and Property Claim	1	8%	1	5%	2	?	13%	21%
2. Unwilling Seller and Injury Claim	1	8	2	10	3	?	18	26
3. Unwilling Seller and Contract Claim	1	8	3	15	4	?	23	31
4. Unwilling Seller and Constitutional Claim	1	8	4	20	5	?	28	36
5. Willing Seller and Property Claim	2	17	1	5	3	W	22	39
6. Willing Seller and Injury Claim	2	17	2	10	4	W	27	44
7. Willing Seller and Contract Claim	2	17	3	15	5	W	32	49
8. Willing Seller and Constitutional Claim	2	17	4	20	6	W	37	54
WHOLE	12	100%	20	100%	32		200%	300%

NOTES:

1. A "W" in the outcome column means the sale is allowed. A "?" in the outcome column means the outcome is unclear. The Shelley case is Casetype 5.
2. The first variable is whether or not the seller is willing to sell. The second variable is the alleged violation which can be a constitutional violation, breach of contract, personal injury, or a property rights violation.
3. Part/whole percentages are added to give a summation score, rather than just adding the raw scores. The raw scores do not take into consideration that there are four categories on the second variable and only two categories on the first variable.
4. The above data generates the following decision rule:
   (1) If a casetype has a sum of weighted p/w%'s of .39 or higher, then the willing seller wins and the sale is allowed.
   (2) If a casetype has a sum of weighted p/w%'s of .36 or lower, then the unwilling seller may be allowed to get out of the sale depending on whether or not the buyer is abusive.
5. If we look to the sum of the raw scores, then we have three inconsistencies out of eight casetypes. If we look to the sum of the unweighted p/w%'s, then we have two inconsistencies, since there are two question-mark cases with higher scores than the lowest winning case.
6. It makes sense to give the variable of being a willing seller more weight than the variable of the alleged violation in cases like these involving restrictive racial covenants.

the nature of the claim is measured in terms of four categories. With two categories on one criterion and four on the other, there are eight case-types, as listed at the left of Table 5–4. Column 1 shows how the eight case-types score on the willingness variable, and column 3 shows how they score on the claim variable. Column 5 adds those raw relation-scores together to obtain an unweighted raw sum. Column 6 shows that the sale will be allowed if the seller is willing. If the seller is unwilling, the outcome depends partly on the other variables that are not included in Table 5–4.

When the predictive variables are measured differently, merely summing the raw scores produces distorted results. That would be more obvious if one predictive criterion were measured in miles and a second predictive criterion were measured in pounds. The results are also distorted if a case receives 4 points for being in the best category on the claim variable and only 2 points for being in the best category on the willingness variable. This is due to the coincidence that the claim variable has four and the willingness variable only two categories. Partially to remedy that situation, the relation scores are transformed into part/whole percentages that are not influenced by whether a variable is measured in miles, pounds, a yes-no dichotomy, or a 1–4 scale.

To transform the relation scores on a given criterion or column, one merely sums the numbers in the column to obtain a total or whole. For example, the sum of the first column is 12. One then divides each number or part in the column by the whole to obtain a part/whole percentage for each relation score. For example, the part/whole percentage corresponding to the first relation score in column 1 is 1/12, or 8 percent. Now instead of adding the raw scores of column 1 to those of column 3 to obtain the unweighted raw sum of column 5, one adds the part/whole percentages of column 2 to those of column 4 to obtain the sum of the unweighted part/whole percentages of column 7. For example, adding 8 percent in column 2 to 5 percent in column 3 gives 13 percent in column 7.

Notice that by just working with the unweighted raw sum there are three inconsistencies out of eight cases. The three inconsistencies are cases 2, 3, and 4. They have unweighted sums that are as high as cases 5, 6, and 7. Cases 2, 3, and 4, however, have unclear outcomes, whereas cases 5, 6, and 7 resulted in the sale being allowed. By working with the sum of the unweighted part/whole percentages (p/w%'s), there are only two inconsistencies. They are cases 3 and 4. They have unweighted part/whole percentages larger than cases 5 and 6. Cases 3 and 4, however, have unclear outcomes, whereas cases 5 and 6 resulted in the sale being allowed. All of the inconsistencies can be eliminated by recognizing that the willingness of the seller is more important than the nature of the claim. If willingness is given a weight of 2, the sum of the weighted p/w%'s for the first case-type is twice 8 percent plus 5 percent for a total of 21 percent. If one does likewise for each of the eight case-types, one obtains the sums of weighted p/w%'s shown in column 8. The percents in that column are in perfect ascending order, such that there are no inconsistencies. If a case-type has a sum of weighted p/w%'s of .39 or higher, the willing seller wins and the sale is allowed. If a case-type has a sum of weighted p/w%'s of .36 or lower, the unwilling seller may be allowed to get out of the sale depending on whether or not the buyer is abusive.[5]

OUTCOME RANGES AND INTERNATIONAL LAW CASES

Table 5–5 contains data for predicting international law cases in which the United States is a party. The object is to predict the probability that the United States will win from at least two predictive criteria. The predictive criteria are the source of law and the industrial power of the U.S. opponent. They are two criteria from a larger list of seven, which also includes (1) the international law subject matter and the U.S. position on it, (2) the decision-making tribunal, (3) the economic interests that may be involved and the U.S. position on them, (4) the civil liberty interests that may be involved and the U.S. position on them, and (5) the nature of the plaintiff as a legal entity.

The source of the law refers to the four categories of (1) domestic law of another country (the United States is victorious in only 25 percent of such cases), (2) an international treaty (47 percent victorious), (3) international law/custom (56 percent), and (4) U.S. domestic law (85 percent). The industrial power of the U.S. opponent refers to the three categories of (1) less industrial power than the United States (the United States is victorious in only 56 percent of such cases), (2) non-countries (70 percent victorious), and (3) about the same in industrial power (100 percent victorious, although that sub-sample is small). The victory probabilities are based on an analysis of the 137 cases contained in four leading international law casebooks.

With four categories on one criterion and three categories on the second criterion, there are 12 case-types, as shown at the left side of Table 5–5. The summation column sums the raw scores for each case-type across the variables. Technically, part/whole percentages should be used since the predictive variables are measured differently via a 1–4 and a 1–3 scale. The scales, however, are close enough to justify working with raw scores at least for this methodological illustration.

Each probability in the outcome column is arrived at by averaging the probabilities for the relevant categories on each predictive variable. Thus Case-type 1 involves foreign law (25 percent U.S. victory rate) and a less industrial U.S. opponent (56 percent U.S. victory rate). The average between 25 and 56 percent is 40 percent rounded to the nearest even number. There are more sophisticated ways of combining probabilities in accordance with Bayesian probability analysis. They are, however, highly complicated, especially when more than two predictive variables are involved. The information for a Bayesian analysis is also almost never available since it requires knowing various details on how the predictive variables relate to each other. Simply averaging the basic probabilities should provide a sufficient approximation to an overall probability, especially if each predictive criterion is worded in the direction of winning and does not

Table 5–5
Data for Predicting International Law Cases with the United States as a Party

CRITERIA / CASETYPES	Source of Law	U.S. Opponent	SUM	OUTCOME
1. Foreign Law and Less Industrial Opponent	1	1	2	40%
2. Foreign Law and Non-Country Opponent	1	2	3	48
3. Treaty and Less Industrial Opponent	2	1	3	51
4. Foreign Law and Equal Opponent	1	3	4	62
5. International Law and Less Industrial Opponent	3	1	4	56
6. Treaty and Non-Country Opponent	2	2	4	58
7. International Law and Non-Country Opponent	3	2	5	63
8. Treaty and Equal Opponent	2	3	5	73
9. U.S. Law and Less Industrial Opponent	4	1	5	70
10. International Law and Equal Opponent	3	3	6	78
11. U.S. Law and Non-Country Opponent	4	2	6	78
12. U.S. Law and Equal Opponent	4	3	7	92

Table 5–5: Continued

NOTES:

1. The decision rule which the above data generates is $Y = .20 + .10(X)$, where Y is the probability of the U.S. winning and X is the summation score.
2. The above decision rule could also be expressed as a series of if-then statements like (1) If X is 1, then Y is .30; (2) If X is 2, Y is .40; (3) If X is 3, Y is .50; (4) If X is 4, Y is .60; (5) If X is 5, Y is .70; (6) If X is 6, Y is .80; and (7) If X is 7, Y is .90.
3. Table 5-4 only deals with two of the seven variables in the international law cases. The two are the main source of law and the industrial power of the U.S. opponent. The source of law includes U.S. law, international law, a treaty, and foreign law. The U.S. opponent can be equal to the U.S., not a country, or less than the U.S. in industrial power.
4. Only two variables are used in Table 5-4 rather than seven partly because of the temporary limitation to 15 alternatives. One can handle all seven variables through multiple runs with 15 case types per run. The number of case types, however, is 163,800 since the number of categories per variable is 4, 13, 6, 5, 5, 3, and 7 respectively. Under those circumstances, one would not want to list all the casetypes. Instead, one would want to know what the probability of U.S. victory is for any combination of seven categories. To estimate that, simply average the seven probabilities of U.S. Victory.
5. The outcome figures shown above come from averaging the two proabilities from the two variables used for each case type. Thus, the combination of U.S. law and equal power has a .92 probability because U.S. law has a .85 probability and equal power has a 1.00 probability. This gives an approximation to a Bayesian conditional, especially where we only have the main probabilities to work with.
6. The above prediction equation comes from observing the relation between the summation scores and the outcome probabilities in Table 5-4. One can determine the prediction equation more accurately by using a statistical calculator that can easily arrive at such an equation for 12 pairs of inputs. One can also think in terms of six pairs of inputs for the summation scores from 2 to 7. Thus a score of 4 had an average outcome of .57 since Casetype 6 had an outcome of .56 and case type 8 had an outcome of .58.
7. Table 5-4 provides a good illustration of an outcome that is not a dichotomy of win or lose, but rather a continuum outcome of 0 to 1.00.

greatly overlap the other criteria. Even if the criteria do overlap, the weights can take that into consideration. Two duplicative criteria, for example, can each be given about half the weight they would otherwise receive if the other criterion in the pair were not also being used.

After determining the criteria, case-types, relations, summation scores, and outcomes, one should develop a decision-rule indicating for various summation scores what outcomes are likely to occur. This example, however, differs from the previous examples in that the outcome is a range between 40 and 92 percent rather than just a dichotomy of winning versus losing. Having an outcome range is common in most court cases as well as a win-lose dichotomy. In damage cases, the dichotomous liability decision is followed by a continuum damages decision when liability is established. Damages can range from a low of $1 in some libel cases to millions of dollars in treble damage antitrust suits. In criminal cases, the conviction decision is followed by a sentencing decision when there is a conviction. Sentences can range from a low of no jail time to life imprisonment or the death penalty.

In Tables 5–1 through 5–5, one could bypass the summation score and formulate a decision-rule that specifies for each case-type or case what the outcome is likely to be. That approach is likely to lead to inconsistencies, as was shown with the redistricting and housing discrimination cases. It is also much more clumsy to have to specify how each case or case-type will be decided, especially if there are many case-types. With a win-lose dichotomy, the decision-rule simply specifies what summation score separates the winners from the losers. In predicting a range outcome, there is no such threshold summation score. Instead, one would like to know (1) the likely outcome at a base summation score of 0 or 1 and how much the outcome is likely to increase for each one-unit or 1 percent increase in the summation score.

Looking at the last two columns of Table 5–5, one tends to generate a decision-rule that $Y = .20 + .10(X)$, where Y is the probability of the United States winning and X is the summation score. One can see that the two case-types with summation scores of 3 average about a .50 probability; the three case-types that score 4 average about .60; and the three case-types that score 5 average about .70. Extending those relations downward implies or extrapolates that a summation score of 0 would have a probability of about .20. One cannot, however, score less than a 2 on the two predictive criteria together. At the other end, that eyeballing approach implies that a summation score of 8 would have a probability of about 1.00. One cannot, however, score more than 7 on the predictive criteria. Thus the eyeballed or linear relation is not subject to the criticism that it leads to probabilities below 0 or above 1.00 since all of the possible summation scores lead to reasonable probabilities when using the decision rule $Y = .20 + .10(X)$.

Greater precision may sometimes be required than the eyeballing approach provides. Under those circumstances, one can insert into a statistical calculator the 12 pairs of numbers, consisting of 2 and .40, 3 and .48, and so on. After keying in those 24 numbers, one can read out the value of the constant, which is .19 rather than .20, and the value of the slope, which is slightly more than .10. The computer program will do that kind of statistical regression analysis directly when the P/G% program is further developed.

One can also obtain a decision-rule that reflects diminishing returns of the form $Y = .24(X)^{.65}$ by inserting the same 24 numbers and asking for diminishing returns output. With that equation, a summation score of 1 predicts a probability of .24, and a summation score of 2 predicts a probability of .38. Each successive increment on the summation score increases the probability but at a diminishing rate. The .65 means that if the summation score doubles (i.e., increases by 100 percent), the probability will increase by about 65 percent. For example, if the summation scores double from 1 to 2, the predicted probability goes up from .24 to .38. The .14 difference is about 65 percent of the .24 base. Diminishing returns is a fact of life in the relation between most input and most output, but linear relations often give good enough predictability. With the aid of the microcomputer program, one can request how one wants the summation scores related to the range outcomes with equal ease, regardless of whether one chooses constant returns, diminishing returns, or other available options.[6]

MULTIPLE WEIGHTS FOR PREDICTIVE CRITERIA AND CRIMINAL CASES

Table 5–6 contains data for predicting criminal cases. The data are purely hypothetical, unlike that in any of the previous four tables. For methodological purposes, however, hypothetical data should be just as usable as real data. These data are not only hypothetical, they are also symbolic, meaning that the cases and criteria have only letters, not names. The advantage of such data is that it enables one to see the methodology more clearly without substance getting in the way. Another advantage is that this particular set of hypothetical data is the first court-case prediction problem with which I dealt in 1960. This example thus illustrates some important changes over the past 25 years in systematic quantitative judicial prediction.

There are five criminal cases called *A, B, C, D,* and *E,* although the data are general enough to represent any kind of cases. There are four predictive criteria called *P, Q, R,* and *S.* There are thus 20 relations. Each relation is a yes-no dichotomy. The criteria are worded in such a way that a yes answer favors the defense, and a no answer favors the prosecution. If one adds the unweighted raw relation scores across each case, one obtains unweighted sums of 5, 8, 6, 6, and 7 for cases *A, B, C, D,* and *E,* respectively. Those raw scores generate one inconsistency out of five opportunities, since both cases *C* and *D* have 6 points, but *C* was decided in favor of the prosecution and *D* in the favor of the defense.

The best way to eliminate inconsistencies is generally by giving the predictive criteria different weights, rather than having the same weight for all criteria. The best way to determine those weights is generally in terms of the relative

Table 5–6
Data for Predicting Hypothetical Criminal Cases

CASES \ CRITERIA	P Criterion (W = +.75)	Q Criterion (W = -.67)	R Criterion (W = +1.00)	S Criterion (W = +.67)	Unweighted Sum	Outcome	Weighted Sum
1. A	1	2	1	1	5	P	1.09
2. C	2	2	1	1	6	P	2.09
3. B	2	2	2	2	8	D	3.50
4. D	2	1	2	1	6	D	3.50
5. E	2	1	2	2	7	D	4.16

NOTES:

1. A "P" in the outcome column means the prosecution wins. A "D" means the defense wins.
2. The decision rule which the above data guarantees is:
   (1) If the weighted summation score is 3.50 or above, the defendant wins.
   (2) With a summation score of 2.09 or below, the prosecution wins.
   (3) If the weighted summation score is between 2.09 and 3.50 the result is unclear.
3. The weighted summation scores are calculated by multiplying the raw scores on each predictive criterion by the weight of the criterion. Those products are then added across each case.
4. There is one inconsistency with the unweighted summation scores, but no inconsistencies with the weighted summation scores.
5. There are various ways in which one can assign weights to predictive criteria. The method used here is to determine the correlation coefficient of each predictive variable with whether the prosecution or defendant wins. In other words, outcome can be considered a dichotomous Y variable to be correlated with the X1, X2, X3, and X4 predictive criteria.
6. This is a good example of the use of weights for the predictive variables.

substantive importance of the variables as known to reasonably knowledgeable people. That is what was once done (1) in the cases dealing with religion in the public schools, in stating that educational purpose is an exemption variable and compulsory participation is a constraint variable; (2) in the redistricting cases, in stating that the presence of an equality requirement is more important than the other variables; and (3) in the housing discrimination cases, in stating that the willingness of the seller is more important than the field of law. The best tests of how well the cases have been weighted are whether the weighting makes substantive sense and results in a perfect separation of the winning from the losing cases.

An alternative weighting method is to weight the criteria in terms of their association with the outcome that one is trying to predict. That is what is done in Table 5–7. This table shows how the weights for Table 5–6 were determined. For example, criterion *P* has a weight of +.75 because 75 percent of the cases that had *P* present resulted in victory for the defense, whereas zero percent of the cases that had *P* absent resulted in victory for the defense. By subtracting those two percentages, one obtains a constant of 0 and a slope of .75 in an equation of the form $Y = 0 + .75(X)$. Y is the case outcome (with 0 for *P* and 1 for *D*), and X is the general predictive criterion (with 0 for absent and 1 for present). Thus if the predictive criterion moves from 0 to 1, the outcome then moves from a probability of zero percent for the defense winning on up to 75 percent. The other four subtables of Table 5–7 can be interpreted the same way to yield equations of the form $Y = 1.00 - .67(Q)$; $Y = 0 + 1.00(R)$; and $Y = .33 + .67(S)$.

Those four slopes or weights can be used to weight the predictive criteria, especially if those variables are independent of one another. If their lack of independence is great enough to produce inconsistencies, the weights can be adjusted in light of the known overlap among the variables until the inconsistencies are eliminated. The weights can also be adjusted in light of the relative substantive importance of the variables. Those weights may not have been adequately measured by the kind of relational analysis shown in Table 5–7 due to problems of (1) reciprocal causation, whereby prior case outcomes influence what evidence variables are subsequently introduced; (2) spurious causation, whereby both the case outcome and the presence of an evidence variable are influenced by other common factors; and (3) multi-collinearity, whereby the predictive criteria influence each other in terms of overlap, interaction, and interference.

Notice that with the weights from Table 5–7 introduced into Table 5–6 the weighted sums for the cases proceed in perfect ascending order. All of the defense cases now have higher weighted summation scores than any of the prosecution cases, which was not so with the unweighted sums. The decision-rule is that the defendant wins with a weighted summation score of at least 3.50 and the prosecution with 2.09 at most. Between 2.09 and 3.50 is a gray area that requires more cases to resolve.[7]

Table 5–7
Weighting Predictive Criteria by Association with Outcome

P Criterion

	No	Yes	
Defense Wins	0 0%	3 75%	+.75
Prosecutor Wins	1 100%	1 25%	
	1 100%	4 100%	5

Q Criterion

	No	Yes	
Defense Wins	2 100%	1 33%	-.67
Prosecutor Wins	0	2 67%	
	2 100%	3 100%	5

R Criterion

	No	Yes	
Defense Wins	0 0%	3 100%	+1.00
Prosecutor Wins	2 100%	0 0%	
	2 100%	3 100%	5

S Criterion

	No	Yes	
Defense Wins	1 33%	2 100%	+.67
Prosecutor Wins	2 67%	0 0%	
	3 100%	2 100%	5

NOTES:

1. There are always five cases regardless of the predictive variable that one is relating to outcome.
2. Each sub-table shows how the five cases are positioned on absence or presence of the variable and whether the defense or prosecution won.
3. Each sub-table has four cells because there are two categories on each variable being related. It is purely coincidental that there happen to be four variables.

MULTIPLE REGRESSION, STAIRCASE PREDICTION, AND P/G% PREDICTION

One might ask, why not do a multivariate regression analysis from the start, instead of doing a set of bivariate regression analyses like those shown in Table 5–7 to obtain the weights for a P/G% prediction analysis? Such a multivariate analysis would have the form $Y = a + b_1P + b_2Q + b_3R + b_4S$. Each b represents a regression weight that statistically controls for multi-dimensionality and overlap. The main advantage of that approach is its mechanical objectivity once the data table has been determined. Multiple regression analysis, however, is more complicated to do and present, although it has recently been made less complicated by the availability of microcomputer floppy discs, which can quickly process a set of data like that shown in tables 5–1 to 5–6 in order to generate the constant and the regression weights for the variables.

Disadvantages of a multiple regression approach are that it cannot guarantee perfect prediction of the past cases on which the equation is based unless one uses the same substantive-reasoning methods for eliminating inconsistencies as the methods associated with P/G% prediction. The same above problems of invalidity occur with multivariate regression as with bivariate regression (including reciprocal causation, spurious causation, and multi-collinearity) since both approaches use the same relatively mechanical methods to arrive at weights, as contrasted to using knowledgeable insiders who can separate out those problems.

Regression analysis cannot meaningfully relate summation scores to winning or losing the way a threshold decision-rule can because a regression equation requires that as the predictor variable increases, the predicted variable must also change. A threshold decision-rule recognizes that the same low scores may all lead to losing, and the same high scores may all lead to winning.

Weighting the predictive criteria substantively as was done with Tables 5–1, 5–2, and 5–4 is much easier methodologically than arranging for a multivariate regression analysis. Likewise, the bivariate analysis of Table 5–6 is much easier than a multivariate analysis even if the criteria are not all measured in yes-no dichotomies. One can then determine a bivariate regression weight with a statistical calculator, as mentioned in discussing Table 5–5, rather than with a four-cell cross-tabulation table.

One could express the idea of summing the unweighted raw scores as a regression equation of the form $Y = a + b_1P + b_2Q + b_3R + b_4S$, where $a = 0$ and each $b = 1$. But that only complicates the summation rule and provides no information about which Y score leads to winning and which to losing.

Multivariate regression analysis may be the most sophisticated and widely used statistical method for predicting incidents or cases from variables. In light of the above points, however, the method is (1) too imperfect in its predictive power, (2) too invalid in its attempt to describe empirical realities, (3) too irrelevant for predicting what is essentially a kinked or threshold relationship rather than a smooth straight or curved line, (4) too complicated, and (5) too incomplete in expressing summation relations.

At the opposite extreme from the mechanical quantification of multivariate statistical regression analysis is the method of staircase prediction. It can be done with no quantification at all. It involves showing one predictive criterion along the horizontal axis of a two-dimensional matrix, with its categories shown as columns in ascending order toward winning. A second predictive criteria is shown along the vertical axis, with its categories shown as rows also in ascending order toward winning. The actual or presumed outcomes are then shown in the cells for each combination of categories expressing the outcomes in words or symbols but not necessarily numbers. One can then see that as one moves from the southwest corner of the matrix toward the northeast, losing changes to winning. One can section off the losing from the winning cells with a thick kinked line that looks like a staircase.

That kind of staircase analysis, like P/G% prediction, does stimulate more careful thinking than multivariate regression analysis about the order of the categories on the variables and what the key variables are. It is also capable of working with a sample size of a few, one, or even no key cases by deducing outcomes for case-types, as contrasted to multivariate regression analysis, which needs many diverse cases with actual outcomes. Such an empirical sample may often be nonexistent. Staircase analysis is also a useful visual aid, like drawing indifference curves in economics or probability analysis.

On the other hand, staircase prediction is limited almost completely to situations in which there are only two predictive variables because it is virtually impossible or at least difficult to use the two-dimensional matrix approach when adding a third or fourth variable. The staircase approach is also incapable of handling the assigning of different weights to the variables without introducing quantitative methods, especially if the variables are measured on different scales.

Multiple regression, staircase prediction, and P/G% prediction all have in common that they are systematic approaches to arriving at predictive decision-rules from a set of cases, criteria for distinguishing the cases, and the relations between the cases and the criteria. Those methods can be contrasted with unsystematic methods that involve relying on a holistic gestalt approach that does not disaggregate the decision-rule components into specific cases, criteria, and relations. A holistic approach tends to lack precision, validity, objectivity, and transferability. Its main advantage is that it requires little thinking, but the quality of results may therefore suffer substantially, although a combination holistic and disaggregated approach may be better than either alone.[8]

P/G% prediction can be considered more meaningful than multiple regression since P/G% has the advantages of quantitative regression without the above disadvantages. It can also be considered more meaningful than staircase prediction since P/G% has the qualitative and verbal advantages of staircase prediction without its limiting disadvantages. In addition, the P/G% approach has the simplicity of being usable with the kind of analysis shown in this chapter or with the readily available P/G% microcomputer program.

Appendix A: Further Examples of P/G% Prediction

Table 5–8
Data for Predicting Welfare Cases

CRITERIA / CASETYPES	Substance Severity	Procedural Severity	SUM	OUTCOME
1. Eligibility Denied and No Attorney Appointed	1.00	0.99	1.99	L
2. Benefits Reduced and No Attorney Appointed	2.00	0.99	2.99	L
3. Eligibility Denied and No Hearing	1.00	2.00	3.00	L
4. Termination and No Attorney Appointed	3.00	0.99	3.99	L
5. Benefits Reduced and No Hearing	2.00	2.00	4.00	?
6. Eligibility Denied and No Reasons	1.00	3.01	4.01	W
7. Criminal Prosecution and No Attorney Appointed	4.00	0.99	4.99	W
8. Termination and No Hearing	3.00	2.00	5.00	W
9. Benefits Reduced and No Reasons	2.00	3.01	5.01	W
10. Criminal Prosecution and No Hearing	4.00	2.00	6.00	W
11. Termination and No Reasons	3.00	3.01	6.01	W
12. Criminal Prosecution and No Reasons	4.00	3.01	7.01	W

NOTES:

1. A "W" in the outcome column means the welfare recipient wins. An "L" means the welfare recipient loses. The Goldberg case is Casetype 7, and the Argersinger case is Casetype 12.
2. The decision rule which the aove data generates is:
   (1) If a welfare case involves a summation score of 4.01 or above, the welfare recipient wins.
   (2) With a summation score of 3.99 or below, the welfare recipient loses.
   (3) With a score of 4.00, the outcome is unclear.
3. The leading case is Goldberg v. Kelly. It involved a summation score of 5.00, and the welfare recipient won. Therefore, one would expect the welfare recipient to win even more with scores higher than 5.00. That covers Casetypes 2, 3, 4, and 8.
4. The outcome of Case 12 is known from the Argersinger case.
5. The outcomes of Cases 1, 5, 9, 10 and 11 are known from things said in the Goldberg case, not from an a fortiori deduction.

Table 5–9
Data for Predicting Equal Protection Cases

CRITERIA / CASETYPES	Score On Rights	Score On Groups	SUM	OUTCOME
1. Consumers/Region	1	1	2	D
2. Consumers/Economic Class	1	2	3	D
3. Employment/Region	2	1	3	D
4. Consumers/Sex	1	3	4	D
5. Employment/Economic Class	2	2	4	D
6. Housing/Region	3	1	4	D
7. Employment/Sex	2	3	5	D
8. Housing/Economic Class	3	2	5	D
9. Schools/Region	4	1	5	D
10. Housing/Sex	3	3	6	D
11. Schools/Economic Class	4	2	6	D
12. Consumers/Race	1	6	7	P
13. Criminal Justice/Region	6	1	7	?
14. Schools/Sex	4	3	7	?
15. Criminal Justice/Economic Class	6	2	8	P
16. Employment/Race	2	6	8	P
17. Voting/Region	7	1	8	P
18. Criminal Justice/Sex	6	3	9	P
19. Housing/Race	2	6	9	P
20. Voting/Economic Class	7	2	9	P
21. Schools/Race	4	6	10	P
22. Voting/Sex	7	3	10	P
23. Criminal Justice/Race	6	6	12	P
24. Voting/Race	7	6	13	P

Table 5–9: Continued

1. The above data can generate two compatible decision rules. One rule is:
   (1) If an equal protection case has a summation score of 7 or higher, then the plaintiff will win.
   (2) If the case has a score of 6 or lower, then the defendant will win.

2. The alternative decision rules is:
   (1) If an equal protection case has a summation score greater than 7, then the plaintiff will win.
   (2) If the case has a score of exactly 7, then the outcome is questionable.
   (3) If the case has a score of 6 or lower, then the defendant will win.

3. Each casetype is defined in terms of:
   (1) The rights that are allegedly being denied which can relate to voting, criminal justice, schools, housing, employment, or consumer rights in that order of importance.
   (2) The group that is allegedly being given unequal treatment, which can relate to race (which generally means being black), sex (which generally means being female), economic class (which generally means being poor), or region (which generally means being urban, inner city, or poor) in that order of importance.

4. To determine the score of each casetype on the rights, the six rights are arranged in rank order with the most important right receiving a score of 6. Slight adjustments are then made to recognize there is more distance between the top two rights and the bottom four than there is between the other rights.

4. To determine the score of each casetype on the groups, the four groups are arranged in rank order with the most important group receiving a ascore of 4. Slight adjustments are then made to recognize there is more distance between the top group and the bottom three than there is between the other groups.

6. The first decision rule implies that the court would decide in favor of the plaintiff if the state provided grossly unequal right to counsel from one county to another, or if women were denied admission to an all-male public school, although the court has not yet done so.

7. The second decision rule implies that being black scores slightly higher than a 6. That causes 12 to score slightly higher than 7, and thus to be distinguishable from the questionable cases

8. Landmark cases or constitutional amendments that correspond to the casetypes include Gomillion v. Lightfoot (Casetype 24), Powell v. Alabama (23), Nineteenth Amendment (22), Brown v. Board of Education (21), Harper v. Virginia (20), Shelley v. Kramer (19), Taylor v. Louisiana (18), Reynolds v. Sims (17), Jones v. Mayer (12 and 16), Gideon v. Wainwright (15), and Rodriquez v. San Antonio (9 and 11).

Table 5–10
Using the P/G% Approach to Synthesize Case Facts

CRITERIA / ALTERNATIVES	(1) Defense Statement (Alibi) W = 2		(2) Prosecution Statement (Scene of Crime) W = 1	(3) SUM (1)+(2)	(4) $\frac{SUM}{N}$ (3)/2	(5) Weighted Sum (1.5)+(2)	(6) $\frac{\text{Weighted Sum}}{\text{Sum of Weights}}$ (5)/3
Defendant is Guilty	.20	(.40)	.70	.90	.45	1.10	.37
Defendant is not Guilty	.80	(1.60)	.30	1.10	.55	1.90	.63
	1.00	(2.00)	1.00	2.00	1.00	3.00	1.00

NOTES:

1. The numbers in columns 1 and 2 are probabilities. They indicate the degree of accuracy or truth associated with the statements in the direction of establishing the defendant's guilt. Thus, the .20 probability means that there is a .80 probability that the defense statement is true, and the .20 complement is in the direction of establishing the defendant's guilt. These are probabilities of truth, not probabilities of guilt.
2. The weights indicate the degree of importance of the evidence items. Thus an alibi statement is quite important (if true) in establishing innocence. A statement saying the defendant was at the scene of the crime is less important because even if it is true, it does not establish the defendant's guilt. The numbers in parentheses in column 1 are weighted probabilities.
3. The numbers in column 3 are the sum of the two unweighted probabilities. The numbers in column 5 are the sums of the two weighted probabilities.
4. The numbers in column 4 are unweighted average probabilities. The numbers in column 5 are weighted average probabilities. The numbers in column 6 are an approximation of Bayesian conditional probabilities especially when one only has probabilities of truthfulness and degrees of importance to work with.

Table 5–10: Continued

5. If the probability in the upper right hand corner is greater than .90, then the judge, juror, or other perceiver of these two items of evidence should vote to convict assuming (1) .90 is accepted as the threshold probability interpretation of beyond a reasonable doubt, and (2) these are the only items of evidence. If the starred probability is .90 or less, then one should vote to acquit.

6. With two alibi witnesses, each might receive a weight of 1.5 if one witness receives a 2. They do not both receive a 2 because they partly reinforce each other.

7. No set of weights will cause the weighted average to exceed .90 with probabilities of .20 and .70. Thus, there is no threshold value for either W1 or W2.

8. The difficulty of obtaining a set of evidence items across the prosecution and the defense that average better than a .90 probability may indicate that jurors and judges generally operate below the .90 threshold, even though judges and commentators say that .90 is roughly the probability translation of "beyond a reasonable doubt."

APPENDIX B: THE COMPUTER OUTPUT FOR GOING FROM CASES, CRITERIA, AND SCORES TO A PREDICTIVE CONCLUSION

Figure 5–1
The Nine Redistricting Cases and How They Were Decided

Alternative	Previous Outcome
1 COLEGROVE	D WINS
2 GRILLS	A
3 MARYLAND	D
4 SCHOLLE	D
5 WMCA	D
6 ASBURY	A
7 DYER	A
8 BAKER	A
9 MAGRAW	A

Figure 5–2
The Four Predictive Criteria and How They Are Measured and Weighted

Criterion	Meas. Unit	Weight
1 = REQUIRED	YES/2 NO/1	1.00
2 STATE LEGIS.	"	1.00
3 = VIOLATED	"	1.00
4 FED.COURT	"	1.00

Figure 5–3
The Scores of the Cases on the Criteria

ALTERNATIVE / CRITERIA SCORING

	= REQUI	STATE LE	= VIOLA	FED.COUR
COLEGROVE	1.00	1.00	1.00	2.00
GRILLS	2.00	2.00	1.00	1.00
MARYLAND	1.00	2.00	2.00	1.00
SCHOLLE	1.00	2.00	2.00	1.00
WMCA	1.00	2.00	1.00	2.00
ASBURY	2.00	2.00	2.00	1.00
DYER	2.00	1.00	2.00	2.00
BAKER	2.00	2.00	2.00	2.00
MAGRAW	2.00	2.00	2.00	2.00

Figure 5–4
The Initial Predictive Conclusion with Equal Weights for the Criteria

Alternative	Combined Rawscores	Previous Outcome
1COLEGROVE	5.00	D WINS
2GRILLS	6.00	A
3MARYLAND	6.00	D
4SCHOLLE	6.00	D
5WMCA	6.00	D
6ASBURY	7.00	A
7DYER	7.00	A
8BAKER	8.00	A
9MAGRAW	8.00	A

Figure 5–5
The Predictive Conclusion with Double Weight for the Most Important Criteria

Alternative	Combined Rawscores	Previous Outcome
1COLEGROVE	6.00	D WINS
2GRILLS	8.00	A
3MARYLAND	7.00	D
4SCHOLLE	7.00	D
5WMCA	7.00	D
6ASBURY	9.00	A
7DYER	9.00	A
8BAKER	10.00	A
9MAGRAW	10.00	A

NOTES

1. On traditional legal prediction, see Harry Jones et al., *Legal Method* (Mineola, N.Y.: Foundation Press, 1980); K. Llewelleyn, *The Common Law Tradition: Deciding Appeals* (Boston: Little, Brown, 1960); W. Statsky and J. Wernet, *Case Analysis and Fundamentals of Legal Writing* (St. Paul: West, 1977); and W. Thode et al., *Introduction to the Study of Law*. (Mineola, N.Y.: Foundation Press, 1970). On behavioral statistical prediction as applied to court cases, see Joel Grossman ed., and Joseph Tanenhaus, *Frontiers of Judicial Research* (New York: Wiley, 1969); Glendon Schubert, *Judicial Behavior: A Reader in Theory and Research* (Chicago: Rand McNally, 1964); Harold Spaeth, *Supreme Court Policy Making: Explanation and Prediction* (San Francisco: Freeman, 1979); and S. Ulmer, *Courts, Law, and Judicial Process* (New York: Free Press, 1981).

2. On the general methodology of policy/goal percentaging analysis as applied to both prescription and prediction, see S. Nagel, *Public Policy: Goals, Means, and Methods* (New York: St. Martin's, 1984), pp. 343–354; idem, "Part/Whole Percentaging as a Useful Tool in Policy/Program Evaluation," 8 *Evaluation and Program Planning* 8 (1985):107–120; idem, "P/G% Analysis: An Evaluation-Aiding Tool Program," *Evaluation Review* 9 (1985):209–214; (1984) and idem, "Policy/Goal Percentaging Analysis: A Decision-Aiding Tool" (Microcomputer manual available through the Political Science Department, University of Illinois, Urbana). The cases to be listed can be found through manual legal search methods or through accessing the microcomputer data bases of systems such as Lexis or Westlaw. Listing predictive criteria generally requires a knowledge of

the cases, the subject matter, and other factors mentioned above. Experiments are now being conducted on the extent to which microcomputer data bases can be used to help generate predictive criteria.

3. Cases dealing with religion in the public schools are discussed in N. Dorsen et al., *Policy and Civil Rights in the United States,* vols. 1 and 2 (Boston: Little, Brown, 1982), and Herman Pritchett, *Constitutional Civil Liberties* (Englewood Cliffs, N.J.: Prentice-Hall, 1984), pp. 150–154. For further details on predicting civil liberties cases quantitatively, see S. Nagel, "Predicting Court Cases Quantitatively," *Michigan Law Review* 63 (1965):1411.

4. The cases dealing with legislative redistricting are discussed in R. Dixon, *Democratic Representation: Reapportionment in Law and Politics* (New York: Oxford University Press, 1968); and Nelson Polsby, ed., *Reapportionment in the 1970's* (Berkeley: University of California Press, 1971). More recent redistricting cases are discussed in J. Nowak et al., *Constitutional Law* (St. Paul: West, 1983), p. 792–802. For further details on this predictive example, see S. Nagel, "Applying Correlation Analysis to Case Prediction," *Texas Law Review* 42 (1964):1006. Other variables that also disfavored *Colegrove* include (1) the intervening case of *Gomillion v. Lightfoot,* which ordered redistricting where blacks were being districted out of the city limits of Tuskegee, Alabama; (2) the partial reliance in the *Colegrove* case on the clause that guarantees a republican form of government, rather than the equal protection clause; (3) the increased public sensitivity to denials of equality between 1946 and 1962; (4) the increased malapportionment between 1946 and 1962, especially as a result of increased urban and suburban growth with virtually no new redistricting; and (5) the request in *Colegrove* for redistricting in time for the next congressional election, which was only a few months away. The threshold weight of -2 is calculated by the computer by solving for W (or the threshold weight) in the equation, $W1 + 1 + 1 + 2 = W2 + 2 + 2 + 2$. That equation simplifies to $W1 + 4 = W2 + 6$, which in turn simplifies to $2W - 1W = 4 - 6$. Thus $1W = -2$.

5. Cases dealing with housing discrimination are discussed in J. Kushner, *Fair Housing: Discrimination in Real Estate, Community Development, and Revitalization* (New York: McGraw Hill, 1984); R. Schwem, *Housing Discrimination Law* (Washington, D.C. Bureau of National Affairs, 1984); and Dorsen et al., vol. 2, *Policy and Civil Rights in the United States,* pp. 940–946. For further details on this predictive example, see Chapter 4 of this book.

6. The international law casebooks that provide the data base for this example are Bishop, *International Law* (Englewood Cliffs, N.J.: Prentice-Hall, 1953); Manley Hudson, *International Law* (St.Paul: West, 1951); Milton Katz and Kingman Brewster, *The Law of International Transactions and Relations* (Mineola, N.Y.: Foundation Press, 1960); and Lester Orfield and Edward Re, *International Law* (Indianapolis: Bobbs-Merrill, 1955). For further details on this predictive example, see S. Nagel, "Judicial Prediction and Analysis from Empirical Probability Tables," *Indiana Law Journal* 41 (1966):403. Working with probabilities of victory and average damages under various circumstances can be facilitated by loose-leaf services such as those published by the Jury Verdict Research Service, Cleveland, Ohio.

7. Cases dealing with criminal law prediction are discussed in Wayne LaFave and Austin Scott, *Criminal Law* (St. Paul: West, 1972). For the forerunner of this predictive example, see S. Nagel, "Using Simple Calculations to Predict Judicial Decisions," *Practical Lawyer* 7 (1961):68.

8. On multiple regression analysis at an introductory level, see A. Edwards, *An Introduction to Linear Regression and Correlation* (San Francisco: Freeman 1976), and Edward Tufte, *Data Analysis For Politcs and Policy* (Englewood Cliffs, N.J.: Prentice-Hall, 1974). On staircase prediction, see Chapter 4 of this book.

6

The Judicial Prediction Service

It has been proposed that a publisher should publish a series of loose-leaf services for use by practicing lawyers that would contain law data and processed data useful in predicting court-case outcomes. The purpose of this chapter is to discuss some aspects of such a judicial prediction service.

Some issues that need to be explored include, in random order:

1. What legal field would be covered?
2. What would be the general format for each loose-leaf service
3. Who would be involved in the general planning?
4. What would be the specific procedures used to maintain each service?
5. How would the services be marketed?
6. What prior related services are there?
7. What bibliographic references are relevant for further ideas?

Preliminary answers to those questions might include the following ideas:

1. The series could start with the most basic legal fields. That would include

tort, criminal, contract, and property cases. The series could also include more specialized legal fields where it has been determined that a market is available. One characteristic that all legal fields probably should have in common is that there is a substantial quantity of trial-court case records or administrative agency case records available for quantitative analysis.

2. A meaningful general format might be for each loose-leaf service to be in two parts. One part would offer lots of data on the relation between a great variety of case elements and the probabiity of victory for the plaintiff (versus the defendant) in personal injury cases, the defendant (versus the prosecutor) in criminal cases, the consumer or buyer (versus the seller) in sales cases, the tenant (versus the landlord) in property cases, and so on depending on what legal fields and sub-fields are involved. The second part would offer lots of data on the relation between a great variety of case elements and the nature of the judgments awarded in terms of damages in personal injury cases, sentences in criminal cases, damages in sales/property cases, and other types of awards in other types of cases. The service would be primarily concerned with prediction, not with citation retrieval. For citation retrieval, lawyers can subscribe to the services of Lexis and Westlaw and use the traditional legal search tools. In light of its purpose, an appropriate name for the loose-leaf series might be ''The Judicial Prediction Service.''

3. The most appropriate people to be involved in the general planning of such a series would be law professors, practicing lawyers, and social scientists who have previously demonstrated a strong interest, knowledge, and innovativeness with regard to systematic court-case prediction. The authors of the bibliographic references cited below may represent an especially good set of sources from whom to draw an advisory group. More specialized advisory groups could be developed for each legal field. Those more specialized groups should include practicing lawyers who would reflect the viewpoints of potential consumers of the services rather than producers or planners.

4. Specific procedures would involve developing a meaningful sample of courthouses across the United States. The number of courthouses would be about 50 if they were chosen in a way so as to maximize their capability of generating national and regional generalizations. The services of survey research centers like those at the University of Illinois, University of Chicago, and University of Michigan could be used in developing the sample. Lawyers, law students, or other qualified people would then be contacted in each of those areas for the purpose of gathering publicly available data from those courthouses or from the attorneys of record in accordance with well-developed forms and rigorous procedures. The data gathered on a monthly basis would be sent for processing to the university survey research centers that participated in the development of the sample. If their processing fees were too expensive, the work could be done by well-trained graduate students or law students. The statistical results, some raw data, and some case studies would be distributed monthly to subscribers across the country.

An alternative or supplementary procedure might involve working with appellate data, compiled in machine-readable form by systems such as Lexis and Westlaw. Programs can be written to process the already compiled data through the following steps for personal injury cases:

1. Separate all of the personal injury cases or a sample of them either by having the cases precoded with a personal injury number or by asking for cases containing certain key words like injury.
2. Divide the cases into those won by the plaintiff and those won by the defendant.
3. Go through the words in the stored summaries for each case to find words that are disproportionately present in the cases that the plaintiff won. Perhaps the word *child* might be such a word. (See Table 6–1.) *Disproportionately present* means that the percentage of cases in which the element word was present and in which the plaintiff won is more than 10 percentage points greater than the percentage of cases in which the element was absent and the plaintiff won.
4. The computerized data retrieval and data processing system could also read out how many cases involved (a) the word being present and the plaintiff won, (b) the word being present and the defendant won, (c) the word being absent and the plaintiff won, and (d) the word being absent and the defendant won. The system would thus be calculating the difference between $a/(a + b)$ and $c/(c + d)$. That difference provides an exact measure of the predictive regression coefficient between the word, or case-element, and the case-outcome. It can be intepreted as indicating how much the probability of plaintiff victory goes up from a probability base of $c/(c + d)$ when the case-element goes from absent to present and the victory probability thus goes from $c/(c + d)$ to $a/(a + b)$.
5. That kind of analysis can also be related to damages awarded by having the computerized system determine for each word what the average damages were when the word was present and when the word was absent. (See Table 6–2.) If the difference is bigger than a certain statistical spread, the computer will read out that information as being worthy of reporting in the prediction service.
6. That same kind of analysis for victory probabilities and judgments can be applied to other types of cases. This system has the advantage of drawing upon already compiled data in machine-readable form. It has the disadvantage of being appellate cases that may not yield the same predictive results as trial cases, although the differences and similarities could be statistically determined.

5. The marketing of the services would involve extensive advertising in the journals published by the American Bar Association, state bar associations, and local bar associations. Direct mail to special mailing lists in each of the relevant legal fields should also be used. The advertising should emphasize how this kind of systematic analysis often reveals relations that conventional wisdom and rules of thumb tend to underestimate, overestimate, or completely miss. The advertising should also transmit the idea that practicing lawyers may be at a disadvantage if the other side has access to this information and also get across the quality of the people who are associated with the service.

Table 6–1
Relating the Word "Child" to Plaintiff Victory

PREDICTOR(X) / RESULT(Y_1)	"Child" Absent (0)	"Child" Present (1)	Totals	Difference
Win (1)	6,350 = a (67%)	150 = c (30%)*	6,500 (65%)	(-37%)*
Lose (0)	3,150 = b (33%)	350 = d (70%)	3,500 (35%)	(+37%)
Totals	9,500 (100%)	500 (100%)	10,000 (100%)	(0%)

NOTES:

1. The numbers in each cell indicate the quantities of cases from the data base of 10,000 cases.
2. The percentages are calculated downward to show the effect of the absence or presence of the predictor. They are not calculated across, which would show how each result is subdivided.
3. The above relation is the equivalent of an equation of the form $Y_1 = .67 - .37(X)$, where Y_1 is losing (scored 0) or winning (scored 1), and X is child-absent (scored 0) or child-present (scored 1).
4. The stars call attention to the most important numbers which are:
   (1) The probability of victory if the word "child" is present (.30).
   (2) The slope or marginal return of going from a child-absent to a child-present case (-.37).

6. The most relevant prior loose-leaf service is called the Jury Verdict Research Service. It is published by a law firm in Cleveland, Ohio, and pertains only to personal injury cases. It is inexpensively produced and charges high subscription fees. The quality of its contents is not very good in terms of the sample used and the data processing. But it does deserve credit for being a pioneer in the field. It can, however, be improved upon, especially in the legal fields other than the personal injury field, where it is not involved. Attached to this chapter is a description and evaluation of the Jury Verdict Research Service under the title "Statistical Prediction of Verdicts and Awards."

7. As for bibliographic references, they can suggest further ideas and also people who might be contacted to participate in the development of such a series.

Table 6–2
Relating the Word "Child" to Damages Awarded

PREDICTOR (X) / RESULT	"Child" Absent (0)	"Child" Present (1)	Difference	Sample Size
Average Damages When Awarded (Y_2)	$20,000	$30,000	$10,000	6,500
Average Damages In All Cases (Y_3)	$13,400 ($20,000)(.67)	$ 9,000 ($20,000)(.30)	-$ 4,400	10,000
Difference	$ 6,600	$21,000	14,400	3,500
Sample Size	9,500	500	9,000	10,000

NOTES:

1. The first row is the equivalent of an equation of the form $Y_2 = \$20,000 + \$10,000(X)$, where Y_2 is damages awarded when the plaintiff wins, and X is the absence or presence of the word "child".
2. The second row is the equivalent of an equation of the form $Y_3 = \$12,000 - \$4,400(X)$, where Y_3 is damages awarded in all cases in the 10,000-case data base.

The following references could serve as a starter, although they could use up-dating, which would involve going through the *Index to Legal Periodicals* and the *Index to Periodicals Related to Law* to find the latest articles. The *Jurimetrics Journal* is probably the best journal in the field. Some references can also be found in issues of the *Rutgers Journal of Computer and the Law*. Some of the following references deal with predicting appellate case outcomes, but the methods used could also be applied to trial case outcomes: (1) Hans Baade, ed., *Jurimetrics* (Dobbs Ferry, N.Y.: Oceana Press, 1964), pp. 143–184, including articles by Fred Kort and Sidney Ulmer; (2) Thomas Gonser, John Soma, and Eileen Wilhelm, "The Computer as a Tool for Legal Decision Making" *Practical Lawyer* 27 (1981):11–17; (3) Joel Grossman and Joseph Tanenhaus, eds., *Frontiers of Judicial Research* (New York: Wiley, 1969), pp. 307–372, including chapters by Werner Grunbaum and Sidney Ulmer; (4) Reed Lawlor, "Analysis and Prediction of Judicial Decisions," in Roy Freed, *Computers and the Law* (Chicago: American Bar Association, 1969); (5) S. Nagel, "Lawyer Decision-making and Threshold Analysis," *University of Miami Law Review* 31

(1983):615–642; (6) S. Nagel, *The Legal Process from a Behavioral Perspective* (Homewood, Ill.: Dorsey, 1969), pp. 125–172; and (7) Glendon Schubert, ed., *Judicial Decision Making* (New York: Free Press, 1963), pp. 111–200, including articles by Joseph Tanenhaus and Fred Kort.

The Judicial Prediction Service could serve many useful purposes such as:

1. Enabling attorneys to have a better idea of which clients to accept in light of the victory probabilities and predicted awards
2. Enabling attorneys to negotiate more realistically with the other side
3. Enabling attorneys to explain to clients the victory probabilities and predicted awards before and after cases are resolved
4. Enabling the publisher to improve its image further as a publisher of quality materials that bridge law and social science
5. Enabling the publisher to have an additional money-making publication

Achieving these purposes will involve imagination and capital as well as hard work. It will be a pleasure to be associated with a quality service like this for modern practicing lawyers.

APPENDIX: STATISTICAL PREDICTION OF VERDICTS AND AWARDS

In 1960 the Jury Verdict Research Company of Cleveland, Ohio, began publishing a little-known, two-volume, loose-leaf service: *Verdict Expectancies* and *Valuation Handbook*. This set of materials is by far the most impressive use of statistical techniques yet devised for predicting litigation outcomes.[1] The material as of now covers only personal injury cases, but the basic techniques involved can be readily applied to almost any field of law at the trial or appellate level. The raw data on thousands of personal injury cases are obtained from various metropolitan reporting services throughout the country and also from a staff of lawyers and newspaper reporters who have been engaged to cover the non-metropolitan areas. Robert Schrage supervises the research staff, which processes the data, and eminent practicing lawyers and legal scholars such as Emile Berman, John Appleman, and Hans Zeisel comprise the advisory board.

The *Verdict Expectancies* consists mainly of more than 500 percentages, each one of which in effect indicates the probability that the plaintiff will win under a given set of circumstances, assuming that the near future will be like the recent past. Being a loose-leaf service, the recent past can be constantly updated. For example, based on 93 verdicts, if a pedestrian is hit by an automobile at a point other than a crosswalk, the pedestrian has only a 34 percent chance of winning a subsequent lawsuit. On the other hand, based on 26 verdicts, if a plaintiff is bitten by a dog, he has a 46 percent chance of winning. The service also covers topics such as intersection collisions, public conveyance accidents, employment injuries, intentional injuries, and the liability of manufacturers, occupiers, and medical practitioners.

The *Valuation Handbook* consists of more than 2,000 monetary amounts representing different kinds of averages and ranges for damages awarded with regard to various types of injuries, again implicitly assuming that the near future will be like the recent past. For example, if the plaintiff wins in a case involving a finger amputation and the claimed special damages (i.e., medical, loss of earnings, and other out-of-pocket expenses excluding property damage) are between $500 and $999, the median amount of damages awarded (half of the awards above, half below) will tend to be about $2,900; the mean amount (total awards divided by number of awards) will be about $4,404; the middle 50 percent of the awards will fall between $2,300 and $4,500; all of the awards will fall between $1,600 and $10,200, and finally the expected award is $4,500.

The expected award is calculated by preparing a line graph for each type of injury with various size awards listed on the vertical axis. Numerous dots are placed on the graph with each dot representing the value of the specials and the award of a given case. A line is drawn through the dots so that the sum of the squared distances from each dot to the line is minimized. With a given amount of specials and this line, one can readily read the expected award from the graph. This expected award has a higher degree of predictive validity than the median or arithmetic mean of the awards.[2] Unfortunately, the number of cases on which the *Valuation Handbook* figures are based is not given, although, unlike the *Verdict Expectancies,* the handbook has an "area value key" to allow for local variations. Thus the area value key indicates that the awards in Chicago are approximately 5 percent higher than the average award in the United States for comparable injuries and specials.

A third set of materials somewhat arbitrarily placed in the *Verdict Expectancies* indicates the effect that different factual circumstances have on damages awarded rather than on victory or defeat. For example, awards are 21 percent lower if the defendant offers a doctor who admits the plaintiff's injury but testifies that the injury is not as severe as the plaintiff claims. This finding is based on 60 cases in which conflicting medical testimony was the main issue. Other topics deal with the effect on awards of multiple parties, of admitting or contesting liability, and of proved misrepresentation or exaggeration by witnesses or parties. A forthcoming section will deal with the relationship between awards and the amount of the suit, and another section will deal with the effect on awards of the occupation, age, sex, ethnic background, and other characteristics of the parties. Later sections will deal with the effect of similar variables on the probability of plaintiff victory.

The publisher recommends that the practicing lawyer integrate this mass of material via a three-step process when he is deciding whether to take a case, negotiating an out-of-court settlement, or deciding how much to sue for. First, he should find the award expectancy amount that corresponds to his provable specials (e.g., $4,500 for a finger amputation with $500 to $999 specials). Then he should multiply this dollar amount by the verdict expectancy percentage that corresponds to his factual situation (e.g. 34 percent if the finger amputation was the result of a pedestrian-auto accident not on a crosswalk). Finally, he should multiply the product of the first and the second steps by the local adjustment (e.g., 105 percent if Chicago) and by other adjustment factors that affect the size of the award or the probability of victory. The resulting figure represents a good monetary estimate of the gross value of the case.

The plaintiff's lawyer can then multiply this gross value by his contingency fee percentage (usually 33 percent) to determine his gross fee, and from this figure he can subtract his expenses to derive his estimated net fee. Defense counsel, on the other hand, can multiply the gross value figure by 67 percent to determine a gross out-of-court settlement value if the potential plaintiff does not have a lawyer, and from this figure defense counsel can derive a net settlement value by subtracting the personal expenses saved by the plaintiff in avoiding trial.

The validity of the *Valuation Handbook* approach was tested by comparing the estimated award expectancy figures for various back and neck injuries and various specials with the average awards in 744 subsequent cases. The average predicted award was only 7 percent away from the average actual award. Unfortunately, no analogous validation is described for the *Verdict Expectancies.* The improvement of the *Valuation Handbook* approach over a commonsense approach was tested by observing that in the 443 back and injury cases on which demand and offer information was available, only one out of every six offers was within 25 percent of the actual award. The comparison with the practicing lawyer's common sense, however, would have been much more meaningful if what was determined was not what the lawyers were demanding or offering but rather what they expected to settle for. Likewise, it would be desirable if the *Verdict Expectancies* could also be systematically compared with commonsense predictions.

The *Verdict Expectancies* and *Valuation Handbook* data can help plaintiff and defense lawyers advise clients, reach settlements, achieve trial and appellate victories, and convince clients of the reasonableness of the case outcome. The materials may also be useful to legislators writing workmen's compensation, wrongful death, and other statutes that specify awards. They may be useful to judges, referees, and adjudicative boards who grant awards or who encourage out-of-court settlements, and they may be useful to social scientists and legal scholars who are interested in the relative weight of various factors that influence litigation outcomes.

In spite of the imaginative format, there are some drawbacks that should be overcome in addition to those already mentioned. For one thing, the handling of multiple fact elements and multiple injuries needs to be strengthened. As a concrete illustration, what is the probability of victory when the plaintiff's auto was struck from behind (73 percent plaintiff victory) but the defendant had some characteristic that generally evoked strong sympathy (say, only 35 percent plaintiff victory)? To determine the overall probability of victory taking into consideration both conflicting factors simultaneously, one could average the two percentages, thereby arriving at a 54 percent probability of victory. But what does one do if the defendant had some characteristic that generally evoked strong antagonism (say 66 percent plaintiff victory)? Would not a combination of two or more fact elements favoring the plaintiff increase his probability of winning more than any one factual element alone, but by how much? Likewise what does one do with a combination of two or more fact elements disfavoring the plaintiff?

A partial solution to this problem can be provided by giving victory percentages for the factual combinations that frequently reoccur. The *Verdict Expectancies* service does this in some instances. Thus in a stoplight intersection collision, if the plaintiff claims the signals were in his favor with or without witnesses, he has a 49 percent chance of winning; but if the plaintiff's version is supported by witnesses, his chances of winning *increase* to 68 percent; whereas if the defendant's version is supported by witnesses, the plaintiff's chances *decrease* to 10 percent; and if both sides are supported by witnesses, the plaintiff has a middling 40 percent chance of winning. This kind of an analysis needs to be used more often than it is. The process of drawing appropriate samples of cases and calculating the combination percentages is greatly simplified by punching and processing all of the characteristics of each case on IBM cards. If this does not satisfactorily handle the problem in terms of predictive validity, what may be needed is a system whereby (1) each fact element is assigned a quantity of points depending on its degree of correlation with victory for the plaintiff, (2) a determination is made of the minimum number of points that is generally needed in each broad type of case to ensure victory for the plaintiff at various degrees of probability.[3]

Likewise, there is the problem of multiple injuries. Obviously, if one suffers two injuries, the award should be greater than if one had suffered just one of the two injuries, but how much greater? When one of these two injuries is relatively insignificant, the publisher recommends that the insignificant injury be ignored in making the calculations. When the second injury cannot be ignored, the publisher recommends as a dubious rule of thumb that one add 33 percent to the highest award expectancy figure and decreasingly smaller percentages for additional injuries. As with the multiple fact-element situation, what is needed are more award expectancy figures for frequently reoccurring multiple injuries.

The service also needs more theoretical explanations of why certain factual situations tend to produce higher probabilities of plaintiff victory and larger awards and why other factual situations have the opposite effect. Without such explanations one finds it hard to have confidence in some of the more unexpected findings. For example, why should the plaintiff recovery rate of 73 percent for general rear-end collisions drop to 64 percent if the plaintiff claims the defendant had defective brakes but rise from 73 to 82 percent if the defendant claims he had sudden and unexpected brake failure? Likewise, why were plaintiff awards reduced by 15 percent if additional defendants were added, when one would think that more defendants would mean less burden per defendant and therefore a higher total award assuming other factors are held constant?

Further drawbacks that will probably be improved with time include the smallness of the sample sizes on which many of the percentages are based and presumably many of the dollar amounts. The sample sizes could also be better evaluated if the publisher would publish a description of how the cases in general are selected and processed. Interpretation of the sample sizes would be still further improved if the publisher would indicate in probabilistic terms how far above or below each verdict percentage or expected award the true percentage or award might be if an infinitely large sample had been drawn.[4] For the sake of providing a more nearly complete picture of the factors influencing personal injury litigation outcomes, the service might also provide data on the effect of the characteristics of the lawyers and judges and more data on the effect of different types of evidence and jury instructions.

In general the *Verdict Expectancies* and *Valuation Handbook* represent the kind of practical application of quantitative techniques to personal injury law practice called for by J. M. Sink at the First National Law and Electronics Conference.[5] The greatest potentiality of this approach to judicial prediction, however, lies in its eventual application to a wide diversity of fields of law and its eventual application to building more realistic theories of the operations of the judicial process.

NOTES

1. Alternative quantitative techniques that have been presented include Fred Kort, "Contingent Analysis of Judicial Opinions and Rules of Law," in Glendon Schubert, ed., *Judicial Decision Making* (New York: Free Press, 1963); and S. Nagel, "Using Simple Calculations to Predict Judicial Decisions," *Practical Lawyer* 7 (1961):68.

2. For a relatively simple explanation of why the expected award has a higher degree of predictive validity than the median or arithmetic mean, see J. P. Guilford, *Fundamental Statistics in Psychology and Education* (New York: McGraw-Hill, 1965), pp. 362–372.

3. For a simplified presentation of this kind of correlation approach, see Nagel, "Using Simple Calculations to Predict Judicial Decisions," p. 68.

4. For a relatively simple explanation of why such confidence ranges are more meaningful than the total range or the middle 50 percent range, see Margaret Hagood and Daniel Price, *Statistics for Sociologists* (New York: Holt, 1952), pp. 115–126, 227–230.

5. Edgar Jones, ed., *Law and Electronics: The Challenge of a New Era* (New York: Matthew Bender, 1962), pp. 334–336.

IV

Litigation Choices

The following material describes systematic ways of making choices in litigation strategy either with or without a microcomputer. Chapter 7, "Applying Decision Science to the Practice of Law," clarifies the kinds of choices that are most likely to occur in litigation strategy broadly defined. They include (1) deciding whether to take a case, (2) dealing with missing information, (3) dealing with delay in being paid, and (4) deciding whether to accept a settlement. Chapter 8 is entitled "Lawyer Decision-Making and Threshold Analysis." Its title should refer to multiple threshold analysis because it emphasizes making choices with missing information on two or more missing variables. It is concerned with go/no-go decisions (such as whether to accept a personal-injury client on a contingent fee basis) and conflicting-choice decisions (such as choosing between clients or projects). It is also concerned with deciding whether to accept a settlement or go to trial, deciding whether to release or hold a defendant before trial, and deciding how to increase police legality in making searches.

Chapter 9 is entitled "Microcomputers, Risk Analysis, and Litigation Strategy." It makes more explicit use of the microcomputer program. It is concerned with both damages litigation and criminal prosecution. It is concerned with a variety of forms of sensitivity analysis whereby one directly or indirectly tries out different inputs to see how changes affect the bottom-line decisions. Those forms of sensitivity analysis include working with (1) threshold values showing to which value the inputs would have to change to enable the second-place alternative to become the first-place alternative, (2) change slopes showing how much the gap changes in the profitability of two alternatives as a result of a one-unit change in each input, and (3) worst- and best-scenario analysis showing for an alternative the worst it could do if all inputs were scored least favorably or showing the best it could do if all the inputs were scored most favorably. Chapter 10 is entitled "Decision Trees and Litigation Strategy." It is particularly concerned with the problem of simplicity of presentation, in contrast to the previous chapters in this part, which emphasize missing information. This chapter can also be contrasted with Part II, which emphasizes multiple dimensions, and Part V, which emphasizes multiple alternatives. The main point of this chapter is that decision trees (which are popular in analyzing litigation choices) may not be as meaningful to produce and understand as PG tables. Those tables show the options or policies along the rows, and they show time benefits, costs, net figures, and other goals along the columns.

7

Applying Decision Science to the Practice of Law

The purpose of this chapter is to describe on an elementary level how one can apply decision science to basic law-practice matters such as deciding whether or not to take a case and deciding whether or not to accept a settlement. *Decision science* can be defined as the study of the principles relevant to determining which of various alternative decisions will most achieve a given set of goals in light of the relations between the decisions and the goals. In the context of lawyer decision-making, the main goal is maximizing income minus expenses (as it is with most business firms), although operating within the constraints of law, ethics, and personal preferences. In the context of basic law practice, the alternative decisions are accept versus not accept a case and accept versus not accept an out-of-court settlement.[1]

DECIDING WHETHER TO TAKE A CASE

The basic principle in deciding to take a case is to take it if the predicted income is greater than the predicted expenses and reject it if the predicted expenses are greater than the predicted income. One can broaden the notion of income to include non-monetary benefits and broaden the notion of expenses to include non-monetary costs. That, however, is discussed elsewhere.[2] Monetary income could include an hourly fee, a flat fee, a contingent fee, or some other income. Expenses for a lawyer are mainly time, measured in hours multiplied by whatever monetary value per hour the lawyer places on his or her time, regardless of the market rate.

For the sake of discussion, this chapter assumes payment on a contingent fee basis, which requires winning an amount from the other side in order for the lawyer to be paid something. One can reason by analogy to other fee arrangements or other forms of income. Under a contingent fee arrangement, deciding whether or not to accept a client implicitly or explicitly involves the following sub-decisions:

1. What damages are likely to be awarded? Suppose the out-of-pocket medical expenses are $300 for this applicant for my legal services. By a rough rule of thumb, that means that if I win the case, we will collect about $3,000 in damages or ten times the medical expenses. That extra money is awarded by juries to cover lost wages, pain, and suffering and possibly the attorney's one-third fee. Predicting damages awarded from medical expenses can be done more accurately by consulting the looseleaf service of the Jury Verdict Research (JVR) Corporation. That service indicates the predicted damages awarded from medical expenses for various types of injuries. The predictions are based on numerous cases that the JVR researchers gather from around the country. The cases are then processed through a statistical-regression analysis to develop prediction information, which is communicated in simple language to practicing lawyers through the looseleaf service.

2. What is the probability of winning this case? By a rough rule of thumb, one can use a 0.65 figure, since that is about the average victory probability in personal-injury cases. Predicting victory probabilities can be done more accurately by also consulting the looseleaf service of the Jury Verdict Research Corporation. The same case samples are used to indicate victory probabilities for various types of cases. A practicing lawyer can combine those probabilities to obtain conditional or joint probabilities, or the lawyer can simply use them in their raw form by finding the single casetype that best fits his or her case.

3. What is the expected value to me of this case? If the predicted damages are $3,000 and the predicted victory probability is 0.65, the expected value to the plaintiff is $1,950. The lawyer, however, gets only one-third of what the plaintiff obtains. Therefore, the expected value of the lawyer's fee would be 0.33 times $1,950, or $650.

4. How much are my expenses likely to be in this case? This requires the lawyer to think in terms of how many hours the case will probably consume. The estimated answer might be 20 hours. Unfortunately, there is no looseleaf service that is helpful on hours consumed for different types of cases or on the more important matter of relating hours consumed and damages awarded, like relating medical expenses and damages awarded. If such information were avail-

Table 7–1
Deciding Whether to Take a Case

I. THE DATA WITHOUT TIME DISCOUNTING

1. Likely damages if the case is won (D)	$ 3,000
2. Probability of winning (P)	.65
3. Expected damages (PD)	$ 1,950
4. Contingency fee rate (F)	.333
5. Expected benefits (PDF)	$ 650
6. Likely hours to win the case (H)	20
7. Hourly rate or worth (R)	$ 30
8. Expected costs (HR)	$ 600
9. Expected profit (PDF-HR)	$ 50

II. GENERAL PRINCIPLES

If the expected profit is greater than zero, then the case should be taken, provided there are no conflicting demands on the attorney's time from more profitable cases, and provided the case is within one's ethical, capability, and other constraints.

able, it could be useful in enabling lawyers to allocate their time better. Answering the expenses question also requires the lawyer to think in terms of how much an hour of his or her time is worth. The answer might be whatever the market rate is, which might be $30 an hour. The lawyer, however, might be willing to work for less than the market rate when it is difficult to fill his or her time with clients at that rate or when the lawyer is receiving non-monetary satisfaction. In light of those numbers, the hourly expenses for this case would be about 20 hours times $30, or $600 in variable expenses, which do not include overhead or other variable expenses beside the lawyer's time. For simplicity, we can ignore the fact that those costs are contingent on the case going to trial and should be discounted by that probability.

5. Should I take the case? If the expected value or incremental income is $650 and the expected incremental expense is $600, the case seems worth taking, as indicated by Table 7–1. Taking cases like this will on the average cover the value of the attorney's time and provide something for other case-related expenses plus overhead. The case, however, should be rejected if other cases are available that are even better on benefits minus costs and the attorney does not have the time for all of them. The important thing for our methodological purposes is that this situation illustrates how the principles of decision science can be applied in a practical way to basic law practice. The same reasoning could be applied to cases in which a non-monetary judgment is involved, such as a criminal prosecution or a civil-liberties defense, but then one would have to decide whether the non-monetary benefits are worth the monetary costs.[3]

DEALING WITH MISSING INFORMATION

Suppose now that one of those key elements is missing in the decision on whether or not to take a case. The key elements are (1) the likely damages, (2) the probability of winning, (3) the contingency fee rate, (4) the likely hours to win the case, and (5) the hourly rate or worth. To be more specific, suppose that the

Table 7–2
Dealing with Missing Information

I. THRESHOLD VALUES

1.	Likely damages (D*)	$ 2,769
2.	Probability of winning (P*)	.60
3	Contingency fee rate (F*)	.31
4.	Likely hours (H*)	22
5.	Hourly rate (R*)	$ 33

II. GENERAL PRINCIPLES

1. Threshold values are the values of the variables when the expected profit is zero.
2. The case should be taken if the perceived value exceeds the threshold value of a benefit component, or goes below the threshold value of a cost component, when other values are held constant.
3. A combination of variables can also have a threshold value.
4. The threshold equation for solving for thresnold values is PDF = HR.

likely damages are unknown. One could try to gather additional information to determine the likely damages. An easier approach is to determine the threshold or breakeven damages and then ask whether the perceived damages are greater or less than the threshold damages.

To determine the threshold damages or any threshold value, one needs to recognize that at the threshold, breakeven point, or point of no profit, the discounted damages multiplied by the contingency rate equals the hours multiplied by the hourly rate. In terms of symbols, that is the same as stating that PDF = HR at the threshold. The next step in determining a threshold value is to substitute numerical values for all known variables. Doing so in this situation would yield the equation, (0.65)(D)(0.333) = (20)(30). The next step is to put the unknown variable on the left side and all of the numbers on the right side, which yields the equation, (D) = (20)(30)/(0.65)(0.333). The next step is to simplify the right side of the equation. Doing this yields the new equation of D* = $2,769, as shown in Table 7–2. This tells us that the threshold value of D (i.e., D*) is $2,769, which in turn tells us that if the perceived damages are greater than $2,769, the case will probably be profitable. If the perceived damages are less than $2,769, the case will probably not be profitable.

Using the basic information from Table 7–1, we can also determine that the threshold probability is 0.60. That means if the perceived probability of winning is greater than 0.60, we should take the case. If the perceived probability is less than 0.60, we should reject it. Likewise, the threshold contingency fee rate is 0.31. The threshold hours are 22, and the threshold hourly rate is $33.

One can apply the same kind of analysis when any combination of variables is missing. For example, suppose that we do not know either the likely damages or the probability of winning. Then the threshold equation becomes (P)(D)(0.33) = (20)(30). Keeping the unknown variables on the left side yields the equation of (P)(D) = (20)(30)/(0.333). That equation simplifies to (PD)* = $1,800. This means that if we perceive the expected value (or the damages discounted by the probability) to be greater than \$1,800, we should take the case. If we perceive the expected value to be less than \$1,800, we should reject the case.

The same kind of analysis can be applied to other two-variable, three-variable, or four-variable combinations. The analysis can even be applied when all five variables are unknown. Then the threshold equation becomes (PDF − HR)* = 0. In other words, if the expected benefits minus the expected costs are greater than zero, take the case; otherwise, reject it. There are visual aids that can be useful to practicing lawyers in prodding their minds into clarifying whether certain variables or combinations of variables are more or less than a threshold value.[4]

DEALING WITH DELAY IN BEING PAID

The above illustration does not take into consideration that the \$3,000 in damages may not be awarded for a few years. There may be no need to consider the future element when deciding whether to accept a client, since the main expenses of working on the case may also not occur for a few years until the case comes to trial. There are, however, many situations in which a personal-injury lawyer should consider the future element. Considering it means making an adjustment to recognize that \$3,000 a few years from now may not be worth as much as \$2,500 at present, since \$2,500 can be invested so that it might earn interest or a profit, making it worth more than \$3,000 in a few years.

For example, suppose that a personal-injury plaintiff could follow the alternative of going to a federal court (on the jurisdictional grounds that the plaintiff and defendant are from different states) or go to the state court in which the defendant can be sued. Suppose further that if the plaintiff goes to the federal court, his case will be heard within one year, and if he wins he will collect about \$15,000, but he only has a 20 percent chance of winning. If, on the other hand, he goes to the state court, his case will be heard within two years, and if he wins he will collect \$10,000, but he has a 40 percent chance of winning. Which alternative should he follow?

The expected value of the federal alternative is \$3,000 (i.e., \$15,000 discounted by the 0.20 probability of winning it) without considering the time element, and the expected value of the state alternative is \$4,000 (i.e., \$10,000 discounted by the 0.40 probability of winning it). If, however, we take into consideration that one has to wait two years for the \$10,000 from the state court, its value substantially decreases. More specifically, the present value of a future amount is calculated by the formula $P = A/(1 + r)^t$, where r is the interest rate that could be obtained by putting money in a savings account for t years. If we assume that the interest rate is 6 percent, the present value of the state's \$10,000 two years from now is \$8,900. If we now discount that present value by the 0.40 probability of achieving it, the expected value of the state case becomes \$3,560. Applying the same formula to the federal case, the present value of its \$15,000 award would be \$14,151 since $\$14,151 = \$15,000/(1 + 0.06)^1$. If we now discount that present value by the 0.20 probability of achieving it, the expected value of the federal alternative becomes $2,830, which is still less than the state alternative but not as much less before taking the difference in time consumption into consideration. We, of course, could have offered a hypothetical example whereby taking the time consumption into consideration reverses the rank order as to which is the better alternative.

Another time-discounting application occurs when, for example, the defendant in a civil case is told by a plaintiff that the plaintiff will withdraw his lawsuit if the defendant will pay $3,000. The defendant figures that if the case goes to trial five years from now and the defendant loses, which he has a ⅔ chance of doing, the plaintiff will be awarded $6,000. The defendant thus perceives the case as having an expected value of $4,000. The question then becomes, is the defendant better off paying the plaintiff $3,000 now or $4,000 five years from now? Answering that question involves working with the equation $A = P(1 + r)^t$ and the current interest rate, which we might assume is 0.06. The equation thus becomes $A = 3000(1.06)^5$, and A thus equals $4,015. The defendant would therefore be better off putting his $3,000 into a savings account at 6 percent, waiting five years, and then paying $4,000 to the plaintiff and having $15 left over than he would be by paying the $3,000 to the plaintiff. For simplicity, we can ignore the fact that the inflation rate may be greater than the interest rate, which means that the invested money would lose value over time, but the damages awarded may need to be adjusted upward.

In this illustration, the defendant is comparing a present benefit with a future one, whereas in the other illustration it was a choice for the plaintiff between two future benefits. In this illustration, the defendant (who is paying) is mainly concerned with the future value of a present investment, whereas in the other one, the plaintiff (who is being paid) was mainly concerned with the present value of a future amount. Both are common examples of time discounting in the legal process. Both have counterparts in numerous public-sector situations in which benefits or costs are substantially delayed. The present value of future benefits is often considered by the Army Corps of Engineers in building alternative dams, some of which can be finished sooner than others. The present value of future costs may be a consideration in postponing the burden of supporting a social security system or postponing the suffering from lack of energy conservation. Unfortunately, the present generation may overly discount those future costs.[5]

DECIDING WHETHER TO ACCEPT A SETTLEMENT

Table 7–3 shows that the present value of the expected damages is $1,457. The $1,457 comes from the fact that the likely damages are $3,000, the probability of winning is 0.65, and the expected value is thus $1,950. The $1,950, however, has to be discounted for the facts that (1) it will take five years to collect the damages and (2) the interest rate minus the inflation rate is 0.06. Doing this

Table 7–3
Dealing with Delay in Being Paid

I. THE DATA WITH TIME DISCOUNTING

1.	Likely damages (D)	$3,000
2.	Interest rate minus inflation rate (r)	.06
3.	Years to collect (t)	5
4.	Present value of the likely damages $(D)/(1+r)^t$	$2,242
5.	Probability of winning (P)	.65
6.	Present value of the expected damages $(PD)/(1+r)^t$	$1,457
1.	Likely damages (D)	$3,000
2.	Probability of winning (P)	.65
3.	Expected damages (PD)	$1,950
4.	Interest rate minus inflation rate (r)	.06
5.	Years to collect (t)	5
6.	Present value of the expected damages $(PD)/(1+r)^t$	$1,457

II. GENERAL PRINCIPLES

1. The plaintiff should be willing to accept anything above $1,457 because if invested for five years, it will yield more than $1,950. Likewise 2/3's of $1,457 in five years at 6% will yield more than 2/3's of $1,950. The 2/3's reflects the fact that the plaintiff gives 1/3 to the attorney. The plaintiff's minimum demand is thus $1,457.
2. The defendant should be willing to offer anything below $1,457 because the defendant will have to tie up $1,457 for five years at 6% interest in order to have $1,950 available to pay off the plaintiff. The defendant's maximum offer is thus $1,457.
3. Note the plaintiff and defendant may not operate with the same perception of PD, r, and t.

discounting yields $1,457 as the present value of the expected damages. We could arrive at the same result by stating that the $1,457 comes from that fact that the present value of $3,000 is $2,242. If we then multiply $2,242 by the 0.65 probability of winning, we also get $1,457.

To determine how much the plaintiff would be willing to settle for, one should take into consideration the plaintiff's litigation costs. The main usual litigation cost·is hiring an attorney. In a personal-injury case, however, the attorney normally collects about one-third of the damages regardless of whether or not the case goes to trial. Assume, however, for the sake of simplicity that the plaintiff has to pay $400 in costs if and only if the case goes to trial. Under those circumstances, the plaintiff should be willing to settle out of court for $1,457 minus the $400 litigation costs, which would be avoided by an out-of-court settlement. That brings the plaintiff's adjusted minimum down from the unadjusted minimum of $1,457 to $1,057. This means that the plaintiff should be willing to settle for any offer on the defendant's part greater than $1,057.

On the other side, the defendant insurance company may incur $500 in litigation costs if the case goes to trial. The defendant should thus be willing to settle for the base $1,457 plus $500. This means that the defendant should be willing to settle for any offer on the plaintiff's part to drop the case for less than $1,857.

Suppose that both sides start with about the same perceived present value of

Table 7–4
Deciding Whether to Accept a Settlement

I. DATA FOR ARRIVING AT A SETTLEMENT

1.	Plaintiff's litigation costs (LP)	$ 400
2.	Plaintiff's adjusted minimum (Original minimum - LP)	$ 1,057
3.	Defendant's litigation costs (LD)	$ 500
4.	Defendant's adjusted maximum (Original maximum + LD)	$ 1,857

II. GENERAL PRINCIPLES

This helps explain why most cases are settled out of court, since the plaintiff's adjusted mimimum tends to be below the defendant's adjusted maximum.

the expected danages at $1,457. The plaintiff then subtracts a discount that he or she is willing to give for early settlement, and the defendant adds a bonus that he or she is willing to give for early settlement. The plaintiff's adjusted minimum is then likely to be below the defendant's adjusted maximum, as is shown in Table 7–4. This helps to explain why most cases are settled out of court.[6]

CONCLUSIONS

From the above analysis, one can perceive four general principles that relate to the four questions or problems that this chapter has discussed as part of a basic law practice. Those conclusions are:

1. In deciding whether or not to take a case, a lawyer should generally do so if and only if the expected benefits are greater than the expected costs, taking into consideration non-monetary benefits and costs and also ethical, capability, and other constraints.
2. In dealing with missing information, a lawyer is generally better off converting the question of what the numerical value of the missing variable is into a question of whether the perceived value is above or below the threshold or breakeven value where the expected benefits would equal the expected costs.
3. In dealing with delay in being paid, a lawyer should generally consider what is the equivalent number of dollars that will yield the future money at the prevailing interest rate minus the inflation rate for the number of years involved. Doing this makes different future amounts more comparable.
4. In deciding whether or not to accept a settlement, a lawyer should compare the present value of the expected judgment with the present offer from the other side. The plaintiff should be willing to give a discount off that present value to avoid litigation costs. The defendant should be willing to give a bonus onto that present value to avoid litigation costs.

To apply these principles, practicing lawyers would benefit from access to the following:

1. Computerized data banks that give likely damages or other judgments for various types of cases
2. Computerized data banks that give probabilities of winning for various types of cases
3. Computerized data banks that give information on billable hours for various types of cases and the relations between billable hours and both judgments awarded and the probability of winning[7]
4. Computer programs that can process the data from the above three data banks in order to answer questions of lawyers about whether or not to take a case and whether or not to accept a settlement.
5. Computer programs that can process the data and answer the questions while taking into consideration missing information, delay in being paid, and how to deal with non-monetary benefits and costs.[8]
6. Workshops or short courses of study which will explain to practicing lawyers how to make use of the above data banks and computer programs.[9]

These data banks and computer programs are not distant possibilities but rather increasingly present realities. Variations on the data banks already exist in the form of looseleaf services. Variations on the computer programs already exist in the form of verbal and quantitative descriptions of the relevant steps or algorithms. A substantial percentage of law firms already have microcomputers for word processing, billing, and/or citation retrieval. It would be relatively easy to supply those firms with a connection to the data banks and a floppy diskette containing the programs. What is needed are some lawyer-entrepreneurs to implement the existing hardware and knowledge in order to make decision science more widely applicable to basic law practice.[10]

NOTES

1. On decision science in general, see Percy Hill et al., *Making Decisions: A Multidisciplinary Introduction* (Reading, Mass.: Addison-Wesley, 1978); Moshe Rubenstein, *Patterns of Problem Solving* (Englewood Cliffs, N.J.: Prentice-Hall, 1975), pp. 311–409; Robert Behn and James Vaupel, *Quick Analysis for Busy Decision-Makers* (New York: Basic Books, 1982); Ruth Mack, *Planning on Uncertainty: Decision-Making in Business and Government Administration* (New York: Wiley, 1971); and S. Nagel, *Policy Evaluation: Making Optimum Decisions* (New York: Praeger, 1982).

2. On dealing with non-monetary benefits and costs, see Mark Thompson, *Benefit-Cost Analysis for Program Evaluation* (Beverly Hills, Calif.: Sage, 1980); Thomas Saaty, *Decision Making for Leaders: Analytical Hierarchy Process for Decisions in a Complex World* (Belmont, Calif.: Wadsworth, 1982); Edward Gramlich, *Benefit Cost Analysis of Government Programs* (Englewood Cliffs, N.J.: Prentice-Hall, 1981); S. Nagel, "Non-Monetary Variables in Benefit-Cost Evaluation," *Evaluation Review* 7 (1983): 37–64.

3. On the decision to accept a client in personal-injury cases, see Murray Schwartz and Daniel Mitchell, "An Economic Analysis of the Contingent Fee in Personal Injury Litigation," *Stanford Law Review* 22 (1970): 1125; and F. MacKinnon, *Contingent Fees*

for Legal Services: A Study of Professional Economics and Responsibilities (Hawthorne, N.Y.: Aldine, 1964). On the decision to accept a client in criminal cases, see J. Jacoby, *Pretrial Screening in Perspective* (Washington, D.C.: Law Enforcement Assistance Administration, 1976); Frank Miller, *Prosecution: The Decision to Charge a Suspect with a Crime* (Boston: Little, Brown, 1969). On how many hours to devote to a case, see Chapter 11 in this book.

4. On dealing with missing information, see Carl Moore, *Profitable Applications of the Breakeven System* (Englewood Cliffs, N.J.: Prentice-Hall, 1971); Bruce Baird, "Sensitivity Analysis," in *Introduction to Decision Analysis* (Boston: Duxbury, 1978): 415–445; and Chapter 8 of this book. The last item emphasizes the use of visual aids to stimulate appropriate decision-making when there are multiple missing items.

5. On dealing with the present value of future money or the future value of present money, see Caroline Dinwiddy, *Elementary Mathematics for Economists* (New York: Oxford University Press, 1967); and Ezra Mishan, *Economies for Social Decisions* (New York: Praeger, 1972), pp. 112–140.

6. On deciding whether or not to accept a settlement in civil cases, see Ronald Greenberg, "The Lawyer's Use of Quantitative Analysis in Settlement Negotiations," *Business Lawyer* 38 (1983): 1557–1586; A. Friedman, "An Analysis of Settlement," *Stanford Law Review* 22 (1969): 67. On criminal case settlements, see W. Landes, "Economic Analysis of the Courts," *Journal of Law and Economics* 14 (1971): 61; and S. Nagel and M. Neef, "The Two Person Bargaining Situation: Plea Bargaining," in *Decision Theory and the Legal Process* (Lexington, Mass.: Lexington-Heath, 1979), pp. 63–180.

7. Perhaps the closest existing service to these computerized data banks is the Valuation Handbook Service (since 1962) and the Jury Verdict Expectancy Service (since 1962). See Chapter 6 of this book. The Associated Faculty Press/Kennikat Press is contemplating the possibility of developing a "Judicial Prediction Service," which will cover more types of cases than just the personal-injury cases covered by the Statewide Jury Verdicts Publishing Company.

8. Perhaps the best existing computerized program for legal decision-making is described in T. Gonser, J. Soma, and R. Wilhelm, "The Computer as a Tool for Legal Decision Making," *Practical Lawyer* (1981): 11–17.

9. Perhaps the most relevant existing short course with national visibility is the one entitled "Computers in the Law Office" offered by the American Law Institute and the American Bar Association Committee on Continuing Professional Education. The course is available on four audiocassettes made in 1982, but they emphasize word processing, billing, and citation retrieval rather than lawyer decision-making.

10. For insightful predictions of the future of decision science in basic law practice, see M. Morrise, "Emerging Computer-Assisted Legal Analysis Systems," *Brigham Young University Law Review* (1980): 116–141; and G. Grossman and L. Solomon, "Computers and Legal Reasoning," *American Bar Association Journal* (1983): 66–70.

8

Lawyer Decision-Making and Threshold Analysis

Lawyers frequently have to make decisions about whether or not to do something, such as accepting or rejecting a client. These matters can be referred to as "go/no-go decisions." Lawyers also frequently have to make decisions involving a choice between alternative projects, such as accepting Client A rather than Client B. These matters can be referred to as "conflicting-choice decisions." In making both kinds of decisions, lawyers (like decision-makers in general) may lack information about key components of the benefits or the costs of the decisional alternatives.

It is the purpose of this chapter to discuss how in the absence of accurate benefit-cost information that lawyer decision-making can be more accurate. The method basically involves determining a threshold value for each missing component or set of components. If the perceived value is above the threshold value, the decision should be affirmative. Otherwise, it should be negative in go/no-go decisions. A similar analysis applies to conflicting-choice decisions.[1]

To illustrate threshold analysis, a good example to start with is deciding whether or not to accept a personal injury client when a contingency fee is involved. One can easily reason by analogy to other go/no-go situations. The client acceptance situation tends to involve five variables, which are:

1. The damages likely to be awarded (*D*), for example, $10,000
2. The probability of winning (*P*), for example, .60, which means six out of ten cases like this tend to win and four out of ten tend to lose
3. The contingency fee rate, which is usually 33 percent or .33 (*F*)
4. The number of hours the case is likely to take (*H*), for example, 40
5. The dollar rate per hour at which the attorney values his or her time (*R*), for example, $30

In light of the above hypothetical data, the expected income from this case would be $2,000 on the average. That amount is arrived at by figuring that if there were ten cases like this, six would result in about $10,000 apiece in damages, and four would result in no liability and thus $0 in damages. If we sum those ten amounts, we get $60,000. If we divide by 10 to arrive at an average, we get $6,000. We could arrive at the $6,000 amount quicker by multiplying or discounting the $10,000 by .60, which is the probability of the $10,000 being received. With that expected, discounted, or average value of $6,000, we then apply or multiply the .33 contingency fee to arrive at the $2,000 average income from a case like this.

In light of the above data, the expected expense from the case would be about $1,200. That simply equals 40 hours multiplied by the $30 rate per hour. There may be other fixed costs like office rent, but those costs get paid regardless of whether we accept this hypothetical client. There may be other variable costs besides the lawyer's time, but they tend to be less important, especially for illustrative purposes. If the expected income is $2,000 and the expected expense is $1,200, this hypothetical case involves an expected profit of $800.

GO/NO-GO DECISIONS: HANDLING ONE MISSING VARIABLE AT A TIME

Determining Predicted Damages and Threshold Damages

To determine predicted damages, one can obtain data on a lot of previous cases of a similar type and then sum their damages and divide by the number of cases. That kind of information is available in loose-leaf services provided by research firms like the Jury Verdict Research Corporation. There are more sophisticated prediction methods that involve multiple ways of categorizing cases on various precise scales. There are also less sophisticated methods that involve multiplying the medical expenses and/or the lost wages by 5 or 10 or using some other rule of thumb. All of the prediction methods, however, generally have a substantial margin of error.

What is needed is a method for being able to make meaningful go/no-go decisions when we are not sure what the damages awarded or some other key components are likely to be. An especially meaningful approach is to attempt to assess the value of all of the components that are relatively easy to assess and then determine the threshold value for the component that is the most difficult to assess. Suppose that component in this case might be the damages to be awarded. Determining a threshold value for *D* involves the following steps:

1. Express the problem in terms of a threshold equation. Such an equation puts the income or benefits components on the left side of the equal sign and the expense or cost components on the right side. In this context, the threshold equation would be $(D)(P)(F) = (H)(R)$.
2. Substitute numbers for the variables for which we have numerical information. That converts the equation into $(D)(.60)(.33) = (40)(30)$.
3. Put the relatively unknown variable on the left side and the relatively known facts on the right side. In this equation, that means dividing both sides of the equation by $(.60)(.33)$. Doing this converts the equation into $(D) = (40)(30)/(.60)(.33)$.
4. Do the arithmetic on the right side of the equation to simplify it. Doing this converts the equation into $D^* = \$6{,}000$. We put a star next to *D* to show that it is the threshold value of the damages awarded.

A threshold damages figure of $6,000 means that if the perceived damages are greater than $6,000, we should take the case because it will generally be a profitable case, assuming the other figures are reasonably accurate. If the perceived damages are less than $6,000, we should reject the case as not being profitable. Having to decide whether the damages are likely to be more or less than a given threshold is generally a lot easier than having to decide exactly what the damages are likely to be. A lawyer can usually say whether the damages in a given case are likely to be more or less than $6,000, even though he or she might not know how much more or less.

Determining Predicted and Threshold Probabilities of Victory

To determine the probability of victory in a given case, one can obtain data on a lot of previous cases of a similar type and observe how many of those cases were won by the plaintiff and how many were lost by the plaintiff. The probability of victory is simply the percentage of cases won by the plaintiff expressed as a decimal. That kind of information is generally available in the same loose-leaf services that provide information on predicted damages. The tricky problem is often that any given case can be classified in a variety of categories, each one of which has a different probability of victory. Combining those probabilities may involve sophisticated mathematical analysis. The probabilities usually cannot be simply multiplied together since that implies that each category is independent of the other. In reality, there may be varying degrees of overlap among the categories. The loose-leaf services can be helpful in giving probabilities for frequently occurring combinations. Even with that kind of good information, there may still be considerable subjectivity in categorizing the cases, especially if the categories involve degrees of being present rather than just present or absent.

In light of the difficulty of determining the probability of victory, this variable is usually the one that is most in need of threshold analysis, even more so than the damages variable. For example, in the above hypothetical data, the threshold probability is .36. That figure was arrived at by following the same general steps mentioned above in arriving at a threshold damages figure. Step 1 is the same, since the threshold equation in this situation is $(D)(P)(F) = (H)(R)$, regardless of which variable is considered to be relatively unknown. Step 2 involves inserting numbers for the variables that we are relatively sure of, which converts the equation into $(10{,}000)(.6)(P) = (40)(30)$. Step 3 involves expressing P in terms of the known facts, which means $P = (40)(30)/(10{,}000)(.60)$. In step 4, we simplify the right side of that equation, which reveals that P^* or the threshold probability equals .36. This means that if we consider the probability of victory to be greater than about 1 in 3, we should take the case, since the expected income outweighs the expected costs. If we consider the probability to be less than 1 in 3, we should reject the case.

One thing that might be noted about probabilities and rational decision-making is that no matter how rational we are in betting on the averages, we can go wrong in any given case because individual cases are not necessarily at the average. In other words, our hypothetical case looks profitable to the extent that the expected income is $800 more than the expected expenses. Even if all of our numbers are perfectly accurate, we can still lose by taking the case since our numbers tell us that four out of ten such cases result in defeat for the plaintiff. On the average, however, we would be rational to take such cases. That is the same as stating that if we have a large number of such potential clients, we will come out ahead by accepting them. It is also the same as stating that if we have a small number of such cases, we may come out behind because we may be unlucky enough to have one of the losers. Nevertheless, the safest and most rational approach in any given case is to assume that it is an average case unless we know otherwise.

Determining Threshold Contingency Fees

The .33 contingent fee rate was considered virtually fixed before the Supreme Court said that minimum fee schedules of bar associations are in violation of the antitrust laws. Now those rates and other lawyer fees can be set by individual lawyers in light of profit-and-loss considerations. Therefore, if a lawyer knows roughly the damages, the victory probability, the hours, and the value per hour, he or she can determine what contingency fee rate to charge to make the case profitable. With the above hypothetical data, the threshold contingency fee is

.20. That can be readily seen since $10,000 × .60 = $6,000. On the cost side, 40 hours × $30 = $1,200. Therefore, the threshold fee is whatever decimal multiplied by $6,000 will yield $1,200. A contingent fee of .20 has that unique characteristic.

Knowing what the threshold contingent fee is can be useful to a lawyer with a client who has been made an offer by another lawyer that is below one's usual rate. For example, in the above case perhaps the lawyer quotes the client a .33 contingent fee. The potential client may truthfully state that he has been offered a .25 contingent fee arrangement by a lawyer down the street. As a competitive lawyer faced with the above facts, you could offer a .20 contingent fee arrangement and still make the case profitable. Some lawyers may consider it beneath their dignity to vary their prices, but doctors often do so in light of the expressed inability to pay by patients, and lawyers are becoming increasingly competitive. Threshold analysis, where the fee is the threshold variable, enables lawyers to be competitive in a more systematic way.

Determining Predicted, Threshold, and Optimum Hours

To determine the number of hours necessary to handle a given type of case, it would be helpful if the loose-leaf services would also provide that kind of information. As of now, they provide only information on damages awards and probabilities of victory for various types of cases because that type of information is available by analyzing court records. To determine how many hours each side expended in a given case would require asking the attorneys of record. It could be done with a postcard inquiry. The attorneys could probably provide that information with reasonable accuracy, since most attorneys do keep good time records. Attorneys in future cases could then estimate predicted time consumption by checking the loose-leaf service in the same way that they check for predicted damages and probabilities. In the absence of such systematic information, attorneys tend to rely on their personal experiences, their memory, and less systematic ways of categorizing cases than a loose-leaf service might be able to provide.

When the necessary quantity of hours is unclear, one can make hours into the threshold variable, just as one can do with any other variable. Doing this with the hypothetical data means determining the quantity of hours that $30 has to be multiplied by to equal the $2,000 on the left side of the threshold equation. That means dividing $2,000 by $30. The threshold number of hours is thus 67 hours. This means that if the lawyer thinks this case is going to take more than 67 hours, he or she should reject it. If the lawyer thinks it is going to take less than 67 hours, he or she should accept it.

The hours variable has a special characteristic different from any of the other variables. It is the only variable that has a causal influence on the other variables. This means that the number of hours can influence the damages awarded and the probability of victory. In other words, the harder we work, the more likely we are to win and the higher the damages are likely to be. The equation that states that (*D*)(*P*)(*F*) = (*H*)(*R*) is true by the definitions of profit and of threshold equation. Profit means income minus expenses. Income is (*D*)(*P*)(*F*) and expenses are (*H*)(*R*). A *threshold equation* is defined as one in which income is on the left side and expenses are on the right side. What we need to determine the optimum number of hours (as contrasted to the predicted or threshold number of hours) is one equation in which damages are statistically related to hours and another equation in which the victory probability is statistically related to hours. Such equations can be obtained by gathering data for a lot of cases in which we can determine the damages awarded, who won, and how many hours the plaintiff's attorney expended. We can then plot the relation between damages awarded and hours expended on a two-dimensional graph. Doing this will probably yield an S-shaped curve showing that adding additional hours at first has little effect, but then the curve gets steeper and finally plateaus out. A similar curve occurs when one relates victory probabilities to intervals of hours expended. A composite curve can show predicted damages awarded, discounted by predicted probabilities. One can superimpose that curve on an upward sloping line relating time costs to hours expended. The optimum number of hours is at the point where there is a maximum positive difference between the discounted damages-awarded curve and the time-cost line.

Determining One's Actual, Threshold, and Derived Hourly Worth

The easiest way to determine one's hourly worth is to observe what the market is paying for an hour of lawyer time in one's type of law practice. The trouble with that figure, however, is that it represents what other people consider one's time to be worth to them, not what one considers it to be worth to oneself. A good test of how much one considers one's time to be worth is to ask a lawyer how much he would be willing to pay another lawyer to free the first lawyer from an hour's worth of work. If the market figure is $50 an hour but the first lawyer would not be willing to buy an hour of free time for anything more than $30, he is in effect stating that he considers his time to be worth about $30 an hour.

That is an important point in threshold analysis in that even if a lawyer is operating at the threshold in a case, he is still coming out ahead if he is covering his hourly worth. In other words, a lawyer in a contingency fee case wears two hats: that of a stockholder in himself, who gets profits in a case only if the income exceeds the expenses, including his labor expenses; and that of a wage earner in the firm who gets full wages if his labor expenses are covered, even though the income in the case equals the expenses.

The hourly rate may be the least subjective of the five variables if the hourly rate is determined by looking to the market rate. If there were a situation in which the hourly rate were questionable, one could convert the problem of determining the exact rate into an easier above-or-below problem by noting in the above facts that the threshold rate is $2,000 divided by 40 hours. That makes the threshold rate $50. This means that the lawyer should take the case if he considers his time to be worth less than $50 an hour and reject it if he considers his time to be worth more.

One could also use this kind of an analysis to work backwards to derive how much lawyers consider their time to be worth. That might involve presenting hypothetical data to lawyers. The data would include figures for predicted damages, probability of victory, the contingent fee rate, and the predicted hours. The lawyers would then be asked for a number of such cases whether or not they would accept each client. By observing which cases they accepted and rejected, one could deduce or derive how much they considered an hour of their time to be worth. One could use the same kind of backward analysis to determine how lawyers perceive damages, probabilities, or hours. Doing this would involve leaving those variables out of the hypothetical data and asking the lawyers whether they would generally accept or reject the hypothetical cases. By noting the ones they accepted or rejected, one could determine within a range how they tend to perceive those variables. One might, however, ask them directly and get more meaningful answers. On the other hand, directly asking the more personal question of how much one considers one's own time to be worth may not produce as meaningful a set of answers as using this indirect approach.[2]

GO/NO-GO DECISIONS: HANDLING MORE THAN ONE MISSING VARIABLE AT A TIME

Two Missing Variables

Often in go/no-go decisions like accepting a contingency client, there is only one variable that is especially missing, to which threshold analysis is particularly applicable. There are, however, many situations where there are two or more variables on which information is so lacking that we cannot position those variables within a narrow range, although we might be able to position them as being above or below a threshold. For example, in deciding whether to accept a contingency client, we may be unable to determine with reasonable accuracy either the damages awarded or the victory probability. Under those circumstances, how might one reach a meaningful decision to accept or reject the client?

A good way of handling that problem is to draw a simple graph showing the relations between the two unknown variables while holding constant the known variables. Doing that involves drawing a graph like Figure 8–1. The vertical axis shows the possible probabilities of victory, and the horizontal axis shows the possible damages. We know that the victory probability cannot be less than 0 or more than 1.00. We know that the damages variable cannot be less than 0, and we probably know roughly what its reasonable maximum is, which in

Figure 8–1
Accepting or Rejecting a Client with Two or More Missing Variables

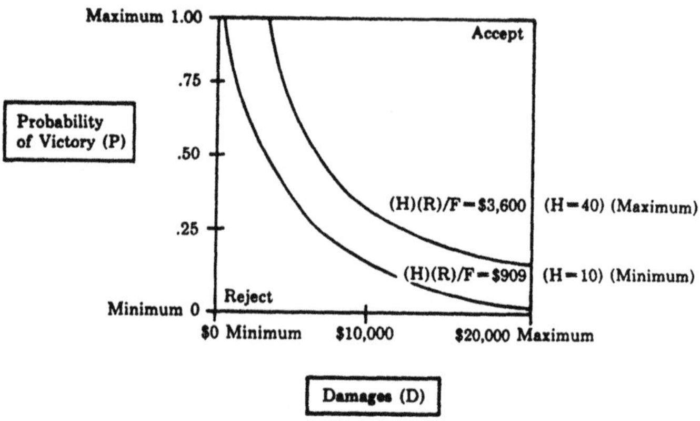

Note at the threshold: PDF = HR
Therefore: P = HR/FD = (40)(30)/(.333)(D) = 3600/D

this case may be $20,000. We also know that at the threshold the following statements are true:

1. $PDF = HR$ (the basic threshold equation).
2. $PD = HR/F$ (putting the unknown variables on the left side).
3. $PD =$ (40)($30)/(.333) (substituting numbers for the known variables).
4. $PD =$ $3,600 (simplifying the right side).
5. $P =$ $3,600/$D$(expressing one unknown in terms of the other).

With that last simple equation, we can substitute any values for *D* and thereby determine the corresponding values for *P*. For example, when *D* is $3,600, *P* is 1.00. When *D* is twice $3,600 (or $7,200), *P* is .50. Likewise, when *D* is four times $3,600 (or $14,400), *P* is .25. Each of those three points can be shown on Figure 5.1. By connecting those three points together, we have a curve showing the relation between victory probability and damages when $F = .333$, $H = 40$, and $R =$ $30, and thus HR/F = $3,600. Note that the curve looks like a children's slide indicating that as the damages increase (i.e., to the right), the victory probability decreases if we are going to continue to be at the threshold where income equals expenses. Likewise, as the victory probability increases, the damages decrease in order to keep $P \times D =$ $3,600.

Note further that the upper right hand corner of the graph is where we would like to be because the damages and the victory probability are high. Call that the "accept-corner" or the "accept-region." The lower left hand corner is where we would *not* like to be because the damages and the victory probability are low. Call that the "reject-corner" or "reject-region." The object now is to try to draw a big circle or other shape on the graph where the combination of damages and victory probability is roughly likely to be. If that circle is mainly above the curve showing HR/F = \$3,600, accept the client or adopt the go/no-go project. If that circle is mainly below the curve showing HR/F = \$3,600, reject the client.

Thus the problem reduces to a relatively simple graph that can serve as a visual aid for determining whether $P \times D$ is more or less than HR/F, even though we do not know the exact location of P, D, or $P \times D$. The same analysis can be applied to situations where we do not know the value of any two of the five or so variables. We simply go through the following more general steps:

1. Draw a two-dimensional graph showing one of the two unknowns on the vertical axis and the other unknown on the horizontal axis. Each axis should extend from the reasonable minimum on the variable to the reasonable maximum.
2. Express one of the two unknowns in terms of the other while holding the relatively known variables constant, as was done in the five steps above.
3. Use that equation to plot about three points on the graph. Connect the points together to create a threshold curve, although sometimes it may be a straight line. That curve shows the relations between the two unknowns, holding the other variables constant.
4. Using that graph, try to estimate the rough location of the combination of the two unknown variables. If that combination is on the accept side of the threshold curve, adopt the project; if it is on the reject side, reject the project.

Three or More Missing Variables

Suppose we change the problem to provide for three unknown variables. The three that tend to be the most likely to be unknown are the damages, the victory probability, and the number of hours needed. In other words, should a client be accepted in a .33 contingency fee case in which we consider our time to be worth \$30 an hour but we do not know the damages that are likely to be awarded, the probability of victory, or the number of hours needed? That sounds like a truly impossible problem with virtually no information on which to base a decision.

The saving feature is that even that kind of problem may provide sufficient latent information that we are capable of teasing out through appropriate stimuli. Figure 8–1 helps in that regard. The only change needed from the way the figure was presented when we dealt with two unknowns is to draw a pair of threshold curves rather than a single threshold curve. That involves a rough awareness of the maximum number of hours (which in this case may be about 40) and the minimum (about 10). At 10 hours, the HR/F amount is (10)(30)/(.333), or \$900.

We can then plot a curve for $P = \$900/D$, just as we previously plotted a curve for $P = \$3,600/D$, as is shown in Figure 8–1. Each of those two curves will be parallel to each other. Note that as the number of hours decreases, the reject-region becomes smaller.

As before, the object now is to draw a big circle or other shape on the graph where the combination of damages and victory probability is roughly likely to be. If that circle is mainly above the maximum hours curve, accept the client. If it is approximately between the minimum and maximum hours curves, one can be considered to be operating roughly at the threshold of zero profits. When dealing with one, two, or three unknowns, one may sometimes find oneself operating at the threshold. Under those circumstances, one can either flip a coin to decide or seek additional information to clarify whether one is more above or below the threshold.

Seldom is one faced with a go/no-go decision involving more than three unknown variables. If there were a fourth unknown variable in this client acceptance situation, it would probably be the hourly rate. When we had one unknown variable, we talked in terms of a threshold point. With two unknown variables, it was a threshold curve. With three unknowns, it was a pair of threshold curves or a threshold band. With four unknowns, we need two graphs like Figure 8–1. The first graph would work with the minimum value on the fourth variable, which might be $20 an hour, and the second graph with the maximum value, which might be $50. We would then draw our rough circle on each graph as to where *P* and *D* might be. If the circle is mainly in the accept-regions on both graphs, we would accept the client. If it is mainly in the reject-regions, we would reject the client. This kind of analysis could be extended to five or more unknown variables by using two sets of paired graphs, rather than just a pair of graphs, a band of curves, a curve, or a point. Each set of graphs would work with a different minimum or maximum value for an unknown variable. That, however, is only of exotic interest since practical situations seldom involve more than one, two, or three unknown variables.

CONFLICTING CHOICE DECISIONS: CHOOSING BETWEEN CLIENTS OR PROJECTS

The Basic Comparisons

Conflicting-choice decisions involve more than one client or project, as contrasted to go/no-go decisions, which involve deciding on a single client or project. When multiple clients or projects are involved, one can apply a similar kind of threshold analysis for making comparisons and for dealing with unknown variables. Suppose we consider our previous hypothetical client to be Client A. We now want to introduce Client B. This client's case has the following characteristics:

1. Damages likely to be awarded are $16,000.
2. The probability of winning is about .20.

3. The contingency fee is still .33.
4. The number of hours is only 15.
5. Our hourly worth is still $30 an hour.

Assume that we have only 40 hours available. Which client should we accept? We cannot accept both, since that would consume 55 hours and we are assuming for the sake of discussion that we have only 40 hours available. At first glance, Client A looks like the better client because he generates a profit of $800 by virtue of $2,000 in expected income and $1,200 in expected expenses. Client B generates a profit of only $606 by virtue of $1,056 in expected income and $450 in expected expenses.

On the other hand, we should note that with Client B, we would have an extra 25 hours available, since Client B consumes only 15 of our 40 hours. Client B would thus be the better client if we can invest that remaining 25 hours in generating more than $194 in profit. The $194 is the difference between the $800 profit of Client A and the $606 profit of Client B. It is the threshold profit, such that if Client B could somehow generate an additional $194 in profit, the two cases would be equally profitable. In order for our remaining 25 hours to generate $194 in profit, those hours would have to average about $8 apiece in terms of profit since $194 divided by 25 hours is about $8. This means that those hours would have to average $38 apiece in income, since our time expense is worth $30 an hour, assuming we expend the whole 25 hours to get the $194 threshold profit. We can thus have a threshold profit of $194 overall, a threshold profit of $8 an hour, a threshold income per hour of about $38, and a threshold income of about $950 overall (25 hours times $38). If the remaining 25 hours or a subset is capable of generating profit that will exceed those thresholds, Client B is the better client. By income and profit in this context, we can also include the monetary value of the satisfaction we might get from going fishing or doing non-lawyering things with that remaining 25 hours.

Missing Variables and Multiple Cases

Thus far we have been talking about choosing between clients when we have complete information for each client on damages, victory probability, contingent fee, hours, and hourly rate. Suppose any *one* of those five variables for either client is missing. What do we then do? Suppose, more specifically, that we do not know the damages for Client B. An appropriate set of steps would be the following.

1. Indicate the threshold equation where both clients are equally profitable. In this context it is $DPF - HR = dpf - hr$, where the capital letters are the variables for Client A, and the small letters are the variables for Client B. The left side of the equation expresses the profit for Client A, and the right side expresses the profit for Client B.

Figure 8–2
Choosing between Two Clients with Two or More Missing Variables

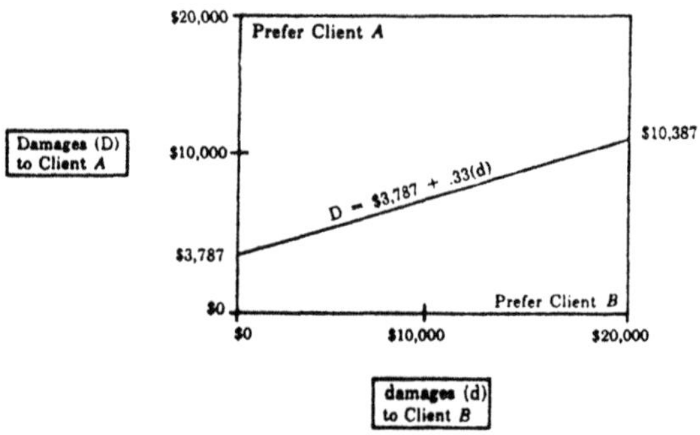

2. Insert numbers for all of the known information. That converts the equation into $800 = (*d*)(.20)(.33) − (15)($30), which simplifies to 800 = (*d*)(.066) − (450).
3. Put the unknown variable on the left side of the equation and the known information on the right side. That converts the equation into *d*(.066) = 800 + 450 by adding 450 to both sides, which then simplifies to *d*(.066) = 1,250. By dividing both sides by .066, we get *d* = 1,250/.066, which then simplifies to 18,750.
4. By doing the arithmetic to simplify the numbers on the right side of the equation, we thereby obtain the threshold value of the unknown damages. That value is $18,750. It means that if the damages in Client B's case could somehow get above $18,750, instead of $16,000, Client B would be the more profitable client.

We could logically extend the above analysis to any missing variable in the threshold equation of *DPF* − *HR* = *dpf* − *hr*. We could also extend the analysis to *two* or more missing variables by using the same graphing approach for dealing with two missing variables as was used in go/no-go decisions. Suppose, for example, that we do not know the damages for either Client A or Client B. Arriving at a decision about which is the more profitable client might involve the following steps:

1. Draw a two-dimensional graph with possible Client A damages (*D*) on the vertical axis and possible Client B damages (*d*) on the horizontal axis, like that shown in Figure 8–2.
2. Express *D* in terms of *d* holding constant all of the other variables by inserting their numerical values into the threshold equation. Doing this means that working with a basic equation of the form (*D*)(.60)(.33) − (40)(30) = (*d*)(.20)(.33) − (15)(30).

It simplifies algebraically and arithmetically to $D = 3{,}787 + .33(d)$, as can be quickly determined with a hand calculator.

3. Plot a few points using that equation. Connect them together to form a threshold curve, which in this case is a threshold straight line.
4. The upper left hand corner of the graph is the region for preferring Client A, and the lower right hand corner is the region for preferring Client B.
5. Try roughly to draw a circle that encompasses where the combination of D and d is likely to be. If that circle is above the threshold line, prefer Client A. If it is below the threshold line, prefer Client B.

We could logically extend the above analysis to any pair of missing variables or any set of three or more missing variables using the same general methods discussed under go/no-go decisions. We could also extend the analysis to any number of cases. Suppose, for example, that we have a potential Client C and that we are still operating in the mutually exclusive context. We can use the above comparison methods for choosing between Client A and Client B. If Client A wins, we then compare Client A with Client C. Whoever wins that comparison is the overall winner. That same system of a series of successive paired comparisons can be applied to any number of cases or projects, with the last uneliminated one being the best.

The above analysis involves mutually exclusive clients or projects. An alternative but possibly more typical situation involves choosing the best combination of clients or projects when they are not mutually exclusive, but not all of them can be adopted. A meaningful procedure for arriving at decisions like that is to (1) determine what all of the possible combinations are, which is usually feasible since the number of projects to choose among is usually not very large; (2) determine for each combination what its expected income, expense, and profit are; and (3) pick the combination that will be the most profitable. Doing this may require going through a set of paired comparisons using threshold analysis, since some of the combinations may involve unknown variables and each combination may involve a different quantity of hours or resources. It is not meaningful simply to pick the combination that is the most profitable in the order of their net profits, just as it was not necessarily meaningful to pick Client A over Client B simply because Client A generates more profit. As previously discussed, Client B could be more profitable if Client B involves fewer hours or resources that could be invested elsewhere to yield enough profit to offset the additional profit of Client A. The same is true with combinations of clients or projects as well as individual clients or projects.[3]

EXTENDING THE ANALYSIS TO OTHER FORMS OF LAWYER OR JUDICIAL DECISION-MAKING

Thus far we have been discussing threshold analysis mainly in the context of accepting or rejecting a client or choosing among clients. We have also referred to adopting/rejecting projects or choosing among projects on a broad level of generality so as to make the analysis more widely applicable. There are many other examples that can be given to illustrate threshold analysis as applied to the decision-making of lawyers or judges. Additional examples might include deciding (1) whether to accept a settlement or go to trial, (2) whether to release or hold a defendant in jail before trial, and (3) how to increase police adherence to legality in making searches.

Deciding Whether to Accept a Settlement or Go to Trial

Lawyers frequently must decide whether to accept a settlement or go to trial. The settlement offer is known. The results of going to trial are not so known. Therefore, this becomes an excellent situation for threshold analysis. An appropriate first step is to develop a threshold equation. In its simplest form, the threshold equation might be $(S) = (P)(D)$. In other words, at the threshold, the settlement is exactly equal to the expected value of going to trial. That equation can apply to either the plaintiff or the defendant in personal injury or criminal cases. In personal injury cases, S and D are expressed in dollars. In criminal cases, S and D are expressed in terms of months in jail. The P stands for probability of plaintiff victory in either type of case. The D could stand for decision in either type of case or for damages in personal injury cases and detention length in criminal cases.

To illustrate the application of that threshold equation to personal injury cases, suppose that as plaintiff's counsel you are offered a settlement in Client A's case of $8,000. Suppose further that you perceive that if the case is won on trial, the damages are likely to be $10,000. What is the threshold probability to make the settlement worth accepting? Answering that question (with the threshold equation in its simplest form) involves:

1. Substituting numbers for the variables for which we have information. That means an equation of the form $\$8{,}000 = (P)(\$10{,}000)$.
2. Putting the unknown variable on the left side and the numbers on the right. That means an equation such as $P = \$8{,}000/\$10{,}000$.
3. Simplifying the right side to determine the threshold probability, which in this case is $P^* = .80$.

The same analysis could be done when we know S and P and we want to solve for threshold D or when we know P and D and want to solve for threshold S. Likewise, the same analysis could be done by counsel for the defendant insurance company in deciding whether to give in to the plaintiff's demand. In the Client A situation, for example, if defense counsel perceives the damages to be $10,000 and the victory probability to be .60, defense counsel should be willing to accept any settlement that involves paying out less than $6,000.

We can also illustrate the application of that threshold equation to criminal cases. Suppose that as the prosecutor you are offered a settlement by the defense counsel whereby the defendant will agree to plead guilty with an 8–month sentence. Suppose further that you perceive that if the case is won on trial, the sentence is likely to be 10 months. What is the threshold probability to make that plea bargain worth accepting? The analysis is the same except the first step is: 8 months = (*P*)(10 months). The second step is *P* = 8 months/10 months, and the third step is *P** = .80. Just as in personal injury cases, here the threshold analysis can be extended to any one of the three variables for either the prosecutor or the defendant. Likewise, we can do a threshold analysis with two or more missing variables, using the graphing approach discussed with go/no-go decisions.

The basic threshold equation needs supplementing to take into consideration the litigation costs. The plaintiff side in either personal injury or criminal cases would generally like to avoid going to trial because there may be expensive fees involved in hiring a personal injury trial lawyer, or there may be expensive administrative costs to the prosecutor's office. The plaintiff, therefore, may be willing to offer a reduction for early resolution of the case the way a seller offers a discount for early payment of an invoice. From the plaintiff's perspective, the initial threshold equation thus becomes (*S*) = (*P*)(*D*)(%*X*), where %*X* is the reduction factor (expressed as a decimal less than 1.00) that the plaintiff is willing to knock off the expected value of the case to avoid a trial. If, for example, the insurance company offers $4,000 and the plaintiff perceives *P* to be .60 and *D* to be $10,000, the threshold reduction factor is .67. That figure was arrived at by solving for %*X* in the equation. It could also be arrived at by asking what reduction or discount has to be given to $6,000 to convert it into $4,000.

Likewise, the defendant would also generally like to avoid going to trial for reasons such as the possibility that there may be a long wait in jail if one is not released on bond, or there may be expensive administrative costs to the insurance company or the public defender's office. The defendant side, therefore, may be willing to offer an increment for early resolution of the case the way that a buyer offers a bonus for early delivery of a needed product. From the defendant's perspective, the initial threshold equation also becomes (*S*) = (*P*)(*D*)(%*X*), but here %*X* is the incremental factor (expressed as a decimal greater than 1.00) that the defendant is willing to add on to the expected value of the case to avoid a trial. If, for example, the prosecutor offers a 4–month jail sentence in return for a plea of guilty and the defendant perceives *P* to be .60 and *D* to be 10 months, the threshold incremental factor is 1.50. That figure was arrived at by solving for %*X* in the equation. It also could be arrived at by asking what increment or bonus has to be given to 4 months to convert it into 6 months.

The basic threshold equation also needs supplementing to take into consideration the fact that a bird in the hand may be worth two in the bush. In this context it means that the right side of the threshold equation needs to be discounted by the number of months we have to wait for the trial results. In other words, a settlement offer of $5,000 may be equal to a $7,500 expected value (i.e., $P \times D$) if we have to wait five years to get the $7,500. This is true if we could invest the $5,000 to bring in $500 a year in profit. In order for $5,000 in principal to make $500 a year in simple interest, the threshold interest rate would have to be .10. What this means in terms of our threshold equation is that it has to be changed to read $(S) = (P)(D)/(1 + RT)$, where R is the simple interest rate, and T is the number of years before the damages are received. The time discounting factor in our case would be $1 + (.10)(5)$, which simplifies to 1.50. When $7,500 is divided by 1.50, it equals $5,000. Likewise, when $5,000 is multiplied by 1.50, it equals $7,500.

With that improved threshold equation, one can now determine the threshold interest rate and/or the threshold number of years to wait, as well as the threshold settlement, victory probability, and damages. By definition, any one of those threshold figures causes both sides of the equation to be equal. This means that a settlement or going to trial is equally profitable at the threshold. The time discounting factor for figuring interest on the interest (i.e., compound interest) is $(1 + R)^T$, instead of $(1 + RT)$. The average personal injury case, however, does not involve enough money and enough trial delay to make that much difference between simple and compound interest. Roughly the same kind of time discounting analysis can be applied to criminal cases (although with more subjectivity) since the average defendant would rather take a 7 1/2 month sentence five years from now than have to go to prison for five months right now.[4]

Deciding Whether to Release or Hold a Defendant in Jail before Trial

Deciding whether to release or hold a defendant in jail before trial is an example of judicial decision-making to which threshold analysis might apply. At the threshold, the costs of holding a defendant in jail (H) equal the costs of releasing the defendant (R). The most important holding costs consist of whatever cost society incurs as a result of the defendant being wrongly held in jail when the defendant would have appeared in court without committing a crime if the defendant had been released. The probability that a defendant would appear in court without committing a crime if released can be symbolized as P. The releasing costs mainly consist of whatever costs society incurs as a result of the defendant committing a crime while released or failing to appear for his or her court date. The probability that a defendant would commit a crime while released or would fail to appear can be symbolized as $1 - P$, which is the complement of the defendant appearing without committing a crime. Thus the expected or discounted value of the holding costs is $(H)(P)$, and the expected value of the releasing costs is $(R)(1 - P)$. At the threshold, $(H)(P) = (R)(1 - P)$. We could make that threshold equation more complicated by adding to the left side of the equation the holding costs for any defendant who is held rightly (i.e., who would be a no-show or a crime-committer) or wrongly (i.e., who would show without committing a crime). That would convert the equation into $(H1)(P) + (H2) = (R)(1 - P)$. For the sake of simplicity, however, we can temporarily ignore the $H2$ holding costs.

To make the threshold equation more usable, we need to determine the threshold probability above which the defendant gets released and below which the defendant gets held. Doing that involves solving for P in the threshold equation. If $HP = R - RP$, then $HP + RP = R$ and $P(H + R) = R$. Therefore $P^* = R/(R + H)$. A more usable way of expressing the threshold probability, however, is first to symbolize the ratio between the holding costs and the releasing costs (i.e., H/R) as being X. Then one can prove by simple algebra that $P^* = 1/(1 + X)$. We are in effect setting R equal to a value of 1 and H equal to a positive number bigger or smaller than 1, depending on how many more times avoiding a holding error is worth relative to avoiding a releasing error.

To use that threshold probability equation involves first deciding the relative value of the holding error costs (H) to the releasing-error costs (R) in a given case. In the average case, the error of wrongly holding a defendant who would appear without committing a crime (H) should be considered more serious than the error of releasing a defendant who would fail to appear or would commit a crime (R). Holding errors should be considered more serious than releasing errors, just as wrongly convicting the innocent should be considered more serious than wrongly acquitting the guilty, although not necessarily with the same ratio of seriousness. If in the average case, we consider the holding error costs to be twice as serious as the releasing error costs, H/R or X is equal to 2. This means that in the average case, the threshold probability should be $P^* = 1/(1 + 2) = .33$. This further means that if the average defendant has a probability of appearing without committing a crime that is greater than .33, the defendant should be released on his own recognizance or a low bond. If the defendant has a P less than .33, the defendant should be held in jail on no bond or a high bond. If the value of X is 1.00 (meaning that H and R are equal), P^* is .50. One can readily see how X can vary from case to case depending on the nature of the defendant and thus how P^* can vary.

Just as one can use a threshold probability for holding or releasing, one can also use a threshold value-ratio between the holding error costs and the releasing error costs. For example, suppose we think we know that a given defendant has a .90 probability of appearing without committing a crime. That is roughly the probability in the average criminal case. With that probability, what is the threshold ratio of H to R above which we should release the defendant and below which we should hold the defendant? To calculate that threshold ratio, we solve for X in the equation $P^* = 1/(1 + X)$. Doing this tells us that $X^* = (1 - P)/P$. If we now substitute the known .90, we get $X^* = (1 - .90)/.90 = .10/.90 = 1/9 = .11$. This means that if the defendant has a .90 probability of appearing without committing a crime, the defendant should be released unless we believe that the releasing costs are nine times as great as the holding costs. Seldom is that likely to be the case, which is a justification for releasing average defendants, since they have a high probability of appearing without committing a crime or at least a known crime.

The threshold equation used in this example of $H(P) = R(1 - P)$ has analogous counterparts in other aspects of the legal process. For example, the threshold equation for a juror deciding whether to vote to convict or acquit is $C(P) = A(1 - P)$. The C represents the conviction-error costs, the A represents the acquittal-error costs, and the P represents the probability that the defendant is truly innocent. Another example is the threshold equation for a would-be criminal deciding whether or not to commit a crime. That threshold equation is $C(P) = B(1 - P)$. Here the C represents the costs of unsuccessfully committing the crime including imprisonment, the B represents the benefits of successfully committing the crime, and the P represents the probability of the costs being imposed. That kind of a threshold equation can be used to arrive at a threshold P, C, B, or X (i.e., C/B). We can calculate the threshold value for any variable in these threshold equations. Doing this can be helpful in (1) making decisions with given values for some of the variables, (2) influencing the decisions of other people such as would-be criminals, (3) predicting decisions in light of changes that have been known to occur in the values of some of the variables, or (4) measuring an individual's decisional propensities (P^*) by knowing the relative value he or she places on H and R, C and A, or C and B.[5]

Deciding How to Increase Police Legality in Making Searches

The previous decision-making examples about out-of-court settlements and pretrial release were basically go/no-go decisions. A good example of a conflicting-choice decision might be deciding between the exclusionary rule and legal action against the police as alternative means of increasing police legality in making searches while not unduly decreasing police morale. That is also a good example of potential legislative decision-making in an area that affects lawyers, judges, and the legal system.

In 1963 a mailed-questionnaire survey was made of one randomly selected police chief, prosecuting attorney, judge, defense attorney, and official of the American Civil Liberties Union in nearly all of the 50 states to determine, among other things, their perceptions of changes in police behavior before and after the Supreme Court required illegally seized evidence to be excluded from all criminal proceedings. Of those who responded from the states that had been newly required to exclude illegally seized evidence, 75 percent reported an increase in police adherence to legality, and 25 percent reported no change or a decrease. Of those who responded from the control group of states that already had the exclusionary rule, 57 percent reported an increase in police adherence to legality, and 43 percent reported no change or a decrease. The .18 difference between 75 and 57 percent can be used to measure the degree of relation (*REL*) between newly adopting the exclusionary rule (*E*) and undergoing improvement in police legality in making searches (*L*). Through the same questionnaire and a similar analysis, we obtain three additional relations, namely, (1) between adopting the exclusionary rule (*E*) and showing a decrease in police morale in making searches (*M*), which is .37 (REM); (2) between the presence of damages/criminal action against the the police (*A*) and increased police adherence to legality (*L*), which is .05 (*RAL*); and (3) between the presence of damages/criminal action (*A*) and decreased police morale in making searches (*M*), which is .09 (*RAM*).

Suppose the goals of increasing legality and not decreasing morale are considered equally important. How then does one phrase the threshold equation, where the exclusionary policy and the legal-action policy are equally profitable or desirable? A simple way would be an equation of the form $REL - REM = RAL - RAM$. If we are unsure of any one of those four relations, we can solve for its threshold value and then try to answer the question about whether the relation is above or below that threshold value. For example, maybe we are unsure of the relation between *E* and *L*. To solve for its threshold value we simply insert numbers for the other relations and express *REL* in terms of those numbers. Doing this gives $REL = RAL - RAM + REM = .05 - .09 + .37$. Simplifying the right side gives $REL^* = .33$. This means that if we are confident that the relation is stronger than .33, the exclusionary rule should be adopted over the legal-action approach, assuming that legality and morale are our only two goals. If the relation is probably below .33, the exclusionary rule should be rejected in favor of the legal-action policy. The threshold equation that contains four variables can be expanded to contain eight variables by showing for each of those relations the 2 percentages on which each one is based. We can then determine the threshold value for any one of those percentages. The threshold equation that contains four variables can be contracted to only the two variables of $REL = REM$ if we are only interested in a go/no-go decision concerning the exclusionary rule.

It would be unrealistic to think that we would weight legality and morale as being of equal importance. Most people believe that police adherence to legality is more important than police morale in making searches. For the sake of discussion, let us assume that people whose values we consider important consider legality three times as important as morale. That converts the threshold equation into $(3)REL - REM = (3)RAL - RAM$. In other words, *REL* and *RAL* get multiplied by 3 because they involve the legality goal, and *REM* and *RAM* get multiplied by 1 because they involve the morale goal. If, however, we are not sure what the relative weight of legality to morale should be, we can substitute a *W* for the 3 and then solve for *W* to find the threshold weight. Doing this involves solving for *W* in the equation $W(.18) - .37 = W(.05) - .09$. Putting *W* on the right side by itself and the numbers on the left side reveals that threshold *W* (or W^*) is 2.15. This means that if we consider legality to be worth more than twice as much as morale (rounding to the nearest whole number), we should prefer the exclusionary rule over legal action, assuming we accept the four relations as being meaningful. If we assume legality is worth less than twice as much, we should prefer the legal action. This assumes that the two policies are mutually exclusive or that there is an issue about which is preferable. The alternative would be to treat each alternative as a separate go/no-go decision, which allows for adopting them both. There is also no need to assume that the four relations or the relative weight are precisely meaningful. We can work with any one of these five variables as unknowns and use the graphing methods for reaching decisions with multiple unknowns, as discussed previously.

The example of deciding how to increase police legality in making searches involves a format that is common in legal or general policy-making. It is a format involving conflicting choices in which the benefits and costs are expressed as decimal or statistical relations with various goals. The relations with desired goals are expressed as positive decimals and the relations with undesired goals as negative decimals. Each decimal relation is preceded by a weight, depending on the relative importance of the goal to which the relation pertains, with the least important goal receiving a relative weight of 1. With that kind of threshold analysis, the highly subjective problem of assigning weights to goals can be greatly simplified by making the goals relative rather than absolute and especially by talking in terms of threshold weights rather than exact weights.[6]

CONCLUSIONS

The simple logic that this chapter proposes under the general idea of lawyer decision-making and threshold analysis can be summarized in a few basic rules.

1. When making a go/no-go decision, develop a threshold equation in which the benefit variables are on the left side and the cost variables are on the right side. Any one of those variables can be considered a threshold variable by expressing it in terms of the numerical values of the other variables. Simplifying those numbers gives the threshold value of the relatively unknown variable, above which the project should be adopted if the variable is a benefit and above which the project should be rejected if the variable is a cost.

2. To reach a go/no-go decision with multiple unknown variables, draw a two-dimensional graph with one variable on the vertical axis and another variable on the horizontal axis. Each axis should extend from the reasonable minimum to the reasonable maximum on the variable. Then draw a curve that holds constant the other variables. If the basic pair of unknown variables is above the threshold curve, adopt the project; otherwise, reject it.

3. To resolve conflicting choice decisions, develop a threshold equation in which the benefits minus costs of one choice are put on the left side of the equation and the benefits minus costs of the second choice are put on the right side of the equation. Any one of those variables can be treated as a threshold variable to be solved in terms of the numerical values of the other variables. Any combination of unknown variables can be dealt with graphically as with go/no-go decisions.

4. When many choices are involved, use a system of successive paired comparisons with the last uneliminated choice declared the winner. The many choices can include combinations of choices as well as the basic choices.

These four principles can be applied to a great variety of legal decision-making situations. Several general examples have been discussed.

1. One might decide whether or not to accept a client on a contingency fee basis where the threshold equation is (Damages) × (Probability of victory) × (Fee percentage) = (Hours) × (Rate per hour), or $DPF = HR$.

2. One might decide between two such conflicting clients where the threshold equation is $DPF - HR$ (for the first client) = $dpf - hr$ (for the second client).

3. One might decide whether to accept something of value that is not contingent on the occurrence of an event versus something of value that is contingent on the occurrence of an event such as the outcome of a trial. The threshold equation for such situations can be symbolized (Net benefits from decision 1) = (Net benefits from decision 2) × (Probability of those benefits being received), or $(B1) = (B2)(P)$.

4. One might decide between two alternatives where they are both discounted by the probability of an event occurring or not occurring, as where doing something can result in one type of error and doing the opposite can result in a second type. The threshold equation for such situations can be symbolized (Type 1 error costs) × (Probability of those costs being imposed) = (Type 2 error costs) × (Complement of the first probability), or $(E1)(P) = (E2)(1 - P)$. Illustrative examples include deciding whether to hold a defendant in jail before trial, whether to convict a defendant, or whether to commit a crime.

5. Deciding between two alternatives where each one has a statistical relation with certain desired and/or undesired goals and each goal has a different importance weight. The threshold equation for such situations can be symbolized $(WB)(RB) - (WC)(RC)$ for the first alternative = $(WB)(RB) - (WC)(RC)$ for the second alternative, where W = Weight factor; B = Benefit variable; R = Relation factor; and C = Cost variable. The illustrative example given involved comparing the rule excluding illegally seized evidence with damages/criminal action against the police as alternative means for increasing police legality in making searches while not unduly decreasing police morale.

Those five types of examples cover a great deal of legal decision-making. All of those forms of decision-making could benefit from the use of threshold analysis to arrive at decisions that could be more effective in achieving desired goals, more efficient in reducing undesired costs, and more equitable in enabling lawyers to compete more equally with one another regardless of their natural decision-making skills. On the latter point, it should be emphasized that the methods presented to a considerable extent represent the codified common sense that good legal decision-makers intuitively use without thinking in these terms. What is needed is more analysis of good decision-making so that what good decision-makers do intuitively can be shared by others who do not have such good intuitive judgment. What is also needed is more communication of the findings of that kind of analysis to lawyers, judges, legislators, and other legal decision-makers to help improve the legal process and its results. It is hoped that this chapter will contribute to those needs and those improvements.

APPENDIX: REPLACING A PAYOFF MATRIX WITH A P/G TABLE

Table 8–1
Deciding Whether to Commit a Crime with Only Monetary Goals

GOALS / OPTIONS	BENEFIT ITEMS			COST ITEMS			NET
	(1) Crime Benefits (B)	(2) Probability of Crime Benefits (PB)	(3) Expected Crime Benefits (B') (1)·(2)	(4) Crime Costs (C)	(5) Probability of Crime Costs (PC)	(6) Expected Crime Costs (C') (4)·(5)	(7) Expected Benefits Minus Costs (B'-C') (3) - (6)
Do Not Commit Crime	$ 0	0	$ 0	$ 0	0	$ 0	$ 0
Commit Crime	$200	.99	$198	$10,000	.01	$100	$+98

Table 8–2
Deciding Whether to Commit a Crime with Monetary and Non-Monetary Goals

GOALS / DECISIONS	Probability of arrest, conviction and imprisonment	BENEFITS				COSTS				SUMS
		Dollars		Gang Prestige		Years in Jail		Missed Opportunities		
		Raw Score ($)	Expected Value	Raw Score (1-5)	Expected Value	Raw Score (Yrs.)	Expected Value	Raw Score (0-10)	Expected Value	
Rob the Store	.10	+$200	$180	+4	+3.6	-3 yrs	-.30 yrs	-2	-.20	
Do not Rob the Store	0	0	0	0	0	0	0	0	0	0

NOTES:
1. The summation question is simply whether or not the benefits exceed the costs in each row.
2. The expected value is calculated by multiplying the raw score by the probability in the benefits columns, and by the complement of the probability in the costs columns.
3. In a go/no-go decision, the no-go alternative could be considered as having all zeros for raw scores, or as having the same raw scores as the go decision but opposite in sign.
4. For most people who rob stores, these benefits do outweigh the costs.
5. The purpose of the table is to stimulate ideas for reducing store robberies (or other socially undesired behavior) by:
   (1) Decreasing the probability of the benefits being received
   (2) Increasing the probability of the costs being imposed
   (3) Decreasing the benefits of the undesired behavior
   (4) Increasing the costs of the undesired behavior
6. One can also reduce undesired behavior by structuring situations so that people are not so likely to be faced with the decision to commit or not commit a wrong. That can be facilitated in the crime-reduction field by gun control, anti-crime architecture, and especially internalized consciences.

Table 8–3
Plaintiff Suing for Damages with a Percentage Fee

GOALS / OPTIONS	BENEFIT ITEMS					COST ITEMS			NET ITEMS		
	(1) Average Damages If One Gets Them	(2) Probability of Receiving Damages	(3) Average Damages or Expected Value (1) x (2)	(4) Percentage Fee	(5) Total Benefits (3) x (4)	(6) Number of Hours	(7) Hourly Cost	(8) Total Costs (6) x (7)	(9) Lawyer B/C (5)/(8)	(10) Lawyer B-C (5) - (8)	(11) Plaintiff B-C (3) x [1.00-(4)]
Reject the Case	$0	$0	$0	0	$0	0	$0	$0	---	$0	$0
Accept a Settlement Predicted	$4,000	.80	$3,200	.20	$640	10	$30	$300	2.13	$460	$2,560
Accept a Settlement Offered	$5,000	1.00	$5,000	.20	$1,000	10	$30	$300	3.33	$700	$4,000
Go to Trial	$10,000	.60	$6,000	.40	$2,400	25	$60	$1,500	1.60	$900	$3,600

Note that the above data can be used to illustrate among other things:

Any payoff arrangement, by just ignoring how the total benefits are calculated.

Either a plaintiff or a defendant perspective, by noting that the benefits to the plaintiff in a damage case are costs to the defendant.

B-C versus B/C, as criteria for choosing among alternatives.

Working with non-monetary benefits, if the dollar benefits are considered as being days in jail.

Missing information, by assuming we do not know the benefits, the costs, or one or more other relevant items in the table.

Multiple alternatives, by separating trials into bench and jury trials, or by considering this an allocation problem for allocating $500 to two activities that are not mutually exclusive.

Time discounting, since the trial benefits may take "t" years to receive, which means they need to be multiplied or discounted by $1/(1+r)^t$, where r is the interest rate minus the inflation rate.

NOTES

1. On threshold analysis in general, see "Sensitivity Analysis," in Bruce Baird, *Introduction to Decision Analysis* (Boston: Duxbury, 1978), pp. 415–445; "Break-Even Analysis," in E. Buffa and J. Dyer, *Management Science/Operations Research* (New York: Wiley, 1981), pp. 69–74; "Switching Values," in P. Dasgupta et al., *Guidelines for Project Evaluation* (New York: Unipub, 1972), pp. 250–259; "Benefit-Cost Analysis with Unknown Variables," in S. Nagel, ed., *Public Policy: Goals, Means, and Methods* (New York: St. Martin's, 1984); and idem, "Decision Making under Complete Ignorance," in Samuel Richmond, *Operations Research for Management Decisions* (New York: Ronald Press, 1968), pp. 535–540.

2. For further details concerning the contingent fee client, see F. Mackinnon, *Contingent Fees for Legal Services* (Chicago: Aldine, 1964); Kevin Clermont and John Currivan, "Improving on the Contingent Fee," *Cornell Law Review* 63 (1978):529; S. Nagel, "Attorney Time per Case: Finding an Optimum Level," *University of Florida Law Review* 32 (1980):424; and Murray Schwartz and Daniel Mitchell, "An Economic Analysis of the Contingent Fee in Personal Injury Litigation," *Stanford Law Review* 22 (1970):1125.

3. On conflicting-choice decisions in the context of choosing among cases, see "Allocating Resources among Court Cases by Legal Counsel," in S. Nagel and M. Neef, eds., *Decision Theory and the Legal Process* (Lexington, Mass.: Lexington-Heath, 1979), pp. 217–253; William Landes, "An Economic Analysis of the Courts," *Journal of Law and Economics* 14 (1971):61; and Brian Forst and Katherine Brosi, "A Theoretical and Empirical Analysis of the Prosecutor," *Journal of Legal Studies* 6 (1977):177.

4. For further details on deciding whether to accept a settlement or go to trial, see Laurence Ross, *Settled Out of Court* (Chicago: Aldine, 1970); Gordon Tullock, *The Logic of the Law* (New York: Basic Books, 1971), pp. 167–191; Judith Lachman and William McLauchlan, "Models of Plea Bargaining," in S. Nagel, ed., *Modeling the Criminal Justice System* (Beverly Hills, Calif.: Sage, 1977), pp. 145–158; A. Friedman, "An Analysis of Settlement," *Stanford Law Review* 22 (1969):67; S. Nagel and M. Neef, "Plea Bargaining, Decision Theory, and Equilibrium Models," *Indiana Law Journal* 51 (1976):987–1024; 52 (1976):1–61; and Richard Posner, "An Economic Approach to Legal Procedure and Judicial Administration," *Journal of Legal Studies* 2 (1973):399.

5. For further details on deciding whether to release or to hold the defendant in jail before trial, see J. Goldkamp, *Two Classes of Accused: A Study of Bail and Detention in American Justice* (Cambridge, Mass.: Ballinger, 1979); W. Landes, "The Bail System: An Economic Approach," *Journal of Legal Studies* 2 (1973):79; and S. Nagel, M. Neef, and S. Schramm "Decision Theory and the Pretrial Release Decision in Criminal Cases," *University of Miami Law Review* 31 (1977):1433.

6. For further information on deciding how to increase legality in police searches, see S. Nagel, *Improving the Legal Process: Effects of Alternatives* (Lexington, Mass.: Lexington-Heath, 1975), 7–26; S. Schlesinger, *Exclusionary Injustice: The Problem of Illegally Obtained Evidence* (New York: Marcel Dekker, 1977); S. Nagel, "Testing the Effects of Excluding Illegally Seized Evidence," *Wisconsin Law Review* (1965):283; and D. Oaks, "Studying the Exclusionary Rule in Search and Seizure," *University of Chicago Law Review* 37 (1970):665.

9

Microcomputers, Risk Analysis, and Litigation Strategy

Litigation strategy mainly refers to deciding whether to go to trial or settle out of court. *Risk analysis* mainly refers to procedures for making meaningful decisions when one alternative provides a reasonably certain benefit or cost (like accepting a settlement) and another alternative provides a benefit or cost that is contingent on the occurrence of a probabilistic event (like going to trial). *Microcomputers* mainly refer to self-sufficient machines that are capable of making probabilistic and other useful calculations quickly and accurately and making them easy to understand.

This chapter covers three important aspects of litigation strategy. The first part is concerned with varieties of sensitivity analysis in civil and criminal cases. *Sensitivity analysis* refers to how the bottom-line conclusion of going to trial, accepting a settlement, or choosing another alternative is affected by changes in the inputs, which mainly relate to matters or criteria such as (1) the predicted damages, (2) the probability of receiving them, (3) the settlement offered, (4) the litigation costs, and (5) the settlement costs.

The second part deals with the use of decision matrices and microcomputers for analyzing litigation-strategy decisions, including sensitivity analysis. A decision matrix involves putting (1) the alternatives to be decided on the rows, (2) the criteria for deciding among them on the columns, and (3) the relations between the alternatives and the criteria in the cells.

The third part deals with the leading alternative to the decision-matrix approach to litigation strategy. That leading alternative is the decision-tree approach. A decision tree tends to involve only two alternatives. At least one of them branches into various paths toward various outcomes. Each path may have different probabilities. Each outcome may have a different monetary value.[1]

SENSITIVITY ANALYSIS AND LITIGATION STRATEGY

The chapter is built around two key civil and criminal examples that are embodied in the first two tables. The first table deals with damages litigation. It illustrates aspects of sensitivity analysis such as (1) the basic data needed, (2) variations possible on the basic data, (3) threshold values above or below which the best alternative changes, (4) insensitivity ranges within which change can occur without affecting the best alternative, (5) change slopes showing how much the gap changes between the first and second alternatives as a result of a one-unit change in each input, (6) multiple threshold values that involve more than one input changing simultaneously, (7) worst and best scenario analysis, and (8) the relevance of microcomputers to these forms of sensitivity analysis.[2]

The second table deals with criminal prosecution. It illustrates aspects of sensitivity analysis such as (1) incremental analysis, which involves comparing the gain of one alternative with the gain of a second alternative on each criterion; (2) percentaging analysis, which converts years, dollars, and other criteria into dimensionless percentages for comparison purposes; (3) criterion weights for indicating the relative importance of criteria measured on different dimensions; (4) convergence analysis, which indicates at what point each input becomes large enough to cause allocation percentages to reach a maximum; and (5) the relevance of microcomputers to these forms of sensitivity analysis.[3]

Damages Litigation

The Initial Analysis. Table 9–1 shows some data for illustrating basic varieties of sensitivity analysis. The problem is one of deciding whether to accept a settlement or go to trial in a damages case from the perspective of a plaintiff's attorney operating under a contingency fee arrangement. The criterion in choosing between those alternatives is to maximize average income minus average expenses. The data is hypothetical for illustrative methodological purposes.

The first cell shows that a settlement offer has been made that will generate $1,000 in income, figuring a 20 percent contingent fee on a $5,000 offer. The second cell reading down shows that going to trial will generate $2,400 in predicted income, figuring a 40 percent contingent fee on an average damage award of $6,000. The $6,000 can be determined by averaging similar previous

Table 9–1
Sensitivity Analysis for Plaintiff Litigation Strategy in a Damages Case

CRITERIA / ALTERNATIVES	Average Income (Y_1)			Average Expenses (Y_2)			Net Gain
	Cell #	Threshold and Range	Change Slope	Cell #	Threshold and Range	Change Slope	
Accept a Settlement (X_a)	a1	$1,000 ($1,200 up to -∞) ($1,200 down to $0)	-$1	a2	$300 ($100 up to ∞) ($100 down to $0)	+$1	$700
Go to Trial (X_b)	b1	$2,400 ($2,200 down to $0) ($2,200 up to ∞)	+$1	b2	$1,500 ($1,700 down to $0) ($1,700 up to ∞)	-$1	$900

NOTES:

1. The symbol in the upper lefthand corner of each main cell shows (1) the alternative under consideration by a lower-case letter, and (2) the criterion under consideration by an arabic numeral.
2. The number in the middle of each main cell shows the average or predicted value of the alternative on the criterion.
3. The number in the lower lefthand corner of each main cell shows the threshold value of the alternative on the criterion. That is the value to which the predicted value would have to change in order for the first and second place alternatives to be tied. The threshold value is always the predicted value plus or minus the profit gap which is the difference between the net gain of trial and the net gain of settlement.
4. The ranges at the bottom of each cell show how much the average or predicted value could change without affecting which alternative is in first place. The first range favors trial, and the second range favors settlement.
5. The number in the upper righthand corner of each main cell shows by how much the gap in net gain would change between the first and second place alternatives if the average or predicted value were to go up by one unit.
6. The numbers in the net gain column show the initial results before doing the sensitivity analyses. They indicate that going to trial is the better alternative by a $200 difference.

cases, including those in which no damages were awarded. A less simple alternative is to note that the prior cases in which damages were awarded averaged $10,000, and 60 percent of the cases resulted in damages awarded. The third cell on the expense column shows that the cost of a settlement would be $300, figuring 10 hours of time that is worth $30 an hour to the lawyer involved. The last cell shows that the cost of going to trial would be $1,500, figuring 25 hours of time that is worth $60 an hour to the lawyer involved.

With that hypothetical data, one can initially conclude that on the average it would be more profitable to go to trial than to accept a settlement in that particular case or that type of case. Going to trial yields a net gain of $900, whereas accepting a settlement yields a net gain of only $700. That conclusion should not be influenced by the initial offer of the defendant. In other words, if the plaintiff succeeds in getting the defendant to move from $1 to $1,000, the settlement should be just as strongly rejected as if the defendant had moved down from $1,100 to $1,000. An acceptable settlement is one that is better than going to trial, not necessarily one that involves hard-won concessions.

The Sensitivity Variations. The situation can be made more realistic, although more complicated, by adding a non-monetary criterion of attitude toward risk by the lawyer. It could be scored highly favorable (5 points), mildly favorable (4), neutral (3), mildly unfavorable (2), and highly unfavorable (1). Using non-monetary criteria will be the key variation in Table 9–2 dealing with criminal cases from a prosecution perspective. One might, however, note that one's attitude toward risk should logically become more unfavorable when the size of the settlement becomes greater. One then not only has the risk of losing the case but also the risk of losing a large settlement and the risk of suffering long-term regret as a result of being unlucky enough to have been on the losing side of an unaverage case with insufficient opportunity to average out over a large set of similar cases.

We could also add to the alternatives by referring to types of settlements and types of trials, such as a bench trial or a jury trial. We could also talk in terms of a different overall goal than maximizing lawyer income minus lawyer expense, such as client income minus client expense or some combination of the two goals. We could also vary the problem to cover cases with an hourly rate or a flat fee, rather than a contingency fee, and to cover cases from the perspective of defense counsel in damages litigation.

The threshold values in parentheses at the bottom of each cell involve applying a sensitivity analysis to Table 9–1. They show, for example, that the second-place alternative would come up to the net gain of the first-place alternative if any one of the following occurrences were to happen:

1. The settlement offer is increased from $5,000 to $6,000. Doing that increases the 20 percent settlement fee from $1,000 to $1,200 and increases the settlement net gain from $700 to $900.

2. The predicted damages from trial is decreased from $6,000 to $5,500. Doing that decreases the 40 percent damages fee from $2,400 to $2,200.
3. The settlement expense is decreased from $300 to $100 by decreasing the hours or the hourly cost.
4. The trial expense is increased from $1,500 to $1,700 by increasing the hours or the hourly cost.[4]

Along related lines, the insensitivity ranges in parentheses at the bottom of each cell also tell us that:

1. The settlement fee can range from $0 to $1,200 and have no effect on which alternative is in first place. This is referred to as the "insensitivity range of an alternative on a criterion."
2. The trial fee can range from $2,200 up to infinity and have no effect on which alternative is in first place. Knowing the insensitivity range is useful in informing one of the range of numbers that are not worth arguing over in terms of the bottom-line conclusion.
3. The settlement expense can range from $0 to $100 without affecting the outcome.
4. The trial expense can range from $1,700 to infinity without affecting the outcome of the trial alternative being in first place. That allows a lot of room for error in estimating the trial expense or in estimating any of the decisional inputs.

Change slopes are another informative measure in sensitivity analysis. They are the numbers in the upper right-hand corner of each of the main cells. They show how much the gap in net gain changes between the first-place and second-place alternatives when each input is increased by one unit. In this table, those numbers tell us that:

1. If the settlement fee increases by $1, the gap decreases by $1.
2. If the trial fee increases by $1, the gap increases by $1.
3. If the settlement expense increases by $1, the gap increases by $1.
4. If the trial expense increases by $1, the gap decreases by $1.

That kind of information can often be helpful in indicating what changes can have the most impact. In this simple situation, however, all of the one-unit changes have the same marginal rate of return, although in different directions. Change slopes can also show by how much the percentage of scarce resources allocated to an alternative will change as a result of a one-unit change in each input. Allocation problems are referred to in connection with Table 9–1.

Multiple threshold values are another form of sensitivity analysis. In Table 9–1 the threshold values for each input assume that the predicted values for the other inputs are held constant. One might, however, ask, what are the combined threshold values of two or more inputs such as trial income and trial expense? The answer to that example is any pair of numbers for b1 and b2 such that b1

Table 9–2
Sensitivity Analysis for Prosecution Litigation Strategy in a Criminal Case

CRITERIA / ALTERNATIVES	Average Sentence		Average Expense		Net Gain		
	Raw Score (Years)	Part/Whole %	Raw Score (Dollars)	Part/Whole %	Raw Score	Sentence P/W% Minus Expense P/W%	Average or Allocation %
	a1		a2				
Accept a Settlement	2 years	36%	$240	25%	NA	+11%	30½%
	(1.38)	(25%)	($346)	(36%)		(0%)	
	b1		b2				
Go to Trial	3½ years	64%	$720	75%	NA	-11%	69½%
	(4.12)	(75%)	($614)	(64%)		(0%)	
Difference	1½ years	28%	$480	50%	NA	22%	39%
Total (Whole)	5½ years	100%	$960	100%	NA	0%	100%

Table 9–2: continued

NOTES:

1. The number in the upper lefthand corner of each main cell shows the average or predicted value of the alternative on the criterion.
2. The percentage in the upper righthand corner of each main cell shows the part/whole percentage of each alternative on each criterion. It is calculated by dividing the predicted value by the total of the predicted values for the criterion.
3. The number in the lower lefthand corner of each main cell shows the threshold value of the alternative on the criterion. That is the value to which the predicted value would have to change in order for the first and second place alternatives to be tied.
4. The number in the lower righthand corner of each main cell shows the threshold part/whole percentage of the alternative on the criterion. It is calculated by dividing the threshold value by the total of the threshold values for the criterion.
5. The symbol "NA" means not applicable. One cannot meaningfully subtract costs measured in dollars from benefits measured in years, although one can meaningfully subtract dimensionless percentages.
6. The numbers in the column labeled "Sentence P/W% Minus Expense P/W%" show the initial results before doing the sensitivity analyses. They indicate that going to trial is the better alternative if the criteria have equal weight.
7. The numbers in the column labeled "Average or Allocation P/W%" indicate what percent of one's scarce resources should be allocated to the projects on rows 1 and 2, assuming being high on both criteria is desired.

minus b2 equals $700. Likewise, the combined threshold values for a1 and a2 are any pair of numbers such that a1 minus a2 equals $900. On a higher level of generality, one could talk in terms of the basic threshold or breakeven equation, which in this context is a1 minus a2 equals b1 minus b2. This means that the combined threshold value of a1 and b1 is any pair of numbers that will preserve the equality. Likewise, the combined threshold values of any three inputs like a2, b1, and b2 are any three numbers that will preserve the equality.

Worst and best scenario analysis is still another form of sensitivity analysis. It involves giving a range to each input value. One end of the range is the reasonable score that most disfavors a settlement, and the other end of the range is the reasonable score that most favors a settlement rather than a trial. With ranges like that for each of the four inputs, the net gain would also be a range. On the settlement row, the net gain might thus be a low of $400 and a high of $1,200. On the trial row, the net gain might be a low of $600 and a high of $1,600. Thus the midpoint on that settlement range would be $800, and the midpoint on the trial range would be $1,100. One could, therefore, conclude the following:

1. If the worst trial net gain is better than the best settlement net gain, going to trial is obviously better.
2. If the net-gain ranges overlap as here, it makes sense to choose the alternative that has the higher midpoint.
3. One does not normally look to which alternative has the highest maximum or the highest minimum in choosing the best alternative.

Criminal Prosecution

The Basic Problem and Data. Table 9–2 shows the basic data for illustrating sensitivity analysis as applied to prosecution litigation strategy in a criminal case. The problem here is one of deciding whether to accept a plea bargain or to go to trial from a prosecutor's perspective. The overall criterion is to maximize benefits minus costs, but here the benefits are non-monetary and the costs are monetary.

The first cell shows that the defense counsel, the public defender, or the defendant has offered to plead guilty to a recommended two-year sentence. The second cell reading down shows that going to trial will generate a predicted sentence of three and one-half years. The three and one-half years can be determined by averaging previous similar cases including those in which there was no sentence due to an acquittal, probation, or a suspended sentence. A less simple alternative is to note that the prior cases in which sentences were given averaged five years, and 70 percent of the cases resulted in convictions and sentences. The third cell on the expense column shows that the cost of a plea bargain would be $240, figuring 12 hours of time that is paid at $20 an hour to the assistant state's attorney. The last cell shows that the cost of going to trial would be $720, figuring 36 hours of time that is paid at $20 an hour.

Handling Non-Monetary Benefits. In Table 9–1 we were able to subtract the costs from the benefits because both were measured in dollars. In Table 9–2 that is not possible since the benefits are measured in years, and the costs are measured in dollars on each alternative. Incremental analysis is one way to approach this data. It involves determining the difference down each criterion rather than across each alternative. Doing this shows that the difference on sentencing is one and one-half years favoring trial, and the difference on expense is $480 favoring settlement. The problem can thus be treated as one of determining whether the prosecutor would prefer to obtain an extra one and one-half years in sentencing or $480 in expenses saved. If the one and one-half years is preferred, the prosecutor should go to trial. If the $480 is preferred, the prosecutor should accept the settlement.

That approach works well for dealing with criteria measured on different dimensions when there are only two criteria and two alternatives, as in Table 9–2. With more than two criteria, one will have more than two differences, some of which will favor the first alternative and some the second alternative. With more than two alternatives, one will have to compare alternative A with B. The winner then gets compared with C. The alternative that wins that comparison then gets compared with alternative D, and so on until one has gone through all of the alternatives. The last uneliminated alternative is the overall winner.

To avoid the complexities of incremental analysis with multiple criteria or multiple alternatives, one can use part/whole percentaging analysis to deal with the problem of criteria measured on different dimensions. That approach involves adding down each criterion to determine the total or whole, which is five and one-half years on sentencing and $960 on expenses. One then divides each score on each criterion by the total or whole for the criterion. Thus two years is converted into 36 percent of five and one-half years, and three and one-half years is converted into 64 percent. Likewise, $240 is converted into 25 percent of $960, and $720 is converted into 75 percent. One can now subtract the percentage cost from the percentage benefits, because percentages have a dimensionless character that years and dollars do not have. Making that subtraction yields a net gain of plus 11 percentage points for accepting a settlement, and minus 11 percentage points for going to trial. One can therefore conclude from this unweighted part/whole percentaging analysis that accepting a settlement is the better alternative.

The defect in this analysis is that it does not consider the relative importance of the two criteria. One way to deal with that is to go through the following steps:

1. Decide which criterion is the least important. Assign it a weight of 1. For example, assign expense a weight of 1.

2. Decide how many more times each other criterion is more important than the base criterion. For example, assign sentencing a weight of 2.
3. Multiply each part/whole percentage by the weight of the criterion to which the percentage pertains. If the criterion is negative like expense, consider the weight as being negative. This means 36 and 64 percent get multiplied by 2, and 25 and 75 percent get multiplied by −1.
4. Add the weighted part/whole percentages across each alternative. This means adding 72 percent to −25 percent for accepting settlement, which yields 47 percent. It also means adding 128 percent to −75 percent for trial, which yields 53 percent.
5. Observe which alternative has the highest or best weighted part/whole percentage. In the above example, trial is the best alternative with a weighted p/w% of 53 percent versus 47 percent for a settlement.[5]

The Sensitivity Variations. Each number in parenthesis in Table 9–2 is the threshold value for the alternative on the criterion to which the threshold value pertains. The threshold values in Table 9–2 can be interpreted as follows:

1. If the 2.0–year settlement were only 1.38 years, there would be a tie between settlement and trial, assuming equal weights for sentencing and expense.
2. If the 3.5–year-average trial sentence were 4.12 years, there would also be a tie assuming the other inputs are held constant.
3. If the $240 for settlement expense were $346, there would be a tie. Put differently, if the settlement expense were more than $346, trial would be the better alternative.
4. If the $720 for trial expense were $614, there would be a tie. Put differently, if the trial expense were less than $614, trial would be the better alternative.

Each of those threshold values can be instantly shown with the floppy-disk program called Policy/Goal Percentaging Analysis, mentioned at the end of the previous section on damages litigation. One can also determine the threshold values with a hand calculator in a simple situation like this with only two alternatives and two criteria. When we were dealing with criteria that were all measured on the same dimension, as in Table 9–1, the threshold equation was $a1 - a2 = b1 - b2$. When part/whole percentaging is involved, the threshold equation is $a1/(a1 + b1) - a2/(a1 + b1) = b1/(b1 + b2) - b2/(b1 + b2)$. Thus in either situation, if one wants to determine the threshold value for any input, one inserts the numerical values for the other inputs into the threshold equation and solves for the value of the input that is represented by a letter.

One can also determine a threshold weight by solving for W in a similar manner. Thus with the date from Table 9–2, the appropriate threshold equation would be $W(36) - (25) = W(64) - (75)$. That equation simplifies to $36W - 25 = 64W - 75$, and to $75 - 25 = 64W - 36W$, and to $50 = 28W$. Thus the threshold weight is 50/28 or 1.79, which rounds off to a threshold weight of 2. This means that if sentencing is less than twice as important as saving money, accept the settlement. If, however, sentencing is at least twice as important as saving money, go to trial. Table 9–2 could also show the insensitivity ranges and the change slopes, as the microcomputer program and Table 9–1 do. One might also note that the program is capable of doing an incremental analysis with any number of alternatives and criteria, but incremental analysis does not lend itself to sensitivity analysis the way that part/whole percentaging does.

Allocation and Sensitivity. Allocating scarce resources is another type of litigation strategy besides accepting a settlement versus going to trial in civil or criminal cases. We could add a Table 9–3 to illustrate allocation analysis and its special forms of sensitivity analysis. For the sake of simplicity, however, assume that the alternatives in Table 9–2 are two different cases or projects, rather than settlement versus trial. Also assume that both criteria are desirable goals rather than benefits and costs. If only the first criterion were being considered, one would allocate 36 percent of one's time, money, or other resources to the first case and 64 percent to the second case, assuming that 36 and 64 percent satisfy the minimum ethical or other constraints. If both criteria were being considered, one would average their respective part/whole percentages. That means allocating 30.5 percent of the resources to the first project and 69.5 percent of the resources to the second project, assuming both criteria are positive. If any criterion is negative, allocate in proportion to the sum of the weighted part/whole percentages, but give nothing but the minimum to any case or project that has a negative or losing sum.

Ordinary threshold analysis is not so applicable to an allocation problem because such an analysis tells us the value of each input at the point where the second-place alternative becomes the first-place alternative. That is useful in a problem designed to determine which alternative is best. In an allocation problem, however, the second place alternative (and even alternatives lower than second place) are generally allocated some portion of the scarce resources. In an allocation problem, one might want to know at what convergence value a disputed weight or other input becomes so large that the alternative which the input favors comes close to its maximum allocation (i.e., within 5 percentage points). For example, if the weight of sentencing were infinity or a huge number, the allocation would be 36 percent to Project 1 and 64 percent to Project 2 since the goal of high sentencing would totally dominate the other goals.

Convergence analysis tells us the weight (short of infinity) at which the allocation will be at least 31.0 and 69.0 percent, which is within 5 percentage points of 36.0 and 64.0 percent. One amazing aspect of convergence analysis is that often a weight of 2 is in effect the equivalent of infinity because it produces virtually the same effect. In the simple example of Table 9–2 a weight of 2 for sentencing does have that effect because a weight of 1 results in allocations of 30.5 and 69.5 percent. Thus moving up to a weight of 2 increases the 30.5 percent over 31.0 percent, and doing this decreases the 69.5 percent below 69.0 percent. The microcomputer program informs the user of the convergence value of each input, with convergence defined as being within 5 percentage points of the maximum or whatever definition the user wants.[6]

Conclusions on Sensitivity Analysis

From the analysis, one can conclude that it is useful in decision-making situations to know the following:

1. The goals one is seeking to achieve, the alternatives available, and the relations between goals and alternatives
2. The threshold value for each goal weight and relation, showing to what value those inputs would have to change to enable the second-place alternative to become the first-place alternative
3. The insensitivity ranges for each input, showing how much the input could range below or above the threshold without affecting the alternative that is in first place
4. The change slope for each input, showing how much the gap changes in the profitability of two alternatives as a result of a one-unit change in each input
5. Multiple threshold values, showing how much two or more inputs need to change to enable the second-place alternative to become the first-place alternative
6. Worst and best scenario analysis, showing for an alternative the worst it could do if all of the inputs were scored least favorably or showing the best it could do if all the inputs were scored most favorably
7. Threshold percentage values, showing for each input the value to which those inputs would have to change to enable the second-place alternative to become the first-place alternative when part/whole percentages are used to deal with goals being measured on different dimensions
8. Allocation change slopes for each input, showing how much the percentage allocation to each alternative would change if there were a one-unit change in each input
9. The convergence value for each input, showing at what value the input reaches a point where the alternative that it favors is within a certain number of percentage points from the maximum that the alternative could be allocated

MICROCOMPUTERS AS DECISION AIDS

Damages Cases

Criteria for Choosing between Settlement and Trial. The criteria for deciding between those alternatives include benefit items such as (1) the average damages in similar cases when damages are awarded, (2) the proportion of similar cases in which defendants are found liable, and (3) the proportion of the damages that goes to the attorney in a contingent fee relation. The criteria also include cost items such as (1) the number of hours likely to be consumed by each alternative and (2) the hourly cost for each alternative. Additional benefit and cost criteria could be added such as number of months to collect and the going interest rate in order to calculate the present value for damages to be awarded later versus a settlement offered now. Once one understands the handling of the criteria in Table 9–3, however, it is relatively easy to add additional criteria.

Within the cells of Table 9–3 are shown hypothetical figures indicating how each alternative scores on each criterion. Reading across the settlement row, an offer of $5,000 has been made. If the percentage fee is 20 percent, the total benefits or income will be $1,000. On the other row, going to trial means an average award of $10,000 if damages are awarded. Only about 60 out of 100 cases like this, however, result in damages being awarded. We therefore discount the $10,000 by 0.60 to obtain an expected value of $6,000. Doing that is the equivalent of stating that six out of ten cases like this would generate an average of $10,000 in damages apiece, and four out of ten cases would generate no damages. We then, in effect, sum those ten amounts to obtain $60,000 and divide by 10 to obtain an average of $6,000. We then apply a 40 percent fee to the average trial damages and obtain a predicted total income of $2,400.

Going to trial thus does better on predicted benefits than accepting a settlement. A settlement, however, does better on having lower costs. Settling would only involve a predicted 10 hours, valued at $30 an hour, for a total cost of $300. Going to trial would involve a predicted 25 hours, valued at $60 an hour, for a total cost of $1,500. If we subtract the predicted total cost from the predicted total income we obtain a $700 profit from accepting a settlement. The predicted profit from going to trial, however, is $900.

Those calculations are from the perspective of the benefits and the costs of the lawyer. Column 10 uses the benefits and costs of the client, which provide an interesting contrast. From the client's perspective, the total benefits from settling are 80 percent of the $5,000 in column 3. That $4,000 figure is the net item for the client in the context of the amounts shown in Table 9–3 since the client does not pay for the lawyer's hours in a contingency fee arrangement. Likewise, on the trial row, the total client benefits are 60 percent of the $6,000. That $3,600 net figure for going to trial is $400 less than the $4,000 for settling. This is in contrast to the lawyer's perspective whereby going to trial is the more profitable alternative.

Under such circumstances, the lawyer has an ethical obligation to put the client's interest ahead of the lawyer's interest. The ideal situation, however, is to make the settlement alternative (which is better for the client) also better for the lawyer or to make the trial alternative (which is better for the lawyer) also better for the client. Sensitivity analysis can be helpful in clarifying how that can be done. Such analysis is helpful even if the same alternative is better from both perspectives. If, for example, the trial alternative were better from both perspectives, the lawyer would go to trial although he might reconsider if (1) avoiding the psychological problems of going to trial is worth more than the $200 difference in profit or (2) some of the amounts in Table 9–3 are subject to change to make the settlement profit higher than the trial profit. That is where sensitivity analysis especially comes in.

The Nature of Tie-Causing Values. Table 9–4 shows the tie-causing values

Table 9–3
Data for Illustrating Microcomputer Analysis Applied to a Damages Case

GOALS / OPTIONS	BENEFIT ITEMS					COST ITEMS			NET ITEMS	
	(1) Average Damages If One Gets Them	(2) Probability of Receiving Damages	(3) Average Damages or Expected Value (1) x (2)	(4) Percentage Fee	(5) Total Benefits (3) x (4)	(6) Number of Hours	(7) Hourly Cost	(8) Total Costs (6) x (7)	(9) Lawyer B-C (5) - (8)	(10) Client (3) x [1 - (4)]
Settle	$5,000	1.00	$5,000	.20	$1,000	10	$30	$300	$700	$4,000
Go to Trial	$10,000	.60	$6,000	.40	$2,400	25	$60	$1,500	$900	$3,600

Note that the above data can be used to illustrate among other things:

1. Any payoff arrangement, by just ignoring how the total benefits are calculated.
2. Either a plaintiff or a defendant perspective, by noting that the benefits to the plaintiff in a damage case are costs to the defendant.
3. B-C versus B/C, as criteria for choosing among alternatives.
4. Working with non-monetary benefits, if the dollar benefits are considered as being days in jail.
5. Missing Information, by assuming we do <u>not</u> know the benefits, the costs, or one or more other relevant items in the table.
6. Multiple alternatives, by separating trials into bench and jury trials, or by considering this an allocation problem for allocating $500 to two activities that are not mutually exclusive.
7. Time discounting, since the trial benefits may take "t" years to receive, which means they need to be multiplied or discounted by $1/(1+r)^t$, where r is the interest rate minus the inflation rate.

Table 9–4
Tie-Causing Values in the Damages Case from the Lawyer's Perspective

GOALS / OPTIONS	BENEFIT ITEMS					COST ITEMS			NET ITEMS
	(1) Average Damages If One Gets Them	(2) Probability of Receiving Damages	(3) Average Damages or Expected Value	(4) Percentage Fee	(5) Total Benefits	(6) Number of Hours	(7) Hourly Cost	(8) Total Costs	(9) Lawyer B-C
Settle	$6,000	1.20	$6,000	24%	$1,200	3.33	$10	$ 100	$900
Go to Trial	$9,167	.55	$6,500	37%	$2,200	28.33	$68	$1,700	$700

NOTE:

1. If any information item in Table 9-3 changes to its tie-causing value in Table 9-4 then the profit from settling will rise from $700 to $900, or the profit from going to trial will drop from $900 to $700.

for each information item in the Table 9–3 analysis. Determining the tie-causing values is the essence of sensitivity analysis. For example, if the settlement offer can be raised from $5,000 to $6,000, there would be a tie between the new profit figures of settlement and trial. This is so because a 20 percent fee applied to $6,000 would generate total income of $1,200. If we subtract the $300 in costs from the $1,200 in income, we get $900, which is the trial profit figure. Thus any settlement offer greater than $6,000 would make settlement more profitable than going to trial assuming (1) the other figures in Table 9–3 remain the same, and (2) those figures are reasonably accurate as known by attorneys who are knowledgeable about the specific kind of damages case that is being considered.

One could check to see that changing any of the amounts in Table 9–3 to any of the amounts in Table 9–4 will result in either (1) raising the settlement profit from $700 to $900 or (2) lowering the trial profit from $900 to $700. For example, suppose that the number of hours involved in going to trial were wrongly estimated at 25.00 when they were really about 28.33. Multiplying $60 an hour by 28.33 gives a total cost of $1,700. That total cost is $200 more than the original total cost of $1,500. The $900 profit from going to trial would thus drop to $700. This means that if going to trial were to consume more than 28.33 hours, it would be better to accept the settlement.

Table 9–5 shows the tie-causing values from the client's perspective. Each figure in the second row of that table shows what it would take to improve the trial alternative to make it as desirable from the client's perspective as the settlement alternative. For example, if the client is offered a 0.33 contingency fee arrangement, rather than a 0.40 arrangement, going to trial would generate for the client the same $4,000 in net profit. This is so because if the percentage fee is 0.33, the client gets 0.67 of the $6,000 expected value, which means the client on the average gets $4,000. Lowering the trial percentage fee from 0.40 to 0.33, however, would then cause settlement to be the more profitable alternative for the lawyer. A better effect would occur if the lawyer can improve the trial alternative sufficiently so that the average damages when awarded are $11,111 rather than $10,000, since $11,111 times a 0.60 probability times the complement of a 0.40 percentage fee is also $4,000. Likewise, raising the probability of receiving damages to 0.67 would generate an expected value (on the $10,000 base) of $6,667, and 60 percent of that is $4,000.

Thus by looking at data such as that shown in Tables 9–4 and 9–5 the lawyer can see what it would take to make a settlement more attractive than going to trial from the lawyer's perspective. If the lawyer can succeed in improving the settlement offer to $6,000, both the lawyer and the client would be better off with that alternative. Likewise, if the lawyer can succeed in improving the trial damages to $11,111, both the lawyer and the client would be better off with that alternative. This kind of sensitivity analysis does help clarify what it would take to bring the second-place alternative up to first-place and, additionally, what it would take to reconcile what otherwise might be a conflict of interest.

Table 9–5
Tie-Causing Values in the Damages Case from the Client's Perspective

GOALS / OPTIONS	BENEFIT ITEMS					COST ITEMS			NET ITEMS
	(1) Average Damages If One Gets Them	(2) Probability of Receiv-ing Damages	(3) Average Damages or Expected Value	(4) Percentage Fee	(5) Total Benefits	(6) Number of Hours	(7) Hourly Cost	(8) Total Costs	(9) Client B-C
Settle	$4,500	.90	$4,500	28%	$3,600	--	--	--	$3,600
Go to Trial	$11,111	.67	$6,667	33%	$4,000	--	--	--	$4,000

NOTE:

1. If any information item in Table 9-3 changes to its tie-causing value in Table 9-5 then the profit from settling will drop from $4,000 to $3,600, or the profit from going to trial will rise from $3,600 to $4,000.

Solving for Tie-Causing Values. All of the amounts in Table 9–4 can be calculated by using simple high school algebra. To do this we need to express the nine criteria in algebraic symbols that could consist of the following:

1. D = average damages if one gets them
2. P = probability of receiving damages or expected value
3. PD = average damages or expected value
4. F = percentage fee
5. FPD = total benefits
6. H = number of hours
7. C = cost per hour
8. HC = total cost
9. FPD − HC = benefits minus costs

We also need to recognize that at the breakeven point, FPD − HC of settling equals FPD − HC of going to trial. Thus to solve for any one of the 18 numbers in Table 9–4 one inserts the estimated values from Table 9–1 for all of the information items except the one for which a tie-causing value is being calculated. For example, if we want to know the tie-causing value of the settlement offer, we solve the equation (D)(1.00)(0.20) − (10)($30) = ($10,000)(0.60)(0.40) − (25)($60). That equation simplifies to (D)(0.20) − $300 = $900. Using the methods of high school algebra, D = ($1,200)/(0.20) = $6,000.

The algebra is even easier for calculating the tie-causing values in Table 9–5 from the client's perspective. The threshold equation is then PD times 1 − F of settling set equal to PD times 1 − F of going to trial. Thus to determine any figure in Table 9–5 each of the variables gets a turn at being the unknown variable to be solved when known or given amounts are inserted for the other variables.

Dealing with Two or More Tie-Causing Values. Tables 9–4 and 9–5 show the tie-causing value for each information item if all of the other information items are held constant at their original values in Table 9–3. Suppose, however, that one wants to know what combinations of D and P will generate a tie between trial and settlement. One could change the question to ask for the tie-causing value of DP, which is $6,500. The answer to the original question, however, is that there are an infinite number of combinations of D and P that generate a tie between settlement and trial. They include $9,167 and 0.60, $10,000 and 0.55, and numerous combinations in between. The fully developed microcomputer program will show all of those combinations as a curve on a graph, with the damages on the vertical axis and the probability of victory on the horizontal axis. One can then decide whether the predicted combination of P and D is likely to be above that tie-causing curve, just as one can decide whether a predicted value is likely to be above or below a tie-causing value in Table 9–4 or 9–5.

The analysis can also be extended to three values by thinking in terms of a tie-causing band across the graph, rather than just a curve, provided that one can indicate a minimum and maximum value for each variable. It is even possible to work with more than three values simultaneously if necessary.

Variations on the Basic Ideas. There are a number of variations on the basic ideas shown in Tables 9–3, 9–4, and 9–5 concerning fee-paying arrangements, a defense perspective, and the introduction of non-monetary criteria. On fee-paying arrangements, Tables 9–3 and 9–4 involve a percentage fee. If a case involves an hourly fee, the total benefits from the lawyer's perspective equal the number of hours multiplied by the hourly fee. If the case involves a flat fee, the total benefits equal the flat fee. From the client's perspective, the benefits minus costs with an hourly fee become PD minus the number of hours multiplied by the hourly fee. If the case involves a flat fee, the net item becomes PD minus the flat fee.

The tables show the perspective of a plaintiff. From a defense perspective, damages and the probability of paying them represent additional cost items rather than benefit items. Thus the defense perspective wants to choose the alternative between settlement and going to trial that will provide the lower total costs where total costs are PD plus the total hourly cost. There is normally no conflict between the defense attorney in damages cases and his or her client. The defense attorney is normally a salaried employee of the client, and they both are interested in keeping down the damages awarded and the total hourly cost.

One could add a non-monetary criterion to Table 9–3 called "psychological case enjoyment." It could be scored on a 1–5 scale, where 5 = great pleasure, 4 = mild pleasure, 3 = no pleasure, 2 = mild displeasure, and 1 = great displeasure. For a lawyer who greatly enjoys trials, going to trial might receive a 5 and settling a 3. A non-monetary variable like that can be handled through part/whole percentaging, the same as the non-monetary variable of average prison sentence. That is a criterion in criminal cases to which we now turn.

Criminal Cases

Criteria for Choosing between Settlement and Trial. Table 9–6 shows relevant data for a criminal case. The alternatives are settle or go to trial. The criteria for deciding between those alternatives include benefit items such as (1) the average sentence in similar cases if defendants are found guilty, (2) the proportion of similar cases in which defendants are found guilty, and (3) the average sentence awarded, which is discounted or multiplied by the probability of a sentence being received. The criteria also include cost items such as (1) the number of hours likely to be consumed by each alternative, (2) the hourly cost for each alternative, and (3) the hours multiplied by the hourly cost.

Within the cells of Table 9–6 are shown hypothetical figures indicating how each alternative scores on each criterion. Reading across the settlement row, an offer to plead guilty with a two-year sentence has been made. The number of hours to consummate the settlement or plea bargain would be 12 hours at $20

Table 9–6
Data for Illustrating Microcomputer Analysis Applied to a Criminal Case

GOALS / OPTIONS	BENEFIT ITEMS			COST ITEMS			NET ITEMS	
	(1) Average Sentence if Awarded (Years)	(2) Probability of a Sentence	(3) Average Sentence or Expected Value (Years) (1) x (2)	(4) Number of Hours	(5) Cost Per Hour	(6) Total Hourly Cost (4) x (6)	(7) Prosecutor %B-%C (3) - (6)	(8) Victim %B-%C (3)
Settle	2	1.00	2.00 (36%)	12	$20	$240 (25%)	? (+11%)	2.00
Go to Trial	5	.70	3.50 (64%)	36	$20	$720 (75%)	? (-11%)	3.50
Increment (Difference)			+1.50			+$480		+1.50
Whole (Sum)			5.50 (100%)			$960 (100%)		

Threshold Raw Score Weight:

B-C of Settle = B-C of Trial
W(2.00) - $240 = W(3.50) - $720
$720 - $240 = 3.5W - 2W
$480 = 1.5W
W* = $480/1.5 = $320/1 year

Threshold Percentage Weight:

B-C of Settle = B-C of Trial
W(2.00/5.30) - ($240/$960) = W(3.50/5.30) - ($720/$960)
W(36%) - (25%) = W(64%) - (75%)
75% - 25% = 64%W - 36%W
50% = 28%W
W* = 50%/28% = 1.79
rounded to 2

an hour for a salaried assistant state's attorney, for a total cost of $240. Reading across the trial row, cases of this type average 5–year sentences where the defendant is found guilty, which is 70 percent of the time. The average or expected value is thus 3.5 years. The number of hours (if the case has to be tried) would be about 36 at $20 an hour for a total cost of $720.

The client of the prosecutor is the state. There normally is no conflict between the prosecutor and the state. The prosecutor is a salaried employee of the state, and they are both interested in obtaining good convictions at low cost. The last column of Table 9–6 shows the benefits minus costs from the victim's perspectives, which may conflict with the prosecutor's perspective. The victim is generally only interested in increasing the sentence length and not especially in reducing the hourly cost.

Handling Criteria Measured on Different Dimensions. Unlike Table 9–3 where $300 in cost can be subtracted from $1,000 in benefits, there is no way of directly subtracting $240 in cost from 2.0 years in benefits. There is likewise no direct way of subtracting $720 in cost from 3.5 years in benefits on the trial row. One can, however, meaningfully subtract downward and note that the increment of trial over settlement is 1.5 years in benefits and $480 in costs. The problem thus could reduce to answering the question of which is more desired by the prosecutor, an incremental 1.5 years or a saving of $480. If 1.5 years is preferred, go to trial since doing so gives the incremental 1.5 years. If saving $480 is preferred, settle since doing so saves the $480.

That approach of comparing increments becomes too complicated when multiple options and/or multiple benefits are involved. It is also too complicated to allow for sensitivity analysis for the calculation of tie-causing values. A generally better approach is to compare the 2.0 years with the 3.5 years by expressing both of them as percentages of their sum, as is shown on column 3. Likewise, one can compare the $240 with the $720 by expressing them as percentages of their sum, as is shown in column 6. One can then subtract the percentage costs from the percentage benefits to obtain the difference shown in column 7. Differences and sums are shown only for the total-benefits column and the total-cost column because the object is to choose the alternative that is better on benefits minus costs rather than better on sentence length, probability of victory, number of hours, or cost per hour.

Column 7 indicates that if the sentence is given equal weight or importance along with the total hourly cost, settling is the better alternative. Its net benefits are a positive 11 percentage points, in contrast to a negative 11 percentage points for going to trial. If, however, one considers that the sentence obtained is at least twice as important as total hourly cost, going to trial is the better alternative. This is shown by the algebra in the lower-right corner of Table 9–5. One could also state that if one would rather achieve an extra year of sentencing than save the prosecutor's office $320, going to trial is the better alternative. This is shown by the algebra in the lower-left corner. That information, however, is the same as asking which is preferred between an extra 1.5 years and an extra $480.

Tie-Causing Values. Table 9–7 shows the tie-causing values for all of the information items in Table 9–6. For example, if the settlement offer goes down from 2.00 years to 1.17 years, there would be a tie. This is so because 1.17 years as a settlement offer in Table 9–7 plus 3.5 years as an average trial result in Table 9–6 adds to 4.67. If those numbers are converted into part/whole percentages, the 1.17 becomes 25 percent of 4.67, and the 3.5 becomes 75 percent of 4.67. If we then add 25 percent as a benefit score to 25 percent as a cost score, settling receives a %B − %C score of zero percent. Likewise, if we add 75 percent as a trial-benefits score to 75 percent as a trial-cost score, we also receive a %B − %C score for going to trial of zero percent. This means that any offer below 1.17 years should be rejected if one gives equal weight to the sentence obtained and the total hourly cost.

One could likewise determine that any of the numbers shown in Table 9–7 (if substituted for the corresponding numbers in Table 9–6) will generate a tie between settling and going to trial on the bottom line of %B − %C. That is the bottom line in this context (rather than $B − $C), since the benefits and costs are measured on the different dimensions of years and dollars. All of the amounts shown in Table 9–7 can be calculated by the algebraic approach shown in the lower-right corner of Table 9–6 which is analogous to the algebraic approach used for calculating the tie-causing values in Table 9–4. Fortunately, the Policy/Goal Percentaging microcomputer program is now available. It can calculate the tie-causing values for any table like Table 9–6 with equal or unequal weights for each benefit goal and each cost goal. One can also by hand or with the microcomputer program determine the tie-causing values (1) from a defense perspective when sentences are additional costs rather than benefits, (2) from a victim perspective when B − C is determined just by the sentence obtained as a benefit, and (3) from a defendant perspective when B − C is determined just by the sentence received as a cost.[7]

Using a Microcomputer for the Sensitivity Analysis

Tables 9–8 and 9–9 show some output for the newly developed personal computer program that can handle most of the sensitivity analysis described in Tables 9–1 through 9–7.

Table 9–8A shows that a jury trial has a higher expected value by 200 monetary units for the lawyer. The four rows of Table 9–8B show that a tie between the alternatives would occur:

1. If the $10,000 predicted damages were only $9,167 or if the combination of the victory probability and the percentage fee were to drop from 0.24 to 0.22
2. If the $5,000 settlement offer were to rise to $6,000 or if the 0.20 percentage fee were to rise to 0.24
3. If the $60 hourly litigation cost were $68 or if the 25 hours were 28 hours

Table 9–7
Tie-Causing Values in the Criminal Case from the Prosecutor's Perspective

GOALS / OPTIONS	BENEFIT ITEMS			COST ITEMS			NET ITEMS
	(1) Average Sentence if Awarded (Years)	(2) Probability of a Sentence	(3) Average Sentence or Expected Value (Years)	(4) Number of Hours	(5) Cost Per Hour	(6) Total Hourly Cost	(7) Prosecutor %B-%C
Settle	1.17 Years	.58 Probability	1.17 Years	20.25 Hours	$32.75	$405.00	0%
Go to Trial	8.57 Years	1.20 Probability	6.00 Years	21.33 Hours	$11.85	$426.67	0%

NOTES:

1. If any information item in Table 9-6 changes to its tie-causing value in Table 9-7, then the %B-%C (from settling) will drop from +11% to 0%, and the %B-%C (from going to trial) will rise from -11% to 0%.

Table 9–8
Using a Microcomputer for the Civil Cases

A. THE BOTTOM LINE FOR THE LAWYER

Alternative	Combined Rawscores
2JURY	900.00
3SETTLE	700.00

B. TIE-CAUSING VALUES FOR THE LAWYER

	THRESHOLD ANALYSIS		
	JURY	SETTLE	Weight
JURY DAMAGES	9166.67		0.220
SETTLEMENT		6000.00	0.240
LITIGATION COSTS	68.00		-28.333
SETTLEMENT COSTS		10.00	-3.333

C. THE BOTTOM LINE FOR THE CLIENT

Alternative	Combined Rawscores
2JURY	3600.00
3SETTLE	4000.00

D. TIE-CAUSING VALUES FOR THE CLIENT

	THRESHOLD ANALYSIS		
	JURY	SETTLE	Weight
JURY DAMAGES	11111.11		0.400
SETTLEMENT		4500.00	0.720

NOTES:

1. The relations between the main tables in the chapter and the sub-tables of Table 9-8 are:

   (1) Table 9-8A corresponds to the bottom line of Table 9-3 for the lawyer.
   (2) Table 9-8B corresponds to the main threshold values of Table 9-5.
   (3) Table 9-8C corresponds to the bottom line of Table 9-3 for the client.
   (4) Table 9-8D corresponds to the main threshold values of Table 9-5.

2. Irrelevant information has been removed from Table 9-8 such as indicating that a $700 settlement constitutes 44% of the total of the damages awarded ($900) plus the settlement ($700). Likewise if one settles, there can be no jury damages or litigation costs, and if one goes through a jury trial, there can be no settlement or settlement costs. Nothing, however, has been added to the above computer displays.

Table 9–9
Using a Microcomputer for the Criminal Cases

A. THE BOTTOM LINE FOR THE PROSECUTOR

Alternative	Combined W P/W
1SETTLE	11.36
2TRIAL	-11.36

B. TIE-CAUSING VALUES FOR THE PROSECUTOR

THRESHOLD ANALYSIS

	SETTLE	TRIAL	Weight
AVG. SENTENCE	1.17	6.00	1.833
TOTAL COST	411.43	420.00	-0.545

NOTES:

1. The relations between the main tables in the chapter and the sub-tables of Table 9-9 are:
   (1) Table 9-9A corresponds to the bottom line of Table 9-6.
   (2) Table 9-9B corresponds to the main threshold values of Table 9-7.
2. Irrelevant information has been removed from Table 9-9 such as indicating that a combined weighted part/whole percentage of +11% is 50% of the sum of the two combined absolute percentages.

4. If the $30 hourly settlement cost were only $10 or if the 10 hours were only 3 hours

Table 9–8C shows that a jury trial has a lower expected value by 400 monetary units for the client. The two rows of Table 9–8D show that a tie between the alternatives would occur:

1. If the jury damages were to rise from $10,000 to $11,111 or if the combination of the victory probability and the percentage fee were to rise from 0.24 to 0.40
2. If the $5,000 settlement offer were to go down to $4,500

Table 9–9A shows that a settlement has a higher value than going to trial for the prosecutor. The two rows of Table 9–9B show that a tie between the two alternatives would occur:

1. If the settlement offer were to drop from 2.00 years to 1.17 years or if the trial sentence were to rise from 5.0 to 6.0 years. The top row also shows that if sentencing

were considered almost twice as important as saving litigation costs there would be a tie.

2. If the settlement cost were to rise from $240 to $411 or if the trial cost were to fall from $720 to $420. Likewise, if saving litigation costs were only considered about half as important as sentencing there would be a tie.

To obtain the bottom-line values for the lawyer in Table 9–8A one inserts into the computer for the trial alternative (1) $10,000 in trial damages weighted by 0.60 times 0.40 and (2) $60 in litigation cost per hour weighted by 25 hours. For the settlement alternative one inserts (1) $5,000 in settlement amount weighted by 0.20 and (2) $30 in settlement cost per hour weighted by 10 hours. To obtain the bottom-line values for the client in Table 9–8C one inserts for the trial alternative $10,000 in trial damages weighted by 0.60 times 0.60. Likewise, one inserts for the settlement alternative $5,000 in settlement value weighted by 0.80. Once those data have been inserted, asking the computer for a sensitivity analysis will yield the tie-causing values of Table 9–8A or 9–8D.

To obtain the bottom-line values for the prosecutor in Table 9–9A one inserts into the computer for the trial alternative (1) 5 years weighted by the 0.70 probability and (2) $20 in litigation cost per hour weighted by 36 hours. For the settlement alternative one inserts (1) 2 years weighted by the 1.00 probability and (2) $20 in litigation cost per hour weighted by 12 hours. Once those data have been inserted, asking the computer for a sensitivity analysis will yield the tie-causing values of Table 9–9B provided that one has previously indicated that part/whole percentaging should be used to deal with the multi-dimensionality of combining years and dollars.

Thus to obtain the initial results or bottom lines, one just has to remember that the probabilities or other multipliers are treated as weights on the dollar-award columns or the dollar-cost columns. This is a much easier method for inputting the information needed for the initial analysis than is the method of decision trees. The trees may look aesthetic, but they are much more complicated to communicate to the computer, and they are generally incapable of doing a comprehensive sensitivity analysis.[8]

Table 9–10
Any Case with an Hourly Rate

GOALS / OPTIONS	BENEFIT ITEMS			COST ITEMS			NET ITEMS			
	(1) Number of Hours	(2) Hourly Fee	(3) Total Fee (1) x (2)	(4) Number of Hours	(5) Hourly Cost	(6) Total Costs (4) x (5)	(7) Lawyer B-C (3) - (6)	(8) Average Judgment	(9) Plaintiff B-C (8) - (3)	(10) Defendant B-C 0-(8)-(3)
Reject the Case	$0	0	$0	$0	$0	$0	$0	$0	$0	$0
Accept a Settlement	10	$50	$500	10	$30	$300	$200	$5,000	$4,500	-$5,500
Go To Trial	30	$100	$3,000	30	$60	$1,800	$1,200	$6,000	$3,000	-$9,000

Column 8 comes from Column 3 of Table 9-3.

Table 9–11
Any Case with a Flat Fee

GOALS / OPTIONS	BENEFIT ITEMS	COST ITEMS			NET ITEMS			
	(1) Flat Fee	(2) Number of Hours	(3) Hourly Cost	(4) Total Cost (2) x (3)	(5) Lawyer B-C (1) - (4)	(6) Average Judgment	(7) Plaintiff B-C (6) - (1)	(8) Defendant B-C 0-(6)-(1)
Reject the Case	$0	0	0	0	$0	$0	$0	$0
Accept a Settlement	$600	10	$30	$300	$200	$5,000	$4,400	-$5,600
Go To Trial	$2,100	30	$60	$1,800	$200	$6,000	$3,900	-$8,100

Column 6 comes from Column 3 of Table 9-3.

Table 9–12
Damages Case for a Salaried Insurance Attorney

GOALS / OPTIONS	DAMAGE COST ITEMS			HOURLY COST ITEMS			NET ITEMS
	(1) Average Damages if Paid	(2) Probability of Paying Damages	(3) Average Damages or Expected Value (1) x (2)	(4) Number of Hours	(5) Hourly Cost	(6) Total Hourly Cost (4) x (5)	(7) Total Cost (3) + (6)
Accept a Settlement	$ 5,000	1.00	$ 5,000	8	$16	$128	$4,072
Go to Trial	$10,000	.60	$ 6,000	25	$16	$400	$6,400

Table 9–13
Suing in a Federal or State Court

CRITERIA / ALTERNATIVES	(1) Probability of Victory(P)	(2) Likely Damages(D)	(3) Expected Value (EV) (1)x(2)	(4) Years to Receive Damages(t)	(5) Present Value(PV) $(3)/1.06^{(4)}$
Suing in a Federal Court	.20	$15,000	$3,000	1 year	$2,830
Suing in a State Court	.40	10,000	4,000	2 years	3,560

NOTES:

1. The present value is calculated by dividing the expected value by 1.06 raised to the value of t, where t is the years to receive damages, and .06 is the interest rate minus the inflation rate.

2. Given these facts, one is better off suing in a State Court in this case, even though it will take twice as long for the damages to be awarded. That is more than offset though by the higher probability of victory after discounting the expected value for the extra time involved.

Table 9–14

Criminal Case for a Salaried Public Defender

GOALS / OPTIONS	SENTENCE COST ITEMS			HOURLY COST ITEMS			NET ITEMS	
	(1) Average Sentence if Awarded (Years)	(2) Probability of a Sentence	(3) Average Sentence or Expected Value (Years) (1) x (2)	(4) Number of Hours	(5) Cost Per Hour	(6) Hourly Cost (4) x (5)	(7) Public Defender $C_1 + C_2$ (3) + (6)	(8) Defendant $C_1 + C_2$ (3)
Accept a Settlement Offer	3	1.00	3.00 (45%)	5	$18	$ 90 (14%)	? (59%)	3.00
Go to Trial	6	.60	3.60 (55%)	30	$18	$540 (86%)	? (141%)	3.60
Increment	3	-.40	.60	20	$ 0	$450		.60
Whole	9	1.60	6.60 (100%)	40	$36	$630 (100%)	(0%)	

1. NOTES: From a defender's viewpoint, long sentences and high hourly costs are both undesirable. They are both cost items.
2. Therefore, the best alternative or option is the one that produces the lowest total cost when those two cost items are added in their part/whole percentaging form. Settling is thus the better alternative here because it has the lowest sum for its part/whole percentages.
3. There is, however, no need to do part/whole percentaging in this specific example because accepting a settlement scores better on both sentence and hourly cost. It therefore is the winner regardless what transformations one uses to deal with the multi-dimensionality of years and dollars.
4. There is a tie-causing value for every relation score and for the weight of every criterion even when one alternative dominates another by being better on all the criteria, although the direction of the weight of a criterion may have to be changed in order for the second-place alternative to become the first-place alternative.

Figure 9–1
The Out-of-Court Civil-Settlement Picture

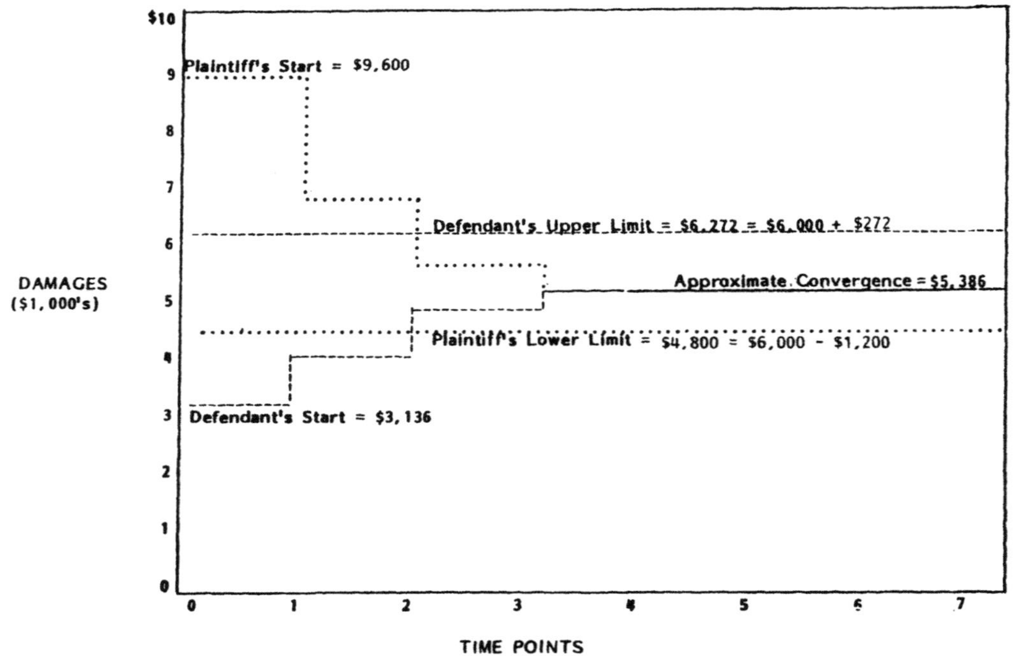

NOTES:

1. The $6,000 is the expected value of going to trial according to column 3 of Table 9-3 and Table 9-7 for both the plaintiff and defendant.
2. The $272 is the bonus that the defendant is willing to give to avoid litigation. It represents the incremental litigation cost which is $400 minus $128 from column 6 in Table 9-7.
3. The $1,200 is the discount which the plaintiff is willing to give to avoid litigation. It represents the incremental litigation cost which is $1,500 minus $300 from column 8 of Table 9-3.
4. The defendant's starting point involves taking approximately 50% of the defendant's upper limit. The plaintiff's starting point involves approximately doubling the plaintiff's lower limit.

Figure 9–2
The Plea-Bargaining Picture

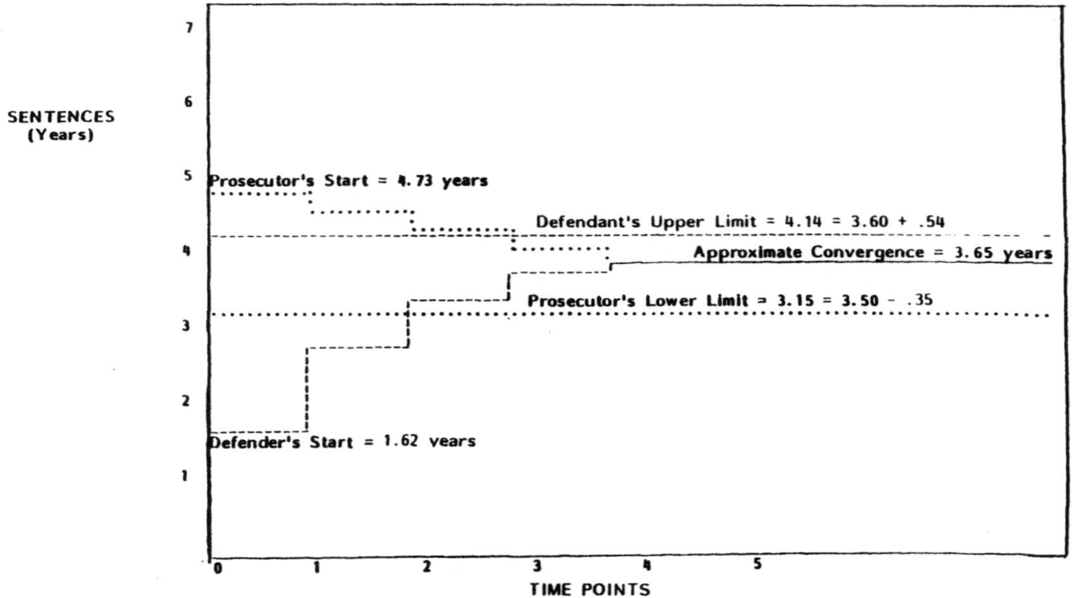

Notes:

1. The 3.60 is the expected value in years of going to trial for the public defender, according to column 3 of Table 9-10. The 3.50 is the expected value for the prosecutor of going to trial, according to column 3 of Table 9-9.
2. The .54 is the bonus that the defendant is willing to give to avoid litigation. It represents 15% of the expected value of 3.60.
3. The .35 is the discount that the prosecutor is willing to give to avoid litigation. It represents 10% of the expected value of 3.50.
4. The defendant's starting point involves taking approximately 40% of the defendant's upper limit. The prosecutor's starting point is approximately 150% of the prosecutor's lower limit.

NOTES

1. On systematic litigation strategy in general, see Gordon Tullock, *The Logic of the Law* (New York: Basic Books, 1971); Ronald Greenberg, "Quantitative Aspects of Legal Analysis," *Insurance Law Journal* (1976): 589–607; S. Nagel, *Applying Decision Science to Law Practice* (Philadelphia: American Law Institute-American Bar Association, 1984); and Chapter 7 of this book. On sensitivity analysis in general, see Carl Moore, *Profitable Applications of the Break-Even System* (Englewood Cliffs, N.J.: Prentice-Hall, 1971); and S. Nagel, "Unknown Variables," in *Public Policy: Goals, Means, and Methods* (New York: St. Martin's, 1984): 296–322.

2. On a decision analysis of damages litigation, see A. Friedman, "An Analysis of Settlement" *Stanford Law Review* 22 (1969): 67; Ronald Greenberg, "The Lawyer's Use of Quantitative Analysis in Settlement Negotiations," *Business Lawyer* 38 (1983): 1557–1587; and S. Nagel and M. Neef, "Out-of-Court Civil Settlements," in *Decision Theory and the Legal Process* (Lexington, Mass.: Lexington-Heath, 1979), pp. 141–146.

3. On a decision analysis of criminal prosecution, see Judith Lachman and William McLauchlan, "Models of Plea Bargaining" in S. Nagel, ed., *Modeling the Criminal Justice System* (Beverly Hills, Calif.: Sage, 1977), pp. 145–158; Richard Posner, "Civil and Criminal Procedures" in *Economic Analysis of Law* (Boston: Little, Brown, 1977), pp. 429–460; and S. Nagel and M. Neef, "The Two-Person Bargaining Situation: Plea Bargaining" in *Decision Theory and Legal Process* (Lexington, Mass.: Lexington-Heath, 1979), pp. 63–149.

4. For further detail on threshold analysis in the legal context, see Chapter 8 in this book.

5. For further details on dealing with non-monetary benefits and other multidimensional goals, see Thomas Saaty, *The Analytic Hierarchy Process: Planning, Priority Setting, and Resource Allocation* (New York: McGraw Hill, 1980); Ward Edwards and Robert Newman, *Multi-Attribute Evaluation* (Beverly Hills, Calif.: Sage, 1982); and S. Nagel, "Part/Whole Percentaging Analysis as a Useful Tool in Policy/Program Evaluation," *Evaluation and Program Planning* 8 (1987).

6. For further details on allocation analysis, see Claude McMillan, Jr., *Mathematical Programming: An Introduction to the Design and Application of Optimal Decision Machines* (New York: Wiley, 1970); Donald Shoup and Stephen Mehay, *Program Budgeting for Urban Police Services* (New York: Praeger, 1971); and S. Nagel, "Finding an Optimum Mix in Allocating Scarce Resources," in *Policy Evaluation: Making Optimum Decisions* (New York: Praeger, 1982), pp. 179–254.

7. For literature describing part/whole percentaging as a means of evaluating alternative decisions that are measured on different dimensions, see Nagel, *Public Policy: Goals, Means, and Methods,* pp. 343–354.

8. For literature describing the new microcomputer program for doing sensitivity analysis in litigation strategy, see Chapters 2 and 3 of this book. The microcomputer program can also calculate the present value for the trial damages, taking into consideration the length of predicted delay and the prevailing interest and inflation rates. The program can also deal with multiple probabilities of victory, but a single holistic or gestalt probability may be more meaningful than disaggregated probabilities that do not capture the total picture.

10

Decision Trees and Litigation Strategy

Joyce Kilmer in his famous poem said that "Only God can make a tree." He was, however, not talking about decision trees. God does not make decision trees for at least two reasons. First, decision trees are for people who think of case outcomes or events in terms of probabilities of occurring, such as 0.70, 1 in 4, or highly probable. Since God is an omniscient being, he thinks of events in terms of either happening or not happening, with nothing in between.

More important for our purposes, even if God did think probabilistically, he would probably not make decision trees to analyze probabilistic events. Since he is an omniscient being, he would use a more insightful tool similar to a policies/goals table, or a PG table. Such a table shows options on the rows, goals on the columns, relations between the options and the goals in the cells, and a bottom line at the right indicating which option is best on benefits minus costs. That is the subject of this chapter.

A DECISION TREE IN NEED OF BEING CUT DOWN

Figure 10–1 shows an impressive decision tree relevant to deciding whether to sue or not to sue. This tree contains two trunks labeled "Litigate" and "Drop

Figure 10–1
A Decision-Tree Approach to Deciding Whether to Sue or Not Sue

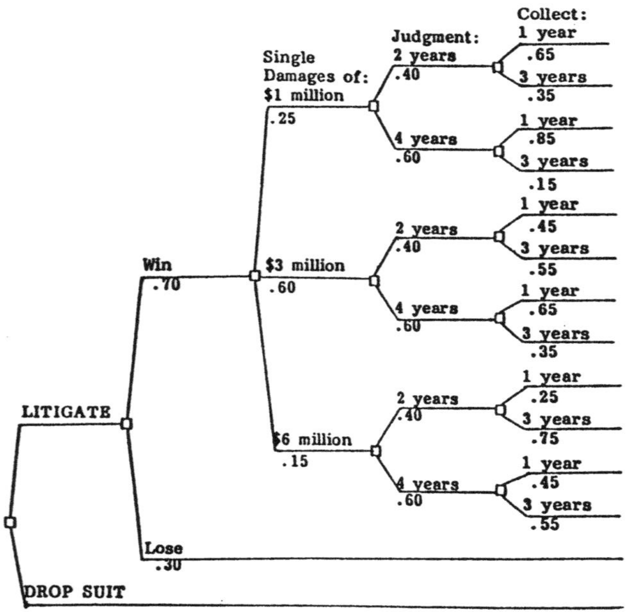

SCENARIO	PROBABILITY	PRESENT VALUE
1	4.6%	$ 2.0M
2	2.4%	$ 1.4
3	8.9%	$ 1.7
4	1.6%	$ 1.2
5	7.6%	$ 6.1
6	9.2%	$ 4.2
7	16.4%	$ 5.0
8	8.8%	$ 3.5
9	1.0%	$12.2
10	3.2%	$ 8.4
11	2.8%	$10.1
12	3.5%	$ 6.9
13	30.0%	$ 0.0
	100.0%	
		Save $ 1.0

NOTES:

1. The above figure is based on the recommendations of Marc Victor as to how to draw a decision tree. See Marc Victor, "Litigation Risk Analysis" (Paper presented at ABA annual meeting, 1982). The above data, however, is purely hypothetical and not meant to reflect any specific case of Marc Victor's or anyone else.
2. The probability for each scenario is the product of the four probabilities along the decision-tree branches of the scenario. Thus, .046 equals .70 x .25 x .40 x .65.
3. The present value for each scenario is equal to 3 times the damages, multiplied by .90 for a 1-year collection (10% collection fee) and by .75 for a 3-year collection (25% collection fee). One then discounts or multiples that figure by $1/(1.10)^t$ where .10 is the discount rate, and t is the years of delay for judgment and collection. Thus, $2.0 equals $\$1 \times 3 \times .90 \times 1/(1.10)^3$.

Suit.'' The litigate trunk branches into win or lose. The win branch sub-branches into damages of \$1 million, \$3 million, and \$6 million. Each of those branches sub-branch into judgments within two or four years, and each of those sub-branches into collecting within one year or three years on the judgments. That adds up to 14 impressive branches or 14 scenarios.

To calculate the probability of any of the 14 scenarios, one multiplies the 4 probabilities along the decision tree branches of the scenario. For example, the 0.046 probability of the first scenario equals $0.70 \times 0.25 \times 0.40 \times 0.65$. To calculate the present value of any of the 14 scenarios, one multiplies 3 times the damages by 0.90 for a one-year collection (10 percent collection fee) and by 0.75 for a three-year collection (25 percent collection fee). One then discounts or multiplies that figure by $1/(1.10)^t$, where 0.10 is the discount rate, and t is the years of delay for judgment and collection. For example, the \$2.0 million of the first scenario equals $\$1 \times 3 \times 0.90 \times 1/(1.10)^3$.

USING THE WOOD OF THE SHAKY DECISION TREE TO MAKE A STURDY PG TABLE

Table 10–1 analyzes the same data from the perspective of averaging rather than probabilities and from the perspective of a PG table rather than a decision tree.

Advantages of the Averaging Approach

On the matter of averaging, one should note that people (including lawyers) have a great deal of difficulty working with probabilities. They do not, however, have much trouble understanding the related concept of an average. A lawyer can easily understand the idea of listing the damages awarded for ten cases (including cases in which no damages are awarded) and then dividing by 10 to get the average damages awarded, which may be \$3,200. That is easier than thinking that the damages awarded are \$4,000 in cases in which liability is found and that \$4,000 has to be discounted by 0.80 to arrive at an expected value of \$3,200. The 0.80 probability is especially confusing if the lawyer is irrelevantly told that such a probability represents four to one odds and a 0.90 probability represents nine to one odds. Table 10–1 only talks in terms of averages. It avoids the word *probability*.

Other advantages of using an averaging approach rather than a probability approach in addition to avoiding confusion include:

1. The averaging approach emphasizes empirical data processing to arriving at average damages, whereas a probability approach tends to overemphasize mathematical probability calculations with independent probabilities or Bayesian conditional probabilities.
2. The data-processing emphasis is also a welcome improvement over the possible overemphasis on subjective intuition of the probability approach.

Table 10–1
Replacing a Decision Tree with Averaging and a PG Table

GOALS / OPTIONS	BENEFIT ITEMS (1) Average Damages	(2) Average Delay to Damages	(3) Damages Discounted for Collection	(4) Damages Discounted for Delay	COST (5) Litigation Cost	NET (6) Benefits Minus Cost (4)–(5)
Not Sue	$0	0 years	$0 ($0 × 1.00)	$0 [$0/(1.10)⁰]	$0	$0
Sue	$6.12 (2.04 × 3)	5.00 years	$5.14 ($6.12 × .84)	$3.19 [$5.14/(1.10)⁵]	$1	$2.19

NOTES:

1. Average damages (column 1) are calculated by noting that a sample of 100 cases shows:
   (1) 30 cases resulted in $0 damages.
   (2) 18 (or .25 × 70) resulted in $1 damages, or $18 in total.
   (3) 42 (or .60 × 70) resulted in $3 damages, or $126 in total.
   (4) 10 (or .15 × 70) resulted in $6 damages, or $60 in total.
   (5) Thus, the 100 cases resulted in $204 in damages for an average of $2.04 apiece.

2. Average delay to damages (column 2) is calculated by noting that in the 70 cases in which damages were awarded:
   (1) 28 cases (or .40 × 70) took 2 years to judgment, or 56 years in total.
   (2) 42 cases (or .60 × 70) took 4 years to judgment, or 168 years in total.
   (3) Thus, the 70 cases took 224 years for an average of 3.2 years to judgment, or 224/70.
   (4) 42 cases took 1 year to collect, or 42 years in total.
   (5) 28 cases took 3 years to collect, or 84 years in total.
   (6) Thus, the 70 cases took 126 years for an average of 1.80 years to collect, or 126/70.
   (7) Thus, the 70 cases took 5.00 years apiece for judgment and collection, or 3.20+1.80.

3. The collection-fee multiplier (column 3) is 1.00 minus the collection fee expressed as a decimal. Thus, if the collection fee is 10%, the collection-fee multiplier is .90. The average collection-fee multiplier is calculated by noting that the 70 winning cases show:
   (1) 42 cases had a .90 multiplier, or 37.8 in total.
   (2) 28 cases had a .75 multiplier, or 21.0 in total.
   (3) Thus, the 70 cases had 58.8 in grand total for an average of .84 as a multiplier.

4. Damages discounted for delay (column 4) equal average damages multiplied by $1/(1.10)^t$ where t is the average delay to damages.

5. The numbers which appear in Table 10-1 and the above notes are all derived from Figure 10-1.

3. To use data processing to get relevant averages, one has to have a big data base that will cover lots of possible types of cases. This may now be possible by using the WESTLAW or LEXIS data base for calculating empirical probabilities by way of quantitative content analysis programs that are now being developed.
4. When no data is available, lawyers can probably generate educated estimates concerning average damages and other averages better than they can generate probabilities. I was recently thinking about the expected value of robbing a grocery store in terms of the monetary crime benefits discounted by the probability of success. I came up with a figure that seemed unrealistic compared to what I generated when I thought in terms of the average monetary crime benefits across a set of ten average grocery store robberies, some of which are unsuccessful.

Because lawyers often think in terms of probabilities does not mean that doing so is the best way to analyze litigation. The best way is the way that (1) maximizes accuracy in consistently arriving at decisions that maximize benefits minus costs and that (2) minimizes the difficulty in arriving at a decision quickly. Thinking in probabilities is not inconsistent with also thinking in terms of averages. The two perspectives may be better than either one alone. My own previous work has used probabilities, such as ''Applying Decision Science to the Practice of Law'' (*The Practical Lawyer* 30 [1984]: 13–22). Observing decision trees like the one in Figure 10–1 has convinced me that there must be an easier way to do it. My previous examples using probabilities were overly simple. The 70 cases that won out of 100 cases averaged about two years to collect after the judgment was awarded. That is simpler to recognize and work with than stating that cases with various probabilities took one year and cases with various other probabilities took three years.

Advantages of the Policies/Goals Table Format

The second main way in which Table 10–1 differs from Figure 10–1 (besides using averages rather than probabilities) is the use of the PG table format, which lists options along the rows, goals along the columns, and relations in the cells. Here the options are to sue or not sue, which is a simple go/no-go decision. The bottom line at the right side of a PG table should always be (1) benefits minus costs, (2) total benefits if all of the effects are stated positively, (3) total costs if all of the effects are stated negatively, or (4) some indirect measure of benefits minus costs.

The advantages of a PG table over a decision tree include:

1. Far easier to type without the artwork of a decision tree.
2. Far simpler in terms of the number of rows since there are only as many rows as there are options.
3. More consistent with the commonsense business practice of picking the option that is most profitable or that is positively profitable in a go/no-go situation.
4. Eliminates virtually all rounding errors.
5. Far easier to read.
6. Allows for an infinite number of degrees of damages, not just \$1 million, \$3 million, and \$6 million. In calculating an average, the damages can be any amount.
7. Allows for an infinite number of degrees of delay, not just two or four years on judgment or one and three years on collection. In calculating average delay, the periods can be any amount.
8. Easily allows for more plaintiff choices than just suing or not suing, such as sue with a jury trial, sue with a bench trial, settle with a structured settlement, settle with a flat payoff, or reject the case altogether.
9. Easily allows for a defendant perspective of defending with a jury-trial request, defending with no jury-trial request, offering various structured settlements, or offering various flat payoffs.

10. Easily allows for sensitivity analysis whereby any of the benefit or cost items can be expressed in terms of a threshold value that would make for a tie between suing and not suing at the bottom line.
11. Easily allows for sensitivity analysis whereby any of the benefit or cost items can be expressed as a range between minimum and maximum values.
12. Easily allows for non-monetary benefits and non-monetary costs that would be involved in criminal cases and possibly civil cases that do not involve damages.
13. The arithmetic is much simpler.
14. There is no unnecessary disaggregation into so many pieces like 14 scenarios. The PG table disaggregates the decision-making into benefit items, cost items, and B − C net items. The PG table thus forces the decision-maker to think about each of those goal components to decide between the two options available. Delay and collection can be considered costs, negative benefits, or simply items that are relevant to determining the true benefits.
15. A PG table could show the degree of risk adverseness as a cost of suing or show the degree of risk preference as a benefit of suing. Being risk adverse is, however, a non-monetary cost, and being a risk preferrer is a non-monetary benefit. PG tables can deal with a mix of monetary and non-monetary variables by methods described in the references at the end of this chapter.
16. Easily allows for making allocation decisions about how much time or money should be invested in alternative case activities or cases.
17. Decision trees tend to encourage lots of branches concerning relatively trivial matters at the ending branches such as how long it takes to collect on a judgment that is already awarded and a slighting of more important matters like the diversity of factors that influence winning and losing at the initial branches.
18. The PG table can be easily handled with a microcomputer program that provides for lots of prompting and sensitivity analysis. Such a floppy disk is now operational in IBM format and can be obtained from me at 361 Lincoln Hall, University of Illinois, Urbana, Illinois 61801.

Spreading PG Tables to Every Lawyer's Office

What may be needed to implement the above ideas and related ideas are entrepreneurial activities like the following:

1. A Judicial Prediction Service. This could be a service charging so many dollars per hour of microcomputer time on a telephone modem or hookup offering systematic predictions of damages, non-damage judgments, averages, and probabilities drawing on WESTLAW, LEXIS, Jury Verdict Research Service, and/or other data bases.
2. A Lawyer Decision-Making Service. This could also be a service charging so many dollars per hour of microcomputer time on a telephone modem but offering an analysis in the form of PG tables by way of an expanded version of the microcomputer program mentioned in point 16 above. Relevant decision-making problems could include:
   a. Choosing among alternative clients, plaintiffs, defendants, firms, or other entities to represent, prosecute, sue, and so on

   b. Deciding whether to go to trial or accept a settlement when tort, contract, or property damages, or other remedies are involved
   c. Deciding on an optimum level of time to spend on big cases or how to allocate one's time resources among many cases
3. A series of training workshops across various U.S. cities each year designed to train lawyers in the use of the Judicial Prediction Service and the Lawyer Decision-Making Service. Those workshops would deal with decision-analysis methods involving mutually exclusive alternatives, combinations of alternatives, decision-making under conditions of risk, decisions when doing too much or too little is undesirable, and decisions that involve allocating scarce resources among people, activities, and places.

The above ideas would have sounded like science fiction a few years ago but not now. The May 1984 issue of the *American Bar Association Journal* (page 161) states that 70 percent of all law offices in the country now have at least one data-processing or word-processing terminal and TV monitor that could be made capable of taking a telephone modem or hookup. I especially welcome comments, questions, and suggestions for improving on the above ideas. Having them implemented would probably be to the mutual benefit of those involved in using and providing the prediction and decision-making services. To the extent that these kinds of developments would make both lawyers and clients better off, the developments would probably be approved by whatever entities are both omniscient and omnibenevolent.[1]

USING A MICROCOMPUTER FOR PROCESSING A PG TABLE OR DECISION MATRIX

Tables 10–2, 10–3, and 10–4 show how the same data from Figure 10–1 can be more meaningfully analyzed by the microcomputer program called Policy/Goal Percentaging than by a decision-tree approach.

The program is called Policy/Goal Percentaging because it relates policies, decisions, or other alternatives to goals or criteria in order to decide which decision or combination is best in light of the alternatives, goals, and relations. The program uses percentaging to deal with the fact that the goals may often be measured on different dimensions like time, distance, attitude scales, dollars, and so on that can be converted to dimensionless part/whole percentages in order to allow for meaningful addition across goals. In this example, however, only dollars are involved.

Alternatives and Criteria

Each table shows one or more computer displays. All of the data come from Figure 10–1. Table 10–2A shows the two alternatives of either litigate or drop the suit. We could easily expand to more than two alternatives such as (1) litigate by a jury trial, (2) litigate by a bench trial, (3) accept numerous forms of

Table 10–2
The Alternatives and the Criteria

A. THE ALTERNATIVES OR AVAILABLE DECISIONS

	Alternative	Budgets Minimum	Budgets Actual
1	LITIGATE	0.00	0.00
2	DROP SUIT	0.00	0.00

B. THE CRITERIA (DAMAGES AND COSTS)

Criterion	Meas. Unit	Weight
1*SCENARIO 1	$	0.05
2*S 2		0.02
3*S 3		0.09
4*S 4		0.02
5*S 5		0.08
6*S 6		0.09
7*S 7		0.16
8*S 8		0.09
9*S 9		0.01
0*S 10		0.03
1*S 11		0.03
2*S 12		0.04
3*LITIGATION COSTS		-1.00

NOTES:

1. There is no minimum budget per decision or past actual budget, since this is a choosing problem, rather than a budget-allocation problem.
2. The measurement unit is millions of dollars for all the criteria. Each criterion is weighted by the probability of its occurring.

settlement, and (4) drop the suit. Columns 2 and 3 of Table 10–2A indicate that this is not a budget-allocation problem. Thus we do not have any minimum budget for each alternative or previous actual budget.

Table 10–2B shows the criteria for judging between the alternatives. In this context, the criteria refer to damages and costs. There are 12 ways of arriving at different damage levels. Damages 1 or Scenario 1 involves (1) litigating, rather than dropping the suit; (2) winning, rather than losing; (3) obtaining damages of $1 million, rather than $3 million or $6 million; (4) obtaining the judgment within two years of winning, rather than four years; and (5) collecting within one year from the time the judgment was awarded, rather than three years. The probabilities of the occurrence of events 2, 3, 4, and 5 are 0.70, 0.25, 0.40, and 0.65, respectively. Multiplying those independent probabilities together gives the probability of Damages 1 or Scenario 1 occurring. That probability is

Table 10–3
The Relations between the Alternatives and the Criteria

A. THE RELATIONS

ALTERNATIVE / CRITERIA SCORING

	SCENARIO	S 2	S 3	S 4	S 5
LITIGATE	2.00	1.40	1.70	1.20	6.10
DROP SUIT	0.00	0.00	0.00	0.00	0.00

	S 6	S 7	S 8	S 9	S 10
LITIGATE	4.20	5.00	3.50	12.20	8.40
DROP SUIT	0.00	0.00	0.00	0.00	0.00

	S 11	S 12	LITIGATI
LITIGATE	10.10	6.90	1.00
DROP SUIT	0.00	0.00	0.00

B. TRANSFORMING THE RELATIONS

```
X' = X *
X = X' /        0.900
Present value : rate=       10
Actual value  : term=     3.00
 F6 exit
```

NOTES:

1. The relations are in millions of dollars, as the measurement unit in Table 10-2B should indicate.
2. The commands in Table 10-3B allow the raw scores of Table 10-3A to be multiplied or divided by any factor. They also enable the present value or future value of any amount in Table 10-3A to be calculated.

0.0455 or 0.05 rounded to two decimal places, which is the figure shown in the "Weight" column. The measurement-unit column indicates that for this problem, all of the criteria are measured in dollars. The litigation costs are not discounted by a probability. They are given a negative weight because being high on cost is undesirable, whereas being high on each of the 12 damage amounts is desirable from a plaintiff's perspective.

Relations and Transformations

Table 10–3A shows the relations between the alternatives and the 12 damages criteria and 1 cost criteria. Scenario 1, for example, states that the damages with that set of events will be \$2 million. That figure is arrived at by tripling the \$1 million in single damages to consider treble damages. The \$3 million is then multiplied by 0.90 to consider the 10 percent collection fee. That figure is then multiplied by $1/(1.10)^3$ to consider the 10 percent interest or discount rate and the three-year waiting period. A similar interpretation should be given to each figure in Table 10–3A. The litigation costs are \$1 million.

Table 10–4
The Initial Decision and the Sensitivity Analysis

A. THE INITIAL DECISION OR ANALYSIS

Alternative	Combined Rawscores
1LITIGATE	2.19
2DROP SUIT	0.00

B. THE SENSITIVITY ANALYSIS

THRESHOLD ANALYSIS

	LITIGATE	DROP SUIT	Weight
SCENARIO 1	-45.59	47.59	-1.049
S 2	-89.82	91.22	-1.540
S 3	-22.90	24.60	-1.199
S 4	-135.62	136.82	-1.808
S 5	-22.71	28.81	-0.283
S 6	-19.60	23.80	-0.429
S 7	-8.35	13.35	-0.274
S 8	-21.38	24.88	-0.537
S 9	-206.72	218.92	-0.169
S 10	-60.01	68.41	-0.229
S 11	-68.09	78.19	-0.189
S 12	-55.65	62.55	-0.282
LITIGATION COSTS	3.19	-2.19	-3.189

NOTES:

1. The combined raw scores in Table 10-4A are calculated by multiplying the probability weights of Table 10-2B against the relations scores of Table 10-3A and then adding the products.
2. The threshold values in Table 10-4B are calculated by setting up a threshold equation in which the sum of the above-mentioned litigating products are set equal to the sum of the above-mentioned suit-dropping products. The equation has 26 terms on each side, including 13 relation scores and 13 weights for litigating, and 13 relation scores and 13 weights for dropping the suit.
3. One then treats each of the 39 inputs as an unknown and asks the question, "To what value would that input have to change in order to make for a perfect equality between the probability of litigating and the profitability of dropping the suit."

Table 10–3B shows how the program can transform the original relations or raw scores. The top line of those transformation commands enables the raw score to be multiplied. This could include multiplying the $1 million by 3 or by 0.90. The second line allows the raw score to be divided by any number. The third line specifies the discount rate for calculating present or future values. The fourth line specifies the term or period. By exercising appropriate options, one can calculate the present value of an amount to be received in the future or calculate the future value of an amount received in the present. Those calculations take into consideration the interest rate, the term, and having the interest remain in the account or the firm to draw compound interest. The amounts shown in Table 10–3A have already been discounted for the collection fee and for the delay in being received.

Initial Analysis and Sensitivity

Table 10–4A shows the initial decision by asking the computer what is the best decision in light of the alternatives available (Table 10–2A), the criteria for judging the alternatives and the weights of the criteria (Table 10–2B), and the relations between the alternatives and the criteria (Table 10–3A). The answer is that the total expected value for litigating is $4.19 million. That represents $3.19 million dollars in damages minus the $1 million in litigation costs. If the suit is dropped, there are no benefits and no costs. The combined raw score for dropping the suit is thus $0.

Table 10–4B provides especially useful information. It shows what the raw scores in Table 10–3A would have to change to in order for the second-place alternative (of dropping the suit) to become tied with the first-place alternative (of litigating). There are 13 criteria and 2 alternatives. This means that there are 26 input scores in Table 10–3A and 13 probabilities in Table 10–2B that could change to enable dropping the suit to become as profitable as litigating. Of those 39 values, only 1 is numerically possible because the gap between litigating and dropping the suit is so large. In a more realistic example in which the two alternatives might be closer in their combined raw scores, any of the 39 or so input values could conceivably change enough to cause the initial best alternative to become second best.

Examples of impossible changes include the impossibility of (1) a scenario bringing in negative damages through litigation, which is what it would take for any one scenario to make a tie between the alternatives in Table 10–4A; (2) a scenario bringing in positive damages through dropping the suit, which is equally meaningless; or (3) a scenario having a negative probability, which is impossible since probabilities only go from zero to 1.00. The only room for eliminating the greater profitability of litigating by way of one input change would be if the litigation costs were to rise from $1.00 million to $3.19 million. Litigating would then be as profitable or unprofitable as dropping the suit. Thus the decision to litigate can be considered firmly in first place, unless there is a possibility that the litigation costs are being so badly misestimated that they may be more than three times the $1 million predicted. One can easily test to see that any of these threshold values will result in a tie between litigating and dropping the suit by inserting any one threshold value in place of its original input value back in either Table 10–3A or 10–2B and then asking for a new initial analysis.

Threshold values can be useful in probability analysis with or without decision trees, especially in deciding litigation strategies. They can indicate to what figure the settlement value has to increase in order for a settlement to be as profitable as going to trial. They can indicate the threshold value for any probability so as to convert questions of the form "What is the probability?" into questions of the form "Is the probability likely to be higher or lower than the threshold value?" The latter type of question is much easier for lawyers and others to handle. If an input score is very close to its threshold score, that tells the decision-maker that he or she should probably seek additional information to be sure the input score is correct since a small change could affect which alternative is best. If all of the input values are substantially different from their threshold values, one can feel more confidence in accepting an initial decision like that shown in Table 10–4A.

Comparing Decision Matrices and Decision Trees

Going from Figure 10–1 to Tables 10–2, 10–3, and 10–4 requires approximately five minutes or less of key strokes. There is no question that a decision-matrix approach like that shown in Tables 10–2, 10–3 and 10–4 is much faster to input and manipulate than a decision-tree approach with or without the aid of computers. There are microcomputer decision-tree programs such as the Arborist developed by Texas Instruments. It requires considerable time and patience to be able to input the information from Figure 10–1. More important, it is almost psychologically impossible to do the algebra needed for calculating a set of threshold values, breakeven values, or indifference points for 39 input items by hand. At present, no other existing microcomputer program seems capable of calculating those useful threshold values.

CONCLUSIONS

The idea of sensitivity analysis includes more than just the calculation of tie-causing values, but that is the most important part of analyzing the effects on decisions of changing items of input information. Other forms of sensitivity analysis that are discussed in the last two chapters (9 and 10) include (1) insensitivity ranges within which scores can vary without affecting the best alternative; (2) change slopes, which show how much the gap between the two leading alternatives is influenced by a one-unit change in each input; (3) best- and worst-case-scenario analysis, whereby one does a version of Table 9–1 that is most favorable toward settling and a version that is least favorable in order to obtain insights into whether one should settle or go to trial; and (4) convergence analysis, whereby one determines how low a figure the weight for a goal can be and yet that the goal will dominate the other goals in determining the best alternative.

The idea of sensitivity analysis and tie-causing values can be a highly useful tool in decision-making. It can be more valuable than the "what-if" analysis that is associated with spreadsheet programs like Lotus 1–2–3. Lotus does what-if analysis whereby one asks what the effect would be of changing a cell or information item in Table 9–3 on the bottom profit for settling versus going to trial. In Table 9–3 there are 16 information items that lead to the two profit figures. Each item may be reasonably capable of taking five different values. This means that if one wants to do a comprehensive what-if analysis, one would have to make approximately 80 changes and observe the effect of each of the separate changes on the profit figures.

The sensitivity analysis of Table 9–4, however, tells us instantly that any offer greater than $6,000 will make settling more profitable, and any offer less than $6,000 will make going to trial more profitable if all of the other numbers are held constant. One does not have to experiment with offers of $4,000, $5,500, $6,500, $7,000, and so on to determine their effects. The same is true of the sensitivity analysis or tie-causing values of the other 15 information items. The what-if system of spreadsheet analysis is totally inapplicable to Table 9–6 dealing with benefits measured in years and costs measured in dollars, since the two profit figures are not arrived at by simply adding and subtracting across the rows. The computerized sensitivity analysis, however, has no trouble calculating tie-causing values under such circumstances.

There are other microcomputer procedures that are useful as decision-making tools for trial lawyers. They include procedures designed to predict the probabilities of victory in civil or criminal cases or to predict damages or sentences likely to be received. The outputs of those programs can be the inputs to the kind of decision-making analysis shown in Tables 9–3 and 9–6, which in turn are the inputs to the sensitivity analysis shown in Tables 9–4, 9–5, and 9–7. There are also systematic procedures designed to enable attorneys to sequence cases and allocate time to cases in order to maximize benefits minus costs.[2] The most useful methodology may, however, be the methodology of calculating tie-causing values in order to make choices between conflicting alternatives, especially whether to go to trial or accept a settlement.

NOTES

1. I thank Marc Victor for having partially inspired this chapter by his stimulating work on litigation risk analysis, such as his 1982 American Bar Association paper referred to in Figure 10–1.

2. For literature describing microcomputer procedures for judicial prediction and attorney-time allocation, see Chapter 9 in this book.

V

Allocating Scarce Resources, Especially Time

The following materials deal with allocating time, money, and people to cases, places, and activities within a law firm or a court system. Chapter 11 deals with allocating attorney time to cases. It is concerned with the optimum time to allocate when being paid a contingency fee, a flat fee, or an hourly rate. Time allocation often involves optimum-level analysis in which doing too much or too little is undesirable.

Chapter 12 deals with the order in which to sequence cases. The emphasis is on sequencing the cases in the order of their benefit/cost ratios. Doing this maximizes the income minus expenses of the firm. Such a system also requires having maximum time constraints whereby cases with low benefit/cost ratios that have been accepted are processed before exceeding a maximum delay. Allocating and sequencing time are discussed in the context of civil and criminal cases from both a lawyer and client perspective.

Chapter 13 is concerned with allocating money to places and activities. The examples deal with government allocation, but the principles can apply to allocating funds within a law firm. This is especially true when the firm maintains multiple offices or budgets in terms of functional activities rather than or in addition to specific cases or traditional formal accounts.

Chapter 14 is concerned with allocating people to tasks in light of their abilities and interests. This involves the development of a division of labor among lawyers within a firm or among judges within a courthouse or allocating other types of people to activities or places.

11

Allocating Attorney Time per Case

The purpose of this chapter is to discuss some basic aspects of how attorneys allocate their time to court cases or other types of cases and especially how they perhaps should allocate their time to increase their total earnings or to maximize benefits minus costs. The chapter uses simple principles from modern allocation theory, which has been developed mainly by management science and operations research. It builds on the increasing availability of computerized and other systems for gathering, retrieving, and processing legal-case data. It is innovative in its perspective, but it has the potentiality for being part of an improved mode of analysis and technology in modern law practice.[1]

Suppose, for example, that a law firm has two personal-injury cases in which it is representing the plaintiffs. Suppose further that Case A has a 0.80 probability of being won, and Case B has a 0.40 probability, although let us leave for later how such information might be determined. For now, a possibly interesting question might be to ask, "How should our hypothetical law firm allocate 100 hours of its time to these two cases?"[2]

HOW NOT TO ALLOCATE

At first glance, one might decide:

1. Allocate all of our resources to the better case.
2. Allocate 80/120, or 0.67, of our resources to the better case and 40/120, or 0.33, to the case less likely to succeed.
3. Allocate as many resources as are needed to win both cases.
4. Allocate as few resources to the case less likely to succeed as one might be ethically obligated to do so and the remainder of one's resources to the better case.
5. Allocate the same amount of resources to Case A as has been allocated in the past to the average case of the Case A type, and do likewise with Case B.
6. Use some other allocation.

All of those possibilities lack common sense, as a little careful thought is likely to indicate:

1. Allocating all of our 100 hours to the better case might be wasteful because we might only need 50 to win. If we allocate 100 hours to Case A we might also miss the possibility of receiving a judgment from Case B and thereby suffer a substantial opportunity cost.
2. Allocating our resources proportionately would mean giving 67 hours to Case A and 33 hours to Case B, which might represent wasted hours since Case A may need less than 67 hours to cross the threshold between being a winner and a loser. Case B may also need more than 33 hours although not necessarily a lot more.
3. Allocating as much resources as are needed to win both cases may be meaningless if by "to win" we mean with a 1.00 certainty since even an infinite number of hours devoted to each case may not be capable of achieving that. The same is true if by "to win" we mean with more than a 0.50 probability since achieving that for Case B may require more than the 100 hours we have available.
4. The fourth alternative of allocating a minimum to the worse case and the rest to the better case would not exceed our hours available (unlike alternative 3) or violate our ethical obligations (unlike alternative 1), but it may represent an excessive allocation to Case A and an opportunity cost for Case B (like alternatives 1 and 2).
5. The fifth alternative of allocating in terms of past averages has the defect that it assumes that what we have been doing on the average in the past has been optimal or rational in allocating our scarce resources.

The answer to our simple hypothetical problem may be that we need more information. For a starter, it might help to know what the damage award is likely to be if Case A results in a victory and likewise for Case B. If the damage award in Case A upon a plaintiff victory is $10,000, that case can be said to have an expected value of $8,000 (or 0.80 times $10,000). If, however, the damage award in Case B upon a plaintiff victory is $30,000, that case has an expected

Figure 11–1
The Relation between Hours Allocated and Damages Awarded

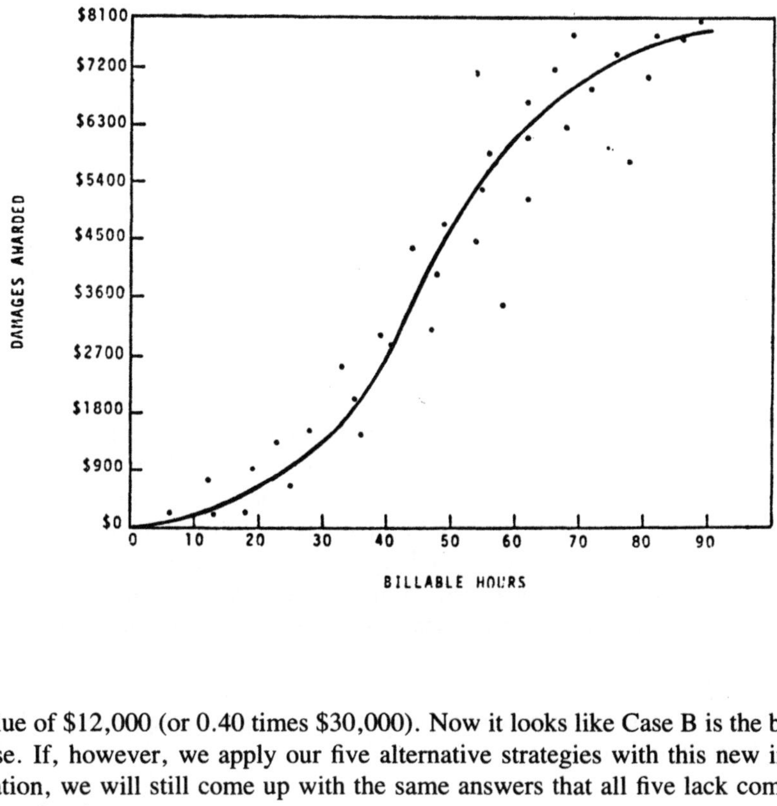

value of $12,000 (or 0.40 times $30,000). Now it looks like Case B is the better case. If, however, we apply our five alternative strategies with this new information, we will still come up with the same answers that all five lack common sense for the same reasons.

At this point, one might perceive that we need to know for each case not what its expected value is, which merely reflects a combination of the victory probability and the average damages awarded for cases of that type. Instead, we might need to know what the relation is between hours allocated and fees received. To obtain that information it would be helpful to know how much damages were awarded in a large quantity of cases that have characteristics similar to those of the cases we are currently considering. Along with the damages-awarded information, we would like to know the quantity of billable hours devoted to each case. "Billable hours" means hours spent on a case for which a client could be legitimately billed if an hourly rate were being charged even though the case may be handled on a contingency fee, flat fee, or salaried basis. That kind of information could be shown in a graph like Figure 11–1. Each dot represents a case. By seeing where the dots are positioned on the vertical axis, we can tell how much damages were awarded in each case. For many cases there were no damages because they were losing cases in which liability was not established. By seeing where the dots are positioned on the horizontal axis, we can tell how many billable hours were devoted to each case.

After graphing such a set of dots, it might then be appropriate to try to fit a meaningful curve to the dots in such a way as to minimize the sum of the distances from the dots to the curve. That can be done by a commonsense eyeballing approach or a more sophisticated computerized analysis.[3] One might expect a well-fitting curve to have a kind of S-shape like that shown in Figure 11–1. Such a curve indicates that before a certain number of hours, putting in additional time is not likely to raise the damages substantially above zero. In other words, cases tend to require an initial minimum number of opening hours before additional time can have an effect on the damages received. Likewise, after some number of hours, additional time probably has little effect in increasing the damages awarded. Thus each type of case probably has a bottom range of hours before hours substantially effect damages and a top range of hours after which the influence of additional hours seems to plateau out.[4]

With that kind of information for Case A and Case B, one might logically give Case A about 75 hours since that is the number of hours roughly corresponding to the upper turning point on the S-shaped curve. We would not want to give the case just 25 hours corresponding to the lower turning point since those 25 hours would be wasted by virtue of the fact that 25 hours only brings us to the point where we first start taking off from a zero damages level. If we devote a number of hours between 25 and 75, at first glance it looks as if we would be suffering some opportunities costs in the sense of missing the additional damages that could be obtained by putting in some additional hours. It may, however, be wasteful to devote 75 hours to such a case because the value of 75 hours to us may be greater than the one-third contingency fee corresponding to a 75–hour allocation.

HOW TO ALLOCATE

Figure 11–2 represents an improvement on Figure 11–1 for viewing the time-allocation problem. First, it shows the relation between hours allocated and cost to the lawyer, not just damages awarded. A lawyer like any business firm or individual is interested not in maximizing income but in maximizing income minus expenses or benefits minus costs. For the sake of simplicity, we assume here that the only cost is our time and that our time is worth $30 an hour. By $30 an hour we are not referring to the charge to clients (which may be $50 an hour) but rather to the fact that we would be willing to work for as low as $30 an hour.[5]

Second, Figure 11–2 talks in terms of fees received rather than damages awarded. We calculate fees received by taking one-third of the damages awarded

Figure 11–2
The Relation between Hours Allocated and Both Fees Received and Time Cost

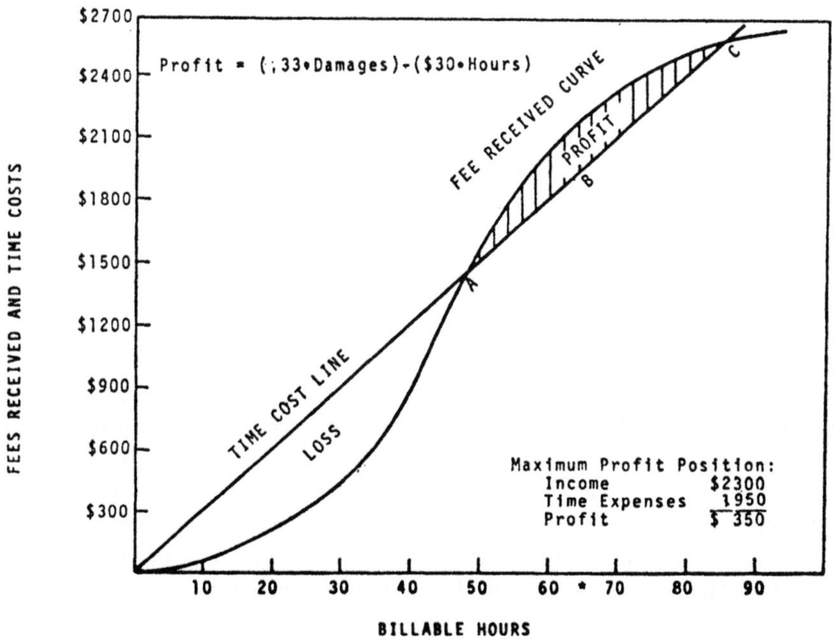

in Figure 11–1, since one-third is the usual contingency fee. The third and most important difference from Figure 11–1 is that with this new information, we should now be able to make a more rational decision concerning how many hours to allocate to a case of the type shown in Figure 11–2. The ideal quantity is about 65 hours, rather than the 75 hours where the fee received approaches the maximum. It makes more sense to allocate only 65 hours because that is where there is a maximum positive difference between the fee received curve and the time-cost line. Either below or above 65 hours would be taking a loss or not making as much profit. Billable hours between points A and C are predicted to yield a profit, but at point B (where an asterisk is show), the profit is at a maximum. Figure 11–1 thus emphasizes how the S-shaped damages-awarded curve is derived, and Figure 11–2 emphasizes what to do with such a curve to make a profit-maximizing time-allocation decision.

When we state that 65 hours is the optimum allocation for cases of type A, we do not mean that when lawyers have put in 65 hours on a case like that, they should then stop whatever they are doing regardless of what is happening.

Likewise, we do not mean that when lawyers have put in only 50 hours on such a case, they should throw in an extra 15 hours regardless of what those 15 hours involve. The 65 hours is just an average optimum that may be meaningfully deviated from in light of aggravating and extenuating circumstances just as with flat-sentencing systems. Relevant variables justifying more or less billable hours might include how experienced the lawyer is, how cautious his or her personality is, and how much help he or she has from assistants, research tools, and counsel for other parties. Also relevant is how difficult the case is in terms of the quantity of factual and legal issues and their newness. The way the cases are classified into types, however, is likely to include some general notions of difficulty in that airline crashes are more difficult than dog bites. Although lawyers are generally seeking to maximize fees minus costs, rather than maximizing fees, it is logical to expect a lawyer to spend more time on a potentially big fee case because the lawyer would regret more losing such a case, but the case classification is also likely to consider that. Although aggravating and extenuating circumstances may influence the extent to which one should deviate from the predicted optimum hours, they should not affect where that optimum generally tends to be for a case with a given set of characteristics.

Figure 11–2 covers cases like Case A. We can do the same kind of analysis for cases like Case B. Suppose, however, that the optimum number of hours for Case B turns out to be about 50 hours given the nature of Case B. This would mean that the sum total of both of our cases would add to 115 hours, or 15 hours more than the 100 we said we had available. One nice thing about allocating time in contrast to allocating a fixed budget is that each day or week we get a new time allocation that we can dip into. In other words, over the next two weeks, we can work 65 hours on Case A and 15 hours on Case B. The week after that, we can finish off the last 35 hours on Case B. In this simplified illustration, we are assuming that it is meaningful to concentrate all of the time devoted to a case within a single week or two weeks, although in reality the 65 hours or 50 hours may have to be stretched over a period of months or even years while waiting for other events to occur such as responses by the other side.

When there is a time conflict between two cases that need working on, it is logical to work on the case that has the closest non-postponable deadline. If both cases are about equally flexible with regard to impending deadlines, a lawyer might choose to work on the case that will bring in the largest profit so the money can be invested while working on the less profitable case. If both cases are also about equally profitable, lawyers might tend to handle the cases on a first come, first serve basis. Doing so, however, would not be ideal from the point of view of minimizing the average time from when a client is accepted to when the case is completed. To minimize that average time, the shortest cases should be taken first, provided that the longer cases are not allowed to exceed a given length of time in light of the legal rules and ethical considerations. For example, in our hypothetical situation, if we were to take the 65–hour case first (Case A), the 50–hour case (Case B) would have to wait 65 hours to begin its

Table 11–1
Alternative Ways of Ordering Two Cases to Minimize Average Total Time

Order Number 1: First Come, First Serve	Waiting Time +	Processing Time =	Total Time
Case A	0	65	65
Case B	65	50	115
	—	—	—
Totals	65	115	180
Averages	32½	57½	90
Order Number 2: Shortest Case First			
Case B	0	50	50
Case A	50	65	115
	—	—	—
Totals	50	115	165
Averages	25	57½	82½

processing. This would mean that Case B would take a total of 115 hours from the time the client was accepted until the case is completed. If Case A takes a total time of 65 hours and Case B takes a total time of 115 hours, the cases average 90 hours apiece from time of acceptance to time of completion, assuming no other distractions along the way. However, if we take the shorter case B first, its total time will be 50 hours. Case A will then have to wait those 50 hours to get started plus 65 hours of processing time, or a total of 115 hours. But then when we add the 50 hours total time for Case B to the 115 hours for Case A, we see that they will average only about 80 hours apiece rather than 90 hours. That is a saving of about 10 percent to the clients, although the lawyer is still putting in a total of 115 hours. The saving would be even greater if there were bigger differences between processing time of the shorter and the longer cases than just 50 and 65 hours, respectively. Table 11–1 shows those relations more clearly.[6]

Although we keep receiving a new allocation of time each week, it does not make sense to state that we should accept an infinite number of cases. For one thing, it does not seem rational to accept unprofitable cases unless, for example,

(1) there is some non-monetary public interest cause being served, (2) we are anticipating that the unprofitable case will later lead to profitable ones, or (3) there are some educational benefits to be gained. By "unprofitable case" in this context, we mean one in which the fee-received curve does not exceed our time-cost line. That concept of unprofitability enables us to rank incoming cases on their predicted profitability. The most profitable ones have a fee-received curve that most exceeds our time-cost line when drawn on the same scale as Figure 11–2. If we were faced with ten prospective clients simultaneously, we would logically pick the most profitable ones until we used up as much time as we were willing to commit in advance.

We normally, however, do not have ten prospective clients approach us simultaneously. Rather, they do so sequentially. Under those circumstances, we might be reluctant to accept the first case even though it is predicted to be profitable because we are anticipating that an even more profitable case will occur later. That problem is like the lawyer exercising his peremptory challenges in picking jurors. He might be reluctant to use his limited peremptory challenges on the first few jurors because he might be anticipating that even worse jurors will come up later in the jury-picking process. The best way to handle the sequential-client problem might be to state that we will accept all profitable cases that exceed a certain threshold. If we wind up accepting too many cases, we will have to hire help or cut back for a while in accepting new clients. If we wind up accepting too few cases, we will have to lower our threshold.[7]

VARIATIONS ON THE BASIC APPROACH

Emphasizing Total Caseload and Probabilities

The above approach to allocating attorney time to court cases in effect treats each case mainly as a separate allocation problem. In the language of decision sciences, we are in effect treating the allocation problem as one of finding an optimum level of time to allocate to each case on a case-by-case basis, rather than treating the problem as one of finding an optimum mix for dividing up a fixed budget of time among a set of cases. The optimum-level perspective makes more sense for a number of reasons. First, there is probably only a relatively narrow range of hours that could be meaningfully allocated to a given case without going below a minimum ethical threshold or above a maximum wastefulness threshold. That is unlike the allocation of a business firm's budget to various advertising methods where any number of budget dollars could be allocated to each of the methods, since there are no ethical minimums and the plateauing phenomenon is probably not so sharp. Second, time allocation has more flexibility by virtue of the possibility of postponing matters and hiring additional help, in contrast to the relative inflexibility of the quantity of money allocated to the advertising department of a business firm for a given period. Third, it is much simpler to think in terms of an optimum level of time to devote to each case (largely out of the context of the other cases) than it is to think in terms of having a total amount of time that is to be allocated among many cases.[8]

The above approach also differs from the decision science approach, which emphasizes making decisions under conditions of risk or uncertainty. Allocating attorney time is an example of that kind of decision-making since each case involves a risk or probability of victory or defeat. The analysis could be modified to take more explicitly into consideration the fact that hours allocated not only influence damages awarded but also the probability of victory. Doing this, however, would substantially complicate the analysis without a commensurate gain in its usefulness. More specifically, doing this would involve eliminating from Figure 11–1 all of the cases in which no damages are awarded that would shift the curve upward and change its slope but probably not change its S-shape. We would also have to generate a figure similar to Figure 11–1 in which the vertical axis would show victory probabilities ranging from zero to 1.00. All of the dots corresponding to the cases would be either at 1.00 or zero, although they would still be above the same billable hours on the horizontal axis, as in Figure 11–1. An S-shaped curve would then be fitted to those dots showing the relation between hours allocated and victory probabilities. We would then create a composite figure by multiplying each point on the Figure 11–1 curve by each point on this new S-shaped curve at each hours mark. That would produce a composite S-shaped curve showing (for each amount of hours allocated) the predicted *expected* damages (which means the predicted damages discounted by the predicted probability of their being received). We could then multiply the points on that composite curve by 0.33 to take into consideration the one-third contingency fee and have a new more sophisticated expected fee-received curve to work with in Figure 11–2.[9]

Flat Fees and Hourly Rates

Instead of talking about more complicated variations that are sometimes referred to in discussing allocation problems, it may be more useful to talk about even simpler situations than the one used to illustrate the basic approach. The simplest (but very common) situation may be that of the salaried lawyer who receives a set salary per year or the flat fee case that involves, for example, a charge of $900 for a particular service. Figure 11–3 shows that the optimum allocation of time to such a case would be whatever minimum amount of time will complete the case. Theoretically, the optimum is zero hours, since any hours allocated above zero means a reduced profit in the sense of a reduction in the positive difference between the fee received and the time-cost line. The breakeven point on a $900 fee is 30 hours figuring time cost at $30 an hour.

The same situation applies if we think in terms of a $30,000 salary for an attorney working for an insurance company defending personal-injury cases, a public defender representing indigent criminal defendants, or an assistant states attorney prosecuting defendants. The $900 would change to $30,000 in the graph,

Figure 11–3
Profit Maximization in a Flat Fee Case

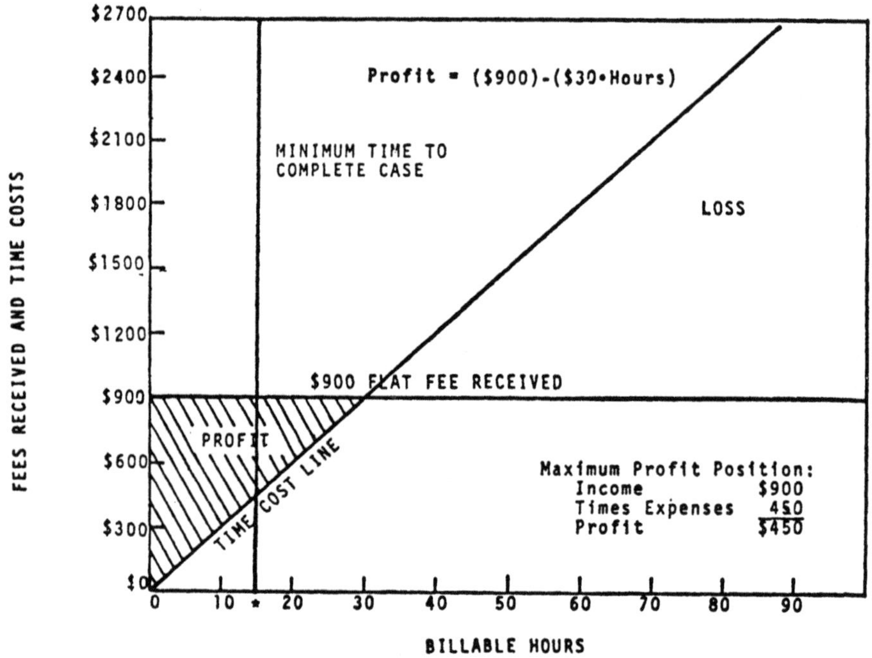

and the breakeven point would change from 30 hours to 1,000 hours. The concept of minimum-time requirement, however, changes when we move from the flat fee case to the salaried attorney. In the flat fee case, the attorney is expected only to complete the case, not to put in any minimum number of hours beyond that. In the salaried situation, attorneys are normally expected to show up at an office for some number of hours per week and weeks per year. Their total working hours may thus add to more than 1,000 hours per year, but salaried lawyers may consider their time per hour to be worth less than lawyers paid by the case since salaried lawyers have the security of a salary. Both the flat fee and the salaried lawyers may seek to put in more than the minimum number of hours required just to complete their cases and retain their jobs if the additional hours are likely to result in increased fees or salary raises. It is, however, difficult to determine the relation between hours allocated and client-employer satisfaction or salary raises. Thus the general strategy of trying to minimize one's hours or time cost when being paid a flat fee or a salary may be the best profit-maximizing strategy.

Another simple but common situation is the hourly rate case. Figure 11–4 graphically shows what is involved there with regard to the optimum time allocation in order to maximize the positive difference between fees received and

Figure 11–4
Profit Maximization in an Hourly Rate Case

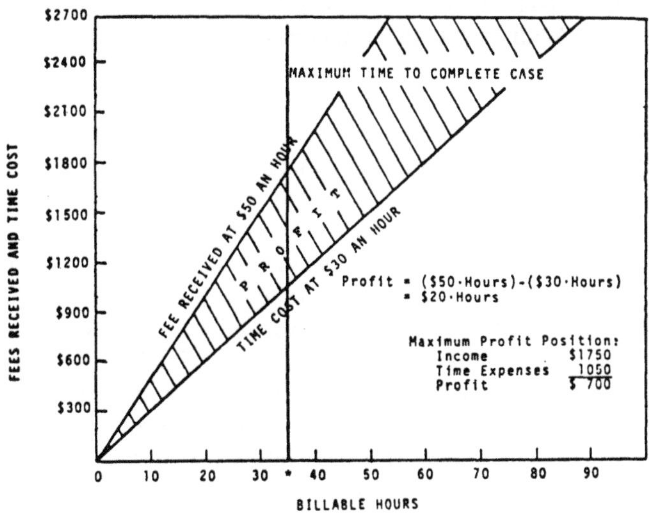

time cost. One can readily see that the optimum allocation of time is the maximum time needed to complete the case. Theoretically, the optimum time is infinite since the more hours allocated, the more the profit is, figuring a billable charge of $50 an hour and a time cost of $30 an hour. For each hour there is a $20 profit between revenue and expenses if for the sake of simplicity we ignore expenses other than the cost of our time. The more hours we put in, the more profit units of $20 we accumulate, thereby building a larger total profit. For 10 hours the total profit is $200, whereas for 30 hours the total profit is $600. At first glance, it looks as if a flat fee case and an hourly rate case would involve diametrically opposed optimum time-allocation strategies, with the former strategy emphasizing time minimization and the latter emphasizing time maximization. However, if the minimum time to complete the case is close to the maximum time, in both situations one may wind up putting in about the same amount of time.[10]

Figures 11–3 and 11–4 could consistently refer to the same case since it is possible for a case to have a 15–hour minimum time and a 35–hour maximum time. One cannot, however, conclude from that hypothetical data that an hourly rate is more profitable than a flat fee. The extent to which it is or is not more profitable depends on (1) the hourly rate, (2) the flat fee, (3) the maximum time, (4) the minimum time, (5) the actual time, and (6) the value of one's time as reflected by the time-cost line. Figures 11–1 and 11–2 are not referring to the same case since the optimum time in Figure 11–2 of 65 hours exceeds the maximum time from Figure 11–4. The profitability of the contingent fee versus the flat fee and the hourly fee depends on the above six elements plus (7) the relation between the fees received and billable hours as illustrated by the dots and curve in Figures 11–1 and 11–2 and (8) the relation between the probability of victory and billable hours as mentioned in the probability variation on the basic approach. With that kind of information one should be able to make decisions not only concerning the optimum hours to allocate but also the optimum payment arrangement between the contingency fee, the hourly rate, the flat fee, or some legitimate combination of two or more of those payment arrangements.

As part of the profit-maximization strategy, one might say something about setting the amount for the flat fee, hourly rate, or contingency percentage. Previously, when the bar associations were enforcing fee schedules, those decisions were largely made by a few influential firms or lawyers in an oligopolistic way. Now that there is more competition in fee setting, flat fees and hourly rates may be more determined by the market forces of intersecting supply and demand curves. To the extent that law practice is a competitive business, the individual lawyer must operate within the market-determined fees. If the lawyer goes above those fees, he or she will lose clients. If the lawyer goes below those fees, he or she is likely to be operating at a loss. Some law practices may be closer to being monopolistic businesses because they are almost the only firm available in their communities or the only firm specializing in a certain field. They are capable of setting their prices as high as the traffic will bear without an offsetting loss of clients. Regardless of the oligopolistic, competitive, or monopolistic market of lawyers' services, the price and the hours allocated would be designed to maximize the positive difference between fees received and expenses incurred especially time costs, while operating within ethical and other constraints. This general rule operates on the assumption that rational lawyers like rational people in general seek to maximize benefits minus costs in their activities, including non-monetary benefits and costs.[11]

Lawyers versus Firms, Society, and Clients

An important variation on this analysis involves talking not in terms of the individual lawyer maximizing his or her benefits minus costs but rather in terms of the law firm, governmental office, or corporation for which the lawyer might work. If each individual lawyer seeks his own profit maximization, doing so will maximize the profits of the firm if he or she is a sole practitioner, or if the lawyer's fees received become part of the income of a partnership. The interests of a law office with salaried lawyers may, however, not be the same as those of the individual lawyers. For example, a prosecutor's office may have as a collective goal to maximize the number and percentage of convictions, with each conviction weighted by the sentence received and possibly divided by the maximum sentence that could have been received. If individual salaried lawyers in such an office seek to minimize their "billable hours" worked while maintaining at least a minimum quality level, what may be goal maximizing to the office may not be goal maximizing for the individual lawyer who may avoid big cases that are likely to involve after-hours work. Under such circumstances, incentive systems need to be established to get the individual lawyers to internalize the office goals into their benefit-cost considerations. The problem moves up to a still higher level if we talk about how to get both the individual lawyer and the group with which he or she is associated to internalize societal or public-interest goals. That is the subject of various articles having more of a political science or governmental orientation than a management-science or economics orientation.[12]

Still another variation on this analysis involves talking in terms of the possible conflict between the profit-maximization position of the lawyer and the individual client, rather than the firm for which the lawyer works. Under a contingency fee arrangement, the client is better off if the lawyer puts in as many hours as possible, assuming that the damages-awarded curve keeps rising even if only to a slight extent as shown in Figure 11–1. Even if the curve eventually becomes totally flat, that point is likely to involve more hours than the maximum profit position shown in Figure 11–2. Under a flat fee arrangement, the client is also probably better off the more hours the lawyer puts in since additional hours should result in higher quality work at least up to a point. The lawyer receiving a flat fee, however, would prefer to put in as few hours as possible as shown in Figure 11–3. Under an hourly rate arrangement, the client may be better off with few hours (provided that the job gets done), whereas the lawyer may be better off in terms of profit with more hours.

Various systems have been proposed to try to reconcile these conflicts. One type of system involves combining different payment arrangements to force the lawyer into a position in which the maximum profit involves neither trying to stretch the work or shorten it, which is the kind of middling position in which the client is usually best off. An example of such a proposed system is the contingent hourly percentage whereby the lawyer charges an hourly rate but receives a percentage of the recovery if the recovery exceeds the total hourly fee. Another type of system involves a fee schedule that specifies average and maximum (1) hours, (2) flat fees, and (3) contingency percentages, in contrast to the now illegal minimum-fee schedules. The averages could be determined by carefully surveying attorneys, and the maximums could represent the response from the upper 20 percent or other percentage. Regardless of what kind of system might someday be adopted to provide client protection from lawyer-client conflict over the allocation of lawyer hours, the lawyer could still follow the general approach and its variations described in this chapter in order to more nearly maximize his or her benefits minus costs. Having a better understanding of how attorneys can maximize those net benefits is also helpful in developing a governmental or bar association system for regulating payment arrangements and thus time allocation.[13]

Legal aid for the poor is a special kind of attorney-client relationship with regard to payment arrangements and time allocation. Three general kinds of payment arrangements have been tried, namely, volunteer or assigned lawyers who do not generally get paid, salaried lawyers whose salaries are generally paid by the Legal Services Corporation or a public defender's office, and lawyers who are reimbursed by the government for their services on a case-by-case basis analogous to medicare. The volunteer attorney is not working to maximize monetary profits but rather for the learning experience or the psychological benefits from contributing one's time. The salaried lawyer for the indigent may also have strong non-monetary motivations, although his heavy caseload may prevent him from allocating as much time per client as hired counsel does. The judicare lawyer is expensive by charging on a case-by-case basis rather than an annual salary, even if there is no overcharging to the government. The salaried system now tends to prevail, for both civil and criminal cases, with the exception of cases that can be handled for the poor on a contingency fee basis and federal criminal cases in which a regulated reimbursement system operates.[14] Insurance systems are now being increasingly developed for people above the classification of being poor but not wealthy enough to be able readily to afford individually hired counsel. Attorneys working for such insurance systems may tend to allocate their time like salaried house counsel rather than like the more idealistic salaried Legal Services Corporation attorney.

IMPLEMENTING THE ALLOCATION SYSTEM

What we have presented so far should make sense at least as a matter of hindsight even though it might be difficult to develop this type of scheme if one were responding to a question of "How should attorneys allocate time to court cases?" The Achilles heel of the system is not that it contains any substantially fallacious or unethical reasoning but rather the problem of how to obtain the data for implementing the system.

An ideal implementation system would be computerized at the three stages of data gathering, retrieval, and processing. With regard to data retrieval, what we would like to have is a business firm compiling data from questionnaires and docket records on thousands of damage cases across the country. For each case, a notation would be made as to information such as (1) billable hours by the plaintiff's attorney, (2) billable hours by the defendant's attorney, (3) damages awarded, (4) the nature of the accident in which the injury occurred, (5) the nature of the injuries, (6) the characteristics of the plaintiff and defendant, (7) the date when and place where the case was decided, and (8) other characteristics of the case that may be relevant to establishing the relation between hours allocated and damages awarded.

If that dataset could be made accessible by a computer terminal, attorneys could ask for all of the cases that have whatever combination of characteristics they are interested in. An attorney, for example could ask for those cases that involve intersection collisions with a whiplash injury by a woman plaintiff. If the attorney gives too much detail in specifying the case characteristics, he or she will receive too few cases and should redefine the request. In other words, the system could work similar to the computerized LEXIS or WESTLAW subscription services for retrieving case citations. Here, however, the attorney does not want citations but rather wants to specify the sub-set of cases to be analyzed. This dataset would also involve trial cases, rather than appellate cases, which makes it more like the data compiled by the Jury Verdict Research Corporation. An important difference from its dataset, though, would be the fact that the data would indicate billable hours for each side, which is not currently compiled by the Jury Verdict people.[15]

After retrieving a sub-set of cases, the same computer system could then process those cases to determine algebraically or graphically the relation between billable hours and fees received in those cases.[16] The result could be a graph like Figure 11–2 when the system is operated off a computer terminal that provides for graphical output. The time-cost line can be superimposed on the graph if the attorney informs the computer how much he considers his hours to be worth in terms of personal cost. If the system merely gives printed output, the attorney could be provided with information such as (1) the general optimum number of hours corresponding to point B on Figure 11–2, (2) the damages likely to be awarded at that optimum number of hours, (3) the range of hours within which a profit is likely to be made corresponding to points A to C in Figure 11–2, and (4) other statistical information such as the equation for the curve and a measure of how well the curve fits the dots. If the computerized system allows for interaction between the attorney and the computer as LEXIS and WESTLAW do, the attorney can vary the characteristics of the case and thereby vary the sub-set of data that gets analyzed. Doing this enables one to see how such variations affect the optimum number of hours and the damages likely to be awarded.

Until a business firm is willing to supply the above-mentioned computerized service or at least a looseleaf binder service, individual attorneys and law firms can try doing the analysis using their own cases and just using a graphical eyeballing approach, rather than the more mathematical approach that a computer would be capable of using. Such a do-it-yourself approach might involve using some form of index cards to record the kind of data-gathering information mentioned above for each case that will be part of the dataset. One can then retrieve any sub-set of those index cards corresponding to the type of case one is interested in. Retrieving such a sub-set is easier if the index cards have some kind of edge notches or colored flags indicating the characteristics of each case. With that sub-set of index cards, one could then plot dots on a pair of axes like that shown in Figure 11–2. Each dot corresponds to a case. Its position from east to west on the graph indicates the number of billable hours, and the dot's position from north to south indicates the fee received. One can then eyeball an S-shaped curve to the dots trying to provide as good a fit as one can. With that curve, one can see the predicted profitability of cases of that sub-set type from the way in which that fee-received curve relates to a predrawn time-cost line reflecting how much per hour one's time is worth. Such a system can be done for a variety of casetypes.

Doing so should provide insights to practicing lawyers regarding the relative profitability of different types of cases.

CONCLUSIONS

The essence of the allocation model presented is simply to try within each case to maximize the positive difference between the fee received and the expenses incurred, especially the time costs while operating within ethical and other constraints. That strategy involves allocating as little time as possible per case when a flat fee or a fixed salary is involved and as much time as possible when an hourly rate is involved. In contingency fee cases, that strategy involves allocating a quantity of hours between the minimum and maximum possible. The exact quantity depends on the relation between billable hours and damages awarded (which indirectly determines the fee received), as indicated by analyzing a set of cases that are similar to the case under consideration. Such an analysis can be facilitated by a computerized system of case data gathering, retrieval, and processing or by a do-it-yourself non-computerized system. The recommended optimum hours from the analysis allows for aggravating and extenuating circumstances. Comparing those optimums across cases can provide insights as to what clients to encourage or accept, as well as how one can improve the allocation of time to cases that are accepted.

A few years ago, lawyers considered the idea of computerized legal searches for case citations to border on science fiction, but it has now become a widespread reality. The next step is to get those computerized data-gathering and retrieval systems to do some processing of the information. A useful first step for such subscription services might be to attempt to relate results to hours allocated. The same systems could also relate results to other case characteristics, but attorneys generally have more control over their hours than over the characteristics of their cases. It is hoped that this chapter may inspire some experimentation along the lines suggested that could help law practices to benefit from some of the management-science developments that have been so helpful to business firms in allocating their scarce resources. Computerized citation retrieval has lessened some of the drudgery of legal research. Computerized case management has the potentiality for further expanding the rational use of attorney time.

APPENDIX: ALLOCATING PER CASE FROM A P/G% PERSPECTIVE

Table 11–2
The Optimum Level of Attorney Time for a Contingency Fee Case

CRITERIA / ALTERNATIVES	BENEFIT ITEMS (1) Predicted Damages	BENEFIT ITEMS (2) Fee Received	COST ITEMS (3) Time Cost	NET ITEMS (4) Benefits Minus Costs
	(1) = f(H)	(2) = .33(1)	(3) = $20(H)	(4) = (2) - (3)
Billable Hours (H)				
0	$ 0	$ 64	$ 0	$ 0
10	0	46	300	-300
20	297	99	600	-501
30	1,302	434	900	-466
40	2,676	892	1,200	-308
50	4,221	1,407	1,500	- 93
60	5,748	1,916	1,800	116
70*	7,050	2,350	2,100	250*
80	7,931	2,646	2,400	246
90	8,208	2,736	2,700	36

NOTES:

Predicted damages is an S-shaped function of hours of the form $Y = b_1X_1 + b_2X^2 + b_3X^3$ where $b_1 = -75.000$, $b_2 = 6.000$, and $b_3 = -.030$. These numbers are accurate to three decimal places.

The numerical values of b_1, b_2, and b_3 are determined by inserting data into a microcomputer for a substantial number of cases showing for each case the billable hours and the damages received. When doing so, there should be a floppy disk in the disk drive that is capable of handling polynomial regression or S-shaped curves.

At 15 hours or below, predicted damages are $0, and so is the predicted fee received. At 90 hours or above, predicted damages cease to increase with additional hours.

The optimum level of time is between 60 and 70 hours since that is where benefits minus costs are maximized. The damages awarded for any given number of hours can be easily determined by the same microcomputer program that gives the formula. Seventy hours is the optimum number of hours rounded to the nearest multiple of ten hours.

One could follow the above format to analyze other decisions that involve finding an optimum decision level where S-shaped curves are involved. An example is finding an optimum bond level to charge arrested defendants. Bond levels tend to have S-shaped relations with the probability of appearing and the probability of being held just as billable hours tends to have an S-shaped relation with damages received. S-shap ed relations tend to be flat at first, then steep, and then flat again

For further details on the contents of the above table, see Nagel, Policy Evaluation Decisions (Praeger, 1982), 89-109.

Table 11–3
The Optimum Attorney Time for a Flat Fee or Hourly Rate Case

CRITERIA / ALTERNATIVES	FLAT FEE CASE			HOURLY RATE CASE		
	Fee Received	Costs $30(H)	Benefits Minus Costs	Fee Received $50(H)	Cost $30(H)	Benefits Minus Costs
HOURS (H)						
0	900	0	900	0	0	0
10	900	300	600	500	300	200
Minimum Time (15)						
20	900	600	300*	1,000	600	400
30	900	900	0	1,500	900	600*
Maximum Time (35)						
40	900	1,200	-300	2,000	1,200	800
50	900	1,500	-600	2,500	1,500	1,000

NOTES:

1. Without a minimum time constraint, the optimum attorney time for a flat fee case would be as close to zero time as possible. With a minimum time constraint, the optimum time is at the minimum time, or above the minimum time but as close to it as possible.
2. Without a maximum time constraint, the optimum attorney time for an hourly rate case is as much time as possisle. With a maximum time constraint, the optimum time is at the maximum time, or below the maximum time but as close to it as possible.
3. In the above example, one cannot be exactly at the minimum or maximum time because the hours are figured in blocks of ten hours apiece. Otherwise, the optimum time in the flat fee case would be 15 hours for a profit of $450. Likewise, the optimum time in the hourly rate case would be 35 hours for a profit of $700.
4. The minimum or maximum time in a case can be defined as the amount of time needed to complete the work in a manner that will satisfy a very high percentage of clients such that they are not likely to complain to the bar association or to withhold referring the attorney to others.

NOTES

1. For a more detailed analysis of some aspects of the problem of allocating attorney time to court cases and clients, see S. Nagel and M. Neef, "Allocating Resources among Court Cases by Legal Counsel," in *Decision Theory and the Legal Process* (Lexington, Mass.: Lexington-Heath, 1979), Chapter 7. That analysis treats time allocation mainly as a problem of finding an optimum division of a fixed budget of time among a set of cases, whereas this chapter considers time allocation more as a problem of finding an optimum level of time to allocate to each case on a case-by-case basis. The present analysis also classifies cases mainly in terms of the payment arrangement as contingency fee, flat fee, salaried, or hourly rate cases, whereas the above book chapter classifies cases mainly in terms of their subject matter as personal-injury, criminal, divorce, and other types of court cases.

2. Other studies (besides the book in note 1) dealing with time allocation among court cases by legal counsel include criminal justice studies like Brian Forst and Katherine Brosi, "A Theoretical and Empirical Analysis of the Prosecutor," *Journal of Legal Studies* 6 (1977): 177; William Landes, "An Economic Analysis of the Courts," *Journal of Law and Economics* 14 (1971): 61; and J. Lachman, "An Economic Model of Plea Bargaining in the Criminal Court System" (Ph.D. dissertation, Michigan State University, 1975). In those studies the time allocation decision is generally only part of a broader economic model of the behavior of prosecutors or the criminal justice system. Like the book in note 1, they emphasize tradeoffs across cases and the substance of the cases.

Still other studies include personal-injury studies like F. MacKinnon, *Contingent Fees for Legal Services: A Study of Professional Economics and Responsibilities* (Hawthorne, N.Y.: Aldine, 1964); Murray Schwartz and Daniel Mitchell, "An Economic Analysis of the Contingent Fee in Personal Injury Litigation," *Stanford Law Review* 22 (1970): 1125; and Kevin Claremont and John Currivan, "Improving on the Contingent Fee," *Cornell Law Review* 63 (1978): 529–639. These studies do focus on the individual case taken out of the context of the other cases in one's caseload. Like the above criminal studies, however, they are primarily concerned with describing and explaining attorney decision-making using an economic model rather than trying to improve the efficiency of attorney decision-making using an implementable management-science or operations-research model.

3. One does not need to know anything about the technical aspects of statistical analysis to plot dots and fit a rough S-shaped curve to the dots using an eyeballing approach. On how that might be done more precisely by a computer, see Edward Tufte, *Data Analysis for Politics and Policy* (Englewood Cliffs, N.J.: Prentice-Hall, 1974), pp. 65–134; and Gorden Hilton, *Intermediate Politometrics* (New York: Columbia University Press, 1976), pp. 186–218. The computer is given (for each case) the damages awarded (the Y score) and the billable hours (the X score). The computer then determines numerical values for the b's in an equation of the form $Y = b_0 + b_1X + b_2X^2 + b_3X^3$. That equation, when plotted by the computer, will appear as an S-shaped curve.

4. An alternative way of conceiving the relation between damages awarded and hours in by a curve that quickly becomes totally horizontal, as contrasted to a curve like that of Figure 11–1 that is always rising at least slightly although at a decreasing rate. See Clermont and Currivan, "Improving on the Contingent Fee." The Clermont-Currivan perspective assumes a flattening of the relation. The type of curve that best fits the empirical reality of actual cases has more than just geometric implications. If the curve does reach

a point where it becomes totally flat, one can state that this is the point of maximum client recovery that dedicated lawyers should be seeking. If, however, there is no total flattening of the curve, there is no point except at an infinity of hours where the client's interest is maximized. The diminishing returns but non-flat curve does seem more reasonable in light of empirical statistical analysis in other subject matter areas. What is obviously needed is a gathering of the kind of data suggested later in this chapter to determine what the relationships are between damages awarded and hours allocated in various types of cases.

5. Clermont and Currivan, "Improving on the Contingent Fee," assume that if a lawyer charges $50 an hour, he or she has then incurred $50 in time expenses. That assumption is essential to their model, which then deduces that lawyers have no incentive to add additional hours under an hourly rate arrangement because they are only covering their expenses by putting in additional hours. They do recognize that lawyers under an hourly rate arrangement may have an incentive to say that they worked ten hours when they only worked eight hours. They do not, however, recognize that lawyers may have an incentive to work ten hours when they could have done the job in eight hours, since they are making a profit or surplus on each additional hour by virtue of the fact that they are getting paid more than they would be willing to pay to have those hours regularly free to do something else. This does not mean that a lawyer can be bargained down from $50 an hour. It simply means that the lawyer considers himself or herself as coming out ahead when working for $50 an hour, that is, as making a net gain of benefits minus costs. A good test for determining the difference between the billable charge per hour and the self-perceived time-cost per hour might be to ask the attorney how much the $50 per hour would have to be lowered before he or she would change occupations. Most lawyers would continue to be lawyers even if there were a substantial reduction in the dollars per hour or per year and no reduction in the hourly or annual incomes of other occupations. That difference between what they are getting and what they would be willing to work for can be considered a producer's surplus.

One could also argue in a Marxist way that lawyers like other wage earners are underpaid in that the client might be willing to pay more than $50 an hour if necessary in view of the benefits the client is receiving. A third perspective states that if lawyers ask $50 an hour, they are worth $50 an hour, because they would not be asking that rate unless they could get it, meaning that by devoting an hour to one client they are suffering a $50 opportunity cost by foregoing $50 that they could receive from another client. In the context of the analysis of this chapter the most reasonable perspective seems to be that lawyers are obtaining a net benefit from every hour worked at the going hourly rate. Otherwise they would be doing something else.

6. On the optimum sequencing of events or cases, see Jack Byrd, Jr., *Operations Research Models for Public Administration* (Lexington, Mass.: Lexington-Heath, 1975), pp. 139–156 and S. Nagel and M. Neef, "Time-Oriented Models and the Legal Process: Reducing Delay and Forecasting the Future," *Washington University Law Quarterly* (Summer 1978): 467.

7. On the problem of making sequential allocations of peremptory challenges, time, or money from a limited total quantity, see Steven Brams and M. Davis, "A Game-Theory Approach to Jury Selection," *Trial* 12 (1976): 47; and Howard Raiffa, *Decision Analysis: Introductory Lectures on Choices under Uncertainty* (New York: Wiley, 1970).

8. On optimum-level analysis, in contrast to optimum-mix analysis, see discussions of inventory modeling and linear programming in any elementary operations research textbook such as Samuel Richmond, *Operations Research for Management Decisions*

(New York: Ronald Press, 1968); H. Theil et al., *Operations Research and Quantitative Economics: An Elementary Introduction* (New York: McGraw-Hill, 1965); and Sang Lee and L. Moore, *Introduction to Decision Science* (New York: Petrocelli/Charter, 1975). For a discussion of optimizing methods with legal process examples, see S. Nagel and M. Neef, *Legal Policy Analysis: Finding an Optimum Level or Mix* (Lexington, Mass.: Lexington-Heath, 1977).

9. On making decisions under conditions of risk or uncertainty, see chapters on that subject in the operations-research textbooks in note 8. For a discussion of that optimizing perspective with legal-process examples, see Nagel and Neef, *Decision Theory and the Legal Process*. For additional sophistication, we could also discount the fees received, not only by the probability of their being received but also by the fact that with some types of cases it takes longer to receive fees than with others. If a type of case tends to take three years for a settlement or a judgment, the present value of the fee received needs to be divided by $(1 + r)^t$, where r is the interest rate, and t is the number of years one has to wait. See Caroline Dinwiddy, *Elementary Mathematics for Economists* (New York: Oxford University Press, 1967), pp. 199–216.

10. See note 5 for the questionable alternative perspective that makes no distinction between hourly fees received and time costs.

11. On the economics of price setting, see any elementary or intermediate economics textbook such as Paul Samuelson, *Economics: An Introductory Analysis* (New York: McGraw-Hill, 1972); and William Baumol, *Economic Theory and Operations Analysis* (Englewood Cliffs, N.J.: Prentice-Hall, 1965), pp. 311–337.

12. On internalizing group and societal goals into individual benefit-cost considerations, see "Using Decision Deterrence Theory to Encourage Socially Desired Behavior," which is Chapter 8 in Nagel and Neef, *Decision Theory and the Legal Process*. To illustrate the problem of getting individual salaried lawyers to internalize law-office goals, that chapter discusses having an incentive system to get assistant prosecutors to move cases faster rather than ask for work-easing continuances. To illustrate the problem of getting a corporation and its house counsel to internalize societal goals, the problem of environmental protection is used.

13. On proposed systems to reconcile the interests of attorneys and clients in allocating time and setting fees, see Murray Bloom, *The Trouble with Lawyers* (New York: Simon and Schuster, 1968); D. Rosenthal, *Lawyer and Client: Who's in Charge* (New York: Russell Sage, 1974); and Clermont and Currivan, "Improving on the Contingent Fee."

14. On alternative methods for paying lawyers to represent indigent clients or defendants and how those methods affect the behavior of lawyers, see Arthur Berney et al., *Legal Problems of the Poor: Cases and Materials* (Boston: Little, Brown, 1975), pp. 499–588; Lee Silverstein, *Defense of the Poor: The National Report* (Chicago: American Bar Foundation, 1965); and S. Nagel, "Effects of Alternative Types of Counsel on Criminal Procedure Treatment," *Indiana Law Journal* 48 (1973): 404.

15. On the computerized data-gathering and retrieval systems of LEXIS, WESTLAW, and related systems, see American Bar Association, Law and Technology Committee, *Automated Law Research* (Chicago: American Bar Association, 1973); and Diane McCabe, "Automated Legal Research: A Discussion of Current Effectiveness and Future Development," *Judicature* 54 (1971): 283. On the Jury Verdict Research Corporation system, see the Jury Verdict Expectancies Service (since 1962) and the Valuation Handbook Service (since 1962) as well as Chapter 6 of this book.

16. See note 3 on how a computer can fit a curve to a set of data using damages awarded and billable hours for a set of cases.

12

Sequencing and Allocating Attorney Time to Cases

The purpose of this chapter is to discuss how attorneys can better sequence and allocate their time in processing cases by making use of modern management-science methods. Such methods can maximize benefits minus costs while complying with ethical constraints. The chapter also emphasizes making use of records that show the amount of time spent on various cases and the results obtained. The records could come from one's own firm or from a set of firms whose time-and-results records are available through a looseleaf service.

The chapter is logically divided into two parts. The first part is concerned with the order in which cases should be efficiently handled. Ordering is necessary unless there are as many lawyers in the law firm as there are cases. Then no case would be taken unless a lawyer is free to work on the case. That way there is no backlog and no need for sequencing. As long as there is a backlog of at least two cases, there is a need for the next available lawyer to decide the most efficient order in which the cases should be processed. Processing them on a first-come, first-served basis may not be the most efficient procedure from the perspective of maximizing the benefits minus the costs of either the firm or the clients.[1]

The second part is concerned with how much time to devote to each case. Time allocating is necessary because devoting too little time to a case may result in losing a contingency fee and may be unethical regardless of the fee-paying arrangement. Likewise, devoting too much time to a case may be wasteful under a contingency fee or a flat fee and may be unethical under an hourly fee. One thus wants to find the optimum-time level for each case where doing too little or too much is undesirable.[2] The time-allocation part is much shorter than the case-sequencing part because the time-allocation problem has been partially discussed in previously published articles, but systematic case sequencing by lawyers has not been previously analyzed.

PRELIMINARY INFORMATION

The Illustrative Data

Table 12–1 provides a set of hypothetical data that can be used to illustrate the principles of this chapter regarding optimum-sequencing and optimum-time-allocation levels. The data is for 12 cases that correspond to four casetypes. The four casetypes might be medical-malpractice, anti-trust, product-liability, and automobile-accident cases or any set of casetypes as defined by the nature of the specialization of the law firm in question.[3]

Column 3 shows the hours spent on each of these 12 cases according to the time and billing records of the law firm. The column provides a measure of the cost incurred in each case figuring that an hour's time is worth $100 to a prominent law firm and also recognizing that the arithmetic is simpler by figuring $100 an hour rather than a less round number. One could also include other variable costs for each case, in contrast to the fixed costs of the law firm that are not attributable to specific cases. For the sake of simplicity, however, other variable costs are left out.

Column 4 shows the fee obtained in each of these cases. The fee is expressed in terms of benefit units, each one of which is worth $100. Thus the first case involved 10 cost units or $1,000 and 21 benefit units or $2,100. The numbers in the benefits column can be considered as benefits that have already been discounted for the probability of their being received and discounted for delay when the payoff does not occur until substantially later.

Column 5 shows the benefit/cost ratio or efficiency ratio for each case by dividing column 4 by column 3. Column 6 shows the benefit minus cost (B − C) difference or profit for each case by subtracting column 3 from column 4. This chapter will help demonstrate that the benefit/cost (B/C) ratios are needed for sequencing cases in order to maximize total benefits minus costs of the firm over the course of a year or other time period. This chapter will also help demonstrate that the B − C differences are needed for allocating time to each case also in order to maximize total benefits minus costs of the firm.

Note that all of the cases are predicted to be profitable in that the B/C ratio

Table 12–1
Sequencing Attorney Time to Cases with One Benefit Measure

(1) IDENTIFICATION	(2)	(3) CRITERIA	(4)	(5) OVERALL SCORES	(6)	(7)
Case	Casetype	Hours (C) (1H=$100)	Benefits (B) (1B=$100)	B/C Ratio (4)/(3)	B-C Difference (4)-(3)	(B-C)/C (6)/(3)
1	A	10	21-	2.10	11	1.10
2	A	20	61*	3.05*	41*	2.05*
3	A	30	80*	2.67	50*	1.67
4	B	10*	20-	2.00-	10	1.00
5	B	20	45	2.25	25	1.25
6	B	30	55	1.83-	25	.83
7	C	10*	30-	3.00*	20	2.00*
8	C	20	45	2.25	25	1.25
9	C	30	45	1.50-	15	.50
10	D	10*	25-	2.50	15	1.50
11	D	20	60	3.00*	40	2.00*
12	D	30	85*	2.83	55*	1.83
TOTALS		240	572	29.00	332	17.00

NOTES:

1. Columns 3 and 4 show hypothetical data which could be obtained from the records of a law firm or a looseleaf service which compiles information on cases as to damages awarded, hours worked, and other characteristics.
2. The stars in columns 3 through 7 show the three best cases on each column from the perspective of the plaintiff lawyer. The hyphens in columns 4 and 5 show the three best cases on each column from the perspective of the defendant lawyer.
3. The B/C ratios in column 5 provide the order for sequencing the cases to maximize total benefits minus costs. The B-C differences in column 6 show the optimum level of hours for each casetype to maximize total benefits minus costs.

is greater than 1.00 and the B − C difference is always positive. Otherwise we would not deliberately take the case to begin with, unless we were taking a loser now in order to get a big winner later from the same client.

Predicting Costs and Benefits

A data table like Table 12–1 can serve two important purposes. One is to make sequencing and allocating decisions when the data table represents incoming cases that have not yet been processed. A second purpose is to make predictions concerning incoming cases with regard to how many hours each case is likely to consume and what the benefits or income is likely to be from each case.

As for the predictive purpose, rather than the decision-making purpose, one can predict future time consumption from a data table like this by the following two steps:

1. Determine the casetype for the incoming case. Narrowly classifying the cases may give precision in describing the cases, but if the categories are too narrow, the sample sizes may be too small to generalize from.
2. Observe the average number of hours for cases of the appropriate casetype. For example, if an incoming case fits Casetype B, it would be reasonable to predict that the incoming case will probably take about 20 hours. We have three examples of Casetype B in our data table. They took 10, 20, and 30 hours respectively, thereby averaging 20 hours for the set of three cases.

There are more complicated ways of predicting how much time cases will consume, but this method is sufficient for later illustrating what one does with predicted case-time.

One can likewise predict benefits or income per case using a similar two-step approach.

1. Determine the casetype for the incoming case.
2. Determine the average benefits or income for cases of the appropriate casetype. For example, if an incoming case fits Casetype B, it would be reasonable to predict that the incoming case will probably bring in about 162/3 benefit units, or 54 benefit units, or $5,400.

OPTIMUM SEQUENCING

Suppose that we now consider the data in Table 12–1 to represent 12 incoming cases, rather than 12 past cases. Suppose further that these cases represent the total backlog of our small law firm, and this is the beginning of the week. In what order should we process these cases.

Some attorneys might suggest processing the cases on a first-come, first-served basis since that rule seems fair and it avoids having to think about how the sequencing could be done better. But first-come, first-served is not necessarily fair since it may mean that short cases and others may have to wait a long time to be processed because a long case came in ahead of them. If the cases are processed with the shortest cases first, the average delay will be substantially reduced without necessarily causing the maximum delay to become unreasonable or unethical, assuming that the long cases are flagged for processing before they exceed a maximum constraint.

Other attorneys might suggest processing the cases by a variety of sequencing methods that make no sense in terms of maximizing the income minus expenses of the firm such as:

1. Take the shortest cases first to get them out of the way, rather than to reduce the average delay to clients.
2. Take the longest cases first to get them out of the way.
3. Take the most profitable cases first to bring in working capital.
4. Take the least profitable cases first to get them out of the way and to have the more profitable cases to look forward to.
5. Use other sequencing methods.

Sequencing by B/C Ratios

Before clarifying the defects in the above methods, we should clarify the method that does make sense. It involves taking the cases in the order of their benefit/cost ratios. Suppose that we have a 40–hour week and one attorney. How should that 40–hour week be most efficiently spent in processing these 12 cases? We should take Case 2 first since it has the highest benefit/cost ratio at 61/20 or 3.05. We should then take Case 7 since it has the second highest benefit/cost ratio at 3.00, although Case 11 also has a 3.00 B/C ratio. When two cases have the same B/C ratio, prefer the case with the shorter hours in order to reduce the average waiting time per client. If we take all three cases, the total number of predictive hours is 50 hours. This means that the second 10 hours of Case 11 are postponed or continued into next week.

If we follow that procedure, we will have incurred 40 hours of cost, or $4,000. We will have obtained predicted benefits equal to 61 plus 30 plus half of 60, for a total of 121 benefit units, or $12,100. We are figuring half of the 60 benefit units for Case 11 because we have put in half of the predicted 20 hours that are needed to complete the case. We could state that there are no benefits until the case is completed. That would be the equivalent of operating on a cash-accounting system, rather than an accrual-accounting system, although the accrual system generally makes more sense. As a compromise we could accrue 30 benefit units when we complete 10 of the 20 hours. After completing the full case and seeing that the case took 15 hours, we could then adjust the benefit units we assigned to the previous week to be $^{10}/_{15}$ or $2/3$ of 60 benefit units, which means 40 units rather than 30. Since reports are normally prepared only on an annual basis, those adjustments would have to be made only once per year in our time-efficiency records. Those adjustments would not have to be made at all if we were just seeking to establish the proper sequencing rule.

Assuming that the predicted benefits are reasonably accurate, we will have made a profit of 121 minus 40 profit units, or a profit of $8,100. There is no combination of cases that can add up to 40 hours that would bring in a bigger profit. By sequencing the cases to bring in bigger profits early, we are not going to change the total profit for the 12 cases. The total profit for the 12 cases will still be 332 profit units. The advantage of collecting fees from the more efficient cases first is that it enables us to obtain more working capital as early as possible to plow into the development of the firm or to invest for obtaining interest. Thus if we add the interest obtainable to the profit figures in column 6, the optimum sequencing of taking the cases in the order of their B/C ratios will give us the greatest total profit plus interest.

Maximum Time Constraints as Supplements

If one strictly follows the optimum-sequencing principle of taking the cases in order of their B/C ratios, a case with a low B/C ratio like Case 9 might never be processed. To prevent that from occurring, maximum constraints are needed on each case. Those maximum constraints should reflect the statute of limitations and whatever the attorneys involved consider to be a reasonable maximum. When the maximum date is approached minus the predicted number of working hours minus some leeway for error, a good scheduling system should flag the cases involved to get them started or completed before the expiration of the time for starting or completing.

Another aspect of optimum sequencing that tends to keep the accepted cases with relatively low B/C ratios from being put off too long is the optional rule that states that at the beginning of each week or other period new cases should be scheduled for getting started. This means that a low B/C case from last week should go ahead of a high B/C case from next week. Thus the sequencing by B/C ratios can be just within a given time cluster or cohort. That rule is designed to supplement the flagging system when optimum sequencing is used by courts to reduce delay, although it does not have to be part of optimum sequencing when used by law firms to improve their cash flow for maximizing income minus expenses.

Sequencing by B − C Differences

The leading contender to sequencing the cases in the order of their B/C ratios is the idea of sequencing them in the order of their B − C differences. At first glance, that sounds reasonable since we want to maximize benefits minus costs, but in terms of our annual or weekly profit-and-loss statement, not in terms of the order in which we process the cases.

If we process the cases in the order of their B − C differences, or their individual profitability, we would process Case 12, not Case 2, first. Processing Case 12 would use 30 hours and bring in 85 benefit units. We would then process Case 3 since it has the second highest B − C difference. Completely processing that case would consume an additional 30 hours, but we only have a 40–hour week. We therefore process only 10 of the 30 hours. As before, we prorate the 80 benefit units by accruing only one-third to this week, or 27 benefit units. Adding 85 and 27 gives a total of 112 benefit units, or $11,200. The B/C sequencing gave $12,100 for the same 40 hours, although sequenced differently. This means that by using B/C sequencing we gained an additional $900 that week to invest in the firm or to draw interest. We could have used hypothetical numbers that would have made the difference between the two approaches equal to $9,000 or $90,000, rather than $900.

If we have the unusual situation in which all of the cases take exactly the same amount of time, sequencing by B − C would give the same result as sequencing by B/C or by B alone. Likewise, if all of the cases produce the same benefits even though they vary in hours required, sequencing by B − C would also give the same result as sequencing by B/C or by C alone. If all of the cases had the same benefits and costs, one could get the same total profit by taking the cases in any order.

Other Alternatives

B/C divided by C is referred to as the "yield ratio." It can be interpreted as a percentage of profit returned to each hour. Thus a yield of 2.00 means a 200 percent return of $2,000 on one's investment of $1,000 worth of time as shown in column 7 for Case 7. Sequencing in order of yield gives the same results as sequencing in order of efficiency. This is so because the yield ratio is always equal to the efficiency ratio minus a constant 1.00. One can show algebraically that $(B/C)/C = B/C - C/C = B/C - 1$, or the reverse. Using yield ratios involves a little more arithmetic, but for many people such ratios are more understandable to use in sequencing because they do include a profit calculation in the numerator. The yield ratio is also useful later when we deal with non-monetary benefits.

At first glance, one might think that the sequencing solution might be influenced by the order of the listing of the cases and that we would obtain a different result if the cases were listed from Case 12 down to Case 1 instead of from Case 1 up to Case 12. There would be a difference in the sequencing but not in the bottom-line profit of total benefits minus costs. If the cases were reversed, the best case to take first would still be Case 2 for 20 hours. The second case, though, would now be Case 11 rather than Case 7. If we take Case 11 for its 20 hours, we have used our 40 hours. The total benefits would be 61 for Case

2 and 60 for Case 11 for the same total of 121 and $1,200. This is so because Case 11 has the same B/C ratio as Case 7, and the B/C ratios do not change as a result of how the cases are listed and thus seen.

To understand optimum sequencing, it is also helpful to show the defects in other forms of non-optimum sequencing. For example, taking the shortest cases first to cover our 40 hours would mean Cases 1, 4, 7, and 10. The total benefits would then be 21 plus 20 plus 30 plus 25 for a low 96 or $960. Taking the shortest cases first is the optimum-sequencing approach for minimizing average waiting time rather than maximizing profit. It is thus a useful sequencing method for the courts to use in sequencing court cases subject to maximum time constraints.

Taking the cases in the order of their benefits and ignoring costs will result in a lower total profit than the $12,100 of B/C sequencing. By coincidence with the data in Table 12–1, the sequencing by benefits is the same as the B − C order because Cases 12, 3, and 2 are the three best cases on both benefits and benefits minus costs, although only Case 2 is in the top three on the more important criterion of the B/C ratio. We could easily change that coincidence by assuming that Case 3 requires 40 hours. Then Case 3 would no longer be in the top three on B − C but would still be in the top three on total benefits. If we then allocate 30 hours to Case 12 and the remaining 10 hours to Case 3, we would receive 85 benefit units plus one fourth of 80 for a total of 105, or only $10,500.

From this analysis of alternatives to B/C sequencing and the previous analysis of the benefits of B/C sequencing, one can conclude that it is the most meaningful way to sequence cases efficiently in a law-firm backlog. That is partially why it is called the "efficiency ratio." One must, however, emphasize that sequencing by B/C ratio is only a means to a higher goal, which is maximizing total benefits minus costs.

SEQUENCING FROM DIVERSE PERSPECTIVES

Lawyers for Civil Defendants

Suppose that Table 12–1 were viewed from the perspective of a law firm that does only defense work in damages cases. Therefore, all of the figures in column 4 are detriments or additional costs and not benefits from the defendant's perspective if they are amounts that are likely to be paid out. Assume also for the sake of simplicity that the defense side has to put in as many hours preparing and conducting each case as the plaintiff side does. How then, should a defense firm sequence these 12 cases?

At first glance, the answer might be to delay the biggest payout cases as long as possible and therefore take the smallest payout cases first, which would mean Cases 1, 4, 7, and 10. The total payout for those four cases would be only $9,600. This can be contrasted with spending 40 hours completing the big payout cases of Case 3 and Case 12. Just as the plaintiff's lawyer wants to bring in the bigger profits early to have the money available for working capital or investment, so also the defendant's lawyer wants to retain the big payouts until later in order to have that money available for working capital or investment.

At second glance, sequencing the cases in the order of their payouts would be as bad from a defense perspective as it would be from a plaintiff lawyer perspective. The defense lawyer who is usually an attorney for an insurance company would be much better serving his or her insurance firm by sequencing the cases in the order of their detriments/costs ratio taking the cases with the lowest ratios first. This means that the insurance-firm lawyers (if they feel an obligation to put in 40 hours) should first work on Case 9, which has a 1.50 detriments/cost ratio. That would consume 30 hours and result in a payout of $4,500. The insurance-company attorney should then work on Case 6 for the remaining ten hours. That will result in a prorated payout of one-third of 55, or 18 detriment units, or $1,800. The total payout will then be only $6,300 in contrast to taking Cases 1, 4, 7, and 10, which generate a payout of $9,600.

If lawyers for plaintiffs seek to maximize their profits, the cases with the highest benefit/cost ratios will get pushed for early resolution. If defense lawyers for insurance companies seek to maximize their profits, the cases with the lowest ratios will get pushed for early resolution, although the insurance companies would prefer to have zero losing cases resolved if that were possible. The important point here is that both sides cannot completely succeed in their opposite strategies. This is a key reason why a plaintiff's attorney cannot start a case on one day and keep working at it until it is finished. That does not happen partially because completing the case may require waiting for the defense, who is in no hurry to cooperate. It may also require waiting for the court system, which has its own backlog and sequencing strategies. Nevertheless, one should still try for optimum sequencing. When one tries for the optimum and only half succeeds, one has still achieved a lot more than if one tries for less than the optimum and only half succeeds.

Lawyers in Criminal Cases

One can also use Table 12–1 to illustrate optimum sequencing in criminal cases from either a prosecutor or defense-attorney perspective. The prosecutor in criminal cases in this context is like the plaintiff in civil cases. The prosecutor gets glory from winning big cases. Prosecutors like to win big cases as early in their terms as possible so as to bask in that glory for as long as possible. Basking in glory is to prosecutors what interest or return on monetary investment is to attorneys who specialize in bringing damage cases. Suppose that the benefits column from the prosecutor's perspective represents years of imprisonment. The prosecutor should thus sequence the cases in the order of their benefit/cost ratios. Doing so will result in maximizing total imprisonment years, which can be used as a rough measure of how well a prosecutor is doing.

From the defense attorney's perspective, the object is to get the sentences down as low as possible when there is going to be a conviction. All of the cases in Table 12–1 involve convictions. We could have added some non-conviction cases by just inserting some zeros in column 4. We could have similarly added some non-liability civil cases. As with the civil-defense attorney, criminal-defense attorneys should be interested in keeping their capital-punishment cases from being consummated more than their shoplifting cases. Likewise, a life-imprisonment case is more of a loss than 30 days in jail, and one would expect defense attorneys to want to delay the embarrassment and regrets that are associated with having one's client sentenced to prison for life or a lengthy term. Assuming that the defense attorney does want to minimize total prison time relative to the hours the defense attorney has available, he or she should push the cases that have the lowest detriments/costs ratios, or ratios of prison years to attorney hours. That means taking Case 9 first and then one-third of Case 6 for the coming 40–hour week.

Sequencing from the Client's Perspective

We have analyzed the sequencing problems of Table 12–1 from the perspective of the civil plaintiff's lawyer, civil defendant's lawyer, criminal prosecutor, and criminal-defense attorney. What about the perspective of the client? In all of these situations, the optimum sequencing from a lawyer's perspective is also the optimum sequencing from the total clientele perspective, although not necessarily from the perspective of any individual client. For example, the optimum strategy of the civil plaintiff's lawyer is to take Case 2 first, then Case 7, and then half of 11. Doing this will maximize benefits gained at 121 units. The benefits column sums to 572 units. This means that other clients will be unhappy to the extent of 572 minus 121 units or 451 units of deprived benefits. There is, however, no better way that the plaintiff's lawyer could sequence the cases in order to provide less than 451 units of unhappiness or more than 121 units of happiness. This assumes working a 40–hour week and that the predicted hours and benefits are reasonably accurate. The same analysis can be applied to showing the harmony between the civil-defense attorney, the prosecutor, and the criminal-defense attorney and their respective clients or salary payers.

The above analysis about the harmony between the interests of lawyers and their clients assumes that the benefits column in Table 12–1 represents benefits for both the lawyer and the client. If, however, the lawyer is getting paid an hourly fee that is dependent solely on the number of hours worked, rather than the benefits achieved, the optimum sequencing might at first glance appear to involve taking the cases that have the most hours first. That, however, would not make sense since the lawyer would presumably be paid so many dollars an hour regardless of whether it is an hour spent on a 10–hour case or 20–hour case. Therefore, even under an hourly rate, the lawyer can justify sequencing the cases in the order of their B/C ratios. Doing that maximizes the client happiness (as mentioned above), which should be an important consideration in lawyer decision-making.

One might also at first glance think that under a flat fee arrangement, a lawyer should sequence the cases to take the shortest cases first. That would make sense if the lawyer were being paid the same flat fee for all 12 cases, with no payment until each case is completed. If, however, the payment is at the time the case is accepted, there is nothing to be gained by taking the shortest cases first. Therefore, the lawyer who is paid flat fees in advance should sequence the cases in the order of their B/C ratios so as to maximize client happiness and thereby increase repeat customers and referrals. The same is true if the lawyer is paid flat fees, but the flat fee tends to correlate with the predicted benefits. Under those circumstances, even if the lawyer is paid only after the case is completed, the sequencing should still be by B/C ratios in order to bring in early the bigger benefits and thus the bigger flat fees.

When sequencing cases, the interests of lawyers and their clients tend to be in harmony. That is not necessarily so when it comes to arriving at an optimum level of time to devote to each case as will be seen in that part of the analysis later in this chapter.

ADDITIONAL CRITERIA LIKE CASE ENJOYMENT

The above sequencing principles operate on the assumption that law firms and lawyers want to maximize their income minus expenses or benefits minus costs subject to ethical constraints, including maximum time constraints on processing the less desirable cases that one has accepted. The sequencing approach needs to be modified, however, if a law firm or a lawyer gets non-monetary pleasures out of certain casetypes or cases more so than others. We might want to add a column to Table 12–1 that seeks to measure enjoyment received on a 1–5 scale. On such a scale, a 5 means strong positive enjoyment, a 4 means mild positive enjoyment, a 3 means neither pleasure nor displeasure, a 2 means mild displeasure, and a 1 means strong displeasure.

If we insert a column called psychological enjoyment-benefits, we could not add the scores in that column to the scores in the dollar-benefits column to obtain a total benefits score. Likewise, we cannot subtract dollar costs from enjoyments benefits. We can, however, convert enjoyment benefits, dollar benefits, and dollar costs into dimensionless part/whole percentages by dividing each criterion figure per case by the total shown in the column. Doing this creates a set of percentages that can be meaningfully added and subtracted. That can be done even better if the lawyers can state how much more psychological enjoyment is worth to them than gaining dollar income or saving dollar costs. If psychological enjoyment is worth twice as much, the part/whole percentages in the enjoyment column all get multiplied by 2. Weighted part/whole percentages are generally easier for people to handle than trying to attach a monetary value to the 1–5 enjoyment units. Those ideas are implemented on columns 4–7 of Table 12–2.

Table 12–2
Sequencing Attorney Time to Cases with Two Benefit Measures

(1)	(2)	(3)	(4)	(5)	(6)	(7)	(8)	(9)
IDENTIFICATION		HOURS	B-C DIFFERENCE		ENJOYMENT SCORE		OVERALL SCORES	
Case	Casetype		$	P/W%	1-5 Scale	P/W%	Sum of the Weighted P/W%'s (5)+2(7)	Sum/Hours (8)/(3)
1	A	10	$11	3%	2	6%	15%	1.50
2	A	20	41	12	3	10	32	1.60*
3	A	30	50	15	3	10	35*	1.17
4	B	10	10	3	1	3	9	.90
5	B	20	25	8	3	10	28	1.40
6	B	30	25	8	4	13	34*	1.13
7	C	10	20	6	1	3	12	1.20
8	C	20	25	8	2	6	20	1.00
9	C	30	15	5	3	10	25	.83
10	D	10	15	5	1	3	11	1.10
11	D	20	40	12	3	10	32	1.60*
12	D	30	55	17	5	16	49*	1.63*
TOTALS		240	332	100%	31	100%	300%	15.06

NOTES:

1. Columns 3 and 4 come from columns 3 and 6 of Table 12-1.
2. The enjoyment scores of column 6 are measured on a 1-5 scale with 5 = strong positive enjoyment, 4 = mild positive enjoyment, 3 = neither positive nor negative enjoyment, 2 = mild displeasure, and 1 = strong displeasure.
3. The enjoyment scores for illustrative purposes are given twice the weight of monetary profit.
4. The sum of the weighted P/W%'s provide a measure of total B-C where multiple criteria are not all measured on the same scale.

When combining monetary and non-monetary goals as Table 12–2 does, one should first combine \$B and \$C into a single monetary goal of \$B and \$C. The non-monetary goals should also be combined if they are measured on the same scale, such as a 1–5 scale. If the non-monetary goals on the same scale differ in importance, one should indicate the relative weight of each non-monetary goal and then multiply the scale scores by those weights when making the non-monetary combination. By combining the monetary goals and the non-monetary goals that can be combined, we thereby reduce the analysis in Table 12–2 to one composite monetary goal and as few non-monetary goals as possible. We can then subject the scores to part/whole percentaging in order to convert the raw scores into dimensionless numbers.

Column 8 shows the sum of the weighted part/whole percentages for each case. Each of those sums is arrived at by taking the part/whole percentage for the B − C difference shown in column 5 and adding it to twice the part/whole percentage for the enjoyment score shown in column 7. Those figures in column 8 can be referred to as showing percentage benefits minus percentage costs or %B − %C. One would, however, not want to sequence the cases in the order of the column 8 numbers any more than one would want to sequence the cases in Table 12–1 in the order of the B − C differences. Sequencing by B − C or %B − %C does not maximize overall benefits minus costs. It does not take into consideration that the case with the highest B − C or %B − %C may also consume a large quantity of hours and inefficiently leave no time for handling other highly profitable cases.

To consider the quantity of hours in sequencing the cases, one needs to divide B − C by hours in Table 12–1 and divide %B − %C by hours in Table 12–2. That is done in column 9. It shows that the best order in which to process the cases for the first 40–hour week is Case 12 first, which uses 30 hours. We then have a choice of either Case 2 or Case 11, both of which have a score of 1.60 on (%B − %C)/Hours. Both cases also happen to take 20 hours. One can therefore complete the 40 hours by doing half of the 10 hours of work on either Case 2 or Case 11. The result will be 49 plus 16 %profit units. There is no other combination of 40 hours that will add to more than those 65 %profit units. If, for example, one were to take Case 23 and the next more profitable case, which is Case 6, that would mean 49 %profit units plus one-third of 34, or 11 %profit units for Case 6. The total would then be only 60 %profit units, rather than 65.

The analysis in Table 12–2 enables one meaningfully to combine criteria that are measured in dollars (like the B − C difference) and other relevant criteria that are measured on a different scale (like psychological enjoyment). The arithmetic, however, requires more effort than Table 12–1, where all of the criteria are measured in dollars. Even so, the arithmetic is no more complicated than calculating and adding percentages rather than raw scores. The arithmetic can be made easier using a microcomputer program called Policy/Goal Percentaging. The user inputs into a microcomputer (along with the program) the predicted benefits and costs for each case and a psychological enjoyment score. The microcomputer then displays information like that shown in Table 12–2 to enable the user-lawyer or legal administrator to schedule the cases accordingly. Doing this will result in bringing in the biggest monetary and non-monetary profits as early as possible so that one can invest the money and enjoy the psychological pleasures with many returns thereafter. That would not be so possible if those profits and pleasures were needlessly delayed through bad scheduling.

ALLOCATING TIME PER CASE

The main purpose of this chapter is to discuss the optimum sequencing of cases, rather than how much time should be optimally allocated to each case. The time allocating problem is interesting, but unlike the sequencing problem, it has been previously discussed in the law-review literature by me and others. Time allocating is also a simpler problem, although one that raises trickier ethical questions.

With the data from Table 12–1, one can logically state that the optimum time for cases of Casetype A is 30 hours; for Casetype B, anything between 20 and 30 hours; for Casetype C, 20 hours; and for Casetype D, 30 hours. Those figures are arrived at by noting which case or time interval gives the most profit. With only three cases per casetype, we do not have a very large sample for generalizing. It would be much better to have a few dozen cases per casetype. We could then arrange the cases in the order of their billable hours and observe through simple graphing at which level of billable hours profit tends to be maximized. For most casetypes, when there is a relation between hours and benefits received, the profit or B − C difference would go up as more hours are devoted to bringing in more benefits, but then profit would go down as the hours become excessive relative to the diminishing returns. The same reasoning applies to Table 12–2 where non-monetary criteria are involved, except that for each casetype, we would pick the level of hours corresponding to the maximum %B − %C, rather than $B − $C.

Ethical problems occur in time allocation because the interests of the lawyer in maximizing the profits of the firm may not be congruent with the interests of clients in maximizing their benefits minus costs, unlike the sequencing situation in which the interests do tend to be congruent. Under an hourly rate, a lawyer might have a tendency to work more hours than under a contingency fee or flat fee to the benefit of the lawyer's income but to the detriment of the client's expenses. Likewise, under a flat fee, the lawyer might have a tendency to work as few hours as possible to the benefit of keeping down the lawyer's expenses but to the detriment of the client's benefits in winning whatever the client is seeking. Even under a contingency fee or a case in which the lawyer gets paid in proportion to the benefits obtained for the client, there may be a conflict of interest, although they share in the benefits. This is so because only the lawyer bears the expenses for the hours put in, not the client. This could cause lawyers to hold back on additional hours in order to maximize their benefits minus costs, which are not the same as the benefits minus costs of the clients. The best remedy for these potential conflicts is probably not stronger ethical guidelines for attorneys but instead more price and advertising competition among attorneys. Consumers are less likely to be taken advantage of when they can do meaningful comparison shopping among attorneys offering different rates and forms of service.

Sequencing the cases to indicate the order in which they should be processed is clearly different from allocating time to each case. Both forms of time management are different from allocating a fixed amount of resources. Time in one sense is not a scarce resource. Individuals have a lifetime of time, which usually means about 70 years from birth, 50 years from beginning law practice, and 25 years from the prime of law practice. Thus if one runs out of time this week, there will be more time available next week. An individual or firm can also hire additional people, thereby acquiring more time for handling incoming cases. Therefore, if a lawyer turns down a case for lack of time, it means that (1) the case could be processed eventually, but the delay would be too long relative to the statute of limitations or other maximum constraints; (2) the case might never be processed because the lawyer anticipates that there will be a continuous inflow of more profitable and more interesting cases such that the case under consideration will always be pushed back; or (3) the case is not worth hiring additional personnel to process.

One should also note that time allocation means allocating time per case not per casetype. For example, suppose that one has two casetypes. Suppose also that the first casetype is twice as profitable as the second in that (1) the average case from the first casetype brings in a profit of $20,000, whereas the average case from the second casetype brings in a profit of only $10,000, or (2) the B/C ratio of the first casetype is 8 to 1, whereas the B/C ratio of the second casetype is only 4 to 1. One would not necessarily allocate twice as much time to the first casetype because the amount of time one would allocate to the first and second casetypes would depend partially on how many cases there were of each type. More important, one always allocates time to cases, not to casetypes. One also allocates the amount of time that analysis of that casetype has shown tends to maximize benefits minus costs, borrowing from next week if necessary.

An important distinction between time allocation to cases and money allocation to activities or places is the fact that case allocation generally involves an optimum-level problem, in which doing too much or too little is undesirable. Allocating to activities or places, however, generally involves an optimum-mix problem, in which the object is to allocate the resources to the activities or places in light of their diminishing marginal returns. It thus makes sense to switch some funding from more efficient activities or places to less efficient ones because the marginal or incremental returns from the more efficient places have plateaued out, but the marginal returns from the less efficient places are still substantial. Under those circumstances, one generally wants to allocate to the activities (X_1 and X_2) in proportion to their elasticity coefficients or exponents in equations of the form $Y = a(X_1)^{b_1}(X_2)^{b_2}$, where Y is a composite goal to be achieved. The activities or places are not so likely to involve diminishing absolute returns whereby profits go up until they reach a peak and then go down as contrasted to tapering off. This is unlike allocating to cases in which the profits do go down as a result of the benefits tapering off while the expenses rise with additional hours or other inputs. This is a more important distinction than stating that more time comes later since in most budgeting problems more money also comes later. Likewise, one can hire or borrow additional money analogous to hiring or borrowing the time of additional people.[4]

CONCLUSIONS

We thus have three kinds of allocation problems covering:

1. Sequencing of cases or activities in order to maximize benefits minus costs for a given period or to reduce delay
2. Allocating to cases in which doing too much or too little is undesirable and each case is viewed as a separate optimum-level problem
3. Allocating to activities or places where an optimum mix across the activities or places is needed to consider their diminishing marginal returns

Those three kinds of allocation can be applied to a wide variety of situations in operating a law firm, a court system, a government agency, or other entities efficiently. One point that needs emphasis is that those methods can bring increased monetary and non-monetary benefits minus costs without incurring substantial risks or investment. Normally, to increase one's net benefits or profits, one has to be willing to take chances or to spend substantial funds or other resources. To obtain the increased net benefits or profits that come from optimum sequencing and optimum-time allocating, however, one simply needs to be more systematic in the processing of cases, especially the scheduling of them. It is hoped that this chapter will contribute to the increased use of those systematic methods for increasing the net benefits of law practice and related activities.

NOTES

1. For literature on optimum sequencing of events as a management-science problem, see Kenneth Baker, *Introduction to Sequencing and Scheduling* (New York: Wiley, 1974); Richard Conway, William Maxwell, and Louis Miller, *Theory of Scheduling* (Reading, Mass.: Addison-Wesley, 1967); and Samuel Richmond, *Operations Research for Management Decisions* (New York: Ronald Press, 1980), pp. 461–480. No literature has been found dealing with optimum sequencing of cases in a law firm, but there are articles dealing with optimum sequencing of cases in the judicial process such as Jack Hausner, Thomas Lane, and Gary Oleson, "Automated Scheduling in Courts," in Sidney Brownstein and Murray Kamrass, eds., *Operations Research in Law Enforcement, Justice, and Societal Security* (Lexington, Mass.: Lexington-Heath, 1976), pp. 217–228; Task Force

on the Administration of Justice, *The Courts* (Washington, D.C.: President's Commission on Law Enforcement and the Administration of Justice, 1967): 88–90, 165–167; and S. Nagel and M. Neef, "Time Oriented Models and the Legal Process: Reducing Delay and Forecasting the Future," *Washington University Law Quarterly* (Summer 1978): 467, 474–482. Optimum sequencing in the judicial process is concerned mainly with reducing the average waiting time, whereas optimum sequencing in law practice is concerned mainly with maximizing income minus expenses.

2. For literature on finding an optimum level of activity where doing too much or too little is undesirable, see Michael White et al. *Managing Public Systems: Analytic Techniques for Public Administration* (Boston: Duxbury, 1980), pp. 278–290; and S. Nagel, *Policy Evaluation: Making Optimum Decisions* (New York: Praeger, 1982), pp. 81–178. For applications to the problem of how much time to allow court cases or stages in court cases, especially criminal cases, see Task Force on the Administration of Justice, *The Courts,* pp. 84–88; and Nagel and Neef, "Time Oriented Models and the Legal Process," pp. 467, 490–494. For applications to the problem of how much time attorneys should allow for civil cases, see F. MacKinnon, *Contingent Fees for Legal Services: A Study of Professional Economics and Responsibilities* (Hawthorne, N.Y.: Aldine, 1964); Michael Kritzer et al., "Understanding the Costs of Litigation: The Case of the Hourly-Fee Lawyer," *American Bar Foundation Journal* 70 (1984): 559–604; and Chapter 11 of this book.

3. I gratefully thank Arthur Robinson, professor, School of Engineering, University of Illinois, for having suggested this data. It was originally part of his class assignment designed to illustrate the use of dynamic programming as a form of operations research. The data, however, can be more easily analyzed by following the principle of choosing the cases in the order of their B/C ratios until one's budget or time runs out. Dynamic programming in this context involves choosing cases by going through a series of stages and doing a separate optimizing at each stage. For literature on a dynamic programming approach to this kind of data see D. Meredith et al., *Design and Planning of the Engineering Systems* (Englewood Cliffs, N.J.: Prentice-Hall, 1985); and G. Nemhauser, *Introduction to Dynamic Programming* (New York: Wiley, 1966).

4. For literature on finding an optimum mix in allocating resources across activities or places, see Claude McMillan, Jr., *Mathematical Programming: An Introduction to the Design and Application of Optimal Decision Machines* (New York: Wiley, 1970); Edward Beltrami, *Models for Public Systems Analysis* (New York: Academic Press, 1977); Walter Helly, *Urban Systems Models* (New York: Academic Press, 1975); and S. Nagel, *Policy Evaluation: Making Optimum Decisions* (New York: Praeger, 1982), pp. 179–254.

13

Allocating Money to Places and Activities

This chapter deals with allocating money, budgets, or other scarce resources to places and activities. It can be contrasted with Chapter 11, which was concerned with allocating attorney time to cases. Chapter 12 was mainly concerned with sequencing or the optimum order in which to process cases. Chapter 14 is mainly concerned with assigning lawyers to types of cases.[1]

ALLOCATING TO PLACES

The purpose of this part of the chapter is to discuss a simple method for optimally allocating resources to places in such a way as to maximize benefits minus costs. The basic method will be illustrated with the example of allocating anti-crime dollars to cities, although one could easily reason by analogy to allocation in any subject matter. The basic method involves clarifying the goals to be achieved, scoring the cities on the goals, weighting the goals, and determining a percentage indicating how much of the total budget each city should receive.

Goals to Be Achieved

In allocating government money to places, there are normally two general types of goals to be achieved. One set of goals relates to the need for money, and the other set relates to the ability to use money efficiently.

Need or equity attributes might be population size, crime occurrence, or wealth of the city. These attributes are similar to allocating national income in accordance with need. Under such a system, each family receives an income in accordance with (1) the number of people in the family, (2) disease occurrence or other variables that require expenditures, and (3) how much wealth or other income the family already has.

An ability or efficiency attribute in the anti-crime context might include the quality of the police-recruitment system measured on a 1–10 scale. This would be analogous to allocating national income on the basis of ability or potential contribution. Under such a system, those with more education or intelligence are allocated higher incomes, anticipating that they will put the money to better use or that such a system will stimulate others to get more education.

Ability can also refer to applied ability, not just potential ability. In the anti-crime context, this might refer to the scoring of cities by knowledgeable people on how well they have been actually fighting crime. This would be analogous to allocating income to people in terms of how much they have actually been contributing to the betterment of society or the economy, as measured by marketplace factors or by a national planning commission.

The need attributes are generally determined through (1) the legislative process, (2) the judicial process, where constitutional equal protection issues may be involved, or (3) the administrative process, where administrative agencies have been delegated authority to make such decisions. Need attributes and their weights can also be determined by surveying relevant people, deducing from other related allocation procedures, or making assumptions and then determining how the allocations are influenced by alternative assumptions.

Ability attributes and their weights can be determined by the same methods. One can also use a relational analysis, whereby proposed ability attributes are correlated with goals such as crime occurrence per capita to see how much statistical weight they have in such relations.

Scoring the Places on the Goals or Attributes

Once an appropriate set of allocation attributes or criteria has been determined, one might then ask what one does with that information. Suppose that we only want to allocate on the basis of one attribute like population between two cities. City A has 40 people, and City B has 10 people, as is shown in Table 13–1. If we have $200 to allocate, we would logically give 40/50 (or 80 percent) to City A, and 10/50 (or 20 percent) to City B. We would not give everything to City A because we recognize the phenomenon of diminishing returns or diminishing

Table 13–1
Allocating Anti-crime Dollars to Cities by Part/Whole Percentages

City	People (Wt=1)	P/W%	Crime (Wt=2)	P/W%	Wealth (Wt=1)	P/W%	Unweighted Sum	Weighted Sum
A	40	80%	90	60%	$500	-83%	57%	117%
B	10	20%	60	40%	$100	-17%	43%	83%
Whole	50	100%	150	100%	600	-100%	100%	200%

City	Police Efficiency	P/W%	Judicial Efficiency	P/W%	Corrections Efficiency	P/W%
A	6	75%	5	50%	3	33%
B	2	25%	5	50%	6	67%
Whole	8	100%	10	100%	9	100%

Symbols

X* = Optimum amount to give to a city.
G = Grand total available to allocate (e.g., $200)
S = Raw attribute score or part.
P = Attribute score expressed as a part/whole percentage of the sum of the scores (P/W%)
W = Relative weight of each attribute (Wt).

Formulas

One attribute: $X^* = (G)(P)$, where $P = S/\Sigma S$
Two or more attributes unweighted: $X^* = (G)(\Sigma P/N)$
Two or more attributes weighted: $X^* = (G)\,[\Sigma(WP)/\Sigma W]$

utility. This means that City A may have more need or ability in general than City B, but the two-hundredth dollar given to City A is likely to produce less need satisfaction or goal achievement than the first dollar given to City B. We thus allocate proportionately, as if we were allocating in accordance with nonlinear elasticity coefficients rather than in accordance with linear slopes.

This kind of analysis can be extended easily to more than two cities. We allocate to each city in accordance with the ratio between its population and the total population of all of the cities or in accordance with the ratio between its attribute score and the sum of the attribute scores of all of the cities.

Suppose that we want to work with two or more attributes such as population and crime. Suppose further that City A has 90 crimes, and City B has 60 crimes. If we are allocating only in accordance with crime, City A will receive 90/150 (or 60 percent) of the $200 and City B will receive 60/150 (or 40 percent) of the $200. Since we are allocating in accordance with two attributes, each of which has equal weight, the logical thing to do is to compromise between the $160 that City A will receive in accordance with the population allocation and the $120 that it will get in accordance with the crime allocation. With these two attributes, City A should thus receive $140, and City B should get $60.

This kind of analysis can be extended easily to more than two attributes. We determine how much each city would be allocated using the proportional allocation for each attribute separately. We then arrive at an average allocation for each city by averaging across those differing attribute allocations. Each attribute should preferably be scored so that a high score indicates a desirable characteristic.

Suppose that one wants to allocate to each place in proportion to the people, crime, and wealth, with all three criteria weighted equally. Wealth has the golflike characteristic that the less of it a city has, the more money the federal government should allocate to the city. A logical way to do this would be to give City A a composite score equal to 80 percent + 60 percent − 83 percent, which equals 57 percent. One would likewise give City B a complementary composite score equal to 20 percent + 40 percent − 17 percent, which equals 43 percent. That tells us that City A should get 57 percent of the $200, and City B should get 43 percent of the $200. If one is allocating to a golflike criterion such as wealth, and it is the only criterion, one can allocate in proportion to the complements of the part/whole percentages. If, however, it is one of a set of criteria, one would calculate a composite score for each place or other object of the allocations. The composite score is the algebraic sum of the positive percentages and the negative percentages. One would then allocate in proportion to those algebraic sums.

To clarify further the distinction between equity or needs criteria and efficiency criteria, the second part of Table 13–1 provides hypothetical data for each place on the efficiency of their police, judicial, and corrections systems. Such data could possibly be obtained by asking knowledgeable police chiefs, state supreme court justices, prison wardens, or other such people to rank order each place on a 1 to N scale or to rate each place on a zero to 100 scale the way political-science department heads have often been asked to rank or rate each other's departments. Perhaps the most knowledgeable people might be those who are officers or staff members of cross-city associations like the International Association of Police Chiefs, the American Judicature Society, or the American Probation and Parole Association. Those scores can be treated arithmetically like the equity scores of population, crime, and wealth. If we allocate only in accordance with efficiency scores, we may thereby get more crime reduction for our $200 than allocating in accordance with the equity scores. We may, however, be violating our sense of fairness that no place should receive less than a certain minimum allocation in view of its population, crime problems, and lack of wealth.

Weighting the Goals or Attributes

Suppose that our initial two attributes of population and crime are not equally important. More specifically, suppose that a survey of legislators, public opinion, or some other relevant group determines that crime is twice as important in allocating as population is. In this situation, City A would receive 80 percent of the $200 budget if population were the only criterion, and 2 times 60 percent of the budget if crime were the only criterion with a weight of 2. This means that we sum 80, 60, and 60 percent, divide by 3 and obtain 67 percent. If the two attributes were weighted equally, City A would get 70 percent. City A gets only 67 percent when crime is given a weight of 2 because City A scores lower on crime than on population compared to City B. In more general terms, we allocate to each city by summing its weighted percentage scores and dividing by the sum of the weights.

The weights should consider the relative importance of each attribute in light of the other attributes that are present. Thus crime would get a greater weight if population were not also included as an attribute, since crime occurrence and population size are closely related. There is no need to consider the measurement units in doing the weighting since 30 days versus 60 days produces the same part/whole percentages as one month versus two months.

On the matter of weighting the equity and efficiency attributes, a compromise might be to weight the three equity allocations equally along with the three efficiency allocations. One can also use a differential weighting, as described above in discussing the weighted composite allocation.

An alternative to allocating with equity and efficiency criteria simultaneously is to allocate with those criteria sequentially. Doing that involves making a decision as to what is roughly the minimum that each place, group, or person needs to be at a minimum level of decency with regard to health, education, freedom from crime, or other societal benefits. If it is determined that City A needs a minimum of $4 beyond what it can afford and City B needs a minimum of $8 beyond what it can afford, the sequential method would allocate that $12 to those two places and then allocate the remaining $188 in accordance with the efficiency criteria. A better sequential method might be to allocate optimally first in accordance with the efficiency criteria and then make adjustments if those allocations do not satisfy the minimum needs.

The simultaneous method may be easier since it does not require determining a minimum constraint level for each city. It is, however, less accurate in guaranteeing that each city will be at or above a minimum level.

The Allocation

In light of all the above considerations, one can summarize the part/whole percentaging approach by stating that it defines the optimum allocation to each city as being the minimum per city and then adding a proportion of the new grand total to be allocated across the cities. The minimum per city is what the city spends on itself plus a federal amount necessary to bring the city up to a minimum level. The new grand total is the original total minus the sum of the amounts needed to bring the cities up to those minimum levels. The proportion that each city gets is then equal to the ratio between the sum of its weighted part/whole percentages divided by the sum of the weights.

There is a need for more research on allocating federal money to cities, or resources to places. Most of the present research relates to (1) descriptions of how much money various cities receive and what they do with it, (2) descriptions of the political process for deciding how to allocate or how a proposal becomes a law, and (3) recommendations for allocations in specific substantive fields, rather than general principles of optimum allocation. Doing research on the effects of alternative allocation systems could pay off in terms of developing ideas for improving allocation procedures and thereby improving the benefit/cost ratio of allocation dollars spent in many subject matters that involve allocating federal money to cities, like crime, housing, transportation, education, health, welfare, and urban development. Such research can also be relevant to improving the more general aspects of allocating scarce resources to diverse places in light of various equity and efficiency criteria.[2]

ALLOCATING TO ACTIVITIES

For a general starter in this illustrative example, there are two budget categories. One is money for the police, and the other is money for the courts. There are two allocation criteria. One is crime reduction, and the other is fair procedure. The scoring of the alternatives on the criteria is purely relative scoring.

Scoring the Activities on the Goals

To score the alternatives on crime reduction, one asks which budget category is less effective on crime reduction. Nearly everyone would say that the courts are less effective than the police in reducing crime.

1. The courts, however, do reduce crime by sentencing convicted criminals. That does have some deterrence effect on the general public, although it may not have much deterrent effect on the specific defendant.
2. Proof that the police are somewhat effective in reducing crime are studies that show highway speeding is reduced by the presence of more visible police cars. The Kansas experiment that found virtually no change in the crime rate of a neighborhood in which the police were temporarily removed is not inconsistent since would-be criminals were not notified that the police were being removed.
3. After giving the less effective category a score of 1, one asks how much more effective the next category is. People might disagree as to how much more effective a 10 percent increase in police expenditures might be relative to a 10 percent increase in court expenditures, but perhaps they might generally say twice as effective. Therefore, give the police a score of 2 on crime reduction.

To score the alternatives on fair procedure one asks which budget category is less effective. Nearly everyone would say that the police are less effective than the courts in separating out the innocent from the guilty, which is the essence of fair procedure.

1. The police, however, do some separation of the innocent from the guilty when they decide who should be given warnings and who should be arrested.
2. Proof that the courts are somewhat effective in separating the innocent from the guilty is the fact that there are so few cases of convicted people who are subsequently found to have been innocent. There are many cases of people who have not been found guilty who subsequently do commit crimes, although that does not necessarily indicate that they were previously guilty. The concept of fair procedure, however, places more weight on freeing the innocent than on convicting the guilty anyhow.
3. After giving the less effective category a score of 1, one asks how much more effective a 10 percent expenditure increase would be for the courts in comparison to a 10 percent expenditure increase for the police. Most people would probably say that there is a bigger gap regarding the effectiveness of the courts on fair procedure than there is regarding the effectiveness of the police on crime reduction. The courts are supposed to be a more substantial part of the crime-reduction system than the police are in the guilt-determination system. Therefore, we tentatively give the courts a score of 3 on fair procedure.

In technical terms, the 2–1 on crime reduction, and the 1–3 on fair procedure are substitutes or proxies for non-linear elasticity coefficients or regression equation exponents.

Weighting the Goals

Table 13–2B differs from Table 13–2A in that the criteria of crime reduction and fair procedure have been weighted in terms of their relative importance. To do the weighting, one asks between those two criteria which criterion is less

Table 13–2
Allocating Anti-crime Resources between the Police and the Courts

A. THE RAW DATA SHOWING THE RELATIVE EFFECTIVENESS OF POLICE AND COURTS ON CRIME REDUCTION AND FAIR PROCEDURE

ALTERNATIVE / CRITERIA SCORING

	Crime re	Fair pro
Police	2.00	1.00
Courts	1.00	3.00

B. THE TRANSFORMED DATA WHEN FAIR PROCEDURE RECEIVES A WEIGHT

WEIGHTED

	Crime re	Fair pro
Police	2.00	2.00
Courts	1.00	6.00

C. THE ALLOCATIONS IN LIGHT OF THE WEIGHTED SUMMATION SCORES OF POLICE AND COURTS

Total Resources = 500.00

Alternative	Actual	Alloc.	Resid
1Police	300.00	181.82	118.18
2Courts	100.00	318.18	-218.18

NOTES:
1. The weighted summation score of police is 4, and the weighted summation score of courts is 7 (see Table 14-2B).
2. The allocation percentage ot police is thus 4/11 or 36.36%, and the allocation percentage of courts is 7/11 or 63.63%.
3. The allocation amounts are arrived at by multiplying the allocation total resources by the allocation percentages. That gives police 36.36% of $500 or $181.82. That also gives courts 63.63% of $500 or $318.18 (see Table 14-2C).

important to the purposes for which the money is being allocated. More people associated with the legal system would say that crime reduction is less important than fair procedure. They would thereby implicitly agree with William Blackstone in direction although not necessarily in magnitude that it is ten times better to acquit the innocent than it is to convict the guilty, or it is ten times worse to convict the innocent than it is to acquit the guilty. After giving the less important criterion a weight of 1, one asks how much more important or desired the next criterion is. Ten to one would be too high in this context since we are not talking about convicting or acquitting a specific defendant but rather about crime reduction and fair procedure, which are only analogous concepts.

For the sake of simplicity and illustrative purposes, we can tentatively state that fair procedure is twice as important as crime reduction to whoever has the responsibility for allocating the $500 budget that needs to be allocated. The relation-scores shown in Table 13–2B are weighted relation-scores. They are arrived at by multiplying the raw scores in Table 13–2 by the 1 and 2 weights of crime reduction and fair procedure. Thus the crime-reduction scores remain the same, and the fair-procedure scores are doubled. For another approach, one could treat all of the criteria as being equally important and then use the sensitivity analysis of the program to determine at what tradeoff magnitude the allocation results become substantially different.

The Allocation

Table 13–2C shows that if one allocates to the police and the courts in proportion to their relative effectiveness of crime reduction and fair procedure (with fair procedure considered twice as important as crime reduction), the police should receive $182 out of this year's $500 budget, and the courts should receive $318. The $182 to the police is arrived at by noting that the grand total of the weighted raw scores in Table 13–2B is 11. Of those 11 points, the police have 4 points, and the courts have 7 points. One therefore allocates 4/11 of the $500 to the police and 7/11 of the $500 to the courts. That means $182 to the police and $318 to the courts. One would not want to give the whole $500 to the activity with the higher score because the scores are proxies for non-linear elasticity coefficients. This means that they reflect the principle of diminishing returns whereby additional money given to a budget category will produce additional good results but at a diminishing rate. After a point, shifting some money to the less effective activity is meaningful because the first $10 spent on the lesser activity is likely to be more effective than the last $10 out of $500 spent on the generally more effective category. One can prove with classical calculus optimization that a goal is maximized by allocating to the goal-achieving means in proportion to their elasticity coefficients. An elasticity coefficient in this context indicates how much of a percentage reduction in crime there would be as a result of a 1, 10, or 100 percent increase in expenditures to the budget category in question. The other elasticity coefficients indicate how much of a percentage increase in fair procedure there would be as a result of a 1, 10, or 100 percent increase in expenditures to each budget category.

Table 13–2C shows that last year, the total budget consisted of $400. From that total, the police received $300, and the courts received $100. Table 13–2C also shows that the police received $118 more than their optimum or proportionate share last year and the courts received $218 less. Those figures could be converted into percentages to allow for the fact that last year's total budget was only $400 compared with this year's $500. Explanations for why the police may be overallocated and the courts may be underallocated are:

1. People doing the allocating may consider crime reduction to be as important or maybe even more important than fair procedure.
2. People doing the allocating may perceive that fair procedure can be bought more cheaply than it can be. They may thus provide only a small allocation to the public

defender's office within the courts thinking that the public defender can adequately represent all potentially innocent defendants on such a small budget.

3. There may be other goals operating in the minds of the decision-makers that we have not included such as the employment goal mentioned later, whereby the police are viewed in some cities as providing important employment opportunities but not so much the courts.[3]

DISTINCTIONS BETWEEN ALLOCATING AND CHOOSING

The most common type of decision-making other than allocation decisions are optimum-choice decisions in which one has a set of alternatives, criteria, and relations between the alternatives and criteria, and the object is to pick the best alternative or combination.

Allocating differs from choosing in a number of important ways. First, the alternatives in allocating are not really alternatives but rather budget categories. For example, if we are allocating $1,000 to two budget categories like police and courts, we would have 1,001 alternative ways of allocating the $1,000 involving only integer amounts. We could allocate $1,000 to the police and $0 to the courts. Another alternative is $999 to the police and $1 to the courts, and so on down to $0 to the police and $1,000 to the courts. If we had a $1,000,000 to allocate, we would have 1,000,001 alternatives. If we had three budget categories, the number of alternatives would become huge. With more budget categories and more dollars to allocate, the number of alternatives becomes astronomical. A large quantity of alternatives is time consuming to analyze even with computers, and distinctions concerning how each alternative scores on the criteria become meaningless. We therefore work with budget categories instead of alternatives when making allocating decisions.

Allocating also differs from choosing with regard to what one does with the bottom-line percentages. In a choosing situation, the bottom-line percentages are used mainly to rank order the alternatives in order to pick the best one or the best five or N alternatives. The percentages could also be divided by cost figures to derive a form of benefit/cost ratios. They in turn could be used to indicate the order in which the alternatives should be chosen until one's budget runs out. In allocating, the bottom-line percentages need to be divided by the sum of the weights in order to have them add to 100 percent, since we cannot allocate more than 100 percent of what we have. Those allocation percentages are then multiplied against the grand total of dollars that we have available to determine how much goes to each budget category.

A third important distinction between choosing and allocating relates to the meaning of the scales on which the relations are measured between the alternatives or budget categories and the criteria. For example, a common scale is a 1–5 scale when no better measurement is available. The 5 means highly conducive to the criterion, the 4 means mildly conducive, the 3 means neither conducive nor adverse, the 2 means mildly adverse, and the 1 means highly adverse. That scale needs no absolute zero point in a choosing problem, regardless of whether one works with raw scores in the absence of multi-dimensionality or with part/whole percentages when multi-dimensionality is present. That is so because the important thing in a choosing problem is getting the alternatives in the proper order or at least determining which alternative is in first place. It is generally not so important to determine how far each alternative is above each other alternative or is above or below an absolute zero on one or more criteria. In allocating on the other hand, if one budget category receives a 5 on a 1–5 scale, and another budget category receives a 1, the first category will receive 5/6, or 83 percent, of the budget and the other category will receive 1/6, or 17 percent, of the budget. That may not make sense if a 1 on the 1–5 scale means that additional money given to the second category will result in a worsening on the criterion. If the part/whole percentages were elasticity coefficients, we would not give more than the minimum required to a budget category that has a negative coefficient with a positive goal. Likewise, relation-scores below an absolute zero should therefore be converted into zeros.

A fourth important distinction relates to the concept of dominance and diminishing returns. In a choosing problem, if one alternative dominates the other alternatives on all of the criteria, that one alternative is obviously the best alternative regardless of multi-dimensionality and diminishing marginal returns. For example, if the police were to receive a higher score than the courts on both crime reduction and fair procedure, the police category is clearly the better category for the purpose of choosing between the categories. That would be so if the police were to receive a score of 2 on crime reduction and a 3 on fair procedure and the courts were to receive scores of 1 and 1. Even though the police receive a higher score on both criteria, we do not give the police the complete $500 allocation available. If we did, we would be allocating dollars to the police when diminishing returns would provide a very low marginal rate of return. At some point, we are better off switching some dollars to the courts. If the police category dominates, it would be better to give all $500 to the police than all $500 to the courts. We would, however, still be better off giving about 5/7, or 71 percent, of the $500 to the police and 2/7, or 29 percent, to the courts. The first $100 given to the police may be more productive than the first $100 given to the courts, but the last $100 between $400 and $500 given to the police may be less productive than the first $100 given to the courts. One can show that if those crime reduction and fair-procedure scores can be treated as proxies for elasticity coefficients, one should allocate the budget to the categories in proportion to those scores and not give all of the budget to the category with the best combined raw scores, even if it is best on all of the criteria.[4]

CONCLUSIONS

From the example of allocating anti-crime dollars to cities and the example of allocating a criminal-justice budget to police and courts, one can conclude that budget allocation can be meaningfully done by using the following principles:

1. Have a reasonably clear notion of the goals one is seeking to achieve and their relative importance.
2. Know what the budget categories are to which the budget is to be allocated, regardless of whether those categories are places or activities.
3. Be capable of indicating how each budget category scores on each goal. Sufficient and valid information can often be obtained by asking knowledgeable insiders to score the relations on 1–5 or 0–10 scales or on scales of relative degrees of relationship.
4. If different scoring systems are used for different goals, weighted part/whole percentaging may be used for dealing with the multi-dimensionality. If the same scoring systems are used on different goals, working with weighted raw scores should be sufficient.
5. By adding the weighted scores across each budget category, one can obtain meaningful aggregate scores to which the budget can be proportionately allocated.

These general principles can be applied in the law firm context to allocating resources to branch offices in different places. The principles can also be applied to allocating a personnel budget to different members of the firm in light of how well they have performed on various criteria. Applying the principles is also likely to result in obtaining insights as to other relevant law-firm applications.

NOTES

1. For further details on allocating to cities, places, activities, or other allocation objects through the use of part/whole percentages and related methods, see Ward Edwards and Robert Newman, *Multi-Attribute Evaluation* (Beverly Hills, Calif.: Sage, 1982); Thomas Saaty, *The Analytic Hierarchy Process: Planning, Priority Setting, and Resource Allocation* (New York: McGraw-Hill, 1980); and S. Nagel, "Multiple Goals and Policies" in *Public Policy: Goals, Means, and Methods* (New York: St. Martin's, 1983), pp. 343–354.

2. For further details on allocating federal money to cities so as to maximize social impact, see George Hale and Marian Palley, *The Politics of Federal Grants* (Washington, D.C.: Congressional Quarterly Press, 1981); Deil Wright, *Federal Grants-in-Aid: Perspectives and Alternatives* (Washington, D.C.: American Enterprise Institute for Public Policy Research, 1968); and George Break, *Intergovernmental Fiscal Relations in the United States* (Washington, D.C.: Brookings Institute, 1966).

3. For further details on allocating a budget to various activities, see John Due and Ann Friedlander, *Government Finance: Economics of the Public Sector* (Homewood, Ill.: Irwin, 1973), pp. 154–197; Thomas Lynch, *Public Budgetting in America* (Englewood Cliffs, N.J.: Prentice Hall, 1985); and Dennis Ippolito, *The Budget and National Politics* (San Francisco: Freeman, 1978).

4. For further details relevant to comparing allocative decision-making with choosing a best alternative or combination, see S. Nagel, *Policy Evaluation: Making Optimum Decisions* (New York: Praeger, 1982), pp. 47–80, 230–254. I thank Gordon Pitz of the Department of Psychology at Southern Illinois University for emphasizing that allocative decision-making may be substantially different from choosing among alternatives.

14

Using Management Science to Assign Judges or Lawyers to Types of Cases

The purpose of this chapter is to discuss the relevance of management science (MS) to assigning lawyers to types of cases. The most relevant MS method in this context is called "linear programming." The relations are "linear" on the assumption that diminishing marginal returns or diminishing incremental output does not occur over a relative short span of time like 30 billable hours a week. The term *programming* in the phrase "linear programming" is synonymous with *optimizing*. It means finding an optimum allocation of scarce resources in the sense of maximizing some goal or goals.[1] The scarce resources are lawyer time. The main goal is to allocate lawyers to different casetypes in light of their abilities and interests and the demand for cases to be processed.

This chapter shows how modern management science can assign lawyers to cases more systematically than the traditional haphazard systems do. The methodology is versatile in taking into consideration any constraints that relate to (1) the range of billable hours each lawyer has on the average per week, (2) the range of billable hours for different types of cases in an average week, and (3) constraints that relate to equity, efficiency, effectiveness, and other considerations. Similar methods could also be used to assign judges more efficiently in a court system to casetypes.[2]

THE PROBLEM OF ASSIGNING TWO LAWYERS TO TWO CASE-TYPES

Expressing the Problem

Table 14–1 shows the basic data for illustrating the management-science methodology and the competing methodology of intelligent trial and error. We have two lawyers named Fox and Wolf. They are each expected to put in 30 billable hours per week. The rest of their time is spent in non-billable activities. In an average week, there are 30 billable hours for each.

These lawyers have been included in a survey of the lawyers who practice in this one firm. The survey involved asking all of the lawyers to score each other lawyer on a 1 to 5 scale as to how well each perceives the abilities of the others in criminal and civil cases. The five points can be expressed in symbols or words consisting of:

1. – or highly incompetent.
2. – or mildly incompetent.
3. 0 or neither competent nor incompetent.
4. + or mildly competent.
5. + + or highly competent in handling this casetype.

Fox received an average score of 4 in criminal cases and a 3 in civil cases. Wolf received a 2 in criminal cases and a 3 in civil cases.

The scores on the 1–5 scale do not have to refer only to competency as determined by a judge survey. They could also be composite scores that take into consideration each lawyer's interests, track record for speed in handling certain types of cases, record on appeal, and whatever else is considered relevant to the systematic assignment of cases to lawyers.

For each lawyer in each type of case, one can calculate an hours-times-quality product. The problem is how to allocate the 60 hours between the two lawyers so as to maximize the sum of all of the hours-times-quality products. In algebraic terms, we would like to solve for a, b, c, and d in Table 14–1.

The problem can also be expressed algebraically or in terms of symbolic logic as a goal or objective function to be maximized subject to various constraints. Table 14–2 states the problem in that manner. The goal to be maximized is the sum of the four products of 4a, 3b, 2c, and 3d. Each lawyer should be assigned 30 hours, which means $a + b = 30$, and $c + d = 30$. Of the 60 hours, 24 hours, or 40 percent, should be criminal and 36 hours non-criminal, which means $a + c + 24$, and $b + d = 36$.

Table 14–1
The Problem of Allocating 60 Hours to Two Lawyers for Two Casetypes

CASES / LAWYER	CRIMINAL		CIVIL		Hours per Lawyer
	Quality Score	Hours Assigned	Quality Score	Hours Assigned	
FOX	4	a	3	b	30
WOLF	2	c	3	d	30
Hours per Casetype		24		36	60

NOTES:

1. The allocation system is shown in its simplest form with two lawyers and two casetypes.
2. Each lawyer is expected to put in thirty hours a week to satisfy the average weekly total of 60 hours of trial time.
3. Criminal cases constitute 40% of the total or 24 hours, and civil cases constitute 60% or 36 hours.
4. Lawyer 1 receives scores of 4 and 3 on the two casetypes, and Lawyer 2 receives scores of 2 and 3.
5. Hours per casetype and hours per lawyer refer to billable hours, as contrasted to hours that cut across cases and are thus not billable to any specific client, such as general background reading.

Table 14–2
Converting the Lawyer-Assignment Problem into a Set of Linear Programming Statements and Coefficients

STATEMENTS \ VARIABLES	Algebraic Form	Linear Programming Coefficients				
		a (1)	b (2)	c (3)	d (4)	Right-Hand Side
Objective Function	4a + 3b + 2c + 3d	4	3	2	3	
Fox Hours	a + b = 30	1	1	0	0	30
Wolf Hours	c + d = 30	0	0	1	1	30
Criminal Hours	a + c = 24	1	0	1	0	24
Civil Hours	b + d = 36	0	1	0	1	36

NOTES:

1. Any variable in an equation in column 2 that has no coefficient is considered as having a coefficient of 1 for that equation. Any variable not in an equation in column 2 is considered as having a coefficient of 0 for that equation.
2. The concept of "statements" in column 1 includes statements of equality, greater than or equal to, less than or equal to, and statements concerning the objective function to be maximized.
3. Variables in columns 3-6 are shown with both letters and numbers. The letters are needed to understand the relation between the equations and the coefficients. The numbers are needed to communicate with the computer since the computer refers to the variables by number.

To communicate the objective function and the constraints to a microcomputer, one needs to express the problem just in terms of the coefficients or multipliers of the variables in the objective function and in the four constraints. The variables are a, b, c, and d. Their coefficients in the objective function are 4, 3, 2, and 3, as indicated in Table 14–2. The first coefficient in the first constraint is a 1 because the variable a is in effect multiplied by 1. The second coefficient is also a 1. The third coefficient is a zero, since variable c is not present in the first constraint. Likewise, the fourth coefficient is also a zero. The right-hand side of the first constraint is 30 hours. One can easily determine the coefficients for the other three constraints by noting that if a letter or a variable appears in a constraint without a multiplier, its coefficient is 1. If a variable does not appear at all in a constraint, its coefficient is zero in that constraint.

The Solutions

Table 14–3 shows most of the alternative possibilities for allocating 60 hours to two lawyers for two case-types. That set of alternative possibilities was determined by working with Cell a. Once any one cell is determined in a four-cell table, the numerical values of the other three cells are automatically determined in order for the rows to add to 30, and for the columns to add to 24 and 36. Alternative #1 sets Cell a at 24 hours. Alternative #2 sets Cell a at 21 hours, and so on through Alternative #9, which sets Cell a at zero hours.

To aid in determining which of those nine alternatives is best, the upper-left corner of each cell indicates the quality score that the lawyer received on the case-type (e.g., 4). In the center of each cell is the assigned hours (e.g., 24). In the lower-right corner of each cell is the product of the assigned hours times the quality score (e.g., 96). The sum of those four products is then shown to the lower right of the four-cell table (e.g., 204). For example, in Alternative #1, the assignments are 24, 6, 0, and 30 hours for the four cells, which generates a grand total of 204.

From those nine alternative allocations, one can easily see which alternative is best. The answer is Alternative #1 because it has a grand total of 204 points in terms of quality-weighted hours. All of the other alternatives have less than 204 points. They each go down by 6 points whenever Cell a is lowered by 3 hours. This tells us that the change slope for Cell a is +2. This means that whenever Cell a goes up by 1 hour, the grand total or objective function goes up by 2 hours. In commonsense terms, that analysis tells us that we should give as many hours as possible to Cell a because it has the highest quality score. That means giving Cell a 24 hours, which is Alternative #1. Another way of arriving at the same result is to state that we should give as few hours as possible to Cell c because it has the lowest quality score. This means giving Cell c zero hours, which is also Alternative #1.

One might also note that Alternative #8 is the worst alternative. It can be considered the malimum alternative, in contrast to Alternative #1, which is the

Table 14–3
Alternative Possibilities for Allocating 60 Hours to Two Lawyers for Two Casetypes

#1 The Optimum

	C quality	C hours	C product	N quality	N hours	N product	Row total
F	4	24	96	3	6	18	30
W	2	0	0	3	30	90	30
Column total		24			36		204

#2

	C quality	C hours	C product	N quality	N hours	N product	Row total
F	4	21	84	3	9	27	30
W	2	3	6	3	0	3	30
Column total		24			36		198

#3

	C quality	C hours	C product	N quality	N hours	N product	Row total
F	4	18	72	3	12	36	30
W	2	6	12	3	24	72	30
Column total		24			36		192

#4

	C quality	C hours	C product	N quality	N hours	N product	Row total
F	4	15	60	3	15	45	30
W	2	9	18	3	21	63	30
Column total		24			36		186

#5

	C quality	C hours	C product	N quality	N hours	N product	Row total
F	4	12	48	3	18	54	30
W	2	12	24	3	18	54	30
Column total		24			36		180

#6

	C quality	C hours	C product	N quality	N hours	N product	Row total
F	4	9	36	3	21	63	30
W	2	15	30	3	15	45	30
Column total		24			36		174

#7

	C quality	C hours	C product	N quality	N hours	N product	Row total
F	4	6	24	3	24	72	30
W	2	18	36	3	12	36	30
Column total		24			36		168

#8

	C quality	C hours	C product	N quality	N hours	N product	Row total
F	4	3	12	3	27	81	30
W	2	21	42	3	9	27	30
Column total		24			36		162

#9 The Malimum

	C quality	C hours	C product	N quality	N hours	N product	Row total
F	4	0	0	3	30	90	30
W	2	24	48	3	6	18	30
Column total		24			36		156

NOTES:

1. Table 14-3 shows all nine possible combinations of hours that would add to 60 hours overall, with 30 hours per lawyer, and 24 plus 36 hours for criminal and civil cases, respectively.
2. The best combination is to give Fox 8 hours of criminal cases per week and 6 hours of civil. Wolf should get zero hours of criminal and 30 hours of civil.
3. Doing so yields a sum of hours-times-quality products equal to 96 + 18 + 0 + 90 or a total of 204. No other combination gives a higher total.
4. "C" Stands for criminal cases and "N" stands for non-criminal or civil cases. "F" stands for Fox and "W" stands for Wolf.
5. The three numbers in each cell are:
   (1) The number in the upper left-hand corner shows how well each lawyer does on each casetype on a 1-5 scale.
   (2) The number in the center of each cell shows the number of hours that could be given to each lawyer on that casetype and be consistent with the other cell allocations, the row totals, and the column totals.
   (3) The number in the lower right-hand corner of each cell is the product of the quality score times the hours in the cell. The number beneath the lower right-hand corner of each four-cell table is the sum of the hours-times-quality products in the cells.

optimum alternative. The malimum can be arrived at by following the opposite rules of those used to arrive at the optimum. This means giving the most hours to the cell with the lowest quality score, which is Cell c. The most hours that it can be given is 24 hours in order to stay within the column total. Once that 24 has been assigned, the other cell entries are automatically determined in order to add properly across to the row totals and down to the column totals. The malimum allocation is thus 0, 30, 24, and 6. Knowing the malimum allocation is helpful because one can then see how close the actual allocation is to both the worst and the best allocation.

One useful purpose in this context that the malimum serves is to show what the overall score would be if the cases were assigned on a random rotation basis instead of an optimizing basis. The results from random assignment would be an overall score of 180 quality hours, rather than 204. The 180 can be arrived at by averaging the optimum and the malimum since there is a symmetrical pattern present in Table 14–3. It can also be arrived at by averaging the nine overall scores of Table 14–3 since they are all equally probable under a random assignment. A more complicated approach would involve randomly assigning via a Monte Carlo computer routine the 24 criminal hours and 36 civil hours to the lawyers in such a way that each gets 30 hours. The important point to note is that by systematically (rather than randomly) assigning the cases there is an improvement of 13 percent as derived from dividing the 24–unit improvement by the 180–unit base. With other hypothetical data, the improvement might be substantially greater (or less) than 13 percent, but there is always a higher amount of quality hours through systematic assignment than through random assignment.

Listing all of the alternative possibilities is too laborious a method of determining the optimum alternative. A simpler way of determining the optimum alternative is to insert the coefficients from Table 14–2 into a linear programming microcomputer routine in response to a series of on-screen questions that ask for the coefficients for each variable in each programming statement. The routine generates the results shown in Table 14–4. Those results indicate that the coefficients in the objective function were 4, 3, 2, and 3, respectively. The results also indicate that the right-hand side of the constraints were 30, 30, 24, and 36, respectively. Those numbers are useful for indicating that the computer was given the proper input. The output refers to those numbers as the original coefficients and the original right-hand side because both are subject to change in the subsequent sensitivity analysis to see the difference that various changes might make in the optimum allocation. The most important part of the results are the optimum assignments, which are 24, 6, 0, and 30. They yield a grand total of 204 quality-weighted hours.

The results also show the change slopes but only for the variables that are assigned zero hours. Thus variable c or Cell c has a change slope of −2, meaning that whenever Cell c goes up one hour, the grand total goes down 2 points. An alternative way of expressing that change slope or coefficient sensitivity is to state that in order to move Cell c from an assignment of zero to an assignment

Table 14–4
The Results of the Linear Programming Analysis and Their Sensitivity

** RESULTS **

VARIABLE	VARIABLE VALUE	ORIGINAL COEFF.	COEFF. SENS.	CONSTRAINT NUMBER	ORIGINAL RHS
X 1	24	4	0	1	30
X 2	6	3	0	2	30
X 3	0	2	2	3	24
X 4	30	3	0	4	36

OBJECTIVE FUNCTION VALUE : 204

SENSITIVITY ANALYSIS

OBJECTIVE FUNCTION COEFICIENTS

VARIABLE	LOWER LIMIT	ORIGINAL COEFFICIENT	UPPER LIMIT
X 1	2	4	NO LIMIT
X 2	NO LIMIT	3	5
X 3	NO LIMIT	2	4
X 4	1	3	NO LIMIT

NOTES:

1. The above computer output indicates that the optimum allocation of hours to cells a, b, c, and d is 24, 6, 0, and 30.
2. Those results are based on the fact that the quality scores for those cells were 4, 3, 2, and 3.
3. Those results also recognize the fact that the row-column totals or constraints are 30, 30, 24, and 36.
4. The objective function value is 204 as determined by adding (24 x 4) to (6 x 3) to (0 x 2) to (30 x 3).
5. The column labeled "coefficient sensitivity" tells us the change slope for any cell whose optimum is zero. It says that if cell c were to go up one unit (i.e., one hour), then the objective function value would go down by two units.
6. The above computer output indicates that the same optimum allocation of 24, 6, 0, and 30 to the four cells would still be the optimum allocation of 60 hours in light of the row and column constraints, even if there were substantial changes in the quality scores in each cell.
7. For example, Fox's score of 4 in criminal cases could go as low as 2 or as high as infinity, without affecting the optimum allocation. A similar interpretation can be given for the insensitivity ranges around the other three quality scores of 3, 2, and 3.

of 1, we would have to be willing to accept a reduction of 2 points in the grand total. One could similarly calculate a change slope for the other three variables by inserting a + 1 hours instead of Cell a into the program and so on for b + 1 and d + 1.

There is a special version of linear programming called the "transportation algorithm," which is easier to apply to the attorney-assignment problem. It treats each lawyer as a warehouse or a supplier of goods and each casetype as a destination or a receiver of goods. The numbers in the cells represent distances from the suppliers to the receivers. Thus each lawyer has 30 units available to supply. The criminal receiver wants 24 units, and the civil receiver wants 36 units. The solution to minimize transportation distances or times is to take 24 units from the Wolf warehouse for the criminal receiver, 30 units from the Fox warehouse for the non-criminal receiver, and 6 units from the Wolf warehouse for the non-criminal receiver. The advantage of using the transportation algorithm is that one has to insert into the microcomputer only the eight numbers shown in Table 14–1, not the 24 numbers shown in Table 14–2. The optimum solution can be generated by telling the microcomputer to maximize rather than minimize the objective function or the overall sum of the quality scores times the hours of each cell.

VARYING THE COEFFICIENTS AND CONSTRAINTS

Varying the Quality Coefficients

An important benefit of the microcomputer approach to assigning lawyers (or judges) to case-types (or people to tasks) is the additional sensitivity analysis shown in Table 14–5. There we see that the quality score of Lawyer Fox on criminal cases could range from a low of 2 to a high of infinity without affecting the optimum allocation. That is known as the insensitivity range. Actually, it only goes from 2 through 5, since the quality scale is a 1–5 scale. To test that insensitivity range, one can insert a 2, 3, or 5 in place of a 4 in Cell a in Table 14–1 and then think about what the new optimum should be. Under any of those changes, Cell a indicates that it would still make sense to give all 24 criminal hours to Lawyer Fox, especially with a score of 3, 4, or 5. Even with a score of 2, which gives Lawyer Fox a tie with Lawyer Wolf, one could give all 24 hours to Lawyer Fox and zero to Lawyer Wolf (or any combination of positive numbers that adds to 24) without affecting which alternative is best.

Those changes will affect the size of the grand total of Alternative #1 but not how it compares to the other possible grand totals. If the size of the grand total for Alternative #1 is lowered by giving Lawyer Fox a score lower than 4, all of the grand totals in Table 14–4 will be lowered, but Alternative #1 will still have the highest grand total. A similar interpretation can be given to the other insensitivity ranges around the original coefficients in the objective function.

Table 14–5
Solutions for Variations on the Constraints

A. Constraints Per Casetype, But Not Per Lawyer

	C	N	
F	4 a 24 96	3 b 18 54	
W	2 c 0 0	3 d 18 54	
	24	36	204*

B. Constraints Per Lawyer, But Not Per Casetype

	C	N	
F	4 a 30 120	3 b 0 0	30
W	2 c 0 0	3 d 30 90	30
			210*

C. Constraint on Total Cases, But Not Per Lawyer or Per Casetype

	C	N	
F	4 a 60 240	3 b 0 0	
W	2 c 0 0	3 d 0 0	60* 240

D. Constraints Per Casetype, Per Lawyer, and on a Cell

	C	N	
F	4 a 24 96	3 b 6 18	30
W	2 c 0 0	3 d 30 90	30
	24	36	204*

NOTES:

1. The underlined numbers are the right-hand side of the equality constraints. Thus for Situation I, the only constraints are a + c = 24 and b + d = 36.
2. The starred number in the lower-right corner of each table is the grand total of the sum of the four products of the quality scores multiplied by the assigned hours.
3. The quality scores are in the upper-left corner of each cell. The assigned hours are in the middle of each cell. The Q times H products are in the lower right corner of each cell.

This shows that there is substantial room for error in scoring the quality of the lawyers on each casetype without affecting the optimum allocation.

Varying the Hours per Lawyer

For some linear programming problems, there are also insensitivity ranges around the numbers that are on the right-hand side of the constraints. That is not so with this problem. If any of the right-hand numbers of 30, 30, 24, and 36 change, that will change the allocations. For example, if Fox is no longer expected to have 30 hours of trial time but instead can have an average of 20, he would not be able to do 24 hours of criminal cases and 6 hours of non-criminal cases in an average week. The allocations must be consistent with the row and the column totals. The row and column totals must also be consistent with each other.

One could, however, ask the sensitivity analysis question of what would be the optimum total hours (other than 30 apiece) to assign Fox and Wolf in light of their four quality scores and the fact that a typical week involves 24 criminal hours and 36 non-criminal hours. The answer is shown in Table 14–5A as 42 for Fox and 18 for Wolf. The optimum allocation for Cells a, b, c, and d reading across is shown as 24, 18, 0, and 18. Those figures could have been arrived at through a linear programming routine using the same objective function of 4a + 3b + 2c + 3d. Actually, any combination of Cells b and d that add to 36 would equally result in the maximum objective function of 204, since the quality scores for Cells b and d are the same. In a tie like that, one can split the column total of 36 among the tied cells, although some computer programs may give all 36 hours to the first cell.

When only dealing with two lawyers and two case-types, one does not need a computer. One can arrive at the optimum allocations by (1) giving as many hours as possible to the high-scoring cells, (2) giving as few hours as possible to the low-scoring cells, (3) giving an intermediate number of hours to the intermediate-scoring cells, and (4) making small trial-and-error adjustments after following those three basic rules. If we add a fifth rule stating that one should minimize the number of casetypes per lawyer, the allocation would be 24, 0, 0, and 36. That way, no lawyer would have more than one casetype. We could also add a fifth rule stating that one should try to give the lawyers roughly equal caseloads when doing so does not decrease the overall objective function. Adding that rule would cause the optimum allocation to be 24, 6, 0, and 30. Both lawyers would then have 30 hours apiece while still achieving the maximum objective function of 204 and satisfying the column constraints.

Varying the Hours per Case-type

One could also ask the sensitivity analysis question of what would be the optimum hours of criminal and non-criminal cases if we operate only under the constraints that say Fox and Wolf should be assigned 30 hours apiece. The answer (as shown in Table 14–5B) is 30, 0, 0, and 30. That solution could also be arrived at by using the microcomputer linear programming approach of Table 14–2 by dropping the last two rows or constraints of that table. With two lawyers and two case-types, one could simply give the first lawyer 30 hours of whatever case-type he or she does best and then give the second lawyer 30 hours of whatever case-type he or she does best. The same analysis could be applied if the constraints were any pair of numbers other than 30 hours and 30 hours.

Table 14–5B shows 30 criminal and 30 non-criminal hours in the average week instead of 24 and 36. A law firm could seek to turn away certain case-types to other firms when the firm lacks lawyers who are especially competent in those case-types or lacks a sufficient quantity of lawyers regardless of their competence. Thus the 36 non-criminal hours per week could be reduced to 30 by diverting or discouraging the extra 6 hours per week. Likewise, if the system has an especially competent lawyer like Fox hearing criminal cases, the firm might therefore encourage more criminal cases. That would mean raising the original 24 hours per week to 30 hours.

The situation shown in Table 14–5B may be the more typical work-assignment situation than the one shown in Table 14–3. Work specialization typically involves each person being assigned to one job as in Table 14–5B and not multiple jobs as in Table 14–3. There is a variation on the linear programming routine called the "assignment algorithm," which generally works with exactly as many tasks as there are people to be assigned.

Other Variations, Inequalities, and Conflicting Constraints

Carrying the variations one step further in dropping constraints, one might ask what the optimum allocation is if there are no constraints per case-type or per lawyer but only a total constraint of 60 hours per week. The optimum allocation then (as shown in Table 14–5C) is 60, 0, 0, and 0. All 60 hours would be assigned to Fox, and the 60 hours would consist only of criminal cases. That is the optimum solution within that one constraint. That set of constraints may, however, be unreasonable if they allow for a lawyer to have no billable hours at all. A lawyer could still do administrative tasks. They and other lawyers in the firm could, however, complain that such an arrangement is not equitable.

Carrying the variations one step in the other direction toward adding constraints, Table 14–5D shows what would happen if in addition to having column constraints for the case-types and row constraints for the lawyers, we also add a cell constraint. A logical cell constraint would be to state that any lawyer who receives a score of 2 or 1 on a case-type should not have any cases of that case-type, since a 2 means that the lawyer is mildly incompetent on that case-type, and a 1 means that the lawyer is severely incompetent. With a four-cell table, adding a cell constraint automatically determines what the other cells have to be without requiring any reiterative trial and error to arrive at the optimum allocations. If a zero is assigned to Cell c in Table 14–5D the optimum allocation is 24, 6, 0, and 30.

An important variation on Table 14–1 is to express the hours per lawyer or the hours per case-type in terms of ranges, rather than specific hours. For example, instead of stating that each lawyer should have 30 billable hours per week, one could express the constraint as from 20 to 30. That is the same as stating that Cell a plus Cell b should be greater than or equal to 20 and less than or equal to 30. Likewise, instead of stating that the case-types should average 24 and 36 hours apiece, one can note that criminal cases range from 9 to 45 billable hours per week, and non-criminal cases range from 24 to 48. Given that information, what is the best allocation for maximizing the sum of the products of the quality scores times the hours assigned?

The answer is an allocation of 45, 15, 0, and 33, arrived at either through the linear programming routine or through logical reasoning. The reasoning approach seeks to push the constraints as high as they will go since the more hours allocated, the more benefits that will be generated, just as in a budgeting problem in which one generally pushes for as big a budget to allocate as possible. The maximum number of hours per week would be 93, which involves 45 criminal and 48 non-criminal hours. Of those 93 hours, 60 should be given to Fox since the sum of his quality scores is higher than the sum for Wolf. Of those 60 hours, give as many as possible to Cell a, which means 45. That determines the other cells as being 15, 0, and 33. Similar reasoning can be applied to arriving at an optimum allocation of hours to lawyers and case-types with other numbers and other combinations of constraints that are equations, ranges, less-than inequalities, or greater-than inequalities.

One could easily introduce conflicting constraints such as stating that (1) Cell c should be zero in Table 14–5D (because Wolf got only a score of 2 on criminal cases); (2) Cell d should be 18, meaning that Wolf should get about half of the non-criminal cases; and (3) Wolf should have 30 hours per week. Whenever there are conflicting constraints, the computer will indicate that the problem is unsolvable. A knowledgeable insider though, may be able to resolve the conflict by prioritizing the constraints in light of the purposes of the system. For example, it is more important to have zero in Cell c than 18 in Cell d. Therefore, we could drop the Cell d constraint more easily than the Cell c constraint. The zero in Cell c is more important for achieving a higher score on the objective function. It is also more important in view of the efficiency of the firm and fairness to clients to avoid lawyers hearing case-types that they do not handle well. A similar analysis could be done wherever conflicting constraints occur.

THE PROBLEM OF ASSIGNING SIX LAWYERS TO FOUR CASE-TYPES

Expressing the Problem

Table 14–6 expands the original problem of only two lawyers and two case-types into six lawyers and four case-types. The new problem is more realistic, and at first glance looks substantially more difficult. It involves solving for 24

Table 14–6
The Problem of Allocating 180 Hours to Six Lawyers for Four Casetypes

CASES / LAWYERS	CRIMINAL		PERSONAL INJURY		FAMILY		MISCEL-LANEOUS		Hours per Lawyer
	Q	H	Q	H	Q	H	Q	H	
BROWN	4	a	3	b	4	c	3.67	d	30
GREEN	5	e	4	f	2	g	3.67	h	30
JONES	4	i	2	j	5	k	3.67	l	30
MILLER	2	m	3	n	4	o	3.00	p	30
SMITH	1	q	4	r	3	s	2.67	t	30
WOOD	4	u	1	v	4	w	3.00	x	30
Hours per Casetype		72		54		36		18	180

NOTES:

1. There are six lawyers in Table 14-6 and four casetypes, as contrasted to two lawyers and two casetypes in Table 14-1. Table 14-6 and the tables which immediately follow are thus designed to illustrate the application of the allocation system to a larger problem.

2. Here the object is to solve for 24 unknowns in order to maximize the sum of the products of the quality scores (Q) times the hours assigned (H) for each lawyer, subject to the row and column constraints.

3. An additional constraint might be that no lawyer should be assigned any hours for a casetype unless the lawyer receives a score of at least 3 on the casetype.

4. The miscellaneous quality score is derived by averaging the other three quality scores for each lawyer.

unknowns since six lawyers and four case-types mean 24 cells or allocations need to be made. Those allocations must also satisfy the six row constraints representing hours per lawyer and the four column constraints representing hours per case-type. The case-types here are criminal, personal injury, family, and miscellaneous.

The problem could be solved with a microcomputer using a linear programming routine. Doing that would involve an objective function of the form 4a plus 3d plus 4c plus 2.67d and so on through 4w plus 3.00x. This would also involve expressing the six row and four column constraints the same way that the two row and two column constraints were expressed in Table 14–2 That is a substantial amount of information, but it can be quickly inputted into the computer in response to a series of simple questions concerning the linear programming coefficients that appear on the computer screen.

The Solutions

Table 14–7B shows the optimum solution as arrived at through the microcomputer program. Table 14–7A shows one trial-and-error solution. That trial-and-error solution was arrived at by following the commonsense rules mentioned at the bottom of the table, which include (1) giving many hours to cells that have a 5 for a quality score, (2) giving few hours to cells that have a 3 and zero hours for cells with a 2 or 1, and (3) giving a middling number of hours to cells that have a 4 for a quality score. Following those rules and making adjustments in light of the row constraints and the column constraints generated the trial-and-error solution shown in Table 14–7B.

The overall objective function of the optimum solution is 750 points after summing the products of the quality scores times the hours assigned for each cell. The overall objective function for the trial-and-error method is almost as close at 738 points. One might state that if trial and error can regularly come within 95 percent of the optimum, it may not pay to go to the extra trouble of obtaining the optimum through a microcomputer program. The total of 738 is 98 percent of 750. Furthermore, one can easily go from the trial-and-error solution of Table 14–7A to the optimum solution of Table 14–7B by adding an additional rule stating that one should try to minimize the number of case-types per judge. The trial-and-error solution in Table 14–7A involves some judges hearing three types of cases, whereas the optimum solution involves no lawyer hearing more than two case-types. Working with a matrix like Table 14–6 and adding that additional rule makes it easy to find the optimum solution through trial and error and a little arithmetic.

CONCLUSIONS

The above analysis should not be interpreted as indicating that the microcomputer approach is not worth pursuing. It may be worthwhile even in problems that are

Table 14–7
Alternative Ways of Allocating 180 Hours to Six Lawyers and Four Casetypes

Cell Letter	Hours Assigned	Quality Score	Quality Times Hours	TOTALS
I. A Trial-and-Error Solution				
a	21	4	88	
b	9	3	27	
e	30	5	150	
k	30	5	150	
n	15	3	45	
o	3	4	12	
p	12	3	36	
r	30	4	120	
u	21	4	84	
w	3	4	12	
x	6	3	18	
				738
II. Optimum Solution				
a	12	4	48	
d	18	3.67	66	
e	30	5	150	
k	30	5	150	
n	24	3	72	
o	6	4	24	
r	30	4	120	
u	30	4	120	
				750

NOTES:

1. The trial and error solution is arrived at by following rules like:
   (1) Give as many hours as possible to cells that have a 5 for a quality score.
   (2) Give as few hours as possible to cells that have a 3 for a quality score.
   (3) Give a middling number of hours to cells that have a 4 for a quality score.
   (4) The exact numer of hours to give as part of rules 1, 2, or 3 depend on the row and column constraints, and what has already been allocated or could be allocated.
   (5) In allocating hours to judges, try to minimize the numer of casetypes per judge. This makes it eaier to find the optimum, and it is in conformity with the idea that specialization is efficient where there are no diminishing returns.
2. The optimum solution is derived by a microcomputer using what is known as the simplex algorithm which guarantees optimality in linear programming situations like this.
3. Both solutions are feasible since they satisfy the row and column constraints. The optimum solution is better since it generates a sum of the quality-times-hours products equal to 750 rather than only 738.
4. With a reasonably big problem of substantially more than two casetypes and more than two lawyers, it may be impossible, or at least difficult to find the optimum solution through trial-and-error and quite time-consuming, as contrasted to using the simplex algorithm in computer or non-computer form.

substantially bigger than six lawyers and four case-types, such as 100 lawyers in a big law firm and 40 case-types or 435 members of Congress and 30 committees to be assigned to. One can also never be sure that one has found the optimum or that one has come within 5 percentage points, unless one uses a computer program or the simplex algorithm behind the program that guarantees an optimum solution. The main benefit of the trial-and-error approach is that it does provide the user with insights into the analysis that are missed by simply accepting the computer output.

On the other hand, the big advantage of the computer output is not that it guarantees an optimum but rather how well microcomputers can do sensitivity analysis. Through trial and error, one may be able to arrive at the optimum solution. It is, however, far more difficult to arrive at the lower limit and the upper limit of the insensitivity range for every quality coefficient like those shown in the bottom of Table 14–4. It is also difficult to arrive at change slopes or coefficient sensitivity scores for every quality coefficient like those shown in the top of Table 14–4. The computer is also helpful in quickly showing how the optimum allocation would change if we make changes in the constraints per lawyer, per case-type, the hours assigned to any cell, or the overall quantity of hours. The computer is at its best not so much in finding the initial solution but in providing useful information on how sensitive that solution is to various changes in the coefficients and constraints. By using that capability, we can arrive at an optimum allocation in light of a possible optimum set of constraints. The computer analysis thus not only provides answers, but it also enables us to improve on the questions we ask.

In the context of using management science to assign lawyers to types of cases, we can conclude that these general methods may enable law firms to operate more effectively, efficiently, and equitably. Effectiveness is improved by having the cases handled better as measured by the objective function of maximizing the products of the quality scores times the hours assigned. Efficiency is improved by building into the quality score the ability to handle cases quickly and inexpensively and thus reduce delay and expense in the system. Equity is improved by treating lawyers more fairly in proportion to their abilities. Their interests could also be taken into consideration in the quality scores. To the extent that equity also means equal treatment, the optimum assignment rules can include equality constraints as well. What is needed is more use of linear programming for optimum assignment of lawyers to case-types and more use of the rational commonsense ideas on which those linear programming routines are based.

NOTES

1. For literature on linear programming and its variations as applied to assigning people to tasks, see Warren Erikson and Owen Hall, *Computer Models for Management Science* (Reading, Mass.: Addison-Wesley, 1983) pp. 23–52, 71–86; Samuel Richmond, *Oper-*

ations Research for Management Decisions (New York: Ronald Press, 1968), pp. 277–285, 314–382; Sang Lee, *Linear Optimization for Management* (Princeton, N.J.: Petrocelli Charter, 1976), pp. 1–246, 307–332. The Erikson and Hall volume is especially useful because it comes with an IBM-compatible floppy disk for applying its versatile linear programming routine.

2. For literature discussing law-firm management, see D. McCarty, *Law Office Management* (Englewood Cliffs, N.J.: Prentice-Hall, 1955); American Bar Association, *The Lawyer's Handbook* (Chicago: American Bar Association, 1975); Bradford Hildebrandt and Jack Kaufman, *The Successful Law Firm: New Approaches to Structure and Management* (New York: Harcourt Brace Jovanovich, 1983); Daniel Remer, *Computer Power for Your Law Office* (Berkeley, Calif.: Sybex, 1983). Also see periodicals such as *Legal Economics* (American Bar Association Section in *Economics in Law Practice*) and *Law Office Economics and Management* (Callaghan and Company). None of the literature examined, however, describes improving law-firm efficiency through more systematic assignment of attorneys to case-types. There is related literature, though, dealing with the assignment of judges to case-types such as *Task Force on the Administration of Justice* (Washington, D.C.: President's Commission on Law Enforcement and the Administration of Justice, 1967); and American Bar Association, *Standards Relating to Trial Courts* (Chicago: American Bar Association, 1976), pp. 86–93.

VI

Facilitating Negotiation and Mediation

Chapter 15 ties many of the ideas together that are presented elsewhere in this book since effective negotiation between lawyers often involves trying to predict what will happen if the negotiations break down and the dispute has to go to court. Effective negotiation also involves litigation strategy since a lawyer receives no favorable points for succeeding in getting the other side to improve its offer from $10,000 to $100,000 if the expected value of going to court minus the expenses is still substantially above $100,000. Effective negotiation also involves rationally allocating one's time since extensive negotiations can be more time consuming than litigation or vice versa. Personal computers can facilitate effective negotiation by enabling each side to simulate what it would take to convince the other side in light of the other side's values and perceptions.

Chapter 15 is also concerned with mediation whereby both sides in a dispute can be brought together such that they both come out winners in achieving more than their worst expectations and sometimes even more than their best expectations. Personal computers can quickly show both sides the effects of new proposals on their respective goals and thereby facilitate the adoption of mutually satisfying proposals. Systematic analysis of alternatives and goals can also aid in making decisions concerning alternative forms of dispute resolution, including alternatives to litigation.

15

Microcomputers, P/G%, and Dispute Resolution

The purpose of this chapter is to describe how a new microcomputer program called Policy/Goal Percentaging can be used to aid in dispute resolution. In that regard, the essence of the program is to be able to show disputants quickly the effects of alternative proposals on their respective criteria. Doing this can facilitate arriving at dispute-resolving compromises, including optimizing compromises in which all of the disputants come out ahead of their original maximum positions.

The program is called Policy/Goal Percentaging because it relates policies (or alternatives) to goals (or criteria), and it often uses part/whole percentaging to deal with goals being measured on different dimensions. The program is designed to process a set of goals to be achieved, alternatives for achieving them, and relations between goals and alternatives in order to choose the best alternative or combination for maximizing benefits minus costs of the disputants or other users.[1]

The kind of dispute resolution with which this chapter is especially concerned is disputes over public policies that ought to be adopted in dealing with various social problems. In such circumstances, the disputants are likely to be liberal and conservative policy-makers, generally serving in a legislative body. They could also be associated with administrative agencies, courts, interest groups, or political parties. Examples could be taken from the public policy fields that relate to environmental protection, poverty, criminal justice, and other social problems.

A good example of the microcomputer program in action is applying it to the highly emotional controversy of how to provide legal services for the poor. That example can be helpful in understanding (1) how to determine initial alternatives, criteria, and relations; (2) how to attempt to resolve deadlocks by weighting the criteria and averaging the alternatives; (3) how to determine what it would take to convince the other side; (4) how to resolve deadlocks by adding an alternative; (5) the concept of optimizing compromise as a goal to seek in dispute resolution; and (6) various other means for achieving optimizing compromises. Other examples will also be given, but all of the examples should be viewed in terms of the general ideas they illustrate and which are applicable to a wide variety of dispute resolutions in public-policy evaluation.

At the outset, one should clarify that the concept of dispute requires persons, groups, ideologies, or other entities to be in conflict over how a matter should be resolved. A problem is not necessarily a dispute, since it may involve only one person or entity trying to decide what to do. The major processes whereby disputes are resolved are through forms of negotiation, mediation, arbitration, or adjudication. In negotiation, the two or more sides interact to try to come to an agreement, which may be considered mutually desirable or may be forced by one party on the other through threats of negative sanctions. In mediation, a non-disputant tries to bring or force the disputants to reach an agreement. If the non-disputants have the power to impose a solution on the parties, they are generally referred to as arbitrators when chosen by the parties or as judges when the non-disputants are imposed on the parties. Mediators generally seek solutions that will be considered mutually satisfying by the parties. Arbitrators and judges seek solutions that are considered correct in accordance with a body of past practice, common sense, or rules, and the solutions may not be mutually satisfying.[2]

The P/G% program can facilitate either individual problem solving or dispute resolution. It can facilitate dispute resolution through negotiation, mediation, arbitration, or adjudication. The emphasis in this chapter is on dispute resolution through microcomputer-facilitated negotiation and mediation. Various articles deal with microcomputer-facilitated arbitration and adjudication.[3]

DETERMINING THE INITIAL ALTERNATIVES, CRITERIA, AND RELATIONS

The basic alternatives in the public-policy dispute over how to provide legal services to the poor are a volunteer system versus salaried government lawyers. The Reagan administration has repeatedly proposed that legal services for the poor should be provided by volunteer lawyers with no federal appropriation. Congress has repeatedly voted in favor of salaried government lawyers working for the Legal Services Corporation. An interesting aspect of this dispute is that the disputants generally agree on (1) the conflicting alternatives, (2) the basic criteria for determining the best alternative, and (3) how the alternatives score on each criterion. Yet they disagree on which alternative is best, largely because they disagree on the relative importance of the various criteria. Until recently, they have not adequately explored dispute-resolving alternatives.[4]

The four basic criteria cover:

1. Inexpensiveness. Both liberals and conservatives favor inexpensiveness or efficiency in that if quality legal services can be provided for $100 million, $150 million should not be spent. Liberals and conservatives may disagree about what should be done with the extra $50 million. Liberals might favor urban programs, and conservatives might favor defense programs. Neither side, however, would favor spending $150 million for what could be obtained for only $100 million.
2. Accessibility. The program should be accessible and visible to poor people. If one is sincerely interested in having a legal-services program for the poor, it should be a program that will be used and not one that is relatively unknown or especially difficult to make use of.
3. Political Feasibility. The program should be capable of (1) getting through Congress and (2) not being vetoed by the president or capable of surviving a veto through a two-thirds congressional vote.
4. Competency. The attorneys in the program should be reasonably competent. They should be willing and able to go to court if necessary to provide adequate representation to their clients.

Table 15–1A shows how the two alternatives score on the four criteria. Each criterion involves a simple 1–2 scale, where 1 means relatively low, and 2 means relatively high. The scoring of the relations between the alternatives and the criteria are as follows:

1. Inexpensiveness. The volunteer system is clearly less expensive than a system of salaried government lawyers.
2. Accessibility. The salaried government lawyer in the context of the Legal Services Corporation (LSC) is especially accessible by way of storefront neighborhood law offices. Volunteer legal aid has traditionally been relatively inaccessible because of the difficult procedures for accessing the volunteer attorneys. For example, in Champaign County before the Legal Services Corporation, poor people would (1) phone the United Fund and (2) be referred to the office of the Bar Association where they would then (3) be referred to the chairperson of the Legal Aid Committee who would then (4) refer them to a member of the committee who might then be unavailable or who would (5) refer them to law students in their office. The system processed about 50 cases a year before LSC, which was almost immediately processing about 100 cases per week largely due to increased visibility and accessibility.

Table 15–1
Volunteer versus Salaried Legal Services

A. WITH UNWEIGHTED CRITERIA

	INEXPENS	ACCESSIB	POLIT.FE	COMPETEN
VOLUNTEER	2.00	1.00	2.00	1.00
SALARIED G	1.00	2.00	1.00	2.00

B. WITH CONSERVATIVE-WEIGHTED CRITERIA

	INEXPENS	ACCESSIB	POLIT.FE	COMPETEN
VOLUNTEER	4.00	1.00	4.00	1.00
SALARIED G	2.00	2.00	2.00	2.00

C. WITH LIBERAL WEIGHTED CRITERIA

	INEXPENS	ACCESSIB	POLIT.FE	COMPETEN
VOLUNTEER	2.00	2.00	2.00	2.00
SALARIED G	1.00	4.00	1.00	4.00

3. Political Feasibility. The volunteer system is more politically feasible in that no one in Congress is likely to object to attorneys being willing to volunteer to help poor people. On the other hand, there are objections to paying government salaries to such attorneys, especially if they spend substantial time developing test cases and new legal policies concerning the legal rights of the poor against landlords, merchants, employers, and government officials, in contrast to more routine family-oriented legal-aid matters.
4. Competency. The salaried system tends to generate more competent attorneys who work full time in the field of poverty law. The volunteer system tends to bring out new attorneys who are looking for experience or older attorneys who are trying to be helpful but who are not so knowledgeable about poverty-law matters.

THE MAJOR APPROACHES FOR RESOLVING DEADLOCKS

Weighting the Criteria and Averaging the Alternatives

Table 15–1A shows that with those four reasonable criteria and with the reasonable scoring of the alternatives on them, there is a deadlock tie of 6 points apiece for each alternative. At first one might think the tie could be broken and the dispute resolved by recognizing that the criteria should not all receive equal weight. Table 15–1B uses conservative weights. Such weights put relatively more emphasis on inexpensiveness and political feasibility. Doing this means doubling the scores on those two criteria to show that those criteria have more importance than accessibility and competency. Doing this in Table 15–1B shows that the volunteer system receives 10 points, and the salaried system receives only 8 points from a conservative perspective.

Table 15–1C uses liberal weights. Such weights put relatively more emphasis on accessibility and competency. Doing this means doubling the score on those two criteria to show that they are more important than inexpensiveness and political feasibility. Table 15–1C then shows that the volunteer system receives only 8 points, and the salaried system receives 10 points from a liberal perspective. If we average the conservative 10 and the liberal 8 for the volunteer system, we obtain an average 9. Likewise, if we average the conservative 8 and the liberal 10 for the salaried system, we also obtain an average 9.

Thus weighting the criteria does not resolve the deadlock here. It might have done so if liberals were to like the salaried system more than conservatives like the volunteer system, or vice versa, assuming that liberals and conservatives have an equal say in this controversy. In this situation, however, their value weights are diametrically opposed in both direction and magnitude.

The results of the weighting here merely tell us that if one has conservative values, one is likely to prefer the volunteer over the salaried system, and that if one has liberal values, one is likely to prefer the salaried over the volunteer lawyers for providing legal services to the poor. One might, therefore, conclude that systematic policy analysis is a sham, especially with microcomputers, because it merely tells us that the results depend on one's values. This Legal Services dispute, however, turns out to be one of the real success stories of systematic policy analysis, as we will see shortly.

Determining What It Would Take to Convince the Other Side

Another way of sometimes resolving such disputes besides the system of weighting and averaging is to have one side convince the other side to adopt the other position. The P/G% software is especially helpful in showing what changes are needed in the scoring of the relations or the weighting of the goals to move the liberals to adopt the volunteer system or the conservatives to adopt the salaried system.

Table 15–2A shows what it would take to bring the salaried system up to the level of the volunteer system, given the conservative values. Table 15–1B previously showed that with the conservative weights, the volunteer system receives a score of 10 and the salaried system receives a score of 8. Thus there is a 2-point gap that the liberals need to make up to convince the conservatives that the salaried system is as good as the volunteer system. Table 15–2A shows 12 ways that this gap could theoretically be made up. Those ways, reading down the columns, are:

1. Inexpensiveness.
    a. The volunteer system receives a "no" on inexpensiveness.

Table 15–2
What It Would Take to Convince the Other Side

A. BRINGING THE SALARIED SYSTEM UP TO THE LEVEL OF THE VOLUNTEER SYSTEM GIVEN CONSERVATIVE VALUES

	INEXPENS	ACCESSIB	POLIT.FE	COMPETEN
VOLUN	1.00	-1.00	1.00	-1.00
SALAR	2.00	4.00	2.00	4.00
Weight	-0.000	3.000	-0.000	3.000

B. BRINGING THE VOLUNTEER SYSTEM UP TO THE LEVEL OF THE SALARIED SYSTEM GIVEN LIBERAL VALUES

	INEXPENS	ACCESSIB	POLIT.FE	COMPETEN
VOLUN	4.00	2.00	4.00	2.00
SALAR	-1.00	1.00	-1.00	1.00
Weight	3.000	0.000	3.000	0.000

b. The salaried system receives a "yes" on inexpensiveness.

c. Inexpensiveness receives a weight of zero.

Any one of those three changes would generate a tie by bringing the volunteer system from a score of 10 down to an 8 (e.g., possibility 1a) by bringing the salaried system from a score of 8 up to a 10 (e.g., possibility 1b) or by bringing both down to a score of 6 (e.g., possibility 1c). All three possibilities, however, are unrealistic. Conservatives are not going to perceive that the volunteer system is really an expensive system, or that the salaried system is an inexpensive one, or that inexpensiveness is of no importance.

2. Accessibility.

   a. The volunteer system receives a −1 on accessibility, but that is impossible since the scale only goes as low as 1 and as high as 2.

   b. The salaried system receives a 4 on accessibility, which is also impossible.

   c. Accessibility receives a weight of 3. That is not impossible. It is, however, unlikely that accessibility would receive more weight than inexpensiveness and political feasibility in the values of conservatives.

3. Political Feasibility. There are three possibilities here. They are the same unrealistic possibilities that were previously discussed under inexpensiveness.

4. Competency. There are also three possibilities here. They are the same impossible and unlikely possibilities discussed under accessibility.

Table 15–2B shows what it would take to bring the volunteer system up to the level of the salaried system given liberal values. Table 15–1C previously showed that with the liberal weights, the salaried system receives a score of 10 and the volunteer system receives a score of 8. Thus there is a 2–point gap that the conservatives need to make up to convince the liberals that the volunteer system is as good as the salaried system. Table 15–2B shows 12 ways that this gap could theoretically be made up. Those ways, reading down the columns, are:

1. Inexpensiveness.
    a. The volunteer system receives a 4 on inexpensiveness. That, however, is beyond the 1–2 scale.
    b. The salaried system receives a −1 on inexpensiveness. That, however, is also beyond the 1–2 scale.
    c. Inexpensiveness receives a weight of 3. It is, however, unlikely that inexpensiveness will receive more weight than accessibility or competency in the values of liberals.
2. Accessibility.
    a. The volunteer system receives a 2 on accessibility. Liberals, however, are not going to perceive that the volunteer system scores as high as possible on accessibility.
    b. The salaried system receives a 1 on accessibility. Liberals, however, are not going to perceive that the salaried system scores as low as possible on accessibility.
    c. Accessibility receives a weight of zero, but liberals are not going to agree that accessibility is of no importance.

3. Political Feasibility. There are three possibilities here. They are the same impossible and unlikely possibilities discussed under inexpensiveness.

4. Competency. There are also three possibilities here. They are the same unrealistic possibilities discussed under accessibility.

Thus the probability seems low that liberals could convince conservatives to accept salaried legal services or that conservatives could convince liberals to accept a volunteer system. The kind of sensitivity analysis shown in Table 15–2, however, is often helpful in indicating to disputants what they should emphasize in order to convince the other side. This is a sensitivity analysis in that it shows how sensitive the conclusion is to various changes in the weights of the criteria and the relations between alternatives and goals. It just so happens in this situation that all of the threshold or breakeven values shown in Table 15–

2 are either conceptually impossible to obtain or they are empirically unrealistic. Thus the deadlock is not likely to be resolved by one side convincing the other.

Resolving Deadlocks by Adding an Alternative

A third alternative that has been discussed in the past is a judicare system analogous to medicare or medicaid whereby poor people would go to existing private-sector lawyers who would then be compensated by the federal government. That alternative, however, is not a compromise in the sense of being a fallback second choice to the volunteer system for conservatives or to the salaried system for liberals. Instead, it is probably a third choice for both sides. Conservatives now reject the judicare system because it is substantially more expensive than salaried legal services. The LSC program tends to pay lawyers an annual salary of about $25,000 for which they process numerous cases, including maybe as many as 300 divorce cases a year. If each case were handled by a private-sector lawyer at approximately $300 apiece, that would be $90,000 just for divorce cases. Liberals reject the judicare system because it tends to handle only routine cases, such as family-law cases. Salaried legal-services attorneys tend to look for precedent-setting test cases that will have high leverage in developing the legal rights of the poor.

Looking at Table 15–1A stimulates ideas about what a deadlock-resolving alternative might involve. It would probably have to build on the existing salaried Legal Services Corporation, since it is already in place, in contrast to starting from scratch. Whatever is built on the existing LSC program should seek to reduce the expensiveness of salaried government lawyers and improve upon their political feasibility, since those are the two criteria on which salaried attorneys admittedly do not do so well. Likewise, whatever is built on the existing LSC program should seek to improve upon the lack of accessibility of volunteer attorneys and their relative lack of competency, since those are the two criteria on which volunteer attorneys admittedly do not do so well.

In 1982 Gerald Caplan, professor, the George Washington University, was appointed acting director of the Legal Services Corporation. He was an excellent compromise for a number of reasons. He could appeal to liberals, being one of the founders of the original Legal Services Program of the Office of Economic Opportunity under Lyndon Johnson and a professor with credentials in both law and social science. He could appeal to conservatives, having been a leader in developing anti-crime policy in the Law Enforcement Assistance Administration under Richard Nixon and Gerald Ford. He is an arch conservative but in a libertarian sense who believes the government should get off the backs of poor people as well as business people. He also made clear that he would be only a temporary acting director long enough to try to salvage what was becoming a shambles at LSC due to the inability of the White House and Congress to resolve their dispute.

Partially following the reasoning suggested by the above analysis of Table

15–1A and also the other tables, Gerald Caplan proposed to require that all Legal Services Agencies spend 10 percent of their budgets for the development of a meaningful volunteer system. The money would be used mainly for two purposes. The first purpose would be to make volunteers more accessible. A survey should be made in each community of all of the attorneys to determine (1) which ones are willing to do some volunteer work, (2) what their specialties are, and (3) what days and times they are available. The second step involves maintaining a well-organized card file of relevant information on volunteers. Appointments can then be scheduled for them with legal-services clients who have problems that relate to their specialties at the regular Legal Services Agency office. The volunteers are therefore just as accessible to the clients as the regular attorneys. The clients are unable to tell the difference. The volunteer attorneys also do not suffer the frustration of having no clients, irrelevant clients, or long waiting periods with nothing to do.

The second purpose of the 10 percent funding would be to provide training to improve the competency of the volunteers. These well-coordinated volunteers, however, would not need so much training since they would be handling cases in fields with which they are already familiar, rather than across-the-board poverty law. Nevertheless, they could benefit from materials and workshops that relate their fields to the problems of poor people. Thus a real estate lawyer may not be completely aware of special statutes and precedents that relate to poverty tenants, and a lawyer who is an expert on the Commercial Code may not be completely aware of procedures that relate to poverty consumers. The volunteers could also benefit from training that relates their fields to the broader context of poverty law.

Even if this works, one might argue that it still shows how arbitrary public policy is since the 10 percent figure seems to have been pulled out of the air. On the contrary, the 10 percent represents approximately the maximum amount that could possibly be spent on coordinating the accessibility and improving the competency of the volunteer attorneys. The Legal Services Program is funded at approximately $300 million a year. Ten percent represents $30 million. For $30 million, one can buy about all of the coordinating surveys, card files, training manuals, and workshops that it is possible to buy. A stubborn skeptic might argue that the $30 million taken away from other LSC activities may mean laying off some regular LSC lawyers or other personnel. That is true, but if spending $30 million brings in $60 million worth of accessible and competent volunteer attorneys, the investment will have been well worth it.

OPTIMIZING COMPROMISES

In the Dispute Over Legal Services for the Poor

Table 15–3A shows how the 10 percent compromise compares with the other two alternatives. The first two rows of Table 15–3A are the same as Table 15–

Table 15–3
The 10 Percent Compromise

A. WITH UNWEIGHTED CRITERIA

	INEXPENS	ACCESSIB	POLIT.FE	COMPETEN
VOLUNTEER	2.00	1.00	2.00	1.00
SALARIED G	1.00	2.00	1.00	2.00
COMPROMISE	1.50	2.00	2.00	2.00

B. WITH CONSERVATIVE VALUES

	INEXPENS	ACCESSIB	POLIT.FE	COMPETEN
VOLUNTEER	4.00	1.00	4.00	1.00
SALARIED G	2.00	2.00	2.00	2.00
COMPROMISE	3.00	2.00	4.00	2.00

C. WITH LIBERAL VALUES

	INEXPENS	ACCESSIB	POLIT.FE	COMPETEN
VOLUNTEER	2.00	2.00	2.00	2.00
SALARIED G	1.00	4.00	1.00	4.00
COMPROMISE	1.50	4.00	2.00	4.00

1A since the scoring of the volunteer and salaried systems have not changed. On all four criteria, the compromise systems does well:

1. On inexpensiveness, the compromise system is not so inexpensive as a volunteer system. It is, however, less expensive than a salaried system in two ways. First, it reduces the appropriation for the purely salaried system by 10 percent. Second, and more important, the 10 percent compromise produces a better benefit/cost ratio. The cost can be considered the same at $300 million. If, however, the amount of valuable attorney labor goes up as a result of adding the volunteer component, the total system is more economic and is less expensive for the value received. Therefore, we score the 10 percent compromise at 1.5 on inexpensiveness, between the 2.0 for the volunteer system and the 1.0 for the salaried system.
2. On accessibility, there is no reduction in accessibility by adding volunteers who meet with poor clients during regular hours at the regular offices of the Legal Services Agency. They are thus just as accessible to the clients as the regular attorneys, as previously mentioned.
3. On political feasibility, that tends to be a matter of being on or off and not so much a matter of degrees. The salaried government-attorney system lacks political feasibility in that (1) it is strongly opposed by the White House; (2) it has some substantial difficulty getting through both houses of Congress without considerable anguish and friction; and (3) it runs into administrative problems due to the White House hostility. The 10 percent compromise system has, however, manifested its

political feasibility by not being so strongly opposed by the White House, by getting through Congress more easily, and by having less administrative sabotage and turmoil.

4. On competency, adding the volunteer component does not substantially lower the competency if the volunteers work primarily in their specialties and receive appropriate training. They may sometimes even add useful specialized knowledge to the regular attorneys who are more generalists in poverty law.

Given those scores on the compromise row of Table 15–3A, the 10 percent compromise receives a total score of 7.5 compared with the 6.0 of the volunteer system and the 6.0 of the salaried system. One might, however, question the value of such a compromise by referring to it as everybody's second choice when the conservative and liberal values are taken into consideration, as is so often the case with compromises.

Table 15–3B shows how the 10 percent compromise scores on the four criteria given the conservative weights that emphasize inexpensiveness and political feasibility. Table 15–3B differs from Table 15–3A in that the raw scores are doubled on the inexpensiveness column and on the political-feasibility column. The result is that the volunteer system receives a score of 10 and the salaried system receives a score of 8, as mentioned in discussing Table 15–1B. Note, however, that the compromise alternative receives a total score of 11, which is even higher than the previous first choice using conservative values.

Table 15–3C shows how the 10 percent compromise scores on the four criteria given the liberal weights that emphasize accessibility and competence. Table 15–3C differs from Table 15–3A in that the raw scores are doubled on the accessibility and competency columns. The result is that the volunteers receive a score of 8.0, salaried attorneys receive a score of 10.0, and the compromise system receives a still higher score of 11.5 using liberal values.

This is a good illustration of the concept of an optimizing compromise, which is an additional alternative that is better than the previous first choice of either set of disputants using their own values to weight the criteria and their own perceptions to score the alternatives on the criteria. Acceptable compromises that are everybody's second choice are often difficult to achieve, although the P/G% microcomputer program does facilitate such compromises by clarifying the criteria, the alternatives, the relations, and especially the effects of changing any of those components on the bottom-line conclusion as to which alternative is best. The incremental difficulty of achieving optimizing compromises should be more than offset by the incremental gain in terms of satisfying conservative and liberal disputants and in terms of benefiting the recipients of the public policies that are adopted.

In Criminal and Civil Cases

Optimizing compromises can even be developed in mediating or negotiating settlements in criminal or civil cases. For example, in a criminal case the prosecutor's optimum position might be five years. This means that the prosecutor considers five years to be the maximum realistic number of years that the defendant would be willing to go to prison. Five years may be less than the maximum that the statute allows. If five years is the prosecutor's optimum, the prosecutor would probably be willing to settle for as little as two years. On the other hand, the defendant's optimum might be one year as the best possible settlement. This means that the defendant might be willing to settle for as much as three years in prison.

An optimizing solution would thus be one that allows the prosecutor to have a settlement of more than five years and allows the defendant to have a settlement of less than one year. That seems impossible, but not necessarily so if the disputants can move on to a different settlement dimension, such as community service instead of prison. On that dimension, they might be able to reach an agreement in which the defendant agrees to serve ten years in a monastery. From the prosecutor's point of view, that may be better than five years in prison. From the defendant's point of view, that might be better than one year in prison. Thus ten years of monastic community service is an optimizing compromise whereby both sides believe they have come out ahead of their original optimum positions.

Likewise, in a damages case the plaintiff may initially demand $100,000, figuring that this amount is substantially higher than the defendant would ever be willing to pay. The defense, on the other hand, might initially offer $10,000, figuring that this amount is substantially lower than the plaintiff would ever be willing to settle for. An optimizing compromise would be one in which the plaintiff believes he or she is getting the equivalent of more than $100,000, and the defendant believes he or she is paying the equivalent of less than $10,000. That kind of a settlement also seems impossible but, again, not necessarily so if the disputants can move on to a different settlement dimension, such as a performance agreement.

Under a performance agreement, the defendant might be willing to promise to comply with certain quality standards in the workplace, in medical practice, or in product manufacturing. The defendant might consider such an agreement to be a victory because of the favorable publicity over his or her competitors by entering into such an agreement. The plaintiff might also consider such an agreement to be a victory because of the benefits received by the plaintiff's constituents. In that sense, the defendant may think he or she is getting more than $100,000 worth of benefits. The plaintiff may, however, believe that he or she is losing less than $10,000 and is actually gaining something of net value.

An optimizing compromise should be distinguished from a Pareto optimum. A *Pareto optimum* in the context of negotiation and mediation means the disputants think they are coming out ahead of what they would have been willing to settle for. If, for example, in the above criminal case, a plea bargain was struck at 2.5 years, a Pareto optimum would have been reached since the prosecutor was willing to go as low as 2.0 years and the defendant was willing to go as high as 3.0 years. They would then each come out ahead of their worst possible positions but not ahead of their best possible positions. If negotiators and mediators seek optimizing compromises, they may not succeed. Just trying, however, may result in a more mutually satisfying dispute resolution than merely seeking a Pareto optimum or forcing an agreement. Seeking an optimizing compromise stimulates imaginative solutions that are mutually satisfying to the mediator as well as the disputants.

Other Public-Policy Examples

Many other examples can be given of emotional public-policy disputes that were resolved by developing an optimizing compromise whereby both sides thought they were better off than what they formerly considered to be their best positions or at least better off than they were under the prevailing policy before the optimizing compromise was reached. For example, in the field of criminal justice, there has been considerable controversy over how to draft sentencing legislation. Conservatives are especially concerned with obtaining severe sentences. Liberals have traditionally been concerned with rehabilitative sentences. Both sides can be considered as optimizing winners under the new determinate sentencing, which many states have adopted. Conservatives have succeeded in obtaining more severe sentences on the average, since the new determinate sentencing often provides for mandatory minimums or relatively high determinate sentences as part of the legislative bargaining. Conservatives have also received a bonus of greater objectivity in the sentencing by virtue of the lessened sentencing discretion and the greater predictability of sentences. Liberals have gained a more rehabilitative system by virtue of the emphasis now placed on community-based corrections, including supervised work-release programs. Liberals have also received the bonus of greater objectivity, with reduced disparities along racial, class, sex, and other lines.

Pretrial release is another example. Conservatives emphasize the need for getting a higher percentage of defendants to appear in court without committing crimes. Their previous first choice was high holding rates as a pretrial-release policy. Liberals emphasize the need for enabling defendants to be able to establish their innocence and to avoid the bitterness generated by pretrial detention. Their previous first choice was low holding rates as a pretrial-release policy. Both sides are optimizing winners with the new bail-reform systems, which emphasize screening, supervising, notifying, selectively prosecuting, and reducing delay. Those reform measures please conservatives because they result in higher appearance rates without crime committing while saving taxpayer money by having less pretrial holding. Those reform measures also please liberals because they result in low holding rates without an undesirable increase in no shows and crime committers.

The housing and urban-development field is another good example of compromises that have been developed that appeal to both conservatives and liberals. Until recently, conservatives have been largely opposed to government programs to provide housing for the poor, arguing that the marketplace could adequately cover the needs involved. Likewise until recently, liberals have been in favor of public-housing projects, arguing that they were needed because the marketplace could not adequately provide housing for the poor. Both sides felt emotional about the subject, as indicated in the congressional debates over public housing from the 1930s to the 1970s. During the 1970s, however, new ways of providing government involvement were developed. The most important new approach has been the rent and mortgage supplements. Those supplements are probably now considered by conservatives to be better than their original first choice of leaving the matter completely to the marketplace because (1) the government subsidies convert anti-social poor people into more respectable tenants and even homeowners; (2) the taxpayer saves money since the rent supplements cost less than building and maintaining public-housing projects; and (3) the rental market welcomes the rent subsidies. Rent supplements are now probably considered by liberals to be better than their original first choice of public housing because rent supplements mean (1) more dignity for poor people and (2) more scattering of poor people with resulting racial and economic integration.

Such optimizing compromises are possible when the disputants emphasize different criteria that can be simultaneously satisfied. That may more often be the case in dispute resolution than is generally recognized. The P/G% approach helps bring out more clearly the criteria, weights, alternatives, constraints, and relations of both sides so as to facilitate such compromises. A simple clarifying example of an optimizing compromise whereby the disputants emphasize different criteria would be a situation in which Disputant A wants a red ball and Disputant B wants a heavy ball. The optimizing solution is to give them a ball that is extra red and extra heavy. One could, however, arrive at an optimizing compromise whereby the disputants all emphasize the same criterion such as color rather than different criteria such as color and weight. For example, if Disputant A wants a red ball and Disputant B wants a blue ball, they could be given a purple ball. That, however, is just a traditional compromise, not an optimizing compromise. It just gives them something better than their worst expectations, not something better than their best expectations. An optimizing compromise in that situation might be to give them a solid gold ball to share. No part of the ball is either red or blue, but they would probably be overjoyed to sell the solid gold ball for $800,000 and to divide the proceeds to buy all of the red and blue balls they might want. The $800,000 is based on gold selling at $500 an ounce and the solid gold ball weighing 100 pounds.

To keep things in perspective, we might also offer an example of a more traditional compromise that is each side's second choice, rather than an optimizing compromise that is considered to be better than each side's first choice. An example is the marketable pollution right in the field of environmental protection. It involves giving business firms permits to engage in various units of non-toxic, biodegradable pollution. Low polluters receive more units than they need, and high polluters receive less than they want. The high polluters therefore buy permits from the low polluters to be operating within the law. Doing this is expensive, which causes the high polluters to reduce their pollution, especially if the purchase means income for a competitor. The previous first choice of conservatives concerning environmental protection has been reliance on the marketplace with no governmental regulation. The previous first choice of liberals has been pollution taxes, which would provide incentives for pollution reduction and provide a clean-up fund. The conservatives like marketable pollution permits better than pollution taxes because the permits rely more on the marketplace and less on government regulation. Liberals like marketable pollution permits better than no regulation because the permits provide incentives for pollution reduction, although no funds to municipal or other governments to pay for water filtration or other clean-up activities.

Clarification is needed as to how each side's second choice is able to become the compromise winner. What happens implicitly, although not explicitly, is a series of paired comparisons. Suppose that there are three alternatives consisting of (1) the conservatives' first choice, (2) the liberals' first choice, and (3) the first choice of those who consider themselves relatively neutral. Suppose also that the conservatives and liberals are about equally strong. Otherwise, there would not be a deadlocked dispute. The first paired comparison might involve the conservative against the neutral choice. The neutral choice would win since it would get the votes of the liberals and the neutrals. The second comparison might involve the liberal against the neutral choice. The neutral choice would win again since it would get the votes of the conservatives and the neutrals. The third, first, or second comparison might involve the conservative against the liberal choice. That comparison would result in a tie if the conservatives and liberals are equally strong and the neutrals equally divided. If the conservative or liberal choice does win in this comparison, it will still lose to the neutral or second-choice alternative. Second-choice compromises are good for resolving disputes but not as satisfying as optimizing compromises that are viewed as being better by the disputants than their original first choices.

OTHER AND GENERAL MICROCOMPUTER-BASED PROCEDURES FOR RESOLVING DISPUTES

Disputes can often be resolved well by adding an alternative, especially an alternative on a new settlement dimension that results in an optimizing compromise. Microcomputers and the P/G% program can facilitate the resolving of disputes by making and testing these and other changes in the alternatives, the criteria, and the relations. Such microcomputer programs can also be used to aid in deciding among alternative processes for resolving disputes.

Changing the Alternatives

As for the alternatives, instead of adding one, subtracting an alternative might be helpful when more than two alternatives are involved. For example, by reducing three alternatives to two, we may have a clear-cut runoff in which one of the two alternatives in effect gets an especially large portion of the votes or points that would otherwise go to the third alternative. This is particularly true when the percentaging method of Policy/Goal Percentaging is used to deal with criteria on multiple dimensions, rather than the raw-score approach used in the legal-services example. Even with the raw-score approach, the raw scores tend to be relative. Thus Alternative B may move from a score of a 4 to a 5 on a 1–5 scale when Alternative B is just being compared with Alternative A after Alternative C has been removed.

Related to adding an alternative is the idea of consolidating two or more alternatives. Doing this in effect creates a new alternative. That new alternative may be a good compromise if there are only two alternatives at the time of the consolidation. If there are more than two alternatives, consolidating can have the beneficial effect of reducing the number of alternatives. Related to consolidating (although in the opposite direction) is sub-dividing one alternative into two or more alternatives. Perhaps one of those newly created alternatives may be a compromise alternative on which the disputants can agree. If not, some of the newly created alternatives might be quickly eliminated as clearly inferior, thereby clarifying the situation although not reducing the number of alternatives. Each time there is an addition, subtraction, consolidation, or sub-division, the P/G% program can quickly show how the new alternatives compare in terms of their overall or summation scores on the criteria, with regard to either raw scores or percentaging scores.

Changing the Criteria

All of the above approaches to making changes in the alternatives can also apply to making changes in the criteria. For example, a dispute might be more capable of being resolved by adding a criterion that brings out that Alternative B is clearly the winner, even though the two alternatives were originally tied. Likewise, subtracting a criterion could make Alternative B clearly the winner. The same effect in terms of clarifying the winner can also occur as a result of consolidating two or more criteria or as a result of sub-dividing a criterion.

Unlike the alternatives, the criteria are subject to different weights to indicate their relative importance, although the alternatives are subject to different overall scores to indicate their relative importance. The overall scores of the alternatives, however, are outputs of the analysis, whereas the weights of the criteria are inputs of the analysis. By changing those criterion weights, Alternative B may become the clear winner. Working with different weights when all of the weights were originally the same can help resolve many disputes, although doing this did not work in the legal-services example. Along related lines, one can work with the weights and criteria of just the first disputant and then just the second disputant. Doing this generates two sets of overall or summation scores for the alternatives. One can average those overall scores to see which alternative might be the winner. The averaging can be a weighted average if one side of the dispute is considered to have more weight or to be entitled to more votes than the other sides or other disputants.

Working with minimum and maximum constraints is another approach that especially applies to the criteria, although it could apply to the alternatives. For example, the subject matter of a given dispute may cause the disputants to agree that a certain criterion is desirable such as the age of the person to be hired but only up to 70 years because of a relevant retirement rule. That could eliminate some alternatives as could a minimum requirement of age 21. Likewise, the subject matter of a given dispute may make it meaningful to have a maximum or minimum constraint on an alternative. Perhaps, for example, the original alternatives are (1) spending $100 on Activity P and $10 on Activity Q versus (2) spending $90 on Activity P and $30 on Activity Q. The alternatives under consideration may be reduced if there is a maximum budget of no more than $115, a maximum expenditure on an activity of no more than $95, or a minimum expenditure on an activity of no less than $20. The P/G% program allows one to determine quickly the effects of changing minimum and maximum constraints on criteria and alternatives, as well as changing the criteria and the alternatives themselves.

Changing the Relations

In resolving disputes, the third big area of change involves the relations between the alternatives and the criteria. What begins as a tie could possibly be resolved by changing the scores for some of the relations. One could also show the overall summation scores for the alternatives when all of the relations are scored from a conservative perspective and a liberal or other perspective. One could then average those two or more sets of overall scores to arrive at a super-overall winner as was discussed in talking about conservative and liberal weights and criteria.

Along related lines, one can change the relations by providing for more refined measurement as when one goes from a 1–2 scale to a 1–5 scale or less refined but clearer measurement as when one goes from a 1–5 scale to a 1–2 scale. One could change the measurement units from a 1–5 scale to a scale measured in dollars, years, miles, or another dimension. Changing the measurement scale may require shifting from a raw-score approach to a percentaging approach if multi-dimensionality is introduced. For example, although one can add the raw scores on two criteria, both of which are measured on 1–5 scales, one cannot so meaningfully add the raw scores from a 1–5 scale to the scores from a scale measured in miles. It may, however, be meaningful to indicate how each alternative scores on each criterion in terms of the percentage relation of each raw score to the maximum raw score possible or to the total of the raw scores on a criterion. The P/G% program works especially well with such multi-dimensionality in view of the program's emphasis on working with part/whole percentages of raw scores converted into percentages of the total points on a criterion.

Using P/G% to Decide among Methods for Resolving Disputes

The discussion thus far has emphasized how P/G% can be used to resolve disputes, especially by quickly showing the disputants the effects of changing the alternatives, the criteria, and the relations between alternatives and criteria. P/G% can also aid by showing the disputants the relevant benefits minus costs of alternative methods for resolving disputes. We are thus talking about two levels of dispute resolution. The lower level might be referred to as subject-matter dispute resolution in which the alternatives could be a volunteer-attorney system versus a salaried government-attorney system. The higher level might be referred to as process dispute resolution in which the alternatives relate to deciding among processes for resolving the subject-matter dispute in question.

As mentioned earlier, the basic processes for resolving legal disputes are negotiation, mediation, arbitration, and adjudication. A frequent choice that has to be made is between a negotiated settlement and going to trial or adjudication. The P/G% program is especially useful under those circumstances. The settlement offer may be $5,000. The average trial damages in similar cases may be $6,000, including cases in which there were no damages. The percentage fee from a settlement may be 20 percent, or $1,000, whereas the percentage fee from a trial may be 40 percent, or $2,400. A trial, however, may be more expensive to the lawyer who is deciding between these alternative dispute-resolution processes. The attorney may predict only 10 hours of work to close the settlement, figuring that such office time is worth $30 an hour for a total of $300. The attorney may predict 25 hours of work to try the case, figuring trial time at $60 an hour for a total of $1,500.

This means that the predicted net profit from settling is $1,000 minus $300 for a net of $700, whereas the predicted net profit from trying the case is $2,400 minus $1,500 for a net of $900. There is thus a $200 gap between the benefits minus costs of the trial alternative versus the negotiation alternative. The P/G% program can facilitate choosing between those two alternatives by indicating for each settlement input item how it would have to change to bring the settlement profit up from $700 to $900. The program also shows how each trial input item would have to change to bring the trial profit down from $900 to $700. That information can be helpful in answering specific questions such as (1) how much does the settlement offer have to increase to make settlement more profitable than trial, (2) how much room for error is there on each of the trial items before going to trial becomes less profitable than settling, and (3) how much would we have to cut our hours, cut the hourly cost, or increase the percentage fee to make settlement as profitable as going to trial.

There are many variations on those basic ideas. Some of them include:

1. Changing the fee-paying arrangement from a percentage fee. If the case involves an hourly fee, the total benefits equal the number of hours multiplied by the hourly fee. If the case involves a flat fee, the total benefits equal the flat fee.
2. Changing the type of lawyer from a plaintiff lawyer. If the lawyer is a defense lawyer, the damages and the probability of paying them represent cost rather than benefit items.
3. Changing the perspective from lawyer to client. The client perspective requires taking into consideration only the benefits and costs that affect the client. In the above example, the client receives 80 percent of the $5,000 settlement but only 60 percent of the $6,000 trial award. The client may thus be better off with the settlement alternative, even though the lawyer is better off with the trial alternative.
4. Changing from civil to criminal cases. Doing this means introducing a non-monetary criterion since prosecutors seek long sentences, not large damages, and defense attorneys seek short sentences, not small damages. The P/G% program is especially designed to deal with multi-dimensional criteria like years and dollars through its provision for part/whole percentaging.

One can also change the choice from negotiation versus trial to other controversies relevant to choosing the best method of dispute resolution. Some of the other choices include:

1. Adjudication versus trial
2. Two-sided negotiation versus bringing in an outside mediator
3. Binding versus non-binding arbitration
4. Jury trial versus bench trial
5. Federal court versus state court
6. Appellate court versus staying with the trial-court decision
7. Any other choices involving two or more alternative methods of dispute resolution

In those choices, the decision-makers want to pick the alternative that will maximize the benefits minus costs of themselves, their clients, society, or some combination of those interests. In those choices, there are likely to be some monetary and some non-monetary benefits or costs. The P/G% program is general enough to be able to handle any of those seven choices, four types of goals, and two types of measurement, provided that the decision-maker is capable of expressing roughly (1) the criteria for choosing among the alternatives and (2) the relations between the alternatives and the criteria. The decision-maker does not have to be very precise because there is often a substantial insensitivity range around each input item. This means that the numerical value of each input item can generally move up or down substantially without affecting which alternative method of dispute resolution will maximize the decision-maker's benefits minus costs.[5]

CONCLUSIONS

In light of the above general principles and specific examples, one can conclude that microcomputers and the P/G% program can help facilitate negotiation and mediation leading to dispute resolution by proceeding in accordance with the following steps or options:

1. Determine the initial alternatives, the criteria, and the relations between the alternatives and the criteria in light of each side's values and perceptions. The P/G% input-format facilitates clarification of those dispute parameters.
2. Determine what it would take each side to convince the other side. The threshold, breakeven, or tie-causing analysis of the P/G% program facilitates that determination. If each side could at least partially convince the other side, encourage it to do so, since the result may be a mutually acceptable alternative or compromise.
3. Experiment with a variety of additional alternatives, in contrast to the original deadlocked alternatives. Use the P/G% program to determine quickly the overall or summation score for each alternative using the criterion weights of each side to the dispute. Look especially for new alternatives that could be endorsed by both sides more strongly than their original first choices. At least find an alternative that could be each side's second choice and thus serve as a compromise winner in a series of paired comparisons.
4. Try changing the alternatives by subtracting some, by consolidating two or more, or by subdividing some. Try doing the same things with the criteria. Use the P/G% program to determine the overall or summation scores of the new set of alternatives.
5. Try changing the criterion weights, or try averaging the alternatives in light of the different sets of weights that the conflicting disputants have.
6. Try working with reasonable minimum or maximum constraints on the criteria or the alternatives to see what difference that makes.
7. Try changing some of the relation-scores and maybe the measurement units on which the scores are based. That may mean experimenting with the procedures in the P/G% program for dealing with criteria measured on multiple dimensions.

With that set of checklist ideas and with the aid of the P/G% program, the negotiators or the mediator in a dispute should quickly be able to try out a variety of ideas toward arriving at an optimizing compromise that will be even better than the disputants' former first choices. That is a high goal to strive for. Getting only partially there, however, may mean more accomplishment in terms of arriving at a mutually satisfying solution than any lesser goal would be capable of achieving.

NOTES

1. For details concerning Policy/Goal Percentaging, see Chapters 2 and 3.
2. For details concerning various aspects of negotiation, see Howard Raiffa, *The Art*

and Science of Negotiation (Cambridge, Mass.: Harvard University Press, 1982); and Gerard Nierenberg, *Fundamentals of Negotiating* (New York: Hawthorne/Dutton, 1973). Many of the ideas contained in the Nierenberg book have been incorporated into a computer program that emphasizes relevant checklists. The program is available from Roy Nierenberg, Experience in Software, Inc. 2039 Shattuck Avenue, Suite 401, Berkeley, Calif. 94704. For another microcomputer program relevant to facilitating negotiation, see Frederick Winter, "An Application of Computerized Decision Tree Models in Management," *Interfaces* 15 (1985): 74–80.

For details concerning arbitration, see Martin Domke, *The Law and Practice of Commercial Arbitration* (Chicago: Callaghan, 1968); F. Elkouri and E. Elkouri, *How Arbitration Works* (Washington, D.C.: Bureau of National Affairs, 1980); and E. Kellor, *American Arbitration: Its History, Functions, and Achievements* (New York: Harper, 1948). These books contain useful comparisons of arbitration and adjudication including commercial, labor, family, and international arbitration and including civil, criminal, and appellate adjudication.

For a broader treatment of alternative methods of dispute resolution, see Steven Vago, *Law and Society* (Englewood Cliffs, N.J.: Prentice-Hall, 1981), pp. 195–237; Robert Kidder, *Connecting Law and Society: An Introduction to Research and Theory* (Englewood Cliffs, N.J.: Prentice-Hall, 1983), pp. 147–182; and Lewis Mayers, *The American Legal System: The Administration of Justice in the United States by Judicial, Administrative, Military and Arbitral Tribunals* (New York: Harper, 1955).

3. On the application of Policy/Goal Percentaging to facilitating judicial and arbitration decisions that are based on prior precedents or instances, see S. Nagel, "Microcomputers and Improving Social Science Prediction," *Evaluation Review* (1986); and Chapter 5 of this book. On the application of Policy/Goal Percentaging to facilitate arbitration and judicial decisions that are based on evaluating consequences, see S. Nagel, *Public Policy: Goals, Means, and Methods* (New York: St. Martin's, 1984), pp. 343–354.

4. For details concerning alternative ways of providing legal services to the poor, see Legal Services Corporation, *The Delivery System Study: A Policy Report to the Congress and the President of the United States* (1980); "Representing the Poor," in Arthur Berney et al., eds., *Legal Problems of the Poor: Cases and Material* (Boston: Little, Brown, 1975), pp. 500–588; and "The Legal System and the Poor," in Eli Jarmel, ed., *Problems in the Legal Representation of the Poor* (New York: Matthew Bender, 1972), ch. 1 p. 1 to ch. 3 p. 19.

5. For examples of P/G% and other quantitative analysis to aid in deciding among alternative methods of dispute resolution, see Jerome Staller, "The Advantages of Alternative Dispute Resolution in Tort Cases," *Practical Lawyer* 31 (1985): 57–66; and Chapter 10 of this book.

Epilogue

Cross-Cutting Principles and Problems

PRINCIPLES THAT CUT ACROSS THE APPLICATIONS

One benefit of dealing with a number of different microcomputer applications simultaneously is to enable one to see more clearly various cross-cutting principles that might otherwise be missed in a more specifically focused analysis. From these three applications one can draw cross-cutting conclusions such as the following:

1. A key value of personal computers as decision-making aids is to enable lawyer users or other users to see easily the effects of changing various inputs on one's initial decisions. That occurs in all three applications:

a. In litigation strategy, one would like to know what changes in the inputs would enable the trial alternative to become equally desirable with the settlement alternative or vice versa.

b. In judicial prediction, one would like to know how to eliminate inconsistencies in the prior cases in terms of a low-scoring case being a winner or a high-scoring case being a loser.

c. In sequencing, one would like to know what changes would move a given case to a higher position in the sequencing line.

2. Personal computers cannot function well as decision aids to lawyers or others without the user adding a good deal of preliminary knowledge to be processed. That occurs in all three applications:

a. In litigation strategy or other evaluative contexts, the user needs to supply (1) the alternatives of settlement, trial, or other alternatives; (2) the benefits, costs, or other goals; and (3) the scores of the alternatives on the goals.
b. In judicial prediction or other predictive contexts, the user needs to supply (1) the prior cases or issues, (2) the predictive criteria, and (3) the scores of the cases on the criteria.
c. In time sequencing and allocation, the user needs to supply (1) the forthcoming cases to be processed; (2) the relevant benefits, costs, and combination of benefits and costs; and (3) the predicted scores of the cases on those criteria.

3. Personal computers can be helpful in dealing with the problems of how to combine goals or criteria that are measured on different dimensions. That occurs in all three applications:

a. Litigation strategy often mean working with some non-monetary criteria (such as sentence length) and some monetary criteria (such as attorney-time cost).
b. Judicial prediction almost always involves criteria requiring different weights to consider the relative importance of different subjects. Percentaging may also be needed to consider the different ways in which the criteria can be measured.
c. Case sequencing and allocation should take into consideration the non-monetary variable of relative case enjoyment. Rational attorneys do not generally sequence cases or allocate time to them purely on the basis of monetary considerations.

4. Personal computers can be helpful in converting complicated problems into relatively simple ones. That occurs in the three applications:

a. The litigation-strategy displays shown in Tables 9–3 and 9–4 for damages cases should be capable of being understood by lawyers who have no special quantitative backgrounds or interests but who understand the substance of settlement versus trial.
b. The judicial prediction display shown in Table 5–2 should also be capable of being understood by lawyers who would not be likely to use statistical regression analysis but who often do traditional case synthesis.
c. The sequencing display shown in Table 12–1 should be meaningful to lawyers who think of law practice as being partially a business activity in which one tries to do

things that will maximize income minus expenses within ethical and other constraints. Once the simpler situations are understood, the other situations also become understandable such as those displayed in the other tables in Chapters 6, 10, and 13. This is especially true if one is able to generate them on a personal computer, as contrast to just reading about them in an article.

5. Using personal computers as decision-making aids in law practice may raise ethical and related problems more clearly than when less explicit analysis is used. That occurs in the three applications.

a. The litigation strategy analysis brings out more clearly that settlement may be the better alternative from the lawyer's perspective, but going to trial may be better from the client's perspective, or vice versa.
b. The prediction analysis as applied by either lawyers or judges can facilitate arguing for a given case being decided in favor of either the plaintiff or the defendant. The sensitivity-analysis facilitates coming up with the best possible arguments for either side.
c. The best way to sequence cases may be best from either the attorney's perspective or the client's perspective, but the optimum quantity of time to allocate to a given case is almost always likely to be different for those two perspectives. This is true regardless of whether the fee-paying arrangement is a flat fee, an hourly rate, or a contingency fee.

THE PROBLEM OF GETTING PERSONAL COMPUTERS ADOPTED

All three applications (and other applications of personal computers for decision-making in law practice) raise problems of how to get the procedures adopted. There is resistance to the use of microcomputers for litigation strategy, judicial prediction, and case sequencing/allocation on grounds such as:

1. Lawyers do not need these tools. They have been getting along well without them ever since there were lawyers. That is true, but perhaps lawyers can function even more effectively with personal computers to supplement their traditional methods. This may be especially true when a computer-aided lawyer deals with a lawyer who is unwilling or unable to make use of personal computers as decision aids. Those uses include the ability to handle sensitivity analysis, multidimensionality, and complexity.

2. The computer is sometimes viewed as replacing the skills of an attorney. In reality, the computer cannot function in these law-practice applications without the skills of an attorney, especially with regard to indicating the (a) evaluative or predictive criteria, (b) the decision alternatives or prior cases, and (c) the relations between the criteria and the alternatives. The personal computer stimulates lawyers to be more explicit in performing their skills, in contrast to the vague ways in which litigation strategy, judicial prediction, and case sequencing/allocation are traditionally performed.

3. Computers are objected to on the grounds that they overly quantify and miss important qualitative considerations. That may be true of computer programs that do what even social scientists refer to as mindless number crunching. The kind of software that this chapter discusses, however, allows great leeway in working with qualitative criteria that are only measured in yes-no terms (as in the redistricting example) or on a 1–5 scale (as in talking about case enjoyment in the sequencing example). The alternatives can also be loosely defined as when one talks about casetypes rather than specific cases. The relations can be especially loose and flexible in view of the sensitivity analysis that allows one to have a large margin of error and still arrive at the correct bottom-line conclusion.

4. Sometimes one hears conflicting objections that quantitative analysis in law practice is old hat because somebody like Jeremy Bentham was doing or advocating it in the 1800s. Self-sufficient personal computers, however, are a new technology, especially with legal decision-making applications. The other side of that objection is to state that using personal computers as decision-aids is a temporary fad that will soon disappear. That seems contrary to the fact that the use of personal computers to aid in decision-making has expanded to virtually all fields of activity since 1980.

5. On the matter of conflicting objections, objection 1 above conflicts with objection 2 since the first objection 1 in effect states that personal computers are not likely to receive much utilization as decision aids, and the second objection states that they are likely to receive too much utilization. Objection 3 states that the computers overly quantify. Yet one also hears that quantitative analysis is too subjective. That may be true compared to the objectivity we might desire, as for example, in talking about the relative weights of evaluative or predictive criteria. It is certainly not true that quantitative analysis is too subjective compared to the more subjective and less systematic traditional decision-making.

What is possibly needed is more recognition of the realities between these conflicting objections. There may be too little utilization for some purposes (like sequencing and time allocation) and too much utilization for other purposes (like litigation strategy that ignores non-monetary considerations). There may also sometimes be too much quantification as in most forms of statistical analysis but also too little quantification in making explicit the hierarchy of one's values. Stating that traditional decision-making is subjective and not so systematic is not meant to disparage traditional decision-making. On the contrary, what may be especially needed is more study of how good lawyer decision-makers implicitly make decisions. The purpose of such study would be to convert their implicit procedures into explicit routines or algorithms that personal computers can use to enable lawyers and other people to improve their decision-making. It is hoped that this book is a step in that direction.

Appendix

Using the Master Files System of the P/G% Program

Version 8.7 of the P/G% Program has an improved system of keeping datafiles. The improvements partially involve using one disk drive for the program and a second disk drive for the datafiles. Option 3 in the file-management menu now asks the user to indicate whether the datafiles are on disk drive A or B. The datafiles can be on either drive. They can also be on a separate disk or on the program disk. The improvements also partially involve having a set of master files that include many sub-files. When selecting, creating, or deleting a sub-file, one must indicate in response to option 1 what the master file is. One must then indicate in response to option 2 what the sub-file or datafile is. These datafiles can only be used with the Policy/Goal Percentaging Program version 8.5 or after, co-authored by Stuart Nagel and John Long of the University of Illinois.

The purposes of this P/G% Datafiles Manual are:

1. To provide examples of problems with alternatives, criteria, and relations for illustrating the P/G% program
2. To show the variety of subject matters to which the P/G% program has been and

can be applied, including political science, law, economics, medical, sociological, and other problems

3. To show the variety of optimizing forms to which the P/G% program has been and can be applied, including optimum choice, risk, level, mix, timing, and variations on those basic forms
4. To show the variety of methodological problems that the P/G% program can overcome, including problems that relate to multiple goals, weights, alternatives, relations, constraints, and conclusions
5. To provide references to where further details can be found concerning applications of the P/G% program

As of January 1, 1986, the existing datafiles include those summarized in Table A–1.Further details on these datafiles can be found mainly in the following books, whose chapters are referred to in the table: S. Nagel, *Public Policy: Goals, Means, and Methods* (New York: St. Martin's, 1984) (Abbreviated PPG); idem, *Microcomputers, Evaluation Problems, and Policy Analysis* (Beverly Hills, Calif.: Sage, 1986) (Abbreviated MPA); idem, "Public Policy Controversies: Relating Options to Goals," (Unpub. Materials, University of Illinois) (Abbreviated PPC); idem, "Legal Policy Controversies: Evaluating Alternatives," (Unpub. Materials, University of Illinois) (Abbreviated LPC). For each of these books, only the key page is cited for each datafile. There may be other relevant pages close to those pages. The last column of the table labeled "Law Activity" refers to the sections of S. Nagel, *Using Personal Computers for Decision-Making in Law Practice* (Westport, Conn.: Greenwood Press, 1986).

Datafiles from other users should be sent to S. Nagel in the form of a P/G table with policies on the rows, goals on the columns, and relations in the cells, along with clarifying documentation. Those datafiles will be added to the list, so that others can put them to use. The main benefits from using the P/G% Program, however, come from creating and applying one's own data, not using other people's data.

As of January 1, 1986, there are ten master files covering the following:

1. There are three general files called DEMO1, DEMO2, and MISC. Each master file contains up to 20 specific datafiles. These four master files emphasize methodological examples, especially the original set of eight datafiles in DEMO1. These files are especially relevant to the books *Microcomputers, Evaluation Problems, and Policy Analysis* and *Public Policy: Goals, Means, and Methods* and also the Political Science 450 course "Methods of Policy Evaluation" and relevant to the second half of the Political Science 350 course "Law and Societal Logic." These general files also include some problems that relate to personal decision-making and business decision-making.
2. There are three master files: POLICY, GOVT, and POLICY3. These master files emphasize public-policy problems. They are especially relevant to the book *Public Policy Controversies: Relating Options to Goals* and to the Political Science 250 course "Introduction to Public Policy." These problems can be sub-divided into

those that emphasize political science, economic policy, poverty/minorities, health care, and so on.

3. There are three master files called LAW, LAW2, and LAW3. These master files emphasize problems relevant to law-practice and legal-policy evaluation. They are especially relevant to the books *Legal Policy Controversies: Evaluating Alternatives* and S. Nagel, *Law, Policy, and Optimizing Analysis* (Westport, Conn.: Greenwood Press, 1986), and also to the course Political Science 354 "The Judicial Process and Social Change," University of Illinois.
4. There is one master file called PREDICT. It emphasizes predicting case outcomes from prior court cases and predicting scores on dependent variables from independent variables. It is relevant to S. Nagel, *Causation, Prediction, and Legal Analysis* (Westport, Conn.: Greenwood Press, 1986), and to the first half of the course Political Science 350 "Law and Societal Logic," University of Illinois. Also see the second half of MISC.

The column labeled "FORM" refers to ten forms of decision optimizing that these datafiles can illustrate. The forms are discussed in further detail in S. Nagel, *Policy Evaluation: Making Optimum Decisions* (New York: Praeger, 1982). The ten forms are:

1. E-Choice. Deciding among lump-sum choices that are mutually exclusive; thus only one can be chosen, but it must be chosen in full, rather than partially or in multiples.
2. C-Choice. Deciding among lump-sum choices that are not mutually exclusive; thus combinations of alternatives can be chosen.
3. N-Risk. Deciding in a go/no-go context and where the benefits or the costs need to be discounted by the probability of their occurring.
4. C-Risk. Deciding among conflicting lump-sum choices and where the benefits or the costs need to be discounted by the probability of their occurring.
5. D-Level. Deciding among lump-sum choices that can be ordered from low to high and where doing too little or too much is undesirable.
6. C-Level. Deciding along a continuum of alternatives and where doing too much or too little is undesirable.
7. $-Mix. Allocating a monetary budget among alternatives.
8. N-Mix. Allocating time, people, 100 percent of something, cases, or scarce resources other than money among alternatives.
9. D-Pred. Predicting from criteria to a dichotomy like winning or losing.
10. C-Pred. Predicting from criteria to a continuum like damages, sentence length, or probabilities.

For each datafile only the dominant form is indicated, although many datafiles can be used to illustrate more than one form. The dominant form is usually obvious from the nature of the subject matter. Sometimes, however, the dominant form reflects the values of the classifier, as when a moderate person states that a given problem is an optimum-level problem or a choice problem allowing for combinations, and a less middling person states that the problem is a mutually exclusive choice problem.

Some of the datafiles are classified as involving a time-optimization element in the Form column. Time optimization is often a subject matter or a problem, as well as a special form. As a special form, it involves methods such as queueing, Markov chains, difference/differential equations, time discounting, time simulation, flow charting, critical-path methods, forecasting, dynamic programming, and optimum sequencing. As a subject matter, time optimization involves subjects such as delay reduction, longevity lengthening, discounting future opportunities, present value of future benefits or costs, job tenure, optimum level of hours, and allocation of time to activities or places. Any of the prediction datafiles can be considered as having a time dimension since they are concerned with what will happen in the future under various factual situations. Many of the datafiles involve some benefits or some costs not received immediately and involve implicit time discounting. A datafile, however, must include time as an explicit goal or alternative in order to be considered a time-optimization datafile.

The column labeled "PROBLEM" shows what decision-optimizing problems the datafile can be especially used to illustrate. The problems are as follows:

1. MD-Goals: The difficulty of working with multiple goals that are measured on different dimensions
2. W-Goals: The difficulty of assigning relative weights to the goals
3. C-Goals: The difficulty of determining minimum or maximum constraints on some of the goals
4. C-Alts: The difficulty of determining minimum or maximum constraints on some of the alternatives
5. M-Alts: The difficulty of working with a large multiplicity of alternatives
6. M-Rel: The problem of missing information on the relations between alternatives and goals
7. DP-Con: The difficulty of drawing and presenting an understandable conclusion

The problem column shows only actual problems of a datafile, not potential problems. Any datafile that involves $-Mix, N-Mix, or C-Level as a form is likely to involve multiple alternatives as a problem. Likewise, any allocation problem that involves a budget constraint can be considered as involving a constrained goal. Any problem can benefit from sensitivity analysis or threshold analysis that implies that all relations and weights are subject to change, although they are not totally missing information. Likewise, almost any datafile can illustrate the problem of determining the goals and the alternatives to be considered.

The column at the far right shows how each datafile relates to the subject of "Using Personal Computers for Decision-Making in Law Practice." That was the theme for the September 27–28, 1985, conference sponsored by the Committee on Continuing Professional Education of the American Law Institute and the American Bar Association. The conference was divided into law-practice activities covering:

1. Litigation Strategy (L): The use of microcomputers for making decisions about whether to (1) go to trial or settle out of court, (2) take an appeal or stick with the trial court decision, or (3) accept or reject a client
2. Negotiation/Mediation (N): Seeking to resolve a litigation dispute or a legal policy dispute by developing new alternatives, goals, or relations that will result in a mutually acceptable settlement
3. Judicial Prediction (J): Using a prior set of actual or hypothetical cases to develop decision-rules for predicting how related future cases will be decided
4. Attorney-Resource Allocation (A): Allocating time, money, or people to cases, activities, or places and also to deciding in what order cases or activities should be processed
5. Legal-Policy Evaluation (P): Choosing among alternative legal policies the one that is best in light of the goals, alternatives available, and relations, including the allocation of government budgets
6. Case Decision-Making (C): Deciding individual cases in light of the goals and the factual circumstances rather than the prior precedents

An X in the last column indicates that the datafile is not especially relevant to any of those activities. The most common reason for an X is that a public-policy evaluation file is involved that would be of interest mainly to political scientists or public administrators rather than to lawyers, judges, or legislators. Many of the legal-policy-evaluation files involve constitutional-law matters that might be of interest to both lawyers and political scientists. Any file that is marked L or P can be used for negotiation purposes if two microcomputers are available whereby one student or person can work with the datafile on one microcomputer and another student or person can work with the same datafile on a second microcomputer, interacting with each other to arrive at a settlement.

Table A–1
P/G% Datafiles Available on a Data Disk

FILE NUMBER	MASTER FILE	DATAFILE NAME	ALTERNATIVES	CRITERIA	CHAPTERS	CROSS-REFERENCE	FORM	PROBLEM	FILE NUMBER	LAW ACTIVITY
1-1	DEMO1	ASPA	14 budget categories	Membership attitude	PPG 16	MISC (BUS)	$-Mix		1-1	X
1-2	DEMO1	diversn	Trials, pleas, diversion	Delay, respect, expense	MPA 3 etc. PPG 16, POL 10, LAS 1 etc JUD 17	LAW/POL	N-Mix	All	1-2	P
1-3	DEMO1	police	Police $, courts $	Crime reduction, fair procedure	MPA3 etc, POL 10 LAS 11 etc. JUD 2 etc	LAW/POL	$-Mix	All	1-3	P
1-4	DEMO1	crime	Trial, settlement	Sentence, lit. & set. cost, for P & D		LAWYER	C-Risk	M-Rel, W-Goals	1-4	L
1-5	DEMO1	damages	Trial, settlement	Damages, litigation cost		LAWYER	C-Risk	M-Rel	1-5	[illegible]
1-6	DEMO1	health	Doctor $, nurse $	Longevity, cost	MPA 13, POL 12 LAS 16	MED/POL	$-Mix	C-Alts	1-6	[illegible]
1-7	DEMO1	SEQUENCE	FIFO, SCF	Delay, equity, predictibability	PPG 4, LAS 20 JUD 2, 20	LAW/POL	E-Choice		1-7	P
1-8	DEMO1	AFFIRM	2 affirmative action programs	Students trained, patients treated	MPA 4, LAS 10	MISC (BUS)	E-Choice	MD-Goals	1-8	X
[illegible]	DEMO1	JURYINST	No inst., reas. doubt., .90 prob., 10-1 tradeoff	Threshold height, uniformity						
1-10	DEMO1	OPTBOND	Under $100, $101-$500, etc.	Appearance, being held	PPG 4					
1-11	DEMO1	GEOALLOC	Wisconsin, Illinois	Linear, log, semi-log, scale coefficients	MPA 9, PPG 12 LAS 16					
1-12	DEMO1	OPTSENT	Probation, one month, six months, etc.	Crime, prior record	PPG 8					
1-13	DEMO1	FP/FT	News items	Editors, police, prosecutors, defenders						

A–1: continued

FILE NUMBER	MASTER FILE	DATAFILE NAME	ALTERNATIVES	CRITERIA	CHAPTERS	CROSS-REFERENCE	FORM	PROBLEM	FILE NUMBER	LAW ACTIVITY
1-14	DEMO1	SENTDISC	High discretion, low discretion	Urban/rural, North/South, white/black, nonpoor/poor disparities	PPG 8					
1-15	DEMO1	+LAWYER	Having, not having a lawyer	Procedural safeguards, sentencing	PPG 8					
1-16	DEMO1	EXPVAL2	Jury, bench, settle	Damages, probabilities, costs			C-Risk			
1-17	DEMO1	NEWTRIAL	Trial, settle	Damages, Probabilities, hours, hourly rates	MPA 13, JUD 17 LAS 13 etc.		C-Risk			
1-18	DEMO1	FARMERS5	7 farm policies	8 judgemental criteria	POL 4					
1-19	DEMO1	DIVERSN2	Trials, pleas	Speed = 1/delay Respect2 = respect1 minus 5						
1-20										
2-1	GOVT	FEDERAL	National-state relations	3 criteria	POL 15	GOVT/POL	D-Level		2-1	P
2-2	GOVT	BRANCHES	Executive-legislative relations	3 criteria	POL 15	GOVT/POL	D-Level		2-2	P
2-3	GOVT	JUDICIAL	Constitutional review	2 criteria: Popular response, minority rights	POL 15, JUD 2	GOVT/POL	E-Choice		2-3	P
2-4	GOVT	PARTIES	1, 2, many	Voters' choice, governing ability	POL 15	GOVT/POL	D-Level		2-4	X
2-5	GOVT	DEMOCRAC	Democracy, dictatorship	Ideas, response, speed	POL 15	GOVT/POL	E-Choice		2-5	P

Table A–1: continued

FILE NUMBER	MASTER FILE	DATAFILE NAME	ALTERNATIVES	CRITERIA	CHAPTERS	CROSS-REFERENCE	FORM	PROBLEM	FILE NUMBER	LAW ACTIVITY
2-6	GOVT	REMAP	Redistricting alternatives	Equality, compactness	POL 8, JUD 12	GOVT/POL	E-Choice	M-Alts	2-6	P
2-7	GOVT	PUB/AID	9 public aid policies	Taxpayer, recipients, feasible, migration	MPA 14, LAS 12, JUD 21, POL 10, 10	POOR/POL	D-Level		2-7	X
2-8	GOVT	-CRIME	6 anti-crime policies	5 goals		LAW/POL	C-Choice		2-8	P
2-9	GOVT	SOLIDWAS	Landfill, incineration recycle	Cost, health, enforcement location						
2-10	GOVT	ROBBING2	Rob store, do not rob	Benefits & costs if succeed or fail	MPA 14					
2-11	GOVT	ROBBING3	Same	Loot, gang prestige, prison, missed future	POL 10, LAS 18 JUD 21					
2-12	GOVT	DETRIMEN	City A, City B	Crime, expenditures	PPG 3					
2-13	GOVT	EVF	Effectiveness, efficiency	Benefits, costs, B-C	PPG 3					
2-14	GOVT	MRRvARR	Agency L, Agency M	Benefits time 1, benefits time 2	PPG 3					
2-15	GOVT	EQUITY	Person G, Person H	12 actual allocations, minimums, 3 goals, negative deviations	PPG 4					
2-16	GOVT	LvM&N	Ward L, Ward M&N	Efficiency, equity	PPG 4					
2-17	GOVT	ENC.REL	9 ways of encouraging pretrial release	Appearing, crime, release,$,feasibility	PPG 8					
2-18	GOVT	ENC.TS	5 ways of encouraging prosecutor time saving	Time,$,& crime	PPG 8					
2-19	GOVT	-DISPAR	3 ways of reducing CJ disparities	Disparities,$, individualizing	PPG 8					

A–1: continued

FILE NUMBER	MASTER FILE	DATAFILE NAME	ALTERNATIVES	CRITERIA	CHAPTERS	CROSS-REFERENCE	FORM	PROBLEM	FILE NUM-BER	LAW ACTI-VITY
2-20	GOVT	GETDATA	Gather data, don't	Benefits, costs	PPG 257					
3-1	POLICY3	POOR	Govt. doctors, reim-burse, & no govt.	4 criteria for medical services	POL 12	MED/POL	E-Choice		3-1	X
3-2	POLICY3	SURGERY	Perform or not	Survive, live normally, personal worth	POL 12	MISC(BUS)	C-Risk		3-2	X
3-3	POLICY3	CANCER	6 levels	Productivity, patient cost, prevention cost	POL 12	MED/POL	C-Level		3-3	X
3-4	POLICY3	INFANT	5 states	Population, efficiency	POL 12	MED/POL	$-Mix		3-4	X
3-5	POLICY3	FS.CAUSE	Modernism, stability	Freedom of speech	PPG 6, JUD 5					
3-6	POLICY3	INCENTIVE	15 incentives not to pollute	7 goals esp. pollution reduction, clean-up,$, feasibility	PPG 3, JUD 9					
3-7	POLICY3	INCENT2	4 more incentives	Same						
3-8	POLICY3	AID-REL	Degrees of govt. aid to religion	11 criteria for de-ciding						
3-9										
3-10										
3-11										
3-12										
3-13										

Table A–1: continued

FILE NUMBER	MASTER FILE	DATAFILE NAME	ALTERNATIVES	CRITERIA	CHAPTERS	CROSS-REFERENCE	FORM	PROBLEM	FILE NUMBER	LAW ACTIVITY
3-14										
3-15										
3-16										
3-17										
3-18										
3-19										
3-20										
4-1	DEMO2	PREDICT	12 welfare casetypes	Substance, procedure		PREDICT	D-Pred		4-1	J
4-2	DEMO2	FLORENCE	Getting married, staying single	Companionship, privacy		MISC (PDM)	E-Choice		4-2	X
4-3	DEMO2	ENERGY	5 energy sources	5 energy goals	MPA 6 etc. POL 10	ECON/POL	C-Choice	M-Rel, W-Goals	4-3	X
4-4	DEMO2	HOUSE	Buy new house, don't	Cost, space		MISC (PDM)	E-Choice		4-4	X
4-5	DEMO2	POSTAL	Private mail, govt. mail	Efficiency, equity		ECON/POL	E-Choice		4-5	P
4-6	DEMO2	COUNSEL	Volunteer, LSC	4 goals for legal services	PPG 12, POL 10 etc. LAS 19 etc. JUD 11	LAW/POL	C-Choice	C-Alts	4-6	P

A–1: continued

FILE NUMBER	MASTER FILE	DATAFILE NAME	ALTERNATIVES	CRITERIA	CHAPTERS	CROSS-REFERENCE	FORM	PROBLEM	FILE NUMBER	LAW ACTIVITY
4-7	DEMO2	BUSING	Hours per week	Integration, $ costs	LAS 11	POLICY	C-Level	MD-Goals	4-7	P
4-8	DEMO2	ENERGY2	5 energy sources	1 energy goal		ECON/POL	C-Choice		4-8	X
4-9	DEMO2	SHRTPROB	Policy 1, Policy 2	Crimes solved, civil cases processed	MPA 1 etc.					
4-10	DEMO2	SLIPFALL	Trial, settle	Lit cost, set cost, award, set smount, enjoyment, net profit						
4-11	DEMO2	COM-SUP	3 community support programs	3 benefits & 3 costs						
4-12	DEMO2	VACATION	New York, Champaign	Expense, fun						
4-13	DEMO3	OCCA-BIF	Invest in P/G% or not	Sales, cgs, expense, & taxes						
4-14	DEMO2	MCDM's	7 programs	6 criteria						
4-15	DEMO2	LAW/SEQ	12 cases	7 criteria for sequencing	LAS 20					
4-16	DEMO2	COURSES	Alternative college courses	Credits, working days, useful knowledge						
4-17	DEMO2	PERSONS	4 faculty members	Achievement, prior earnings						
4-18	DEMO2	CRIMPOOR	Volunteers, assigned counsel, public defender (L,C)	Expense, access, feasibility, competence, const. (L,C)						
4-19	DEMO2	GIDEON	No, capital, felony, misd., pre/post trial, civil	Acquit, convict, expense, respect, truth						
4-20	DEMO2	CVL.POOR	No, special, all civil cases	+right liab., -wrong liab., respect, truth						

Table A–1: continued

FILE NUMBER	MASTER FILE	DATAFILE NAME	ALTERNATIVES	CRITERIA	CHAPTERS	CROSS-REFERENCE	FORM	PROBLEM	FILE NUM-BER	LAW ACTI-VITY
5-1	PREDICT	PREDICT	12 welfare casetypes in detail	Substance, procedure		POOR/POL	D-Pred		5-1	J
5-2	PREDICT	RELIGION	8 casetypes	Time, place, purpose	MPA 13, LAS 4 etc.	GOVT/POL	D-Pred	C-Alts, C-Goals	5-2	J
5-3	PREDICT	REDIST	9 cases	4 redistricting criteria		GOVT/POL	D-Pred	M-Rel, W-Goals	5-3	J
5-4	PREDICT	INTLAW	14 casetypes	Source of law, U.S. opponent (1-N Scale)	LAS 5	GOVT/POL	C-Pred	M-Alts	5-4	J
5-5	PREDICT	INTLAW2	14 casetypes	Source of law, U.S. opponent (0%-100%)		GOVT/POL	C-Pred	M-Alts	5-5	J
5-6	PREDICT	CRIMINAL	5 hypo cases	4 hypo criteria	LAS 5, 5	LAW/POL	D-Pred		5-6	J
5-7	PREDICT	DISCRIM	8 housing casetypes	Willingness, law field	LAS 4, 5	POOR/POL	D-Pred	MD-Goals	5-7	J
5-8	PREDICT	PREDICT2	12 Welfare casetypes (with outcomes)	Substance, procedure	POL 8, LAS 4 etc. JUD 12, 12	POOR/POL	D-Pred		5-8	J
5-9	PREDICT	DISCRIM2	8 housing casetypes (with outcomes)	Willingness, law field	LAS 11, JUD 14 LAS 4	POOR/POL	D-Pred	MD-Goals	5-9	J
5-10	PREDICT	REDIST2	9 cases(with outcomes)	4 redistricting criteria	MPA 10 etc, JUD 7, LAS 4 etc.	GOVT/POL	D-Pred		5-10	J
5-11	PREDICT	EQL/PRO	11 casetypes	Rights, groups	LAS 4, 5 JUD 7	POOR/POL	D-Pred		5-11	J
5-12	PREDICT	EQL/PRO2	13 casetypes	Rights, groups	JUD 7	POOR/POL	D-Pred		5-12	J
5-13	PREDICT	JC&JDM	Defense oriented, prosecution oriented	Democrat, Republican Catholic, Protestant	PPG 8, LAS 8	LAW/POL	D-Pred		5-13	J
5-14	PREDICT	UNP.REP	Representing unpopular clients	Opportunities attitudes	LAS 8		D-Pred			
5-15	PREDICT	RELIG2	15 case types on religion in schools	4 predictive criteria	MPA 13, LAS 17 JUD 6					
5-16	PREDICT	LABORLIT	Affirmed, reversed Supreme Court decisions	Southern, Northern cases Pro, anti-labor	LAS 7, 7					

A–1: continued

FILE NUMBER	MASTER FILE	DATAFILE NAME	ALTERNATIVES	CRITERIA	CHAPTERS	CROSS-REFERENCE	FORM	PROBLEM	FILE NUMBER	LAW ACTIVITY
5-17	PREDICT	RODRIGEZ	4 kinds of equality of $ per student	Educated pop., adminstration, consistency, etc.						
5-18	PREDICT	PR.CHAIN	Before, after bail reform. Weights are probs.	ROR, bond, jail, plead guilty, innocent, get PD no PD						
5-19	PREDICT	PR.CH2	Same. Weights are Q of cases.	Same						
5-20	PREDICT	CHILD	Win, lose, dams when awarded, dams all cases	Child absent, present						
6-1	POLICY	ROBBING	Rob a store, don't	Money, prestige, jail, future	MPA 14 LAS 18	MISC (BUS)	N-Risk	DP-Con	6-1	P
6-2	POLICY	JOBS/$	8 economic policies	Unemployment, inflation equity, free enterprise	POL 1, JUD 13	ECON/POL	C-Choice		6-2	X
6-3	POLICY	CONSUMER	5 consumer policies	Business, consumer, taxpayer, equity	POL 3, JUD 15	ECON/POL	C-Choice		6-3	X
6-4	POLICY	SOC-CAP	Capitalism, mixed, socialism	Equality, opportunity, GNP, security, initiative	POL 3	ECON/POL	C-Choice		6-4	X
6-5	POLICY	SOC-CAP2	Capitalism, mixed, socialism	Political freedom, enterprise freedom	POL 3	ECON/POL	C-Choice		6-5	X
6-6	POLICY	FARMERS	7 farm policies	Effect on well-off/poor farmers, well-off/poor consumers		ECON/POL	C-Choice		6-6	X
6-7	POLICY	FARMERS2	7 farm policies	Taxpayer, middleman, other countries, moralists		ECON/POL	C-Choice		6-7	X
6-8	POLICY	FARMERS3	7 farm policies	Both sets of goals combined		ECON/POL	C-Choice		6-8	X

Table A–1: continued

FILE NUMBER	MASTER FILE	DATAFILE NAME	ALTERNATIVES	CRITERIA	CHAPTERS	CROSS-REFERENCE	FORM	PROBLEM	FILE NUMBER	LAW ACTIVITY
6-9	POLICY	$/CITIES	Anti-crime $ to City A, City B	Equity, efficiency	MPA 8, PPC 4, LAS 11, 14, JUD 20	LAW/POL	$-Mix	All	6-9	P
6-10	POLICY	GUNS/BUT	Guns, butter	National Defense, quality of life		GOVT/POL	$-Mix		6-10	X
6-11	POLICY	ENV. PRO	Marketplace, regulation, pollution taxes	Reduce pollution, political feasibility	POL 6, JUD 9	ECON/POL	D-Level	C-Goals	6-11	P
6-12	POLICY	ARMSCONT	9 defense policies	Economy, nuclear war, avoid conquest, feasibility	POL 14	GOVT/POL	D-Level		6-12	X
6-13	POLICY	F/SPEECH	5 speech policies	Ideas, criticism, other rights, taxpayer, feasibility	POL 13, JUD 5	GOVT/POL	D-Level		6-13	P
6-14	POLICY	RACE/REL	6 race policies	Minorities, merit, minimums	POL 9, JUD 8	POOR/POL	D-Level		6-14	P
6-15	POLICY	FED/ENV	7 levels of federal-state relations	Business, municipal govt., coordination, localism	POL 6, JUD 9	GOVT/POL	C-Choice		6-15	P
6-16	POLICY	HOUSING	6 housing policies	Taxpayer, incentives, development, feasibility	POL 7, JUD 14	POOR/POL			6-16	P
6-17	POLICY	LABOR	9 labor policies	Workers, business, taxpayers, consumers	POL 5, JUD 13	POOR/POL	D-Level		6-17	
6-18	POLICY	MRR/ACT	Police $, judicial $, corrections $	Crime reduction		LAW/POL	$-Mix		6-18	P
6-19	POLICY	MPR/PLA	10 cities	Crime reduction	MPA 8	LAW/POL	$-Mix		6-19	P
6-20	POLICY	FARMERS4	7 farm policies	8 judgemental criteria						
7-1	LAW	SEARCH	Exclusionary rule, legal action	Police adherance, morale	MPA 362, PPC 253, J AS 454, JUD 27, 28f	LAW/POL	E-Choice	DP-Con, W-Goals	7-1	P

A–1: continued

FILE NUMBER	MASTER FILE	DATAFILE NAME	ALTERNATIVES	CRITERIA	CHAPTERS	CROSS-REFERENCE	FORM	PROBLEM	FILE NUMBER	LAW ACTIVITY
7-2	LAW	SUING	Sue, don't sue	Discounted damages, costs		LAWYER	C-Risk	DP-Con	7-2	L
7-3	LAW	%HOLD	% of defendants to hold in jail pretrial	Holding costs, releasing costs	MPA 14, PPG 17, LAS 18	LAW/POL	C-Level	M-Alts, DP-Con	7-3	P
7-4	LAW	HOURRATE	Settle, go to trial	Total fee, costs, avg. damages		LAWYER	E-Choice	C-Goals	7-4	L
7-5	LAW	FLATFEE	Settle, go to trial	Flat fee, costs, avg. damages		LAWYER	E-Choice	C-Goals	7-5	L
7-6	LAW	GUILT	Defendant is guilty, is not	Alibi, scene of crime		PREDICT	C-Pred		7-6	C
7-7	LAW	PRETRIAL	Preventative detention, money bond, Vera system	4 liberal goals	MPA 14, POL 10, LAS 16, JUD 18	LAW/POL	E-Choice		7-7	C
7-8	LAW	PRETRY/N	PD, MB, Vera	3 neutral goals		LAW/POL	E-Choice		7-8	C
7-9	LAW	PRETRY/C	PD, MB, Vera	2 conservative goals		LAW/POL	E-Choice		7-9	C
7-10	LAW	IND/REL	Release, hold	Type 2 error, type 1 error		LAW/POL	N-Risk		7-10	C
7-11	LAW	JUDGES	Appointed-elected, long-short term	Economic liberalism, civil liberties	PPG 13, JUD 19	LAW/POL	C-Choice		7-11	P
7-12	LAW	JURIES	Jury size	Innocent convicted, guilty not convicted	PPG 11 etc. JUD 19 LAS 9 etc.	LAW/POL	C-Level	M-Rel	7-12	P
7-13	LAW	OPT/TIME	Billable hours	Damages, fee, time cost		LAWYER	C-Level	DP-Con	7-13	A
7-14	LAW	FLATTIME	Billable hours	Fee, costs		LAWYER	E-Choice	C-Alts	7-14	A

Table A–1: continued

FILE NUMBER	MASTER FILE	DATAFILE NAME	ALTERNATIVES	CRITERIA	CHAPTERS	CROSS-REFERENCE	FORM	PROBLEM	FILE NUMBER	LAW ACTIVITY
7-15	LAW	ALLOCATE	4 casetypes	B/C ratio, regression, coefficient		LAWYER	N-Mix	M-Alts	7-15	A
7-16	LAW	SENTENCE	Mandatory minimum, determinate guidelines, discretionary	3 liberal goals, 1 neutral goal	POL 10, JUD 21	LAW/POL	E-Choice		7-16	P
7-17	LAW	SENTENCE2	The same	4 conservative goals	JUD 21	LAW/POL	E-Choice		7-17	P
7-18	LAW	JUVENILE	3 methods of disposition	Rehabilitation, costs, prediction		LAW/POL	N-Mix		7-18	P
7-19	LAW	PATH	Federal court, State court	Victory, damages, years		LAWYER	C-Risk	DP-Con	7-19	L
7-20	LAW	DELAY	Days consumed from arrest to trial	Speed-up cost, delay cost	PPG 12, JUD 20	LAW/POL	C-Level		7-20	P
8-1	MISC	COURSES	3 college courses	Credits, working days, useful knowledge		PDM	E-Choice	DP-Con	8-1	X
8-2	MISC	WHOMARRY	Fred, Joe, Neither	Companionship, interests, security, age		PDM	E-Choice	DP-Con	8-2	X
8-3	MISC	PROF.X	Political science, public administration	Colleagues, travel funds, professionalism		PDM	E-Choice		8-3	X
8-4	MISC	CAMPAIGN	Media $, Organization $	8 two-party vote, dollar cost	MPA 14 etc., LAS 18 etc.	BUS	$-Mix	DP-Con	8-4	X
8-5	MISC	COMP.WOR	3 jobs for comparable worth	2 criteria in months and 0-10 scale		ECON/POL	$-Mix			
8-6	MISC	MUL.OBJ	Multi-objective programming with 4 policies	3 goals with decimal weights	MPA 14 etc., LAS 18 etc.		$-Mix			
8-7	MISC	B-C.B/C	5 projects	Benefits, costs, B/C	PPG 3 etc.					
8-8	MISC	UNKN.VAR	Go, no/go	B,C,Prob.,EV,C/B	PPG 15 etc., LAS 13 etc.					

A–1: continued

FILE NUMBER	MASTER FILE	DATAFILE NAME	ALTERNATIVES	CRITERIA	CHAPTERS	CROSS-REFERENCE	FORM	PROBLEM	FILE NUMBER	LAW ACTIVITY
8-9	MISC	OPSEQ1	9 Optimum sequencing alternatives	Avg. time, max. time, cost						
8-10	MISC	OPSEQ7	6 winners	Same						
8-11	MISC	TORT	Negligence, no fault	Deserts, costs, deterrence fees		LAW/POL				
8-12	MISC	CHILD2	Child absent, present	Damages when child absent, present						
8-13	MISC	PRAC.LAW	Take case, reject case. Go trial, settle	Dams, hours, offer (P,D) (Best civil analysis)						
8-14	MISC	CRIM.PO2	PD, assigned, volunteers, PD big, apptd small, regional small	Expense, access feasibility, competence, const.						
8-15	MISC	CIV.LIB	8 casetypes for civil liberties cases	8 predictive criteria						
8-16	MISC	ASSIGN	Fox vs. Wolf. Criminal vs. civil quality	Criminal vs. civil quality. Fox vs. Wolf						
8-17	MISC	PRETRY4	Prevent. detention Money bond system Vera system	9 criteria for choosing						
8-18										
8-19										
8-20										
9-1	LAW2	LSC	Case handling $, law reform $	Evaluator satisfaction	MPA 14 etc. LAS 18 etc	LAW/POL				

Table A–1: continued

FILE NUMBER	MASTER FILE	DATAFILE NAME	ALTERNATIVES	CRITERIA	CHAPTERS	CROSS-REFERENCE	FORM	PROBLEM	FILE NUMBER	LAW ACTIVITY
9-2	LAW2	CONV.ACQ	Convict, acquit	EB,EC,guilt, rightness, wrongness			N-Risk			
9-3	LAW2	CON.AC2	Acquit, convict	Acquit innocent, acquit guilty, prob I/G			N-Risk			
9-4	LAW2	GF.EXCEP	Good faith exception to exclusion	Police illegality, convictions						
9-5	LAW2	MarcVic	Litigate, drop wuit	12 scenarios, Litigation costs	MPA 13 etc. LAS 18 etc.					
9-6	LAW2	PARTNERS	12 law partners	15 criteria for dividing profits	MPA 13 etc.					
9-7	LAW2	PARTNER2	Same	11 more criteria						
9-8	LAW2	WILL	Son,daughter,spouse	Need, deservingness						
9-9	LAW2	IND/REL2	Released defendant or hold	Benefits & costs if D shows or no show	JUD 18					
9-10	LAW2	CON.AC3	Acquit (go), convict (no go)	Benefits & costs if innocent or guilty						
9-11	LAW2	ETHICS	Quantity of hours to spend on a case	Lawyer profit, client profit	MPA 13, LAS 17, JUD 17					
9-12	LAW2	SEARCH2	4 ways to encourage legal searches	Reduce illegality, lying, crime	MPA 14, POL 10, LAS 18, JUD 3,					
9-13	LAW2	PRE.DAMS	4 damage cases	Medical expenses as a predictor	PPG 17					
9-14	LAW2	SETTLE	D upper limit, P lower limit	Exp. damages, net lit. costs						
9-15	LAW2	BARGAIN	D upper limit, P lower limit	Esp. sentence, $ bonus discount						

A–1: continued

FILE NUMBER	MASTER FILE	DATAFILE NAME	ALTERNATIVES	CRITERIA	CHAPTERS	CROSS-REFERENCE	FORM	PROBLEM	FILE NUMBER	LAW ACTIVITY
9-16	LAW2	JURYvJUD	No, limited, full jury trials	Reduce crime, delay, disparities, increase separation, partic., & pred.	JUD 4					
9-17	LAW2	CAP.PUN	All, special, none on capital punish.	Same	JUD 4					
9-18	LAW2	FACTS	Guilty, not guilty	Alibi wit. for D, scene wit. for P	LAS 5, JUD 19					
9-19	LAW2	MARBURY	10 issues in Marbury v. Madison	4 goals, esp. jud. review federalism						
9-20	LAW2	MARBURY2	Same, but with previous outcomes	Same						
10-1	LAW3	NAACP	Schools, voting, CJ, employment, housing, pubaccom	Equality improvement						
10-2	LAW3	HYPOTEST	Accept, reject	#1, #2 error, #1, #2 accuracy, hypo true, hypo false	PPG 17		N-Risk			
10-3	LAW3	EXPVAL	Trial, settle	Trial damages, settlement probabilities			C-Risk			
10-4	LAW3	DISPAR	Black, white defendant		PPG 8, LAS 8					
10-5	LAW3	LITSTRAT	Bench, jury, settle	Damages, costs, probabilities, enjoyment			C-Risk			
10-6	LAW3	CONFLICT	Budgets, minimums	Economic feasibility, equity satisfaction	MPA 13, LAS 16					
10-7	LAW3	CRIME2	Settle, trial	Average sentence, total cost	LAS 13, 13, 13, 13, 11, JUD 17, 13		C-Risk			
10-8	LAW3	GIFTED	Itinerant teacher, resource room	Cost, effectiveness, school impact						
10-9	LAW3	HYPO2	Accept hypo, reject hypo	Benefits & costs if true or false						

Table A–1: continued

FILE NUMBER	MASTER FILE	DATAFILE NAME	ALTERNATIVES	CRITERIA	CHAPTERS	CROSS-REFERENCE	FORM	PROBLEM	FILE NUMBER	LAW ACTIVITY
10-10	LAW3	%PREDICT	Case 1, case 2	1-5 scale, 1-2	MPA 10					
10-11	LAW3	%WEIGHT	4 criteria in redistricting cases	# yes, # no, % yes who win, % no who win	MPA 11, 11					
10-12	LAW3	CRIME3	Settle, trial	Expected sentence, total cost, P & D	LAS 9					
10-13	LAW3	PAROCH	7 types of aid to parochial schools	Const. percent, const. trichotomy	LAS 4					
10-14	LAW3	PAROCH2	Same, plus prior outcomes	Const. on 0%-100%						
10-15	LAW3	RACIAL	5 relations between blacks and whites	Const. on 0%-100%	LAS 4					
10-16	LAW3	DIVORCE	Law severity, divorce rate	Law severity, divorce rate, % Catholics, predicted severity	LAS 8					
10-17	LAW3	-JAILPOP	7 ways to decrease jail population	Delay trials, pleas, expense, crime, jail pop.	LAS 9, PPG 11					
10-18	LAW3	MISINFO	Go to trial, don't go	Dams, prob., fee, hours, rate, combinations	LAS 13, 13					
10-19	LAW3	MISINFO2	Client A, Client B (Best missing info)	Damages, hours, minimums, maximums (A,B)	MPA 7, LAS 13					
10-20	LAW3	JURY, GEN	Plaintiff wins or loses, Deviation from avg. dams.	Female, male juries & Female, male plaintiffs						

A–1: continued

FILE NUMBER	MASTER FILE	DATAFILE NAME	ALTERNATIVES	CRITERIA	CHAPTERS	CROSS-REFERENCE	FORM	PROBLEM	FILE NUMBER	LAW ACTIVITY
11-1	DEMO3	EVAL.CIT	City A, City B	15 criteria to snow multiplying, logging & MD						
11-2	DEMO3	MD.EQUA	12 multi-dimensionality equations	8 criteria for handling MD						
11-3	DEMO3	P/W%vMUL	P/G% vs. multiplying approach	8 criteria for handling MD						
11-4	DEMO3	B/C.SEQ	Arranging law cases in a law firm	1st and 2nd week profit	LAS 20, 20					
11-5	DEMO3	TOMSAATY	Job A, B, C	Research, growth, benefits, colleagues, location, reputation						
11-6	DEMO3	EDWARDS	Thauma. Dept., other departments	Teaching, research, & service						
11-7	DEMO3									
11-8	DEMO3									
11-9	DEMO3									
11-10	DEMO3									
11-11	DEMO3									
11-12	DEMO3									
11-13	DEMO3									

Table A–1: continued

FILE NUMBER	MASTER FILE	DATAFILE NAME	ALTERNATIVES	CRITERIA	CHAPTERS	CROSS-REFERENCE	FORM	PROBLEM	FILE NUMBER	LAW ACTIVITY
12-1	POLICY4	ANTI-POL	Large, moderate, & no pollution program	Health, recreation, esthetics, agri., ind., poverty, & $						
12-2	POLICY4	ENV.SEP	Judicial, Legis, or Admin. emphasis	9 criteria of good government						
12-3	POLICY4	ABORTION	None, lst trimester, 2nd, 3rd & post-birth	Save babies, anti-sex, women's rights, privacy, life sanctity, etc.						
12-4	POLICY4	ABHOR.SP	Allow abhorrent speech; prohibit	Precedent, expose, counter, safety valve, violence, acceptance, disgrace, psycho harm, publicity, etc.						
12-5	POLICY4	LEGALPOT	Prohibit, allow possession, reg. sale, unreg. sale	Policing, crimes, productivity, cancer, fgn. rel., addiction, privacy, cash crop, accidents, taxes, minors						
12-6	POLICY4	OPT.CQ	Zero, low, medium, high & runaway crime	Crime reduction costs & crime damage costs						
12-7	POLICY4	ATOMBOMB	Develop atom bomb, do not	Worst, best $ midpoint, lives saved & dollar cost						
12-8	POLICY4	LANDPOL	9 controversial land policy issues	See datafile 16-7						
12-9	POLICY4	TAXPOL	8 tax sources	7 criteria of good taxes						
12-10	POLICY4									
12-11	POLICY4									
12-12	POLICY4									
12-13	POLICY4									

A–1: continued

FILE NUMBER	MASTER FILE	DATAFILE NAME	ALTERNATIVES	CRITERIA	CHAPTERS	CROSS-REFERENCE	FORM	PROBLEM	FILE NUMBER	LAW ACTIVITY
13-1	LAW4	MAR.DISP.	Stay married, agreemt, live apart, divorce	Alcohol, violence, remarriage, privacy, $, reputation, child., compnionshp						
13-2	LAW4	PROP.SET	Sell, keep some, keep all	Equal division, child interest, H or W needs						
13-3	LAW4	CUSTODY	Mother all, some kids or time to each, father all	Child, mother, father, interests						
13-4	LAW4	CSUPPORT	From $50/2 weeks to $500	No less, nor more than child needs or spouse ability						
13-5	LAW4	CCOMPLY	7 ways of const. compliance	Compliance, ease of doing						
13-6	LAW4	NOFAULTD	No divorces, adultery, physical/mental cruelty incompatibility	Public, honesty, freedom, wrong div., wrong staying, 2 par., $, remarr.						
13-7	LAW4	CHIABUSE	Take away or leave child	-abuse, + family love, -taxes						
13-8	LAW4	ENC.REP	9 ways of encouraging representation of poor & unpop.	+Rep of poor & -expenses						
13-9	LAW4	PERF.PB	6 ways of making PB results jury-like	Reduce trials & taxes but constitutional						
13-10	LAW4	CON.AC4	Vote acquit, convict	Acquit innocent, convict guilty						
13-11	LAW4	OPT.SEQ	6 ways to sequence 3 cases	Waiting time, processing time, total time, avg. time, gains, losses, & maximum time						
13-12	LAW4	INSA.DEF	Insanity as a broad defense, irrelevant, or only for treatment	Law compliance, rehabilitation, & truth determination						
13-13	LAW4	ADV.SYS	Adversary system, inquisitorial, & modified							

Table A–1: continued

FILE NUMBER	MASTER FILE	DATAFILE NAME	ALTERNATIVES	CRITERIA	CHAPTERS	CROSS-REFERENCE	FORM	PROBLEM	FILE NUMBER	LAW ACTIVITY
13-14	LAW4	LAW.SEQ	6 ways of ordering 3 law firm cases	Income, cost, profit for Ist & 2nd week						
13-15	LAW4	C-A.NEG	Computer-aided negotiation. Trial vs. settle.	Damages, costs, & offer from lawyer & client perspective						
13-16	LAW4	TORT.CON	Intent, negligence, & strict liability	Intent, damages, standard violation, cause, contrib., waiver, 3rd party, etc.						
13-17	LAW4	K.CONCEP	Binding, not binding contract & present occurrence	Agreement, consideration, competence, form, legal, & conscionable						
13-18	LAW4	CONS.CON	Constitutional, unconst., & present occurrence	Authority, federalism, separation, 1st amend., due process, & equal pro.						
13-19	LAW4	CRIM.CON	Criminal act, not criminal, & present occurrence	Intent, statute, behavior, cause, proof, capability, justification, & proper procedure						
13-20	LAW4	CR.CLASS	Crimes against persons, property, & public obstraction	Homocide, bodily attack detention, house crimes personal property, sex crimes, & others						

A–1: continued

FILE NUMBER	MASTER FILE	DATAFILE NAME	ALTERNATIVES	CRITERIA	CHAPTERS	CROSS-REFERENCE	FORM	PROBLEM	FILE NUM-BER	LAW ACTI-VITY
14-1	PREDICT2	EQU.PRO3	15 equal protection case types	4 types of groups, 6 types of treatment, with each type weighted in terms of importance						
14-2	PREDICT2	EQU.PRO4	Case types 16-24	Same scored no-yes						
14-3	PREDICT2	RES.UTIL	15 examples of policy evaluation research	13 factors facilitating utilization						
14-4	PREDICT2	INTLAW3	12 international law casetypes	Source of law US opponent power						
14-5	PREDICT2									
14-6	PREDICT2									
14-7	PREDICT2									
14-8	PREDICT2									
14-9	PREDICT2									
14-10	PREDICT2									
14-11	PREDICT2									
14-12	PREDICT2									
14-13	PREDICT2									

Table A–1: continued

FILE NUMBER	MASTER FILE	DATAFILE NAME	ALTERNATIVES	CRITERIA	CHAPTERS	CROSS-REFERENCE	FORM	PROBLEM	FILE NUMBER	LAW ACTIVITY
15-1	MISC2	HOUSEBUY	House 1, 2 & 3	14 house buying criteria						
15-2	MISC2	HB2	Same	14 more criteria						
15-3	MISC2	HB3	Same	10 more criteria						
15-4	MISC2	ETH.DILS	9 ethical dilemmas in policy evaluation	Effectiveness, efficiency equity, public partic., predict, due process & feasibility						
15-5	MISC2	RAISES	4 faculty members	Earnings, merit scores						
15-6	MISC2									
15-7	MISC2									
15-8	MISC2									
15-9	MISC2									
15-10	MISC2									
15-11	MISC2									
15-12	MISC2									
15-13	MISC2									

A–1: continued

FILE NUMBER	MASTER FILE	DATAFILE NAME	ALTERNATIVES	CRITERIA	CHAPTERS	CROSS-REFERENCE	FORM	PROBLEM	FILE NUM-BER	LAW ACTI-VITY
16-1	LAW5	WIN+CIV	P's best, D's best, win+ solution in civil case	P and D happiness						
16-2	LAW5	WIN+CRIM	P's best, D's best win+ solution in criminal case	P and D happiness						
16-3	LAW5	CRIMCASE	5 criminal cases	Felony, high GNP, Dem. judge, white defendant predictive criteria						
16-4	LAW5	CRIM2	5 criminal cases	same, but different scores						
16-5	LAW5	WHATSLAW	Law present, absent, this situation	Behavioral ought, govt. source, potential sanction						
16-6	LAW5	CRIM3	6 criminal cases with sentences	4 predictive criteria and 2 outcomes						
16-7	LAW5	LANDUSE	7 possible uses	9 criteria, especially fitness for use, but also jobs, taxes, consumer, pollution, balance, congestion, aesthetics, business						
16-8	LAW5	PI.CASES	5 cases with awards	4 criteria as to elected judge, no-fault, urban, male						

Bibliography of Books Cited

The following alphabetized bibliography includes all of the books cited in *Using Personal Computers for Decision-Making in Law Practice*. Other items cited in the footnotes that are not included in this bibliography include journal articles, book chapters, and unpublished papers.

American Bar Association. *The Lawyer's Handbook*. Chicago, 1975.

——— Commission on Standards of Judicial Administration. *Standards Relating to Trial Courts*. Chicago, 1976.

——— Law and Technology Committee. *Automated Law Research*. Chicago, 1973.

Baade, Hans, ed. *Jurimetrics*. Dobbs Ferry, N.Y.: Oceana Press, 1964.

Baird, Bruce. *Introduction to Decision Analysis*. Boston: Duxbury, 1978.

Baker, Kenneth. *Introduction to Sequencing and Scheduling*. New York: Wiley, 1974.

Baumol, William. *Economic Theory and Operations Analysis*. Englewood Cliffs, N.J.: Prentice-Hall, 1965.

Becker, G. and William Landes, eds. *Essays in the Economics of Crime and Punishment*. New York: Columbia University Press, 1974.

Behn, Robert, and James Vaupel. *Quick Analysis for Busy Decision-Makers*. New York: Basic Books, 1982.

Beltrami, Edward. *Models for Public Systems Analysis*. New York: Academic Press, 1977.

Berney, Arthur, et al., eds. *Legal Problems of the Poor: Cases and Material*. Boston: Little, Brown, 1975.

Bishop, Warner. *International Law*. Englewood Cliffs, N.J.: Prentice-Hall, 1952.

Bloom, Murray. *The Trouble with Lawyers*. New York: Simon and Schuster, 1968.

Bohigian, Haig. *The Foundations and Mathematical Models of Operations Research with Extensions to the Criminal Justice System*. Yonkers, N.Y.: Gazette, 1971.

Break, George. *Intergovernmental Fiscal Relations in the United States*. Washington, D.C.: Brookings Institution, 1966.

Brounstein, Sidney, and Murray Kamrass, eds. *Operations Research in Law Enforcement, Justice, and Societal Security*. Lexington, Mass.: Lexington-Heath, 1976.

Buffa, E., and J. Dyer. *Management Science/Operations Research*. New York: Wiley, 1981.

Byrd, Jack, Jr. *Operations Research Models for Public Administration*. Lexington, Mass.: Lexington-Heath, 1975.

Conway, Richard, William Maxwell, and Louis Miller. *Theory of Scheduling*. Reading, Mass.: Addison-Wesley, 1967.

Cooper, G., et al. *Law and Poverty*. St. Paul: West, 1973.

Dasgupta, P., et al. *Guidelines for Project Evaluation,* New York: Unipub, 1972.

Dinwiddy, Caroline. *Elementary Mathematics for Economists*. New York: Oxford University Press, 1967.

Dixon, Robert. *Democratic Representation: Reapportionment in Law and Politics*. New York: Oxford University Press, 1968.

Domke, Martin. *The Law and Practice of Commercial Arbitration*. Chicago: Callaghan, 1968.

Dorsen, Norman, et al. *Political and Civil Rights in the United States*. 2 vols. Boston: Little, Brown, 1979.

Due, John, and Ann Friedlander. *Government Finance: Economics of the Public Sector*. Homewood, Ill.: Irwin, 1973.

Easton, A. *Complex Managerial Decisions Involving Multiple Objectives*. New York: Wiley, 1973.

Edwards, Aron. *An Introduction to Linear Regression and Correlation*. San Francisco: Freeman, 1976.

Edwards, Ward, and Robert Newman. *Multi-Attribute Evaluation*. Beverly Hills, Calif.: Sage, 1982.

Elkouri, F., and E. Elkouri. *How Arbitration Works*. Washington, D.C.: Bureau of National Affairs, 1980.

Erikson, Warren, and Owen Hall. *Computer Models for Management Science*. Reading, Mass.: Addison-Wesley, 1983.

Freed, Roy, ed. *Computers and the Law*. Chicago: American Bar Association, 1969.

Goldkamp, J. *Two Classes of Accused: A Study of Bail and Detention in American Justice*. Cambridge, Mass.: Ballinger, 1979.

Gramlich, Edward. *Benefit-Cost Analysis of Government Programs*. Englewood Cliffs, N.J.: Prentice-Hall, 1981.

Greenberg, Jack. *Race Relations and American Law*. St. Paul: West, 1959.

Grossman, Joel, and J. Tanenhaus, eds. *Frontiers of Judicial Research*. New York: Wiley, 1969.

Guilford, J. P. *Fundamental Statistics in Psychology and Education*. New York: McGraw-Hill, 1965.

Hagood, Margaret, and Daniel Price. *Statistics for Sociologists*. New York: Holt, 1952.

Haimes, Yacov, and Vira Chankong, eds. *Decision Making with Multiple Objectives*. New York: Springer-Verlag, 1985.

Hale, George, and Marian Palley. *The Politics of Federal Grants*. Washington, D.C.: Congressional Quarterly Press, 1981.

Helly, Walter. *Urban Systems Models*. New York: Academic Press, 1975.

Henderson, T., et al. *Spreadsheet Software: From VisiCalc to 1–2–3*. Indianapolis: Que, 1983.

Hill, Percy, et al. *Making Decisions: A Multidisciplinary Introduction*. Reading, Mass.: Addison-Wesley, 1978.

Hilton, Gordon. *Intermediate Politometrics*. New York: Columbia University Press, 1976.

Hirsch, W. *Law and Economics: An Introductory Analysis*. New York: Academic Press, 1979.

Hudson, Manley. *International Law*. St. Paul, Minn.: West Publishing Company, 1951.

Ippolito, Dennis. *The Budget and National Politics*. San Francisco: Freeman, 1978.

Jacoby, J. *Pretrial Screening in Perspective*. Law Enforcement Assistance Administration, 1976.

Jarmel, Eli, ed. *Problems in the Legal Representation of the Poor*. New York: Matthew Bender, 1972.

Jones, Edgar, ed. *Law and Electronics: The Challenge of a New Era*. New York: Matthew Bender, 1962.

Jones, Harry, et al. *Legal Methods*. St. Paul: West, 1980.

Katz, Milton, and Kingman Brewster. *The Law of International Transactions and Relations*. Mineola, N.Y.: Foundation Press, 1960.

Keeney, Ralph, and H. Raiffa. *Decisions with Multiple Objectives: Preferences and Value Tradeoffs*. New York: Wiley, 1976.

Kellor, E. *American Arbitration: Its History, Functions, and Achievements*. New York: Harper, 1948.

Kidder, Robert. *Connecting Law and Society: An Introduction to Research and Theory*. Englewood Cliffs, N.J.: Prentice-Hall, 1983.

King, D., and Charles Quick. *Legal Aspects of the Civil Rights Movement*. Detroit: Wayne State University Press, 1965.

Kushner, J. *Fair Housing: Discrimination in Real Estate, Community Development, and Revitalization*. Colorado Springs, Colo.: Shepard's/McGraw-Hill, 1983.

LaFave, Wayne, and Austin Scott, eds. *Criminal Law*. St. Paul: West, 1972.

LaFrance, A., et al. *Law of the Poor*. St. Paul: West, 1973.

Lee, Sang. *Linear Optimization for Management*. New York: Petrocelli/Charter, 1976.

Lee, Sang, and L. Moore. *Introduction to Decision Science*. New York: Petrocelli/Charter, 1975.

Legal Services Corporation. *The Delivery System Study: A Policy Report to the Congress and the President of the United States*. Washington, D.C., 1980.

Lewis, P., and K. Peoples. *The Supreme Court and the Criminal Process*. Philadelphia: Saunders, 1978.

Llewelleyn, Karl. *The Common Law Tradition: Deciding Appeals*. Boston: Little, Brown, 1960.

Lynch, Thomas. *Public Budgeting in America*. Englewood Cliffs, N.J.: Prentice-Hall, 1985.

Mack, Ruth. *Planning on Uncertainty: Decision-Making in Business and Government Administration*. New York: Wiley, 1971.

MacKinnon, F. *Contingent Fees for Legal Services: A Study of Professional Economics and Responsibilities*. Hawthorne, N.Y.: Aldine, 1964.

Mayers, Lewis. *The American Legal System: The Administration of Justice in the United States by Judicial, Administrative, Military, and Arbitral Tribunals*. New York: Harper, 1955.

McCarty, D. *Law Office Management*. Englewood Cliffs, N.J.: Prentice-Hall, 1955.

McMillan, Claude, Jr. *Mathematical Programming: An Introduction to the Design and Application of Optimal Decision Machines*. New York: Wiley, 1970.

Meredith, D., et al. *Design and Planning of Engineering Systems*. Englewood Cliffs, N.J.: Prentice-Hall, 1985.

Miller, Frank. *Prosecution: The Decision to Charge a Suspect with a Crime*. Boston: Little, Brown, 1969.

Mishan, Ezra. *Economics for Social Decisions*. New York: Praeger, 1972.

Moore, Carl. *Profitable Applications of the Breakeven Systems*. Englewood Cliffs, N.J.: Prentice-Hall, 1971.

Nagel, S. *The Legal Process from a Behavioral Perspective*. Homewood, IL: Dorsey, 1969.

———. *Improving the Legal Process: Effects of Alternatives*. Lexington, Mass: Lexington-Heath, 1975.

———. *Policy Evaluation: Making Optimum Decisions*. New York: Prager, 1982.

———. *Equity as a Policy Goal*. Ohio: Bowling Green State University, 1983.

———. *Applying Decision Science to Law Practice*. Philadelphia: American Law Institute-American Bar Association, 1984.

———. *Public Policy: Goals, Means, and Methods*. New York: St. Martin's, 1984.

———. *Microcomputers as Decision-Making Aids in Law Practice*. Philadelphia: American Law Institute-American Bar Association Committee on Continuing Professional Education, 1985.

———. *Causation, Prediction, and Legal Analysis*. Westport, Conn.: Greenwood Press, 1986.

———. *Law, Policy, and Optimizing Analysis*. Westport, Conn.: Greenwood Press, 1986.

———. *Microcomputers, Evaluation Problems, and Policy Analysis*. Beverly Hills, Calif.: Sage Publications, forthcoming.

———, ed. *Modeling the Criminal Justice System*. Beverly Hills, Calif.: Sage Publications, 1977.

Nagel, S., and M. Neef. *Legal Policy Analysis: Finding an Optimum Level or Mix*. Lexington, Mass.: Lexington-Heath, 1977.

———. *Decision Theory and the Legal Process*. Lexington, Mass.: Lexington-Heath, 1979.

Nemhauser, G. *Introduction to Dynamic Programming*. New York: Wiley, 1966.

Nierenberg, Gerard. *Fundamentals of Negotiating*. New York: Hawthorn/Dutton, 1973.

Nowak, John, et al. *Constitutional Law*. St. Paul: West, 1983.

Orfield, L., and E. Re. *Cases and Materials on International Law*. Indianapolis: Bobbs-Merrill, 1955.

Polsby, Nelson, ed. *Reapportionment in the 1970s*. Berkeley: University of California Press, 1971.

Posner, Richard. *Economic Analysis of Law*. Boston: Little, Brown, 1977.

Pritchett, Herman. *Constitutional Civil Liberties*. New York: McGraw-Hill, 1984.

Raiffa, Howard. *Decision Analysis: Introductory Lectures on Choices under Uncertainty*. New York: Wiley, 1970.

———. *The Art and Science of Negotiation*. Cambridge, Mass.: Harvard University Press, 1982.

Remer, Daniel. *Computer Power for Your Law Office*. Berkeley, Calif.: Sybex, 1983.

Richmond, Samuel. *Operations Research for Management Decisions*. New York: Ronald Press, 1968.

———. *Operations Research for Management Science*. New York: Ronald, 1968.

Roesch, Ronald, and R. Corrado, eds. *Evaluation and Criminal Justice Policy*. New York: Russell Sage, 1981.

Rosenthal, D. *Lawyer and Client: Who's in Charge*. New York: Russell Sage, 1974.

Ross, Lawrence. *Settled Out of Court*. Hawthorne, N.Y.: Aldine, 1970.

Rubenstein, Moshe. *Patterns of Problem Solving*. Englewood Cliffs, N.J.: Prentice-Hall, 1975.

Saaty, Thomas. *The Analytic Hierarchy Process: Planning, Priority Setting, and Resource Allocation*. New York: McGraw-Hill, 1980.

———. *Decision Making for Leaders: Analytical Hierarchy Process for Decisions in a Complex World*. Belmont, Calif.: Wadsworth, 1982.

Samuelson, Paul. *Economics: An Introductory Analysis*. New York: McGraw-Hill, 1972.

Schlesinger, Steven. *Exclusionary Injustice: The Problem of Illegally Obtained Evidence*. New York: Dekker, 1977.

Schubert, Glendon, ed. *Judicial Decision-Making*. New York: Free Press, 1963.

———. *Judicial Behavior: A Reader in Theory and Research*. New York: Rand McNally, 1964.

Schwem, R. *Housing Discrimination Law*. Washington, D.C.: Bureau of National Affairs, 1984.

Shoup, Donald, and Stephen Mehay. *Program Budgeting for Urban Police Services*. New York: Praeger, 1971.

Silverstein, Lee. *Defense of the Poor: The National Report*. Chicago: American Bar Foundation, 1965.

Sindler, Allan. *Bakke, Defunis, and Minority Admissions: The Quest for Equal Opportunity*. New York: Longman, 1978.

Spaeth, Harold. *Supreme Court Policy Making: Explanation and Prediction*. San Francisco: Freeman, 1979.

Statewide Jury Verdicts. *Jury Verdict Expectancies Service*. Cleveland, Ohio: Statewide Jury Verdicts, 1962.

Statewide Verdicts. *Valuation Handbook Service*. Cleveland, Ohio: Statewide Jury Verdicts, 1962.

Statsky, W., and J. Wernet. *Case Analysis and Fundamentals of Legal Writing*. St. Paul, Minn.: Weidenfeld and Nicolson, 1977.

Tapper, C. *Computers and the Law*. New York: Longman, 1973.

Task Force on the Administration of Justice. *The Courts*. Washington, D.C.: President's Commission on Law Enforcement and the Administration of Justice, 1967.

Theil, H., et al. *Operations Research and Quantitative Economics: An Elementary Introduction*. New York: McGraw-Hill, 1965.

Thode, W., et al. *Introduction to the Study of Law*. Mineola, N.Y.: Foundation Press, 1970.

Thompson, Mark. *Benefit-Cost Analysis for Program Evaluation*. Beverly Hills, Calif.: Sage, 1980.

Tufte, Edward. *Data Analysis for Politics and Policy*. Englewood Cliffs, N.J.: Prentice-Hall, 1974.

Tullock, Gordon. *The Logic of the Law*. New York: Basic Books, 1971.

Ulmer, Sidney. *Courts, Law, and Judicial Process*. New York: Free Press, 1981.

Vago, Steven. *Law and Society*. Englewood Cliffs, N.J.: Prentice-Hall, 1981.

White, Michael, et al. *Managing Public Systems: Analytic Techniques for Public Administration*. Boston: Duxbury, 1980.

Whitebread, C. *Criminal Procedure: An Analysis of Constitutional Cases and Concepts*. Mineola, N.Y.: Foundation Press, 1980.

Wright, Deil. *Federal Grants-in-Aid: Perspectives and Alternatives*. Washington, D.C.: American Enterprise Institute for Public Policy Research, 1968.

Zeleny, Milan. *Multiple Criteria Decision Making*. New York: McGraw-Hill, 1982.

Name Index

Subject Index

About the Author

STUART S. NAGEL, a Professor of Political Science at the University of Illinois, is Secretary-Treasurer and Publications Coordinator of the Policy Studies Organization. He has served as a consultant both to the President's Reorganization Program and to the Office of Personnel Management, and has served as attorney to the U.S. Senate Subcommittee on Administrative Practice and Procedure to the National Labor Relations Board, and to the OEO Legal Services Program. Among his most recently authored books are *Causation, Prediction, and Legal Analysis* (Quorum Books, 1986), *Law Policy and Optimizing Analysis* (Quorum Books, 1986), *Microcomputers, Evaluation Research, and Policy Analysis, and Public Policy: Goals, Means, and Methods*. His major edited books include *Law and Policy Studies, Public Policy Analysis and Management*, and *The Policy Studies: Its Basic Literature*. His articles have appeared in the *American Bar Association Journal, American Political Science Review, Judicature*, and other law and professional journals.

www.ingramcontent.com/pod-product-compliance
Ingram Content Group UK Ltd.
Pitfield, Milton Keynes, MK11 3LW, UK
UKHW020906190926
475560UK00010B/302